UNTAXED

One of the most common complaints about the tax system in the United States is that rich taxpayers are able to lower their tax liabilities through abusive tax practices, often outmaneuvering the Internal Revenue Service (IRS). *Untaxed* offers a fresh perspective on the long-standing dilemma of tax avoidance and evasion by the rich by proposing a new legal response: means-based adjustments to the tax compliance rules. These compliance rules govern interactions between taxpayers and the IRS, from filing tax returns to responding to audit letters to paying tax penalties. *Untaxed* shows how tax compliance rules can be adjusted based on taxpayers' means to level the playing field between the rich and everyone else. Timely and innovative, this book is a must-read for legal scholars, policymakers, tax students, and anyone interested in tax policy and administration.

Joshua D. Blank is Professor of Law at the University of California, Irvine School of Law. His scholarship focuses on tax administration, tax transparency, and agency communications.

Ari Glogower is Professor of Law at the Northwestern Pritzker School of Law. He is a scholar of progressive tax theory and design.

Untaxed

THE RICH, THE IRS, AND A NEW APPROACH TO TAX COMPLIANCE

JOSHUA D. BLANK
University of California, Irvine School of Law

ARI GLOGOWER
Northwestern Pritzker School of Law

CAMBRIDGE
UNIVERSITY PRESS

Shaftesbury Road, Cambridge CB2 8EA, United Kingdom

One Liberty Plaza, 20th Floor, New York, NY 10006, USA

477 Williamstown Road, Port Melbourne, VIC 3207, Australia

314–321, 3rd Floor, Plot 3, Splendor Forum, Jasola District Centre, New Delhi – 110025, India

103 Penang Road, #05-06/07, Visioncrest Commercial, Singapore 238467

Cambridge University Press is part of Cambridge University Press & Assessment, a department of the University of Cambridge.

We share the University's mission to contribute to society through the pursuit of education, learning and research at the highest international levels of excellence.

www.cambridge.org
Information on this title: www.cambridge.org/9781009198745
DOI: 10.1017/9781009198707

© Joshua D. Blank and Ari Glogower 2025

This publication is in copyright. Subject to statutory exception and to the provisions of relevant collective licensing agreements, no reproduction of any part may take place without the written permission of Cambridge University Press & Assessment.

When citing this work, please include a reference to the DOI 10.1017/9781009198707

First published 2025

A catalogue record for this publication is available from the British Library

Library of Congress Cataloging-in-Publication Data
NAMES: Blank, Joshua D., author. | Glogower, Ari, author.
TITLE: The rich, the IRS, and a new approach to tax compliance / Joshua D. Blank, University of California, Irvine; Ari Glogower, Northwestern Pritzker School of Law.
OTHER TITLES: Rich, the Internal Revenue Service, and a new approach to tax compliance
DESCRIPTION: Cambridge, United Kingdom ; New York, NY, USA : Cambridge University Press, 2024. | Includes index. | Summary: "Offering a critical perspective on tax enforcement and economic inequality, this book sheds light on the challenges of tax noncompliance by the rich and proposes innovative legal rules to address the tax gap. It is a must-read for legal scholars, policymakers, and students interested in tax policy and administration"– Provided by publisher.
IDENTIFIERS: LCCN 2024011214 (print) | LCCN 2024011215 (ebook) | ISBN 9781009198745 (hardback) | ISBN 9781009198714 (paperback) | ISBN 9781009198707 (epub)
SUBJECTS: LCSH: Tax returns–United States. | Tax collection–United States. | Tax administration and procedure–United States. | Taxpayer compliance–United States. | Taxation–Law and legislation–United States. | United States. Internal Revenue Service.
CLASSIFICATION: LCC KF6310 .B53 2024 (print) | LCC KF6310 (ebook) | DDC 343.7304–DC23/eng/20240506
LC record available at https://lccn.loc.gov/2024011214
LC ebook record available at https://lccn.loc.gov/2024011215

ISBN 978-1-009-19874-5 Hardback
ISBN 978-1-009-19871-4 Paperback

Cambridge University Press & Assessment has no responsibility for the persistence or accuracy of URLs for external or third-party internet websites referred to in this publication and does not guarantee that any content on such websites is, or will remain, accurate or appropriate.

To my wife and children
– Josh
To Katy, Lilah, and Simon
– Ari

Contents

Acknowledgments		*page* ix
	Introduction	1
1	Tax Noncompliance at the Top	13
2	How the Tax System Addresses Noncompliance	38
3	Means-Adjusted Tax Compliance: A New Approach	64
4	When Are Means Adjustments Fair and Efficient?	101
5	From Theory to Legal Design	122
6	Tax Penalties	138
7	Tax Advice	161
8	The Statute of Limitations	183
9	Tax Information Reporting	201
10	Closing the Tax Information Gap	223
	Conclusion	239
Index		243

Acknowledgments

Since we first started to think together about the tax compliance rules in the fall of 2018, many people have helped us develop those initial ideas into this book.

First, we are grateful to our families for their love, support, and patience throughout the writing and publication process.

We would also like to thank many colleagues who helped us think through the arguments in this book, including Ted Afield, Ellen Aprill, Reuven Avi-Yonah, Jordan Barry, Lily Batchelder, Ilan Benshalom, Leslie Book, Tom Brennan, Heather Field, Victor Fleischer, Keith Fogg, Brian Galle, Jacob Goldin, Paul Gowder, Philip Hackney, Nigar Hashimzade, Daniel Hemel, Kathryn James, David Kamin, Mitchell Kane, Ariel Jurow Kleiman, Sarah Lawsky, Michelle Layser, Leandra Lederman, Omri Marian, Ruth Mason, Shu-Yi Oei, Leigh Osofsky, Miranda Perry-Fleischer, Katie Pratt, Jim Repetti, Diane Ring, Kyle Rozema, Ted Seto, Fadi Shaheen, Dan Shaviro, Joel Slemrod, Kathleen DeLaney Thomas, Joe Thorndike, Manoj Viswanathan, Clinton Wallace, and James Wexler. We also thank participants at the Boston College Law School Tax Policy Workshop, the 2019 Junior Tax Scholars Workshop, the 2019 Law and Society Association Annual Meeting, the Loyola Law School Tax Policy Colloquium, the New York University School of Law Tax Policy and Public Finance Colloquium, the 2020 National Tax Association Annual Conference, the UC Law San Francisco Tax Speaker Series, the University of San Diego School of Law Tax Law Speaker Series, the Junctures/Critical Perspectives and Tax Reform Symposium (Monash University, Faculty of Law, Melbourne, Australia), the University of Chicago Law School Seminar on Tax Policy and Economic Inequality, the Tax Administration Research Centre Seminar Series, the 2022 Association for Mid-Career Tax Law Professors Annual Conference, the 2022 Law & Society Annual Meeting, the 2023 ABA Tax Section Midyear Tax Meeting, and faculty workshops at Emory Law School, Northwestern Pritzker School of Law, the Ohio State University Moritz College of Law, the University of California, Irvine School of Law, the

University of Wisconsin Law School, and Vanderbilt Law School for thoughtful suggestions and comments.

We are especially grateful to Matt Gallaway and the other members of the editing and production team at Cambridge University Press for helping us navigate the publication process and for transforming our draft manuscript into a published book. We also thank the anonymous peer reviewers who provided invaluable suggestions and comments on early versions of our work. We are grateful to Jennifer Allison and Holly Qin for their incredibly helpful editing and research assistance. We thank the University of California, Irvine School of Law, the Northwestern Pritzker School of Law Faculty Research Program, and the Ohio State University Moritz College of Law for providing funding for research assistance and summer research grants.

We also express our gratitude to law review editors who have reviewed our work and offered suggestions, both stylistic and substantive. This book includes discussion that has been adapted or excerpted from the following articles: Joshua D. Blank & Ari Glogower, *Progressive Tax Procedure*, 96 N.Y.U. L. REV. 668 (2021); Joshua D. Blank & Ari Glogower, *The Trouble with Targeting Tax Shelters*, 74 ADMIN. L. REV. 69 (2022); Joshua D. Blank & Ari Glogower, *When Should Means Matter? The Case of Tax Compliance*, 42 VA. TAX REV. 241 (2022); and Joshua D. Blank & Ari Glogower, *The Tax Information Gap at the Top*, 108 IOWA L. REV. 1597 (2023).

Finally, we thank our many students who have studied with us at different institutions and who have challenged us to think about the tax compliance rules in new ways.

Introduction

Tax enforcement against the rich in the United States is in crisis. Consider the following examples:

- In December 2022, the House of Representatives Committee on Ways & Means released six years' of President Donald J. Trump's federal income tax returns to the public.[1] An accompanying report found a host of potentially abusive tax positions on these returns, but also that the IRS had failed to adequately challenge, or in some cases to even audit, the returns. The report found that the IRS agents had only audited one of Trump's returns while he was president. When the IRS did audit Trump, its agents were quickly overwhelmed with his complex tax dealings, which involved hundreds of "flow-through returns" filed by tiers of entities.[2] In fact, in some cases, the IRS agents appeared to have simply deferred to Trump's advisors, noting that he had used a professional accounting firm and counsel to prepare his returns.[3] One senator commented that wealthy and high-income taxpayers like Trump are "more likely to get struck by lightning than have [their] hundreds of partnerships audited."[4]
- In May 2021, the Treasury Department released a proposal that would have empowered the IRS to observe more information about the financial activities of taxpayers, especially the rich.[5] Under the proposal, banks and other financial institutions would report to the IRS information on business and personal accounts, including banking, loan, and investment accounts, with exceptions for those with low gross cash flow and fair market value. According to the Treasury, the purpose of the measure was to enable the IRS to "better target enforcement activities" by "increasing scrutiny of wealthy evaders."[6] Despite these arguments, the proposal faced a backlash from legislators, taxpayers, and financial institutions. Opponents warned that the proposal would introduce a new "surveillance state" and lead to an "outrageous and blatant" violation of privacy.[7] Ultimately, Congress did not take up the reform.[8]

- In August 2022, after years of pleas by the IRS, Congress passed, and President Biden signed, legislation providing nearly $80 billion of new funding to the agency.[9] IRS officials stated that they would use part of this funding to increase its tax enforcement against "high-dollar noncompliance," especially by focusing on the returns of "high-income and high-wealth individuals."[10] However, when Republicans gained majority control of the House in the 2022 midterm election, they quickly threatened to repeal the legislation. In June 2023, as part of the perennial debt-ceiling negotiations, Congress and the president agreed to reduce the IRS's annual appropriations by $10 billion in each of the next two fiscal years.[11] The IRS itself acknowledged that the increased tax-enforcement funding, including the portion it would use to increase tax enforcement against the rich, was uncertain.[12]

These three different events all illustrate a pressing challenge for the US tax system. Not only do many high-income and wealthy taxpayers pursue complex strategies and transactions that enable them to engage in abusive tax avoidance and evasion, but also the IRS often has greater difficulty enforcing the tax law against them. High-end taxpayers account for a disproportionate share of the total US tax revenue lost from tax noncompliance. According to one recent study, tax noncompliance by the top 1% of taxpayers alone costs the federal government approximately $175 billion of lost tax revenue each year, or nearly $2 trillion over a decade.[13] As one particularly costly example of this phenomenon, economist Gabriel Zucman highlights the role of "tax havens" in facilitating global tax evasion by wealthy taxpayers.[14] He estimates that unreported foreign accounts resulted in approximately $35 billion in lost revenues in 2014 alone.[15]

This noncompliance also contributes to the low overall effective rates of tax paid by many high-end taxpayers. In 2021, ProPublica, a nonprofit news organization, released otherwise confidential details of tax returns of multibillionaires, including Elon Musk, Michael Bloomberg, Mark Zuckerberg, Bill Gates, Warren Buffet, and Rupert Murdoch. The report showed that in many years, they paid little, if any, federal income tax.[16] During the period when many of these returns were filed, from 2011 to 2018, the IRS audit rate of millionaires plummeted by 80%.[17] For instance, from 2017 to 2018, the IRS's audit rate of households with adjusted gross income between $5 million and $10 million dropped from 7.95% to 4.21%, and its audit rate of households with adjusted gross income between $1 million and $5 million dropped from 3.52% to 2.21%.[18]

Designing and administering rules that prevent aggressive and abusive tax avoidance by the rich is not easy. IRS officials have repeatedly stated that their agency is committed to "enforcing tax laws in a manner that is fair and impartial."[19] But what should the government do when high-income and wealthy taxpayers are subject to the same tax rules that apply to everyone else, but somehow are able to achieve very different tax outcomes? How can the government design rules and policies that address tax noncompliance by the rich in a manner that is fair, impartial, and, importantly, effective?

To combat tax noncompliance and underenforcement involving high-end taxpayers, policymakers usually adopt two familiar approaches. The first approach is to seek to bolster the IRS's funding so that the agency can improve and increase enforcement. Congress took this step in 2022 when it passed the historic $80 billion investment in the IRS described above, through the enactment of the Inflation Reduction Act.[20] But this approach is unpredictable and unstable, especially as political control of Congress changes. When the IRS does seek to increase its enforcement of the tax law, political opponents often accuse the agency of using heavy-handed tactics to invade taxpayers' privacy or even to settle political scores. More importantly for this book, increased IRS funding also does not change the underlying tax rules that often benefit high-end taxpayers, including in their interactions with the IRS.

The second response is to design rules that target specific activities that may enable tax noncompliance by the rich. When it comes to the structure of the tax law, Congress has responded to the problem of tax noncompliance through what can be described as "activity-based rules." These rules target specific activities that enable or signal tax noncompliance. Under an activity-based approach, when taxpayers participate in a particular activity, they may be subject to different tax administration and compliance requirements, such as increased information reporting requirements and potential penalties.[21] While these activity-based rules play an important role in the tax system, they can also target the *wrong* taxpayers while the rich escape their reach. Further, the IRS faces administrative law hurdles in implementing activity-based rules, which have grown in recent years as the agency has faced increased judicial scrutiny in light of legal challenges from high-end taxpayers and their attorneys.[22]

This book shows why these two traditional approaches are not enough to combat the problem of tax noncompliance by the rich. Both IRS enforcement and activity-based rules can only achieve so much in dealings with sophisticated taxpayers. In contrast to these traditional approaches, this book proposes a new legal response to address the long-standing dilemma of tax noncompliance by the rich: a system of means adjustments to the tax compliance rules.

Under current law, the tax compliance rules, ranging from filing tax returns to responding to audit letters to paying tax penalties, apply in the same way to all taxpayers, regardless of their income or wealth. For example, every taxpayer faces the same civil tax penalty rates and interest rates on underreporting and underpayments. All of them, regardless of their income level or wealth, can also raise the same defenses against penalties, and benefit from the same statutes of limitations for IRS assessments.

In contrast to current law, we argue that Congress and the IRS should adopt a new approach to the tax compliance rules, and adjust certain rules based on taxpayers' means, such as their income and wealth, in order to level the playing field between the rich and everyone else. Under our approach, high-end taxpayers would face higher tax penalty rates, longer periods where the IRS could assess tax deficiencies, and higher standards for claiming defenses against penalties, among many other means-adjusted rules. Rather than focusing solely on regulating specific activities, such as a particular abusive tax strategy, we propose that the government should also account for a taxpayer's means in the design of the tax compliance rules.

The problem of tax noncompliance by the rich is as old as the United States tax system itself. Despite waves of tax reform throughout the country's history, lawmakers have struggled to design tax systems that can tax the rich progressively. In the 1800s, rich taxpayers undermined the collection of general property taxes by state and local tax authorities by holding intangible financial assets, including stocks bonds, and other instruments that were harder to tax.[23] When taxing jurisdictions relied instead on indirect taxes that were not as easily avoidable – such as excises and tariffs – it soon became clear that these taxes, in fact, placed higher burdens on lower-income consumers. In the early 1900s, progressive reformers advocating for a national income tax faced the frequent objection that rich taxpayers would simply avoid the new tax by manipulating how their income is measured.[24]

While the public release of the Trump tax returns in 2022 drew denouncement of the IRS's failure to audit and challenge wealthy and high-income taxpayers, this critique also is not new. In the mid-1800s in the United States, during the Civil War period, individual tax returns were open to public inspection. In fact, in 1865, the *New York Times* regularly published a front-page feature titled *Our Internal Revenue*, which listed the income tax liabilities of prominent New Yorkers.[25] A July 8, 1865 feature, for example, listed the tax liabilities of rich and famous citizens such as William B. Astor ($1.3 million), Cornelius Vanderbilt ($576,551) and Samuel Lord ($183,630).[26]

During this period, reporters noted that many tax collection districts in New York, and the United States in general, were behind in enforcing the tax law, especially against wealthy and powerful taxpayers. In one 1865 column, *Times* reporters chronicled their own discovery of unchallenged taxpayer abuses, such as one tax return where "a person returned his income at $11,000, when his books revealed the delightful figuring of $80,000 to his credit," among many other "wonderful frauds" that were only "discernable to the close observer."[27] The reporters argued that this was "partly because the investigation of frauds and 'insufficiencies' occupied time which should have been otherwise employed, but to a very great degree it was due to the lack of brain and physique in the officers themselves – brain with which to comprehend the mysteries of the law, physique with which to drive work and workmen and secure results."[28]

Public disclosure of this information fell out of favor for a period of time, only to return in 1924, when the *Times* published lists of wealthy individuals who had paid no tax at all. The editors dubbed this list of citizens the "non-taxables" and questioned why they had not been investigated for "suspicious" tax positions.[29]

This book offers a new approach to addressing the persistent problem of tax noncompliance at the top. Before describing how our new approach to tax compliance would work, we should pause to define some key terms.

First, what do we mean by "rich" taxpayers? In this book, we focus on the taxpayers at the very highest income and wealth levels, who often have unique advantages to avoid paying their taxes under the current rules. For example, we will describe how taxpayers in the top 0.1% of the income distribution have very different opportunities to avoid or evade taxes than even other high-income taxpayers, such as those in the top 10% of earners. Throughout the book, we refer to high-income and high-wealth taxpayers as "high-end" taxpayers.

Second, what do we mean by the "tax compliance rules"? In this context, these rules govern critical aspects of not only taxpayers' obligations to report and remit federal taxes but also those governing the federal government's administration and enforcement of these obligations. These rules include taxpayers' obligations to file returns correctly and on time, the IRS's ability to review and assess reported tax liabilities, civil tax penalties and interest on underpayments, and reporting requirements of taxpayers and third parties, among other items. Beyond these statutory provisions, the tax compliance rules include the formal and informal rules governing interactions between taxpayers and the IRS. For example, the IRS follows certain practices in conducting taxpayer examinations. Similarly, the appeals procedures govern the taxpayer's right to appeal decisions of the US Tax Court, as well as the right to representation and to informal conferences with IRS Appeals Office personnel.

Unlike the current tax compliance rules, our proposed means-adjusted tax rules would vary depending upon a measure of taxpayers' income or wealth, just like the graduated individual tax rate schedule and other features of our progressive federal tax system.

For example, with means-adjusted tax penalty rules, high-end taxpayers could be subject to higher penalty rates for understatements and fraud that vary according to their income. Current law imposes an "accuracy-related" penalty of 20% on underpayments resulting from either negligence or the taxpayer's disregard of rules or regulations, as well as from substantial understatements of income tax and certain other cases.[30] This 20% penalty applies to all taxpayers, irrespective of their income or wealth. Under means-adjusted tax compliance rules, on the other hand, this penalty rate would increase for high-end taxpayers. For illustration, a taxpayer with $5 million or more of adjusted gross income in the taxable year could be subject to an accuracy-related penalty of 40% rather than 20%.[31]

For another example, consider the defenses that taxpayers can use to avoid federal civil tax penalties. Under current law, all taxpayers can rely on a "reasonable cause and good faith" defense, which they can satisfy by showing that a tax advisor provided them with a written opinion on which they reasonably relied. As many high-end taxpayers and their advisors know, the tax opinion can effectively serve as a tax penalty shield. Here too, the law adopts an activity-based approach and denies this defense of reliance on an advisor for certain transactions, such as for transactions that lack "economic substance." Well-advised taxpayers can still use the defense, as long as they can avoid this economic substance exception. A system of means-adjusted tax compliance rules, in contrast, could prevent high-end taxpayers from taking advantage of this defense – and from avoiding activity-based limitations – irrespective of the specific activity in which they engaged.

The statute of limitations is yet another area where the policymakers could introduce means adjustments. By limiting the number of years during which a tax noncompliance investigation can take place, this statute of limitations restricts the IRS's ability to assess additional tax against taxpayers.[32] High-end taxpayers often enjoy a strategic advantage as a result of this rule, including by engaging in structuring that may be hard for the IRS to detect and challenge before the clock runs out. Under the current default rule, the IRS must assess additional tax within three years from the time a taxpayer files the tax return. In this case as well, current law adopts an activity-based approach. For example, the period is doubled to six years where the return reflects a "substantial omission" of gross income.[33] Under means-adjusted tax compliance rules, the length of the statute of limitations could also vary with a taxpayer's income or wealth. For example, the default rule could increase to six years for taxpayers with income and underpayments above the threshold levels and to nine years in the case of a statutory substantial omission.

We argue that adjusting the tax compliance rules for high-end taxpayers offers several advantages that could improve the administration of the tax system:

1. This approach can equalize the effect of tax compliance rules for taxpayers at varying income levels. These adjustments can counter the specific advantages many high-end taxpayers have under the current rules, including their greater access to complex tax-avoidance strategies and sophisticated legal counsel. For example, higher penalty rates for high-income taxpayers can improve their deterrent effect and account for these taxpayers' lower chance of detection.
2. Means adjustments would redress the limitations of activity-based responses to tax noncompliance. With a system of means-adjusted tax compliance rules, sophisticated taxpayers could not, for instance, simply restructure their transactions to avoid a tax information reporting obligation.
3. Means adjustments would address the unique effects of high-end noncompliance in a progressive tax system, where the dollars of revenue lost from noncompliance at the top represents a greater social cost than the dollars lost from noncompliance lower on the income distribution.
4. Means-adjusted tax compliance rules can be more efficient than relying exclusively on increasing IRS audits and enforcement, which can be costly and limited in effect.

5. Means adjustments can improve tax morale, which is the intrinsic willingness of individuals to pay taxes and comply with their tax return reporting and filing obligations. Some studies find that the perception that the government is enforcing the tax law and that other taxpayers are compliant can affect tax morale for other taxpayers.

Importantly, policymakers should *not* introduce means adjustments to punish or burden rich taxpayers. Rather, they should use these adjustments to improve the administration of the tax system and to enable the collection of taxes that are already owed. In pursuing this goal, it is possible that a system of means-adjusted tax compliance rules could also impose additional burdens on high-end taxpayers. For example, a high-end taxpayer who does not comply and is subject to a higher penalty rate could end up paying more than a lower-income taxpayer with a similar deficiency, or than a taxpayer with the same income who simply complies with the tax law. This outcome should only be considered an ancillary effect of means adjustments, rather than their primary purpose. The purpose of means-adjusted tax compliance rules – like the purpose of penalties and other procedural rules in general – is not to impose additional substantive tax burdens ex post on taxpayers. Rather, means-adjusted tax compliance rules should be designed to deter acts of noncompliance ex ante, and thereby narrow the gap between what high-end taxpayers report and pay and their tax liabilities prescribed by the substantive progressive tax rules.

The tax compliance rules should also not subject high-end taxpayers to unwarranted scrutiny or harassment, and no one should have to face onerous legal burdens just because they have more wealth. The tax compliance rules must preserve basic procedural protections for all taxpayers in their interactions with the IRS. They should also not subject high-end taxpayers to unnecessarily burdensome procedures and penalties for minor offenses. Even when committed by high-income taxpayers, minor tax offenses do not pose the same threats to the tax system as do major ones, and therefore do not warrant the same adjustments to the tax compliance rules. As this book describes, policymakers could address the potential for overburdening smaller offenses by creating an exception for low-value amounts of understatements of income or underpayments of income tax. For example, policymakers could include an exception from means-adjusted tax penalty rules when the amount of a taxpayer's underpayments for the year fall below a particular dollar value.

In addition to presenting the practical advantages of means-adjusted tax compliance rules, we also offer a broader normative case for why policymakers should make these adjustments.[34] Prior academic work in legal theory and in public finance considers the question of when it is appropriate, or not, for the law to subject taxpayers at different income levels to different legal rules. We explain how these debates can inform the design of the tax compliance rules, and also what the case of the tax compliance rules can teach us about these broader questions for legal theory.

In the case of tax compliance, these adjustments can be designed not to penalize one group of taxpayers through different legal rules, but rather to better tailor these rules for taxpayers in different economic circumstances, and to thereby improve the operation of the tax system. Similarly, we explain how means adjustments can be made in a manner that is consistent with constitutional principles of due process and equal protection.

Introducing formal means adjustments to the tax compliance rules would also address important equity concerns. In recent years, the lack of IRS enforcement against high-end taxpayers has been striking when compared to the IRS audits of the poor. In 2021, for example, low-income taxpayers were over five times as likely to be audited by the IRS as other taxpayers.[35] Many of these taxpayers claim the federal Earned Income Tax Credit (EITC), a program designed to replace traditional welfare that is administered through the tax system.[36] When questioned regarding the IRS's focus on taxpayers who claim this credit, the then IRS Commissioner Charles Rettig commented that "EITC correspondence audits are the most efficient use of available IRS examination resources with the average time to complete the audit of 5 hours per return."[37] His response to congressional inquiries regarding this issue suggested that, compared to the tax returns of high-end taxpayers, tax audits involving the EITC and low-income taxpayers are often simply easier for the IRS to conduct than audits of high-income and wealthy taxpayers.

In 2023, in its strategic operating plan, the IRS stated that it would address inequities in tax enforcement and devote more resources to prevent high-end tax noncompliance.[38] That same year, IRS Commissioner Daniel Werfel also commented that the IRS would reevaluate the agency's approach to selecting returns for audit and consider changes to its methodology, which would include exploring the impact of "optimizing on broader issues rather than focusing on EITC overclaims."[39] As we describe, means adjustments to the tax compliance rules could assist these IRS initiatives to improve equity in tax enforcement. These adjustments would increase the potential tax revenue from pursuing audits of high-end taxpayers, and would help the IRS enforce the tax law more evenly across income levels.

After outlining the advantages of means adjustments to the tax compliance rules and their theoretical dimensions, we offer a practical guide for policymakers who may seek to implement these adjustments. We take a deep dive into the structure of the current tax compliance rules and explain how high-end taxpayers can often take advantage of these rules, as well as how they can be improved through means adjustments. This guide offers options for designing the adjustments and explains when they would and would not be suitable. We also consider the roles of both Congress and the IRS in making these adjustments. We then offer analysis of how these adjustments could be implemented in four critical areas of tax compliance: (1) civil tax penalties; (2) statutory and regulatory defenses to civil tax penalties; (3) statutes of limitation and restrictions on assessment; and (4) tax information reporting rules. These examples highlight what we argue are the essential components of effective adjustments while allowing policymakers flexibility in choosing the thresholds of income, wealth, and other indications of means that may trigger them.

The book develops its analysis and proposals as follows. We begin in Chapter 1, *Tax Noncompliance at the Top*, by describing the consequences of high-end tax noncompliance and their impact on the progressive tax system. As this chapter explains, high-end taxpayers have more money at stake and greater opportunities for tax noncompliance than other taxpayers. In Chapter 2, *How the Tax System Addresses Noncompliance*, we describe the basic models of taxpayer compliance in the tax literature – including the behavioral effects of deterrence and detection – and general considerations in balancing the costs and benefits of tax enforcement in order to achieve the optimal level of tax compliance. The chapter then describes the conventional policy and scholarly responses to high-end noncompliance as well as the limitations of these responses. Chapter 3, *Means-Adjusted Tax Compliance: A New Approach*, presents a novel approach to the problem of high-end tax noncompliance: a system of means adjustments to the tax compliance rules governing critical aspects of tax administration and enforcement. In Chapter 4, *When Are Means Adjustments Fair and Efficient?*, we address two areas of legal theory – the "double distortion" principle and the "generality" principle – that consider when means adjustments to legal rules may not be desirable.

We then transition from theory to implementation in Chapter 5, *From Theory to Legal Design*, where we describe general design considerations that policymakers should adopt when implementing our approach, based on the theoretical analysis we developed in earlier chapters. In Chapter 6, *Tax Penalties*, we describe how Congress should enact means-adjusted civil tax penalties to attack abusive tax avoidance and tax evasion by high-end taxpayers. Following up on this proposal and analysis, Chapter 7, *Tax Advice*, proposes that policymakers should revise current law to prevent high-end taxpayers from asserting the reasonable cause defense against any accuracy-related tax penalties. In Chapter 8, *The Statute of Limitations*, we propose means adjustments to the statute of limitations, which limits the period of time in which the IRS can assess taxes. In Chapter 9, *Tax Information Reporting*, we show how the government's activity-based approach to tax information reporting often allows high-end taxpayers to engage in noncompliance with the tax law, while most other taxpayers are subject to significant automatic IRS review. In Chapter 10, *Closing the Tax Information Gap*, we propose means-adjusted reforms to tax information reporting as an additional tool to address high-end noncompliance. This chapter proposes a series of means adjustments to the information reporting rules for high-end taxpayers, including an annual wealth reporting form and increased information reporting by banks and financial institutions.

The costs of high-end tax noncompliance are significant and far-reaching. Lost tax revenue means higher taxes for everyone else, a ballooning national debt, and less money for critical public investments such as in infrastructure, education, and healthcare. Further, tax noncompliance by high-end taxpayers undermines progressive taxation, one of the defining features of the federal US tax system, since these taxpayers have the greatest ability to pay taxes. Tax noncompliance by the rich can also reduce tax morale by fostering a perception that taxes are only "for the little people."[40] Tax noncompliance also makes it harder for legislators to improve the tax system through new reforms that can raise needed revenue and advance fairness.

This book does not offer a complete solution to the problems of high-end noncompliance but shows how the tax compliance rules can be redesigned to help narrow the tax gap at the top. Economist Joel Slemrod once noted that "it is impossible to understand the true impact of a country's tax system by looking only at the tax base and the tax rates applied to that base ... [a] critical intermediating factor is how the tax law is administered and enforced."[41] This book takes a new look at this crucial insight by highlighting how high-income and wealthy taxpayers can often take advantage of our current tax compliance rules and how means adjustments to these rules can help to stop them.

NOTES

1 House Comm. on Ways & Means, Report on the Internal Revenue Service's Mandatory Audit Program under the Prior Administration (2017–2020) (Dec. 20, 2022). See Presidential Tax Returns archive hosted by Tax Analysts. For copies of President Donald J. Trump's 2015–2020 US federal income tax returns, see *Presidential Tax Returns*, Tax Notes, https://www.taxnotes.com/presidential-tax-returns.
2 See Joint Comm. on Taxation, Report to the House Committee on Ways & Means, Chairman Richard Neal 21 (Dec. 15, 2022).
3 House Comm. on Ways & Means, *supra* note 1, at 21.
4 Press Release, US Senate Committee on Finance, *Wyden Statement on Ways & Means Investigation of Presidential Audit Program* (Dec. 21, 2022).
5 See U.S. Dep't of the Treasury, General Explanations of the Administration's Fiscal Year 2022 Revenue Proposals 88–90 (2021).
6 U.S. Dep't of the Treasury, The American Families Plan Tax Compliance Agenda 2 (May 2021).
7 Press Release, House Comm. on Ways & Means, *Ways & Means Republicans Introduce Bill Prohibiting Biden's Invasive IRS Bank Surveillance Plan* (Oct. 15, 2021).
8 See, e.g., Sarah Kolinovsky & Trish Turner, *Biden Admin Backs Down on Tracking Bank Accounts with over $600 Annual Transactions*, ABC News (Oct. 19, 2021, 4:37 PM).
9 Pub. L. 117-169, 136 Stat. 1818.
10 IRS, Internal Revenue Service Inflation Reduction Act Strategic Operating Plan, FY 2023–2031 (2023).

11 Fiscal Responsibility Act of 2023, 118th Cong., Pub. L. No. 118-5, §§ 102, 251, 137 Stat. 10 (2023); see also CONG. RES. SERV., CHANGES TO IRS FUNDING IN THE DEBT LIMIT DEAL (June 6, 2023).
12 IRS, supra note 10, at 123.
13 See John Guyton et al., *Tax Evasion at the Top of the Income Distribution: Theory and Evidence* 10–11 (NBER Working Paper No. 26542, Mar. 2021).
14 See generally GABRIEL ZUCMAN, THE HIDDEN WEALTH OF NATIONS: THE SCOURGE OF TAX HAVENS (2015).
15 See id.
16 See Jesse Eisinger et al., *The Secret IRS Files: Trove of Never-before-Seen Records Reveal How the Wealthiest Avoid Income Tax*, PROPUBLICA (June 8, 2021).
17 See Paul Kiel, *It's Getting Worse: The IRS Now Audits Poor Americans at about the Same Rate as the Top 1%*, PROPUBLICA (May 30, 2019).
18 2018 IRS DATA BOOK 27 tbl.9b (2019), https://www.irs.gov/pub/irs-prior/p55b–2019.pdf; 2017 IRS DATA BOOK 27 tbl.9b (2018), https://www.irs.gov/pub/irs-soi/17databk.pdf.
19 Alan Rappeport, *I.R.S. Acknowledges Black Americans Face More Audit Scrutiny*, N.Y. TIMES (May 15, 2023) (*quoting* Commissioner of Internal Revenue Daniel Werfel).
20 Pub. L. 117-169, 136 Stat. 1818.
21 See, e.g., Treas. Reg. § 1.6011-4(b)(2), (6) (rules governing listed transactions and transactions of interest); I.R.C. §§ 1471–1474 (2018) (information reporting rules for offshore bank accounts). For more discussion of these activity-based rules and others, see Chapter 2, section "Traditional Responses to High-End Noncompliance."
22 See, e.g., CIC Services, LLC v. Internal Revenue Service, 141 S. Ct. 1582 (2021).
23 See AJAY K. MEHROTRA, MAKING THE MODERN AMERICAN FISCAL STATE: LAW, POLITICS, AND THE RISE OF PROGRESSIVE TAXATION, 1877–1929 (2013).
24 See id.
25 See, e.g., *Our Internal Revenue: The Eighth Collection District and Its Official Lists*, N.Y. TIMES (July 11, 1865), at 1; *Our Internal Revenue: The Fifth Collection District in Full*, N.Y. TIMES (July 16, 1865), at 5; *Our Internal Revenue: The Sixth Collection District in Full*, N.Y. TIMES (July 8, 1865), at 5.
26 *Our Internal Revenue: The Sixth Collection District in Full*, N.Y. TIMES (July 8, 1865), at 5.
27 *Our Internal Revenue: The Third (Brooklyn) District Complete*, N.Y. TIMES (June 30, 1865), at 1.
28 Id.
29 *Names of Wealthy on Non-Taxable List*, N.Y. TIMES (Sept. 4, 1925), at 1.
30 I.R.C. § 6662(a).
31 See Chapter 6, section "Redesigning Civil Tax Penalties."
32 I.R.C. § 6501(a).
33 I.R.C. § 6501(e).
34 See Chapters 3 and 4.
35 See *IRS Audits Few Millionaires but Targeted Many Low-Income Families in FY 2022*, TRANSACTIONAL RECORDS ACCESS CLEARINGHOUSE (Jan. 4, 2023).
36 See id.
37 Letter from Charles P. Rettig, IRS Comm'r, to Sen. Ron Wyden (D-OR) 2 (Sept. 6, 2019).

38 *See* IRS, *supra* note 10.
39 Letter from IRS Commissioner Daniel Werfel to Senator Ron Wyden, Chairman, Committee on Finance (May 15, 2023), https://www.finance.senate.gov/imo/media/doc/werfel_letter_to_sen_wyden.pdf.
40 *See* Enid Nemy, *Leona Helmsley, Hotel Queen, Dies at 87*, N.Y. TIMES (Aug. 20, 2007) (*quoting* Leona Helmsley).
41 Joel Slemrod, *Why People Pay Taxes: Introduction, in* WHY PEOPLE PAY TAXES 1 (Joel Slemrod ed., 1992).

1

Tax Noncompliance at the Top

How much tax revenue is lost each year as a result of noncompliance? How much of this lost revenue is from the richest taxpayers? How do the rich avoid paying taxes and why does it matter?

This chapter considers these basic and important questions. The answers explain our motivation for writing this book and provide a starting point for the arguments that follow. This discussion also begins to explain why this book focuses on high-end tax noncompliance as a distinct challenge for the tax system.

To answer these questions, we begin by describing exactly what we mean by tax noncompliance. The discussion then presents research findings on the scope of tax noncompliance and how it is shared across the income distribution. It then explains how high-end taxpayers can often avoid paying the taxes they owe by taking advantage of strategies that are not available to low- and middle-income taxpayers. Finally, we discuss why high-end noncompliance is so harmful to the tax system, and why policymakers should treat it as a pressing challenge.

WHAT IS TAX NONCOMPLIANCE?

What do we mean by "tax noncompliance"? In some cases, the answer is easy: Taxpayers fail to comply with the tax law when they do not report and pay the taxes that they legally owe. Simply defined, the Internal Revenue Code states that any taxpayer who "willfully attempts in any manner to evade or defeat any tax imposed" can be subject to fines or criminal prosecution.[1] For example, taxpayers may fail to report taxable income or transactions, or they might hide their assets in foreign accounts or as cryptocurrency. Noncompliant taxpayers might also claim tax positions that are clearly contrary to the law, such as that filing a tax return is voluntary, or that the US Constitution does not authorize an income tax.[2]

Taxpayers are free to minimize their tax liabilities as long as they comply with the law. Indeed, the tax law offers taxpayers many legal opportunities to reduce their tax liabilities by carefully structuring their transactions and activities. For example, a taxpayer with an appreciated asset can legally avoid paying the capital gains tax by simply holding the asset instead of selling it,[3] and they can entirely eliminate all income tax on the asset's gains by holding it for their entire life and then, after death, leaving it to their heirs.[4] While policymakers may question the wisdom of these rules, taxpayers can use them to lower their tax bills and still be fully compliant with the tax law.

Economists and legal scholars often distinguish in this way between illegal tax *evasion*, on the one hand, and legal tax *avoidance* on the other.[5] Some activities clearly constitute tax noncompliance, while others represent perfectly legal tax planning. In many cases, however, the distinction between tax compliance and noncompliance is not so simple. Between the clear cases of legal and illegal behavior, the many ambiguities in the tax law make it impossible to define precisely when a taxpayer is compliant or not. Economists Joel Slemrod and Shlomo Yitzhaki observe that while "the distinguishing characteristic of evasion is illegality ... in practice ... there are many areas where the dividing line is not clear, and sometimes the tax authorities inappropriately characterize certain cases."[6]

In 1935, the United States Supreme Court decided a case, *Gregory v. Helvering*, that illuminates this basic challenge in distinguishing between tax avoidance and evasion.[7] The taxpayer Ms. Gregory sought to reduce her tax liability on a stock sale by taking advantage of the corporate reorganization rules applicable at the time, which allowed for nonrecognition of gain in certain reorganization transactions. The Court ultimately held that the taxpayer's transaction fell outside the "plain intent" of the statute and disallowed the tax benefits.

Despite the holding, however, the *Gregory* opinion also affirmed the basic principle that taxpayers are free to reduce their tax liabilities through legal means. Justice Sutherland famously stated that a taxpayer has the legal right "to decrease the amount of what otherwise would be his taxes, or altogether avoid them, by means which the law permits."[8] Justice Sutherland's pronouncement in the *Gregory* case has become a staple of introductory tax courses and a mantra for advisors helping clients to legally minimize their tax liabilities.

The *Gregory* case also exemplifies the inevitable ambiguities in the tax law, where there is no simple answer to the question of whether a taxpayer has complied or not. These ambiguities arise in cases where it is uncertain how the tax law should apply to specific transactions or activities, such as Ms. Gregory's combination of a corporate reorganization and a stock sale.

As in the *Gregory* case, the question of whether a taxpayer has complied with the tax law or not will often only be determined in retrospect. In many cases, a taxpayer taking an aggressive but not clearly illegal tax position will only be found noncompliant *if* the IRS decides to challenge the taxpayer's position *and* a court ultimately agrees with the IRS's interpretation of the applicable law.

In many cases, taxpayers can avoid these enforcement efforts and judicial determinations, even when they push or overstep the boundaries of the tax law. As a result, sophisticated and well-advised taxpayers can often take advantage of the many ambiguities in the tax law to reduce their taxes through strategies that will not even be characterized as tax noncompliance. In other cases, taxpayers can bend the law to suit their needs by discouraging or defeating IRS challenges to their positions.

HOW BIG IS THE "TAX GAP"?

The IRS defines the gross "tax gap" as the amount of tax liability for a given tax year "that is not paid voluntarily and timely."[9] Researchers face two basic challenges in estimating the size of the tax gap. First, tax noncompliance is often hard to observe. If the lost tax revenue was easy to identify and measure, the IRS could readily recover it and there would be little to no tax gap at all. As a result, estimates of the tax gap necessarily rely on assumptions and inferences in calculating how much tax revenue is in fact lost to noncompliance. Further, it is not always even clear what counts as tax noncompliance in the first place, given the inevitable ambiguities in the tax law.

The IRS periodically publishes estimates of the tax gap, which it calculates by comparing the total amount of all federal taxes voluntarily paid on time with an estimate of the "total true tax" owed by taxpayers.[10] The IRS estimates the total amount of true taxes owed each year by analyzing data from audit and enforcement actions conducted in the succeeding years. For this reason, the IRS publishes its tax gap estimates retrospectively, typically with a lag of six to eight years after the applicable tax years. The IRS estimates both the "gross" tax gap, which is the total amount of taxes not paid voluntarily and on time, as well as the "net" tax gap after accounting for additional receipts that are paid late or recovered through IRS actions. The estimate of the net tax gap does not, however, account for the additional costs the government incurs when it recovers these additional receipts, such as enforcement expenditures and the lost time value of money, and there may not be an accurate and objective way to account for all these additional costs.

In its 2022 tax gap study, the IRS estimated an annual gross tax gap of $496 billion for tax years 2014–2016, and a total annual "true tax liability" of around $3.3 trillion. These estimates imply a voluntary compliance rate of approximately 85% for those years, and that approximately 15% of federal tax revenues were not paid voluntarily and timely. The IRS also estimated that approximately $68 billion was ultimately paid annually with respect to these tax years, resulting in an annual net tax gap of $428 billion for that period, implying an 87% net compliance rate. The IRS also projected that the tax gap increased after 2016, rising to a gross tax gap of $540 billion annually for tax years 2017–2019.

The IRS notes the challenges and limitations in estimating the total tax gap and its components. First, the tax gap estimate excludes certain categories of unpaid taxes entirely, such as those owed on income earned from illegal activities. Relying on data from IRS examinations may also not fully account for forms of noncompliance that are under-detected on these examinations. These estimates may be particularly challenging in the case of emerging or sophisticated noncompliance strategies that take more time to identify, such as the use of digital assets. Finally, the IRS methodology does not account for taxes not paid due to aggressive – but not clearly illegal – positions taken by taxpayers exploiting ambiguities in the law, and that are not subsequently detected and successfully challenged.[11]

The IRS tax gap studies also find that noncompliance with the federal individual income tax in particular plays an outsize role as the primary driver of the total tax revenue lost to noncompliance. The IRS estimates that underpayment of the individual income tax and employment taxes accounted for more than 90% of the total net tax gap from 2014 to 2016. Underpayment of corporate income taxes and the estate tax, in contrast, only account for approximately 8% and 0.5% of the net tax gap, respectively.

Other studies similarly find that the tax gap has continued to grow in subsequent years. In a 2019 article, economists Natasha Sarin and Lawrence Summers estimated that the tax gap would reach $630 billion in 2020, and over $7.5 trillion over the following decade.[12] They were not the only ones to sound this alarm. In a speech the following year, IRS Commissioner Charles Rettig warned of the increasing challenges in countering tax noncompliance and estimated that the true tax gap could reach up to $1 trillion every year.[13]

THE DISTRIBUTION OF NONCOMPLIANCE

How much do taxpayers at different income levels contribute to the total tax gap? Of course, at every income level, some taxpayers avoid paying their taxes, while others fully and voluntarily comply with the tax law. That said, the data suggest that the richest taxpayers account for a substantial and disproportionate share of the total tax revenue lost from noncompliance. As this section explains, however, estimating the exact distribution of noncompliance is not easy. Further, studies do not always find that noncompliance rates rise consistently and proportionally with taxpayer income.

Methodology. Like the IRS's studies of the tax gap, studies on the distribution of noncompliance are necessarily imprecise, and rely on important assumptions and inferences. Understanding these factors is critical to interpreting their findings.

First, these studies can express the distribution of noncompliance in different ways, which can shape perceptions of how taxpayers at different income levels contribute to the tax gap. The distribution of noncompliance can be expressed as the total dollars of lost revenue attributable to each income group, or by comparing the proportions of income or taxes underreported at each income level. The income distribution can also be sliced in different ways to focus on different bands of taxpayers. For example, studies can focus on the share of tax noncompliance by all higher-income taxpayers, such as the top 10% of earners, or at the very top of the income distribution, such as by the top 1% or the top 0.1%.

These studies also reflect researcher choices in how they interpret the available data, and in the adjustments and inferences they employ to derive estimates of noncompliance rates from the chosen datasets. One basic challenge in determining the distribution of noncompliance is estimating the amount of taxes underpaid across the income distribution.

Distribution of noncompliance estimates typically begin by inferring the total amount of tax noncompliance based on IRS audit data, using a Detection Controlled Estimate (DCE) adjustment. Some researchers argue, however, that this method can systematically underestimate the amount of noncompliance at the top of the income distribution, to the extent that the IRS under-detects certain forms of high-end evasion.[14]

Importantly, unlike the IRS tax gap studies, these studies face the further challenge of estimating how this noncompliance varies at different income levels. For this purpose, income can be defined either as total taxable income or as a broader measure of overall economic income, whether it is taxable or not. The estimates of taxpayers' true income will then necessitate a reshuffling of the taxpayers in each income band, since some of them will have previously appeared to have lower incomes because a portion of their true income was not observed.[15] Finally, these studies focus on the distribution of clearly illegal tax noncompliance, but do not account for the lost revenue when taxpayers exploit ambiguities in the law and adopt tax positions that are neither clearly legal nor illegal.

Findings. Studies on the distribution of tax noncompliance generally find proportionally higher rates of noncompliance at the top of the income distribution. An influential study by economists Andrew Johns and Joel Slemrod, published in 2010, found that, for the 2001 tax year, the proportion of underreported income increased with the taxpayers' income level and peaked among taxpayers in the 99.0–99.5 percentile range.[16] According to the study's findings, that year taxpayers with true taxable income above $100,000 in 2001 misreported an average of 15.2% of their income, while taxpayers at lower income levels misreported only 7% of their income, or less than half this amount.

In the same study, Johns and Slemrod also found that the ratio of underreported tax to true taxes owed is highest at the bottom of the income distribution. This result is less surprising, however, since in the case of a lower-income taxpayer with a lower total tax liability, every dollar of taxes unreported represents a greater proportion of their total taxes owed.

More recent studies of the distribution of noncompliance also find that underreporting is highly concentrated at high income levels. In 2021, a group of economists and IRS researchers estimated a distribution of tax noncompliance that also accounted for "sophisticated evasion," which not only may not be detected on random audit data but is also highly concentrated at the top of the income distribution.[17] This study finds that the bottom 50% of earners underreport their income by an average of 7%, while the top 1% of taxpayers fail to report 21% of their true income. Within the top 1%, the study finds that the underreporting rate declines slightly at the very top of the income distribution, to just under 15% for the top 0.01% of earners. In terms of how the tax gap is shared across income groups, the study estimated that the top 1% of earners accounted for 36% of all federal taxes underpaid, amounting to approximately $175 billion in lost tax revenue every year.

Also in 2021, economists Natasha Sarin and Lawrence Summers similarly found, based on their analysis of the sources of income in the IRS tax gap data, that higher-income taxpayers account for a disproportionate share of the total tax gap.[18] They also estimated that the very highest earners underreport at even higher rates than moderately high-income taxpayers, finding that the average tax underreporting percentage for taxpayers with income under $200,000 is just 2.6%, but more than doubles to 6.7% for taxpayers with income between $500,000 and $1 million, and grows to 13.9% for taxpayers with income of $10 million or more. In a separate 2021 study, Sarin calculated that the top 1% of earners accounts for approximately $163 billion in lost tax revenue each year, or 28% of all unpaid taxes.[19] These findings support the contention that Sarin and Summers, together with Charles O. Rossotti, made in 2020: The true proportion of all taxes unpaid by the richest taxpayers may in fact be higher, because official estimates "likely miss some of the opaque income that high earners accrue."[20]

As previously stated, and as the literature has shown, measuring the distribution of noncompliance in different ways can significantly affect the findings. For example, an alternative study using data from 2006 to 2014 finds that when taxpayers are classified by their reported income rather than their true adjusted income, under-reporting rates may actually decline across the income distribution.[21] Of course, the measure of reported income will be misleading to the extent that taxpayers under-report their true income, and therefore this finding does not indicate how rates of noncompliance vary across the distribution of real economic income.

These studies offer different estimates of how the tax gap is shared across income groups, based on different approaches to interpreting the data and measuring the distribution of noncompliance. Despite their differences, however, they provide a few consistent insights on how tax noncompliance changes at different income levels. First, these studies typically find that the highest earners account for a disproportionate and substantial share of all tax revenue lost to noncompliance, particularly when taxpayers are ranked according to their true economic income.[22] Second, while the rate of tax noncompliance does not necessarily increase continuously and proportionally to income, evidence also suggests that the very highest earners account for an even greater share of all tax noncompliance.

These findings do not suggest that the rich are innately predisposed to tax noncompliance, nor that any individual high earner is more likely to not comply just because of their income level. To the contrary, most taxpayers at every income level are motivated to pay taxes as their civic duty and legal obligation. For example, studies find that "within any group defined by income, age, or other demographic category, there are some who evade, some who do not, and even some who overstate tax liability."[23]

While some studies suggest that tax honesty or the motivation to comply with tax laws may decline at higher income levels,[24] high-end noncompliance often has a simpler explanation. Specifically, high-end taxpayers who *are* inclined to skirt the tax law, or to avoid it altogether, simply have more opportunities to do so under the current patchwork of tax compliance rules and IRS enforcement practices. The final section in this chapter describes these unique opportunities for tax noncompliance at the top, which explains why earners in this category represent a significant share of the total tax gap. But first, it is important to ask why the distribution of noncompliance matters, and why we should be particularly concerned with tax noncompliance at the top.

WHY THE DISTRIBUTION OF NONCOMPLIANCE MATTERS

Noncompliance by any taxpayer at any income level costs the public tax revenues, which means less money for important public investments, higher taxes on other taxpayers, and a larger public debt. To illustrate the scale of this lost revenue, consider again the projections of a total tax gap of $7.5 trillion from 2020 to 2029, which translates to a cost of almost $5,000 for every tax-filing household in the United States.[25] This lost revenue, if it were all recovered, would be enough to cut the projected federal deficits for these years nearly in half, or to fully fund all federal expenditures for the Medicaid program.[26] For reasons described later in this book, policymakers cannot realistically seek to entirely eliminate the tax gap.[27] Recovering even just 15% or less of the tax gap, however, could fully fund tuition at all public colleges and universities.[28]

If we just look at the dollars lost from tax noncompliance – and what we could do with them – we might assume, however, that it does not matter if the government recovers the lost revenue from one noncompliant taxpayer or another. For the same reason, we might assume that policymakers should not be particularly concerned with the distribution of noncompliance, but should instead focus exclusively on the size of the tax gap and the easiest ways to narrow it.

This section describes why the distribution of tax noncompliance also matters. High-end noncompliance imposes unique and often heavier costs to the fiscal system and to society, and policymakers should treat it as a fundamentally different policy challenge, even as they seek measures to narrow the tax gap at every income level. As this discussion demonstrates, there are different ways of thinking about the problems with high-end tax noncompliance. Further, these different understandings of the problem can have different implications for how, and to what degree, policymakers should take measures to help close the tax gap at the top.

Lost Revenue and Higher Enforcement Costs

One simple reason to be concerned with high-end tax noncompliance is the substantial amount of lost revenue at stake. The richest taxpayers account for a large proportion of total revenues lost to noncompliance. The studies cited earlier indicate that the top 1% of earners likely account for between 28% and 36% of the total tax gap, and somewhere between $163 billion and $175 billion in lost revenue annually.

The IRS has a harder time recovering lost tax revenues at the top of the distribution because high-end noncompliance is often more difficult and costly for the IRS to detect. As a result, the IRS encounters what we might term the "enforcement cost gap" when it seeks to equitably enforce the tax law. The IRS must incur greater costs to enforce the tax law against high-end taxpayers, while it can often enforce the tax law against lower- and middle-income taxpayers at a lower cost. By prioritizing enforcement against lower-income taxpayers, the IRS can often earn a higher yield of recovered tax revenues per enforcement dollar spent.

In a 2019 letter to the Senate on challenges to tax enforcement, IRS Commissioner Charles Rettig underscored this point, observing that it is often much cheaper and faster for the IRS to instead target noncompliance by lower-income taxpayers.[29] He noted that the average time to complete a correspondence audit for a lower-income taxpayer claiming the EITC is only five hours per return. In contrast, a highly trained IRS agent requires anywhere from 61 to 251 hours to complete the audit of a tax return by a filer with an adjusted gross income of $10 million or more.

If we set aside correspondence audits – which are often cost-effective ways to recover taxes unpaid by lower-income taxpayers – the IRS can likely earn substantial returns from increasing audits of higher-income taxpayers. A 2023 study found that in-person audits of high-income taxpayers can generate more tax revenue per additional dollar spent on enforcement, as compared to similar audits of low-income taxpayers.[30] A 2023 study by the Treasury Inspector General for Tax Administration similarly suggested that the IRS's Large Business and International (LB&I) Division could increase its productivity by shifting resources from audits of taxpayers earning under $200,000 to examinations of higher-income taxpayers.[31]

Throughout this book, we reconsider how the tax compliance rules can help narrow the enforcement cost gap among taxpayers at different points in the income distribution. During a period of renewed IRS focus on high-end tax enforcement, a reimagined tax compliance system can enable more equitable and cost-efficient enforcement efforts for taxpayers at different income levels.

Tax Noncompliance and Progressivity

Even if we ignore enforcement cost differences, a dollar of lost revenue from a low-income or middle-income taxpayer due to tax noncompliance does not represent the same social cost as a dollar of lost revenue from a high-income taxpayer. A basic principle of progressive taxation is that not all tax dollars are valued equally. The progressive tax system – in which higher-income taxpayers pay tax at proportionally higher rates – is most commonly justified under a principle of declining marginal utility.[32] This principle recognizes that an additional dollar of income will be more valuable for a low-income taxpayer, who may need that income to cover basic needs such as food or shelter. In contrast, a higher-income taxpayer could use the same dollar for discretionary purchases, rather than having to spend it on necessities. Professor Louis Kaplow observes that, in the ordinary case, "as one increases an individual's income, marginal utility falls as utility rises, and conversely when income is reduced."[33] Further, in a welfare economics framework, a greater social weight may be placed on maximizing the utility of those who are less well off, which would imply even greater social welfare gains from marginal dollars of income at lower points on the income distribution.[34]

For this reason, aggregate social welfare can be maximized through a progressive rate structure, which asks more of the taxpayers with a greater ability to pay. Collecting an additional dollar of revenue from a high-income taxpayer will, setting aside other potential costs of taxation,[35] entail relatively lower social welfare cost to the taxpayer, as compared to collecting the marginal dollar of revenue from a lower-income taxpayer.[36] This dollar of tax revenue can increase aggregate welfare if it is used to improve the welfare of an individual at a lower point on the utility curve.

High-end noncompliance directly undermines tax progressivity, and scholars have long recognized its threat to progressive taxation. In a 2017 book, economists Joel Slemrod and Jon Bakija observed that tax evasion "makes it difficult to achieve whatever degree of progressivity we deem to be consistent with vertical equity."[37] Professor Leandra Lederman offered a similar argument in a 2016 article: Noncompliance with the tax laws can undermine their progressive effect and "if the tax laws are not adequately enforced, the net effect of a progressive tax system may be to increase income inequality."[38]

The same marginal utility analysis underlying progressive taxation also explains the higher social costs from high-end noncompliance, and the increased social benefits from recovering dollars of lost tax revenue at the top of the distribution. Reducing the noncompliance of a high-income taxpayer will, all things being equal, result in a larger social welfare gain than if the IRS recovered the same amount of revenue lost to noncompliance from a lower-income taxpayer.

This consideration suggests two additional reasons why policymakers should be uniquely concerned with high-end compliance in a progressive tax system. First, the principle of declining marginal utility underlying progressive taxation explains why, when seeking to maximize social welfare, they should prioritize reducing noncompliance by the highest earners, regardless of the specific distribution of noncompliance at different income levels. That is, even if the degree of noncompliance did not vary at different points in the income distribution, as measured in terms of lost tax revenue, this principle explains why there could still be the greater social costs resulting from noncompliance by the highest earners, as measured in terms of lost social welfare.

This consideration also explains why policymakers setting tax-enforcement priorities should not only consider which enforcement actions will yield the greatest amount of revenue recovered at the lowest monetary costs to the government and taxpayers; rather, policymakers should also consider which taxpayers, at which relative income levels, are engaging in noncompliance when setting enforcement priorities. Only by taking these additional considerations into account can policymakers optimize the trade-offs between enforcement costs and the social welfare effects of lost tax revenue at different points on the income distribution scale.

Racial Equity

Tax noncompliance and enforcement priorities can also reinforce racial injustice. Black taxpayers and other non-white taxpayers comprise a greater proportion of lower- and middle-income earners than white taxpayers.[39] As a result, enforcement measures targeted at tax noncompliance by taxpayers at these income levels can often disproportionably burden these taxpayers, and compound racial inequity in the tax system.

In many cases, the IRS can also more easily target the types of tax noncompliance conducted by lower- and middle-income taxpayers. Professor Dorothy Brown has argued that "it is simply easier for the IRS to go after the most vulnerable among us."[40] A 2019 *ProPublica* report found that "the counties with the highest audit rates were poor, rural, mostly African American and in the South, a reflection of the high number of EITC claims there."[41]

As Professor Brown and others have noted, economic disparities in tax enforcement can also compound the effects of other racial disparities. For example, a 2023 study by a group of economists and IRS researchers found that Black taxpayers are audited at between 2.9 and 4.7 times the rate of non-Black taxpayers, notwithstanding the IRS's race-blind audit selection procedures.[42] Importantly, the study found that the disparity was primarily attributable to "differing audit rates by race" even within the group of all lower- and middle-income taxpayers claiming the EITC. In 2023, IRS Commissioner Danny Werfel affirmed that the findings in this study were concerning and that, despite the complexities in the audit selection process, the agency would redouble its commitment to "fair and equitable tax administration."[43] These findings, and the IRS's response to them, illustrate the complex interactions of economic and racial disparities in tax enforcement, and the need for careful and constant attention to equity in tax administration.

The Effect on Tax Morale

High-end noncompliance can also undermine both "tax morale," which is the intrinsic motivation to comply with the tax laws,[44] and public support for the tax system.[45] Motivations to pay taxes include moral values, social norms or community attitudes, and, importantly for our purposes, "perceptions of and attitudes towards evasion."[46] Policymakers have long recognized the critical role of public perceptions in maintaining the integrity of the tax system.[47] For example, the IRS National Taxpayer Advocate has suggested that voluntary tax compliance depends in large part on taxpayers' "faith and trust in the fairness of the tax system."[48]

Studies have found a correlation between tax morale and tax compliance,[49] and that countries with low tax morale tend to experience higher rates of tax noncompliance.[50] It has also been found that a perception that some taxpayers are evading their taxes can reduce tax morale – and therefore discourage compliance – among other taxpayers. For example, in a 2004 paper, Professor Benno Torgler offered evidence that, when individuals believe that they know or have heard about other taxpayers who engage in tax avoidance and evasion without being detected by the taxing authority, they report lower tax morale than others.[51] While identifying a causal link between tax morale and tax compliance is difficult, a 2014 review of the tax morale literature by Erzo F. P. Luttmer and Monica Singhal argues that individuals' perceptions of "peer compliance directly affects the individuals' own compliance."[52]

Studies also find that high-end noncompliance in particular can erode public trust and morale for taxpayers at all income levels. In a paper published in 2020, Professors Katharina Gangl and Benno Torgler cite evidence that high-end noncompliance "not only directly impacts a state's capacity to finance public goods, but ... also influences the tax compliance of the general population and can be the cause of social and political turbulence."[53] Gangl and Torgler also argue that high-end noncompliance can also have a particularly strong effect on tax morale among the public because the rich often serve as role models, stating that "the wealthy's tax behavior is also socially important because they, by personifying society's measures of success, prompt other citizens to imitate their tax behavior."[54]

Finally, studies find that that progressivity in the tax system can also positively influence tax morale.[55] High-end noncompliance, which erodes the progressivity of the tax system, can have the opposite effect and depress tax morale among all taxpayers. It does this both by fostering a perception that certain privileged taxpayers can more easily avoid their tax responsibilities, and by undermining the progressive structure of the tax system.

A Barrier to Tax Reform

Finally, high-end tax noncompliance operates as a barrier to structural reforms, which can improve the fairness and efficiency of the tax system. Estimates of the tax gap and noncompliance do not include the many ways that taxpayers can avoid taxes through perfectly legal means. Many of the most advantageous legal tax-reduction opportunities disproportionately benefit the wealthiest taxpayers. For example, wealthy taxpayers who earn a greater proportion of their income from investments can take the greatest advantages of preferences in the tax law for capital income.[56] Rich taxpayers may also legally shield their income from taxation through the strategic use of vehicles such as specialized trusts,[57] life insurance policies,[58] and tax-favored retirement accounts.[59]

In some cases, policymakers can target certain strategies that deliver oversized benefits to high-income taxpayers.[60] High-end noncompliance, however, can also frustrate policymakers' efforts to enact broader structural reforms that would create a fairer and more efficient tax system. Any such reforms will not have their intended effects if well-advised taxpayers can easily avoid complying with the changes. In formal terms, the availability of tax avoidance (whether through legal or illegal means) increases the elasticity of the tax instrument, which in turn increases the efficiency costs of taxation while reducing its revenue-raising potential.[61]

High-end noncompliance can be a critical factor for lawmakers in structural tax reform. In 2019, Senator Elizabeth Warren (D-MA) proposed a federal wealth tax on large fortunes, designed to raise revenue for healthcare reform.[62] To a large extent, the subsequent debate over the viability of the reform focused on the question of whether policymakers could adequately ensure compliance with the new rules. When assessing both sides of the debate, economist Alan Viard noted that "most economists believe that the wealth tax would face significant administration and compliance challenges."[63] Proponents, on the other hand, argued that combining the reform with robust tax-enforcement measures would minimize tax noncompliance, which was critical to their claim that the reform would have its intended economic effects.[64]

This book does not address the policy wisdom of any particular tax reform proposal such as a wealth tax. Rather, this example illustrates the central importance of tax compliance in debates over the structure of the tax system, and how high levels of noncompliance can weaken the economic rationale and political support for structural tax reform.

HOW THE RICH AVOID TAXES

Why is the tax gap at the top so large? And why is it so difficult and costly for the IRS to close it? The final section of this chapter explains how the richest taxpayers often take advantage of the current tax compliance rules to escape their taxpaying responsibilities.

Of course, taxpayers at every income level have opportunities to avoid complying with the tax laws. Lower-income taxpayers may be able to inappropriately claim qualifications for tax benefits such as the EITC,[65] and it is possible for wage earners and small business owners in certain industries to underreport their income and accept payments in cash to avoid detection.[66]

Because of their economic resources, however, the richest taxpayers have a broader menu of opportunities to avoid paying taxes. They benefit from a larger economy of scale: With more income and tax liabilities at stake, they can afford more sophisticated structuring and legal advice, options that are simply not available to lower-income taxpayers. These opportunities for noncompliance explain not only why the highest earners account for a substantial share of the total tax gap, but also why it is often more difficult and costly for the IRS to detect and prevent abusive tax planning at the top.

Later chapters in this book detail many specific examples of the opportunities for tax noncompliance available to the richest taxpayers and the challenges the IRS faces in stopping them. This chapter introduces five interrelated factors that explain these varied opportunities, all of which are enabled by high-end taxpayers' access to greater economic resources. Specifically, high-end taxpayers can often take the greatest advantage of (1) complexity, (2) flexibility, (3) reduced visibility, (4) sophisticated tax advice, and (5) ambiguities in the tax law. Because of these factors, high-end taxpayers often have lower chances that their noncompliance will be detected by the IRS, and, even if they are caught, higher chances of success in a dispute with the IRS.

Complexity

Lower- and middle-income taxpayers typically earn taxable income in relatively simple ways, primarily through salaries or wages. These activities only offer limited avenues for tax noncompliance, such as by overstating deductible expenses, understating cash income, or improperly claiming tax benefits such as the EITC. Tax noncompliance by lower-income taxpayers through strategies such as nonreporting of cash or EITC fraud undoubtedly cost the government lost revenues. When the IRS does suspect noncompliance, however, the agency can often address these issues through cost-effective single-issue correspondence audits.

High-end taxpayers, in contrast, can often afford to engage in tax noncompliance through more complex and varied tax structuring, which can be harder for the IRS to successfully detect and challenge. These taxpayers can invest in more complex financial products and asset classes, and they can also hold their assets through intricate and bespoke structures, such as tiered partnerships and offshore accounts.[67] These complex structures available to the rich can multiply the opportunities for tax noncompliance and more effectively conceal noncompliance from IRS detection.

For an example of how complexity factors into tax noncompliance, IRS Commissioner Rettig contrasted the difficulty in identifying tax avoidance for both lower-income and wealthy taxpayers in his 2019 letter to the Senate.[68] Rettig observed that tax noncompliance by lower-income taxpayers can often be detected through relatively inexpensive single-issue correspondence audits conducted by mail. In contrast, high-income taxpayers typically file more complex tax returns, in which tax noncompliance can assume many forms and structures, and which often require lengthy and complex in-person audits by specialized IRS agents. For example, Rettig identified the challenges in detecting tax avoidance through "cash intensive businesses, transfer pricing, executive compensation, research and development credits, cryptocurrencies, partnerships and flow through entities, micro captives, offshore transactions, and syndicated conservation easements."[69] In its 2023 "dirty dozen list," the IRS also highlighted complex forms of tax abuse through the use of charitable remainder annuity trusts (CRATs) and monetized installment sale structures.[70]

The House Committee on Ways & Means' 2022 investigation of President Trump's tax returns illustrates the central importance of complexity in tax avoidance.[71] The Committee identified a host of questionable, and possibly abusive, positions on Trump's returns for tax years 2015 through 2020, but also critiqued the IRS for failing to adequately audit these returns as required by law. The report found that the responsible IRS agents recommended only a limited-scope examination for critical years because of, among other factors, "the complexity of issues."

Taxpayers can also design complex business structures that can mask noncompliance. For example, the 2021 distributional study of "sophisticated evasion" conducted by John Guyton and his colleagues, described earlier in this chapter, identified tax evasion through complex pass-through business structures as a primary driver of the tax gap at the top.[72] They observed that "partnerships create a specific additional challenge to the audit process, because partnerships can be owned by other entities, sometimes leading to complex ownership structures involving numerous partnerships, corporations, trusts, or other intermediaries."[73] This study was not the first time this phenomenon was observed. In 2016, a group of economists and Treasury researchers similarly found that pass-through income is not only highly concentrated among the highest earners but also that much of this income is "opaque," with 20% of the total pass-through income earned by "unclassifiable partners."[74]

The complexity of pass-through structures has also helped them to avoid becoming targets of IRS examinations. A 2014 Government Accountability Report found that the IRS was auditing only a very small proportion of large and complex partnerships, and that the complexity of these structures limited the effectiveness of those audits that the IRS did conduct.[75] In 2015, Congress and the IRS sought to address the challenges in auditing large partnerships by establishing a statutory centralized partnership audit regime and introducing new IRS enforcement initiatives.[76]

Complexity can stack the deck against the IRS at every stage of the tax enforcement process, from audits and detection through the controversy stage. As the following sections explain, complexity can also interact with additional factors that further enable tax noncompliance.

Flexibility

Complexity often also allows high-end taxpayers greater flexibility in structuring their transactions. Further, high-end taxpayers benefit from a wide range of investment opportunities that are not available to those with less income. This flexibility, in turn, often allows high-end taxpayers to stay one step ahead of IRS enforcement actions. Chapter 3 describes how the IRS often finds itself in the position of reacting to the latest market developments – instead of preempting future abuses – and scrambling to quickly challenge tax noncompliance while there is still time. For example, the IRS has sought to crack down on many of the specific complex transactions identified by Commissioner Rettig in 2019, such as cryptocurrency and syndicated conservation easements.[77] By the time the IRS took these actions, however, many high-end taxpayers had moved on to new and different tax-avoidance opportunities.[78]

Chapter 3 also describes in detail how additional legal obstacles can prevent the IRS from acting quickly to counter evolving tax-avoidance strategies.[79] Following the Supreme Court's 2021 holding in *CIC Services, LLC v. IRS*, taxpayers can potentially bring preemptive challenges to a wide range of the IRS's regulatory efforts to prevent tax abuse.[80] These IRS actions can also now be subject to more lengthy procedural requirements under the Administrative Procedure Act,[81] which can slow down the IRS's efforts to quickly challenge abusive structures before taxpayers have moved on.

Visibility

The IRS can more easily detect noncompliance when it knows more about taxpayers' transactions and activities. Low- and middle-income earners typically engage in transactions that are more visible to the IRS and present fewer opportunities for avoidance. High-income taxpayers, in contrast, often earn income through less-visible forms, which can be harder for the IRS to detect and investigate. Due to this "visibility gap," it is often easier for the IRS to detect noncompliance by low- and middle-income taxpayers.

Chapter 9 describes in detail how third-party information reporting increases the visibility of taxpayer transactions, and consequently improves tax compliance.[82] Tax compliance is typically much higher for transactions subject to information reporting, which allows the IRS to more easily detect any abuses or underreporting.[83] For example, the IRS's 2022 report on the tax gap finds that, while the misreporting percentage for income not subject to information reporting is 55%, it is only 6% or less for income that is subject to substantial information reporting.[84] The underreporting percentage drops to only 1% for income subject to both information reporting *and* withholding.

Low- and middle-income taxpayers typically earn forms of income that are most visible to the IRS, and that are generally subject to comprehensive information reporting and withholding.[85] For example, employers report their employees' wage income to the IRS on the annual Form W-2 and withhold the employees' estimated income tax liabilities. Higher-income taxpayers, in contrast, earn a higher proportion of income that is not currently subject to information reporting or withholding, such as pass-through business income and rental income. The Congressional Budget Office (CBO) estimates that in 2019 lower- and middle-income taxpayers earned between 60% and 70% of their total income as labor income (predominantly wages and salaries). Conversely, the highest income taxpayers earn proportionally less labor income, and a higher proportion of less visible capital and business income. The CBO estimates that, in 2019, the top 1% of taxpayers earned less than one-third of their income from labor. For the top 0.1%, that figure was less than 20%.[86]

The different avoidance opportunities for labor income, on the one hand, and capital and business income, on the other, also illustrate the interaction between the different factors in high-end tax avoidance. Taxpayers earning capital and business income also often have greater opportunities to take advantage of more complex tax structuring. As Chapter 9 describes in greater detail, high-end taxpayers can also take advantage of flexibility in structuring their transactions to avoid or minimize information reporting or withholding.

Other factors can also affect the visibility of a taxpayer's activities. Even among activities that are not subject to information reporting, some transactions are less visible than others, including those that do not leave any transaction record or "paper trail," those that are shrouded through complex transactions and tiered entities, and those that are conducted through the use of cryptocurrency or in offshore jurisdictions. Here, as well, high-end taxpayers often have the further advantage of being able to engage in those activities not subject to information reporting that also have the lowest visibility. For example, the 2021 study on "sophisticated evasion" conducted by John Guyton and his colleagues identifies offshore evasion as an additional major factor in the tax gap at the very top.[87] As we describe in Chapter 3, Congress and the IRS have gone to great lengths to address the challenges of offshore evasion; however, they have often done so in a manner that has created further challenges for the tax compliance system.[88]

Finally, high-end taxpayers often derive the greatest benefit from less-visible activities that are in principle available to all taxpayers. For example, some have argued that Bitcoin and other digital currencies offer a "democratized" form of investment available to taxpayers at all income levels.[89] These digital currency transactions are also often hard for the IRS to observe, particularly when conducted outside of centralized exchanges.[90]

Despite their democratic promise, the largest benefits from digital currency often accrue to the very richest taxpayers. For example, a 2021 study analyzing the Bitcoin network estimated that just the top 0.01% of Bitcoin owners held approximately 27% of the entire asset class.[91] A 2022 study also found that lower-income individuals were more likely to use cryptocurrency for regular transactions, while higher-income individuals were more likely to use it for long-term investment and as a store of wealth.[92] A 2023 study similarly found that cryptocurrency holdings are highly concentrated among the very wealthy, with potentially tens of billions of dollars of income tax revenues at stake.[93]

Sophisticated Advisors

Sophisticated advisors help provide high-end taxpayers with the greatest opportunity to manipulate the tax compliance system and its shortcomings. At the planning stage, these advisors can design complex and flexible structures that not only facilitate noncompliance but also increase the likelihood that high-end taxpayers will avoid paying taxes owed even if the IRS successfully detects and challenges their tax noncompliance. High-end taxpayers can also rely on the opinions of advisors in many cases to avoid penalties or other noncompliance consequences.[94]

Due to not only their greater resources but also their economy of scale, high-end taxpayers can afford high-powered and expensive advisors whose services would be cost-prohibitive for lower- and middle-income taxpayers. "Highly-experienced" attorneys working on sophisticated matters often cost more than $1,000 an hour.[95] In a 2019 article, Professor Heather Field argued that high-end taxpayers can often afford to purchase sophisticated tax counsel as a form of "insurance" against tax challenges by the IRS, and the fees paid may be calculated based on billable hours or "on the financial exposure and the estimated likelihood of liability."[96] Not only can these taxpayers afford sophisticated counsel, but they also have higher potential tax liabilities at stake, which justifies engaging expensive tax advisors. Professor Field's subsequent research highlights the emerging market for actual tax insurance products, which can fully insulate taxpayers against potential tax liabilities or penalties.[97] With this type of insurance coverage, the taxpayer bears only the cost of the premiums, and the IRS instead collects any resulting liabilities or penalties from the insurer.[98]

Even if the IRS detects noncompliance, having a sophisticated tax advisor can increase the likelihood that the taxpayer will prevail in a dispute with the agency. In some cases, even the presence of a tax advisor can discourage the IRS from examining or challenging the taxpayer's positions in the first place. For example, the 2022 House Ways & Means Committee Report on the IRS's handling of President Trump's tax returns also highlights the effect of his legal advisors on the agency's examination. The report found that one of the reasons why the IRS did not properly examine the returns was that Trump had a "professional accounting firm and counsel" working for him.[99] Evidently, the IRS determined that the presence of high-powered advisors reduced the agency's chance of success even if they did find evidence of noncompliance, and, as a result, decided not to conduct a full examination at all.

Even if the IRS can successfully detect noncompliance by high-income taxpayers, it may not be able to recover the applicable tax liabilities and penalties due. These taxpayers have greater resources to spend not only on sophisticated tax advisors and representation in disputes with the IRS, but also on procedural actions such as negotiations and appeals.[100] These advantages reduce the amount of taxes and penalties that the IRS ultimately recovers through enforcement actions against high-end taxpayers.[101] For these reasons, Professor David Schizer has argued that the IRS faces an "entrenched mismatch between the government and the private bar" at every stage of tax compliance, from the drafting of rules through the auditing of returns and the litigation of cases.[102]

The disappointments of the IRS "Wealth Squad" illustrate the challenges the agency faces when taxpayers hire sophisticated counsel and engage in complex transactions. In 2009, the IRS formed a "Global High Wealth Industry Group" (commonly referred to as the "Wealth Squad"), which consisted of expert agents dedicated to investigating high-end tax noncompliance. At the time, IRS Commissioner Douglas Shulman announced that the new group would take a comprehensive and global approach to tax examinations, in order to counter sophisticated and complex forms of tax evasion.[103] A subsequent report found, however, that the new program "never came close to having the impact its proponents envisaged," as IRS agents had to "contend with battalions of high-priced lawyers and accountants that often outnumber and outgun even the agency's elite SWAT team."[104] Although the IRS subsequently reconstituted its Global High Wealth program,[105] the challenges faced by the original Wealth Squad illustrate how sophisticated advisors can stack the deck in favor of high-end taxpayers.

Exploiting Ambiguities

Sophisticated tax advisors can incorporate greater complexity in the tax-planning process for their wealthy clients, which in turn can also allow high-end taxpayers to exploit ambiguities in the tax law. The report on Trump's returns reveals how the IRS may not only defer to the judgment of sophisticated tax advisors but also fail to properly investigate their clients' returns. In the cases where the IRS does bring a challenge, sophisticated legal advisors can also increase the chances of a taxpayer prevailing in the dispute, when the proper application of the law is unclear. For this reason, access to sophisticated tax advice also allows high-end taxpayers to take advantage of ambiguities in the law, and to reduce their taxes further through strategies that are neither clearly legal nor illegal.

Because they do not account for ambiguities in the tax law, the official estimates of the tax gap – which measures only clear instances of tax noncompliance – offer an incomplete picture of tax avoidance. In some cases, especially when facing sophisticated legal counsel, the IRS may defer to a taxpayer's position, even though the agency might have prevailed on the merits if the position was challenged. In other cases, the IRS may challenge a taxpayer position that pushes the limits of the legality, only to fall short because of the ambiguities in the law and the role of the taxpayer's legal counsel. In both situations, the taxpayer can take advantage of legal uncertainties to shape the definition of what constitutes tax noncompliance in the first place.

As an example of this interaction between complex tax planning, skilled and knowledgeable counsel, and legal ambiguity, in recent decades the managers of private equity funds have made aggressive use of what is called a "management fee waiver" to maximize the tax benefits of their private equity profits interests.[106] Through these complex arrangements, the fund managers forego their management fees, which are typically taxed at higher rates, so they can instead classify their earnings as "carried interest" profits from the fund, which are more preferentially taxed. The most aggressive forms of these arrangements almost certainly extend beyond the limits of the tax law. By the time the IRS began to target the most egregious abuses with proposed regulations that clarified the proper application of the law to these structures, however, the practice had already cost the government "hundreds of millions of dollars in lost revenue."[107]

Similarly, a 2023 *ProPublica* report detailed how sophisticated taxpayers often take advantage of ambiguities in the Section 1091 "wash-sale rules" to reduce or eliminate their taxes through complex transactions.[108] Through this strategy, taxpayers skirt the wash-sale rules to accelerate the recognition of tax losses without exiting their underlying financial positions. Because of the ambiguities in the underlying law, the IRS has not aggressively challenged these positions, even when they push or exceed the limits of the law.

In some cases, sophisticated advisors can also take advantage of legal ambiguity to shape interpretations of the tax law. In a 2016 article, Professor Sloan Speck describes how high-end taxpayers and their counsel often exercise a "first-mover advantage" in interpreting new laws by structuring transactions in accordance with their own interpretations.[109] Through this process of "planning drift" that Professor Speck describes, sophisticated advisors can entrench interpretations of ambiguous tax laws that Congress never intended.

* * *

High-end tax noncompliance accounts for a large share of the growing tax gap. It imposes unique costs on the fiscal system and is enabled by a confluence of factors that often gives the richest taxpayers the greatest opportunities to take advantage of the current tax compliance rules. In Chapter 2, we take a closer look at the structure of the tax compliance system and the traditional responses to the challenges presented by high-end noncompliance.

NOTES

1. I.R.C. § 7201.
2. IRS, The Truth about Frivolous Tax Arguments (2022), https://www.irs.gov/privacy-disclosure/the-truth-about-frivolous-tax-arguments-introduction.
3. Ari Glogower, *Taxing Capital Appreciation*, 70 Tax L. Rev. 111 (2016) (describing how taxpayers can take advantage of the "realization rule" to reduce or eliminate their taxes on capital income).
4. Edward J. McCaffery, *A Voluntary Tax? Revisited*, 93 Proc. Ann. Conf. Tax'n Minutes Ann. Meeting Nat'l Tax Ass'n 268, 271 (2000).
5. *See, e.g.*, Annette Alstadsæter et al., *Tax Evasion and Tax Avoidance*, 206 J. Pub. Econ. 104587 (Feb. 2022).
6. Joel Slemrod & Shlomo Yitzhaki, *Tax Avoidance, Evasion, and Administration*, in 3 Handbook of Public Economics 1423, 1428 (Alan J. Auerbach & Martin Feldstein eds., 2002).
7. Gregory v. Helvering, 293 U.S. 465 (1935).
8. 293 U.S. at 469.
9. IRS, Pub. 1415 (Rev. 10-2022), Federal Tax Compliance Research: Tax Gap Estimates for Tax Years 2014–2016 (2022).
10. *Id.*
11. *See* Daniel Hemel et al., *The Tax Gap's Many Shades of Gray*, Urban Inst. & Brookings Inst. Tax Pol'y Ctr. (2022).
12. Natasha Sarin & Lawrence H. Summers, *Shrinking the Tax Gap: Approaches and Revenue Potential*, 165 Tax Notes Fed. 1099 (Nov. 18, 2019).
13. David Lawder, *IRS Chief Says $1 Trillion in Taxes Goes Uncollected Every Year*, Reuters.com (Apr. 13, 2021), https://www.reuters.com/article/us-usa-treasury-irs/irs-chief-says-1-trillion-in-taxes-goes-uncollected-every-year-idUSKBN2C0255.
14. *See* John Guyton et al., *Tax Evasion at the Top of the Income Distribution: Theory and Evidence* 10–11 (NBER Working Paper No. 26542, Mar. 2021).
15. *See id.* at 10 (describing how taxpayers must be re-ranked based on the estimates of their corrected income).
16. Andrew Johns & Joel Slemrod, *The Distribution of Income Tax Noncompliance*, 63 Nat'l Tax J. 397, 406 tbl.3 (2010).
17. Guyton et al., *supra* note 14.
18. Sarin & Summers, *supra* note 12.
19. Natasha Sarin, *The Case for a Robust Attack on the Tax Gap* (U.S. Dept. of Treasury) (Sept. 7, 2021), https://home.treasury.gov/news/featured-stories/the-case-for-a-robust-attack-on-the-tax-gap.
20. Charles O. Rossotti et al., *Shrinking the Tax Gap: A Comprehensive Approach*, 169 Tax Notes Fed. 1467 (2020).
21. Jason DeBacker et al., *Tax Noncompliance and Measures of Income Inequality*, 166 Tax Notes Fed. 1103 (Feb. 17, 2020).
22. *See also* U.S. Dep't of Treasury, The American Families Plan Tax Compliance Agenda 5 (May 2021).
23. Joel Slemrod, *Cheating Ourselves: The Economics of Tax Evasion*, 21 J. Econ. Persp. 25, 31 (2007).

24 For a survey of this research, see Katharina Gangl & Benno Torgler, *How to Achieve Tax Compliance by the Wealthy: A Review of the Literature and Agenda for Policy*, 14 SOC. ISSUES & POL'Y REV. 108, 114–15 (2020).
25 The IRS reported approximately 160 million income tax returns filed for the 2020 tax year. IRS, STATISTICS OF INCOME – 2020 INDIVIDUAL INCOME TAX RETURNS (2022).
26 CONGRESSIONAL BUDGET OFFICE, THE BUDGET AND ECONOMIC OUTLOOK: 2023 TO 2033 (2023).
27 *See* Chapter 3, section "The Costs of Enforcement."
28 David Deming, *Tuition-Free College Could Cost Less Than You Think*, N.Y. TIMES (July 21, 2019), at BU.
29 Letter from Charles P. Rettig, IRS Comm'r, to Sen. Ron Wyden (D-OR) (Sept. 6, 2019), https://www.documentcloud.org/documents/6430680-Document-2019-9-6-Treasury-Letter-to-Wyden-RE.html.
30 William C. Boning et al., *A Welfare Analysis of Tax Audits across the Income Distribution* (NBER Working Paper No. 31376, June 2023).
31 TREASURY INSPECTOR GEN. FOR TAX ADMIN., REPORT NO. 2023-30-019, THE IRS LARGE BUSINESS AND INTERNATIONAL DIVISION SHOULD CONSIDER SHIFTING INDIVIDUAL EXAMINATION RESOURCES TO MORE PRODUCTIVE EXAMINATIONS 5–6 (May 25, 2023).
32 *See, e.g.*, JOEL SLEMROD, INTRODUCTION TO TAX PROGRESSIVITY AND INCOME INEQUALITY 1–3 (Joel Slemrod ed., 1996) ("The modern approach to evaluating progressivity focuses on the trade-off between the potential social benefit of a more equal distribution . . . and the economic costs caused by the disincentive effects of the high marginal tax rates required by a redistributing tax system.").
33 LOUIS KAPLOW, THE THEORY OF TAXATION AND PUBLIC ECONOMICS 49 (2008).
34 *Id.* at 42–43 (describing these two different effects as separate factors in the social welfare function).
35 Chapter 2 describes these other potential costs of taxation in greater detail. *See* Chapter 2, section "An Integrated Understanding of Tax Rules."
36 *See* KAPLOW, supra note 33, at 41–47.
37 JOEL SLEMROD & JON BAKIJA, TAXING OURSELVES: A CITIZEN'S GUIDE TO THE DEBATE OVER TAXES 256 (5th ed. 2017).
38 Leandra Lederman, *The IRS, Politics, and Income Inequality*, 150 TAX NOTES 1329, 1333 (2016).
39 *See* DOROTHY BROWN, THE WHITENESS OF WEALTH: HOW THE TAX SYSTEM IMPOVERISHES BLACK AMERICANS-AND HOW WE CAN FIX IT (2021).
40 Dorothy A. Brown, *The IRS Is Targeting the Poorest Americans*, THE ATLANTIC (July 27, 2021).
41 Paul Kiel, *It's Getting Worse: The IRS Now Audits Poor Americans at about the Same Rate as the Top 1%*, PROPUBLICA (May 30, 2019), https://www.propublica.org/article/irs-now-audits-poor-americans-at-about-the-same-rate-as-the-top-1-percent.
42 Hadi Elzayn et al., *Measuring and Mitigating Racial Disparities in Tax Audits* (Stan. Inst. Pol'y Rsch., Working Paper, Jan. 30, 2023).
43 Letter from Daniel I. Werfel, IRS Comm'r, to Sen. Ron Wyden (D-OR) (May 15, 2023), https://www.finance.senate.gov/imo/media/doc/werfel_letter_to_sen_wyden.pdf.

44 Bruno S. Frey & Benno Torgler, *Tax Morale and Conditional Cooperation*, 35 J. COMP. ECON. 136, 140 (2007). Tax morale has also been defined as a "social norm of tax compliance" and as all "nonpecuniary motivations for tax compliance." *See* Erzo F. P. Luttmer & Monica Singhal, *Tax Morale*, 28 J. ECON. PERSP. 149, 149–50 (2014).
45 For more discussion, see also Chapter 2, section "Factors in Tax Compliance."
46 STEVEN M. SHEFFRIN, TAX FAIRNESS AND FOLK JUSTICE 161 (2013); Michael Doran, *Tax Penalties and Tax Compliance*, 46 HARV. J. LEGIS. 111, 131–38 (2009) (describing the social norms model of taxpayer compliance).
47 *See, e.g.*, Marjorie E. Kornhauser, *A Tax Morale Approach to Compliance: Recommendations for the IRS*, 8 FLA. TAX REV. 599 (2007).
48 1 NAT'L TAXPAYER ADVOCATE, 2018 ANNUAL REPORT TO CONGRESS 117 (2019), https://www.taxpayeradvocate.irs.gov/wp-content/uploads/2020/07/ARC18_Volume1.pdf.
49 *See* BENNO TORGLER, TAX COMPLIANCE AND TAX MORALE: A THEORETICAL AND EMPIRICAL ANALYSIS 64–78 (2007); SHEFFRIN, *supra* note 46, at 169, 178–80.
50 *See, e.g.*, Luttmer & Singhal, *supra* note 44; Christian Daude et al., *What Drives Tax Morale?* 2 (Org. for Econ. Co-operation & Dev., Working Paper No. 315, 2013).
51 Benno Torgler, *Tax Morale, Trust and Corruption: Empirical Evidence from Transition Countries* 11–12, 18, 20–21 (Ctr. for Rsch. in Econ., Mgmt. & the Arts (CREMA), Working Paper No. 2004-05, 2004) (finding through a cross-country empirical analysis that tax morale significantly increases with trust of the legal system and decreases with perceived corruption); Benno Torgler & Friedrich Schneider, *What Shapes Attitudes toward Paying Taxes? Evidence from Multicultural European Countries*, 88 SOC. SCI. Q. 443, 465 (2007) (finding the same effect in a within-country empirical analysis).
52 Luttmer & Singhal, *supra* note 44, at 158.
53 Gangl & Torgler, *supra* note 24, at 108.
54 *Id.*
55 *See* Philipp Doerrenberg & Andreas Peichl, *Progressive Taxation and Tax Morale*, 155 PUB. CHOICE 293 (2013).
56 *See* Glogower, *supra* note 3, and accompanying text.
57 *See* Jeff Ernsthausen et al., *More Than Half of America's 100 Richest People Exploit Special Trusts to Avoid Estate Taxes*, PROPUBLICA (Sept. 28, 2021), https://www.propublica.org/article/more-than-half-of-americas-100-richest-people-exploit-special-trusts-to-avoid-estate-taxes.
58 *See* Luís Calderón Gómez, *Too Good to Be True: Private Placement Life Insurance Policies*, 178 TAX NOTES FED. 55 (Jan. 23, 2023).
59 *See* DAVID MITCHELL, RETIREMENT TAX INCENTIVES SUPERCHARGE THE FORTUNES OF WEALTHY AMERICANS (Wash. Ctr. for Equitable Growth, 2022), https://equitablegrowth.org/retirement-tax-incentives-supercharge-the-fortunes-of-wealthy-americans.
60 For example, in spring 2023, the IRS addressed one particularly advantageous strategy where taxpayers would structure an "intentionally defective grantor trust" to avoid both income and estate taxes. IRS, Rev. Ruling 2023-2.
61 *See* Emmanuel Saez et al., *The Elasticity of Taxable Income with Respect to Marginal Tax Rates: A Critical Review*, 50 J. ECON. LIT. 3 (2012); Ari Glogower & David Kamin, *The Progressivity Ratchet*, 104 MINN. L. REV. 1499 (2020).

62 *See* Press Release, Elizabeth Warren, Senator, Senator Warren Unveils Proposal to Tax Wealth of Ultra-Rich Americans (Jan. 24, 2019), http://perma.cc/2MA2-N87C.
63 Alan D. Viard, *Wealth Taxation: An Overview of the Issues*, in MAINTAINING THE STRENGTH OF AMERICAN CAPITALISM, 180–200 (Melissa S. Kearney & Amy Ganz eds., 2019).
64 *See, e.g.*, Emmanuel Saez & Gabriel Zucman, *Progressive Wealth Taxation*, 2019 BROOKINGS PAPERS ECON. ACTIVITY 437, 437 (2019).
65 *See, e.g.*, IRS, COMPLIANCE ESTIMATES FOR THE EARNED INCOME TAX CREDIT CLAIMED ON 2006–2008 RETURNS (2014). Some analysts have argued, however, that the majority of EITC overpayments result from the "complexity of the rules" and "reflect unintentional errors, not fraud." ROBERT GREENSTEIN, JOHN WANCHECK & CHUCK MARR, REDUCING OVERPAYMENTS IN THE EARNED INCOME TAX CREDIT (Ctr. on Budget and Pol'y Priorities, 2019).
66 *See* Susan C. Morse et al., *Cash Businesses and Tax Evasion*, 20 STAN. L. & POL'Y REV. 37 (2009).
67 *See* U.S. DEP'T OF TREASURY, *supra* note 22, at 7.
68 Rettig, *supra* note 29.
69 *Id.*
70 IRS, Press Release IR-2023-71, IRS Wraps Up 2023 Dirty Dozen List, Reminds Taxpayers and Tax Pros to Be Wary of Scams and Schemes, Even After Tax Season (Apr. 5, 2023), https://www.irs.gov/newsroom/irs-wraps-up-2023-dirty-dozen-list-reminds-taxpayers-and-tax-pros-to-be-wary-of-scams-and-schemes-even-after-tax-season.
71 JOINT COMM. ON TAX'N, REPORT TO THE HOUSE COMMITTEE ON WAYS AND MEANS CHAIRMAN RICHARD NEAL (Dec. 15, 2022).
72 Guyton et al., *supra* note 14.
73 *Id.*
74 Michael Cooper et al., *Business in the United States: Who Owns It, and How Much Tax Do They Pay?*, 30 TAX POL'Y & ECON. 91 (2016).
75 GOV'T ACCOUNT. OFF., GAO-14-746T, LARGE PARTNERSHIPS: GROWING POPULATION AND COMPLEXITY HINDER EFFECTIVE IRS AUDITS (2014).
76 H.R. 1314, Bipartisan Budget Act of 2015, 114th Cong., Pub. L. No. 117-74, § 1101 (codified at I.R.C. §§ 6221–6241); Greg Armstrong et al., *IRS Launches Large Partnership Audits*, BLOOMBERG TAX (Nov. 3, 2021), https://news.bloombergtax.com/tax-insights-and-commentary/irs-launches-large-partnership-audits.
77 Rettig, *supra* note 29.
78 For further discussion of this dynamic, see Chapter 3, section "Limitations of Activity-Based Rules."
79 *See* Chapter 3, section "Administrative Constraints on the IRS."
80 CIC Servs., LLC v. IRS, 141 S. Ct. 1582 (2021).
81 For an introduction to the Administrative Procedures Act, see TODD GARVEY, CONG. RESEARCH SERV., R41546, A BRIEF OVERVIEW OF RULEMAKING AND JUDICIAL REVIEW (2017).
82 *See* Chapter 9, section "The Role of Tax Information Reporting."
83 GOVT. ACC'T. OFF., GAO-14-746T, TAX GAP: MULTIPLE STRATEGIES ARE NEEDED TO REDUCE COMPLIANCE 7–10 (2019).

84 IRS, *supra* note 9.
85 Tips and cash payments earned by informal and self-employed workers, however, can often be more difficult for the IRS to identify. *See* Slemrod, *supra* note 23, at 26–29.
86 CONG. BUDGET OFF., THE DISTRIBUTION OF HOUSEHOLD INCOME, 2019 (2023).
87 *See* Guyton et al., *supra* note 14; *see also* EMMANUEL SAEZ & GABRIEL ZUCMAN, THE TRIUMPH OF INJUSTICE: HOW THE RICH DODGE TAXES AND HOW TO MAKE THEM PAY 63–66 (2019).
88 *See* Chapter 3, section "Limitations of Activity-Based Rules."
89 *See, e.g.,* Stephen Stonberg, *Cryptocurrencies Are Democratizing the Financial World. Here's How,* in THE DAVOS AGENDA 2021 (Jan. 22, 2021), https://www.weforum.org/agenda/2021/01/cryptocurrencies-are-democratising-the-financial-world-heres-how.
90 *See* Omri Marian, *Are Cryptocurrencies Super Tax Havens?*, 112 MICH. L. REV. FIRST IMPRESSIONS 38 (2013).
91 Igor Makarov & Antoinette Schoar, *Blockchain Analysis of the Bitcoin Market* (NBER Working Paper No. 29396, 2021); *see also* Paul Vigna, *Bitcoin's 'One Percent' Controls Lion's Share of the Cryptocurrency's Wealth,* WALL ST. J. (Dec. 20, 2021), https://www.wsj.com/articles/bitcoins-one-percent-controls-lions-share-of-the-cryptocurrencys-wealth-11639996204.
92 BOARD OF GOVERNORS, FED. RS. SYS., ECONOMIC WELL-BEING OF U.S. HOUSEHOLDS IN 2021, at 45–46 (2022).
93 Katherine Baer et al., *Taxing Cryptocurrencies,* 39 OXFORD REV. ECON. POL'Y 478 (2023).
94 *See* Chapter 7, section "Tax Advice as Tax Penalty Insurance."
95 *See, e.g., How Much Does a Tax Attorney Cost,* CROSS L. GRP. (Jan. 16, 2017), https://www.crosslawgroup.com/blog/hiring-tax-attorney-worth-cost.
96 Heather M. Field, *Tax Lawyers as Tax Insurance,* 60 WM. & MARY L. REV. 2111 (2019).
97 Heather M. Field, *Tax Enforcement by the Private Sector: Deputizing Tax Insurers,* 99 IND. L. J. (forthcoming 2024); *see also* Kyle D. Logue, *Tax Law Uncertainty and the Role of Tax Insurance,* 25 VA. TAX REV. 339 (2005).
98 Researchers have also observed that the presence of sophisticated tax advisors can also affect taxpayer motivations and can transform an individual compliance decision into a group decision characterized by different forms of ethical decision-making. Gangl & Torgler, *supra* note 24, at 121–22.
99 JOINT COMM. ON TAX'N, *supra* note 71.
100 *See* Alex Raskolnikov, *Crime and Punishment in Taxation: Deceit, Deterrence, and the Self-Adjusting Penalty,* 106 COLUM. L. REV. 569 (2006).
101 *See* Doran, *supra* note 46, at 111.
102 David M. Schizer, *Enlisting the Tax Bar,* 59 TAX L. REV. 331, 335–36 (2006).
103 *See* IRS Press Release, IR-2006-116, Prepared Remarks of Douglas H. Shulman, George Washington University Law School, 22nd Annual Institute on Current Issues on International Taxation, Washington, DC (Dec. 10, 2009), https://www.irs.gov/newsroom/prepared-remarks-of-commissioner-douglas-shulman-before-the-22nd-annual-george-washington-university-international-tax-conference.
104 Jesse Eisinger & Paul Kiel, *Gutting the IRS: The IRS Tried to Take on the Ultrawealthy. It Didn't Go Well,* PROPUBLICA (Apr. 5, 2019), https://www.propublica.org/article/ultrawealthy-taxes-irs-internal-revenue-service-global-high-wealth-audits.

105 *See* IRS, IRM 4.52.1 GLOBAL HIGH WEALTH PROGRAM PROCESSES AND PROCEDURES (May 3, 2022); CHARLES RETTIG, IRS, A CLOSER LOOK: IMPLEMENTING THE TAX GAP 11–12 (Dec. 3, 2020), https://www.irs.gov/pub/foia/ig/cl/tax-gap-for-web.pdf.
106 *See* Gregg Polsky, *A Compendium of Private Equity Tax Games*, 146 TAX NOTES 615 (2015).
107 Gretchen Morgenson, *I.R.S. Targets Tax Dodge by Private Equity Firms*, N.Y. TIMES (July 22, 2015), https://www.nytimes.com/2015/07/23/business/irs-targets-tax-dodge-by-private-equity-firms.html.
108 Paul Kiel & Jeff Ernsthausen, *How the Wealthy Save Billions in Taxes by Skirting a Century-Old Law*, PROPUBLICA (Feb. 9, 2023), https://www.propublica.org/article/irs-files-taxes-wash-sales-goldman-sachs. The "wash-sale" rules in I.R.C. § 1091 generally seek to prevent taxpayers from accelerating their taxable losses before exiting their investment positions.
109 Sloan Speck, *Tax Planning and Policy Drift*, 69 TAX L. REV. 549 (2016).

2

How the Tax System Addresses Noncompliance

Chapter 1 described the research on tax noncompliance, its costs to the government and society, and how high-end taxpayers often have greater tax-avoidance opportunities. This chapter turns to the structure of the tax compliance system and how it attempts to address high-end noncompliance. Broadly speaking, these rules govern the administration and enforcement of the tax laws. The tax compliance system spans statutes, regulations, and both formal and informal IRS guidance and procedures.

This chapter begins by situating the tax compliance rules within the broader tax system. The discussion considers what they share with all tax rules and what sets them apart. The following sections begin a more detailed dive into the structure of the tax compliance system. After addressing what motivates taxpayers to comply with the tax law, the discussion considers the main components of the tax compliance system and how these components leverage taxpayer motivations to improve compliance. Subsequent chapters in this book explore in greater detail many of the rules surveyed in this chapter.

With this important context on the tax compliance system established, the discussion then returns to the challenges of high-end noncompliance. The final part of this chapter describes the two most prominent approaches in current law and reform proposals. The first general approach is to increase funding of the IRS, so it can more effectively deter noncompliance and recover unpaid taxes. The second general approach is what this book terms "activity-based" rules, targeting the specific taxpayer activities that can either indicate or enable tax noncompliance.

THE ROLE OF THE TAX COMPLIANCE RULES

The tax *compliance* rules, as defined in this book, broadly encompass the laws and procedures governing the administration, enforcement, and collection of tax revenues. These rules may all be contrasted with what this book terms the *substantive* tax rules, which determine tax liabilities by defining an applicable tax base (such as income or estates[1]), a rate schedule,[2] and additional adjustments, such as credits.[3]

This section describes the defining features of the tax compliance rules and their role within the broader tax system. The section first considers the similarities shared by both the tax compliance rules and substantive tax rules, and then describes how the tax compliance rules serve a different function in the tax system, which sets them apart from other tax rules.

An Integrated Understanding of Tax Rules

If we just consider how different tax rules can affect taxpayers and the government, we might conclude that there is no reason to distinguish among various categories of rules. We also might conclude there is no reason to single out the tax compliance rules as distinct and unique components of the tax system. After all, any tax rule, regardless of how it is categorized, can affect the total amount of tax revenues collected and the various costs borne by taxpayers and the government. Further, any tax rule can impact both the distribution and the allocation of economic resources and activity.

Policymakers can change the amount of tax revenue collected, or who bears the tax burden, by making changes to any number of legal rules or processes. For example, they can adjust the amount of taxes owed by changing applicable tax rates, the calculation of the taxable base (such as through deductions or exclusions), or the availability of special credits against tax. Policymakers can also change the rules for the reporting, collection, and enforcement of tax liabilities. Methods of doing this include imposing penalties for unpaid taxes, or establishing recordkeeping requirements for taxpayers to substantiate their tax positions. Policymakers can also change the amount of tax revenue collected by adjusting the frequency, extent, and prioritization of enforcement actions.

To illustrate the potentially comparable effects from both substantive rules and tax compliance rules, consider the interaction between the substantive rules for calculating corporate income and the tax compliance rules governing "listed" and other "reportable transactions." If an individual organizes a business as a corporation, the business income will be subject to corporate income tax liabilities.[4] If the business subsequently engages in a listed or other reportable transaction, but does not disclose it, then this activity will result in additional liabilities owed to the government in the form of a civil tax penalty.[5] The first rule (the corporate income tax) would be characterized in this book as a "substantive" tax rule, while the second rule (the nondisclosure penalty) would be characterized as a tax compliance rule. However, both rules simply define additional liabilities to be paid to the government when a taxpayer conducts certain activities.

Both substantive tax rules and tax compliance rules can also impose different costs on taxpayers and the government. Tax rules can impose costs by changing taxpayers' real behavior. For example, a higher tax on labor income may induce some people to supply less labor than they would otherwise, resulting in "excess burden" or lost welfare from the changed behavior.[6] Taxpayers may also incur costs to change the form in which their activities are reported, without changing their underlying activities. For example, they might pay a tax professional to help identify tax benefits to report on a return, or they might operate a business through a tax-preferred business entity.[7] Similarly, tax reporting obligations cause taxpayers to spend time and even psychic strain on tax compliance, or to spend money on professionals to do it for them.[8] The government also incurs costs to enforce and administer the tax rules, such as by funding the IRS and other agencies involved in tax collection.[9] Tax-enforcement efforts that make the substantive tax rules more effective can also change the degree to which these substantive rules affect taxpayers' behavior.

Economists Joel Slemrod and Shlomo Yitzhaki argue that policymakers should therefore conduct a comprehensive evaluation of the different possible configurations of tax rules and the various costs they may entail:

> [E]xcess burdens, administrative costs, and compliance costs are all components of what we shall refer to as the social costs of taxation: the costs incurred by society in the process of transferring purchasing power from the taxpayers to the government.... All these components of social cost should be included in a proper model of the costs of taxation, and they should affect the design of an optimal tax system.[10]

Building upon this core insight, economists Michael Keen and Joel Slemrod offer an integrated framework for evaluating changes to both tax enforcement and the substantive tax rules.[11] Adjusting both substantive tax rules and tax compliance rules can change the distributional burden of tax liabilities, and different combinations of tax rules and procedures can result in different aggregate tax burdens on each income group. For example, the distributional effects of adjustments to the corporate tax rate will depend on how the incidence of the corporate tax is borne across income groups.[12] Similarly, the distributional effect of the penalties for listed and reportable transactions will depend on the frequency with which taxpayers at different income levels bear these penalties.

In sum, any tax rule or procedure, whether it is labeled as a substantive or a compliance rule, can affect the total amount of tax revenue raised, the costs borne by taxpayers and the government, and the distribution of tax burdens. For this reason, policymakers should, in principle, adopt the configuration of substantive and compliance rules that optimizes for the realization of specified policy goals: and particularly for raising a desired amount of revenue according to a certain distributional pattern, while minimizing costs to taxpayers and the government. Joel Slemrod consequently argues for a "tax-systems approach" that takes a comprehensive view of not only the substantive tax law and the tax compliance system but also the "multiple margins of behavioral responses to taxes."[13] Within this unified framework, before accounting for distributive goals, "all tax policy instruments – not just the standard instruments such as tax rates – should be utilized so as to equalize the marginal efficiency cost per dollar of revenue raised, which should in turn equal the marginal social benefit of raising revenue."[14]

The Function of Tax Compliance Rules

Any conceivable mix of tax rules and procedures will raise some amount of revenue according to some distribution pattern, at some cost to taxpayers and the government. Even the Internal Revenue Code often treats tax compliance rules the same as substantive tax rules. For example, under the Internal Revenue Code, both civil tax penalties and interest on underpayments are treated like all other taxes for purposes of statutory interpretation.[15]

In that case, when would it ever be helpful for policymakers to view the tax compliance rules as a distinct component of the tax system? What common features do these rules share and what sets them apart from other tax rules?

One starting point is to consider tax rules' various functions, and why they are part of the tax system. All tax rules or procedures can have an ultimate ex post, or "after the fact," effect on the amount of tax revenues raised, costs to taxpayers and the government, and the distribution of resources. In practice, however, different tax rules are often designed to achieve different policy objectives, when viewed from an ex ante, or "before the fact," perspective.

The public finance literature identifies a basic distinction between two functions of fiscal policy: an "allocative" function and a "distributive" function.[16] Professor Daniel Shaviro defines this distinction as follows: "Allocation affects the amount, use, and character of all assets in society, while distribution affects who has what."[17]

Professor Shaviro argues that this distinction can help to explain the function of different tax rules. Distributive rules, in general, are designed to adjust tax liabilities in accordance with the taxpayer's ability to pay, and thereby to implement the tax system's distributive function.[18] For example, the progressive rate schedule adjusts applicable tax rates based on the level of the taxpayer's income.[19] Allocative tax rules, in contrast, are designed to affect taxpayer behavior and the allocation (rather than the distribution) of resources and economic activity.[20] For example, the "clean vehicle credit" in Internal Revenue Code Section 30D provides a credit for new electric plug-in vehicles placed in service during the taxable year.[21] This provision serves the primary purpose of influencing the reallocation of resources from internal combustion to electric vehicles, rather than affecting the distribution of taxpayers' income.[22]

As an extension of this functional approach to categorizing tax rules, the tax compliance rules can be defined as those rules that are not designed ex ante to serve either an allocative or a distributive function. Instead, these rules can be characterized as primarily serving an "implementing" function: Their purpose is to facilitate the collection of tax liabilities prescribed by the substantive tax rules, rather than to impose additional burdens on taxpayers.[23] Even if these rules may have the ex post consequences of readjusting the burden of tax liabilities, their primary function ex ante is to implement the substantive tax rules, which specify the socially desirable distribution of tax burdens. Understanding this different purpose of the tax compliance rules helps to explain much of the analysis in the following chapters, as well as this book's system of means-adjusted tax compliance rules.

In principle, policymakers could design tax compliance rules to have the expected effect ex ante of imposing additional tax liabilities on a subset of taxpayers. For example, subject to constitutional limitations, policymakers could impose onerous penalties on high-income taxpayers for even minor offenses, solely for the purpose of raising even more revenue from these taxpayers than would be prescribed under the substantive tax rules. Similarly, some jurisdictions impose non tax fines and fees, such as those for motor vehicle violations, for the intended purpose of raising revenue from persons who are subject to these penalties, rather than for the intended purpose of deterring the undesirable activities.[24]

Policymakers have expressed the view that the tax compliance rules should not be designed for the purpose of adjusting the distribution of tax burdens, but rather to ensure that taxpayers pay the amounts owed as provided in the substantive tax rules. That is, from this perspective, the tax compliance rules should be designed ex ante to serve only an implementing function, rather to make further adjustments to the distribution of tax burdens.

For an example of this view that the tax compliance rules should serve a primary implementing function, the Treasury Department has long maintained the position that tax penalties should *not* be designed from an ex ante perspective to extract additional money from taxpayers. In a 1999 report on the design of tax penalties and interest charges, the Treasury articulated this key distinction between the purpose of tax compliance rules and the purpose of the substantive tax rules:

> Penalties may raise revenue collaterally but this should not be a deliberate objective of penalty design and doing so can create perverse incentives. Rather, the penalty regime should raise revenue by encouraging taxpayers to remit the appropriate amount of tax in the proper fashion. Thus, although it is appropriate to consider the cost to the government associated with noncompliance in designing penalties, fostering compliance and deterring noncompliance should be the overriding goals.[25]

Distinguishing between the tax compliance rules and the substantive tax rules based on their different primary functions does not mean that any particular tax rule will fall neatly into one role or the other. A single tax rule can serve multiple functions and have multiple purposes embedded in its provisions. For example, the clean vehicle credit in Internal Revenue Code Section 30D includes a phase-out rule, which denies the benefit to higher-income taxpayers.[26] This phase-out will cause the provision to have different distributive effects, by denying the credit to higher-income taxpayers, even as the provision primarily serves an allocative function.

Similarly, any given tax provision can have multiple ex post effects. For example, Internal Revenue Code Section 6662 imposes an accuracy-related penalty for certain understatements, including a 20% penalty for any "substantial understatement" of income tax.[27] In the case of individual taxpayers, the provision defines a substantial understatement as one that exceeds the greater of 10% of the taxes that should have been reported, or $5,000.[28] This $5,000 cutoff has the effect of essentially excluding many low-income taxpayers from the penalty, whose understated tax liabilities are unlikely to exceed this amount. As a result, this provision and many other tax compliance rules analyzed in this book will inevitably have varying ex post effects on taxpayers who are affected by these rules, such as a taxpayer who is subject to an additional penalty. In this case as well, the relevant consideration for policymakers is rather the ex ante purpose of this provision, and whether it succeeds in more effectively implementing the substantive tax rules and their intended effects. In the case of the tax penalties, this primary purpose is to discourage tax avoidance – and therefore to avoid the imposition of penalties at all – rather than to extract additional revenue from those taxpayers who do not comply ex post.

Why should policymakers primarily design the tax compliance rules to serve this narrow implementing function, rather than to have an explicit distributive function? Tax policy implicates fundamental questions of fairness in the allocation of tax burdens. Hiding these distributional effects of government policies in less visible and salient tax compliance rules could undermine public debate on these critical questions and policymaker accountability.[29]

Adjusting the distributional effects of the tax system through IRS administrative policies and enforcement discretion could also raise other concerns. The perception that the IRS uses its discretion to shift the distributive policies set by Congress could similarly erode public trust in both the agency and in the legislative process. For this reason, the IRS has publicly stated that its objective is not to impose new burdens on taxpayers, but rather to ensure that every taxpayer pays what they owe. For example, in its 2023 Strategic Plan, the IRS affirmed this basic principle that the tax compliance system should not be designed to affect the distribution of tax burdens:

> The IRS has an obligation to administer the law in a fair manner. This is central to the agency's mission and essential to fostering public trust, as everyone must play by the same set of rules. Taxpayers must see that the IRS addresses all types of noncompliance and does not focus disproportionately on any particular area or population.[30]

Designing tax compliance rules to adjust the distribution of taxes collected could also have uneven effects on different groups of taxpayers. For example, consider again the possibility of a rule that imposes heavy penalties on high-income taxpayers when they engage in relatively minor offenses. From an ex ante perspective, this rule might equally deter all such taxpayers so that policymakers might raise additional revenue from all members of this income group. From an ex post perspective, however, this approach would only collect additional penalty revenue from a subset of taxpayers who violate the tax rules, are caught, and are subject to the penalties. This adjustment would, in effect, move the tax system from a principle of taxation in accordance with a taxpayer's "ability to pay" to a principle of taxation in accordance with a taxpayer's "level of compliance and detection."

Other economic sanctions regimes designed to raise additional revenue ex post face this same problem. Policymakers could design an income-based speeding ticket to raise more revenue from higher-income taxpayers.[31] This income-based fine, however, would only raise additional revenue from offenders who speed and are subsequently caught, rather than from all higher-income individuals.[32]

Similarly, Professor A. Mitchell Polinsky gives the example of a pollution-control rule designed to also advance distributional goals. This kind of rule could impose heavier ex post burdens on higher-income offenders, on the assumption that "there may be a closer correspondence between the income of a party and whether that party is a victim or an injurer." Polinsky argues, however, that in this case, "the legal rule used to control the pollution dispute will, at best, redistribute income from a subset of one income class to a subset of another[,]" since the only parties affected would be higher-income parties subject to the rule and lower-income parties who are compensated victims.[33]

Chapter 4 returns to the implementing function of the tax compliance rules and considers how this function should inform the design of means adjustments to these rules. For now, this preliminary discussion helps to set the stage for understanding the role of the tax compliance rules, and how the current system seeks to address high-end noncompliance.

FACTORS IN TAX COMPLIANCE

How does the tax compliance system perform its implementing function? This section begins by surveying the most important reasons underlying why people pay taxes. The following sections describe how the structure of the tax compliance rules leverages these factors to serve its implementing function. Subsequent chapters also describe many of these factors in greater detail, when they explain this book's different approach to designing the tax compliance system.

Voluntary Compliance

The large majority of taxpayers comply with their obligations to report and pay taxes. The IRS's most recent study of the tax gap finds that the estimated voluntary compliance rate, which it defines as the proportion of taxes paid "voluntarily and timely," was approximately 85% for the tax years 2014–2016.[34] This voluntary compliance rate has also remained relatively steady since the time the IRS started estimating the tax gap despite intervening rounds of legislative tax reform. If anything, the estimated voluntary compliance rate has crept up slightly over time. The IRS estimated a voluntary compliance rate of approximately 83.6% for the tax years 2011–2013,[35] 83.1% for the tax years 2008–2010,[36] 83.1% for 2006,[37] and 83.7% for 2001,[38] although these estimates also reflect changes to the IRS's methodology in estimating the tax gap and compliance rates over time.

Tax Morale

What drives this relatively high and stable voluntary compliance rate? At least in part, voluntary compliance is driven by tax morale, or a taxpayer's intrinsic motivation to pay taxes without regard for the threat of penalties or enforcement actions. Studies of tax morale suggest that many taxpayers voluntarily comply with their tax obligations for a variety of reasons. Some taxpayers are motivated by the benefits the government provides through tax revenues. This reciprocal view of taxpaying is best encapsulated in the famous quote by Oliver Wendell Holmes Jr.: "Taxes are what we pay for civilized society."[39] Some taxpayers are motivated by a desire to comply with their legal obligations because they believe in the legitimacy of the lawmaking authority.[40] Other taxpayers are also motivated by a sense of civic duty or social norms,[41] or an altruistic motivation to support the needs of those who have fewer resources.[42]

Studies find that taxpayers may also be motivated to comply with the tax law when they believe that the government is acting in their interests and follows fair procedures when administering the tax law.[43] Professor Marjorie Kornhauser argues that the IRS can positively influence tax morale and "activate compliance norms" through various strategies, including "education, properly framing communications, and fair procedures."[44]

The IRS faces a delicate balance, however, in its efforts to foster tax morale. On the one hand, the IRS must seek and maintain positive relations with taxpayers so that taxpayers perceive paying taxes as a responsibility rather than just as an obligation. On the other hand, the IRS must adequately enforce the tax laws, and both deter and punish tax avoiders, in a way that does not undermine tax morale. For this reason, the IRS National Taxpayer Advocate has argued that the IRS must build trust with taxpayers, even while it enforces the tax law, to promote tax morale and voluntary compliance.[45]

Involuntary Compliance

Of course, most of the taxpaying reflected in the voluntary compliance rate is not in fact voluntary. In many cases, taxpayers have no choice but to have their taxes remitted for them. For example, workers who earn wages and salaries are typically required to file an IRS Form W-4 (Employee's Withholding Certificate). In this case, employers withhold from the employees' paycheck an amount equal to their estimated taxes and remit this amount directly to the IRS. Many state and local tax payments are similarly involuntary. Consumers bear the burden of consumption taxes, such as sales taxes, whenever they purchase products from retailers responsible for remitting the tax.[46] Mortgage lenders also often remit property taxes on behalf of homeowners automatically.[47]

Scholars have recognized that the withholding system has not only played a crucial role in the evolution of the modern tax system but has also guaranteed stability in the tax compliance rates over time.[48] The IRS study of the 2014–2016 tax gap found only a 1% misreporting percentage for income subject to both substantial information and reporting, which is significantly lower than even the 6% rate for income subject to substantial information but not withholding.[49]

As described in Chapter 9, however, the current withholding rules do not consistently ensure the same level of "involuntary" compliance for all taxpayers in equal measure. As a result, the tax system has relied more heavily on involuntary compliance at the bottom and middle of the income distribution, and more heavily on voluntary compliance at the very top.

Sanctions for Noncompliance

Many taxpayers are also motivated, at least in part, to comply with the tax law so they can avoid legal consequences. Taxpayers who do not comply with the tax laws can face monetary sanctions, such as civil penalties or other charges.[50] They may also face other nonmonetary sanctions, such as losing a passport[51] or public shaming.[52] They could also be subject to additional IRS scrutiny, or backup withholding, to ensure future compliance.[53] Finally, in severe or egregious cases of noncompliance, taxpayers may be subject to criminal sanctions, including imprisonment.[54]

This section describes basic principles of how different forms of sanctions may deter noncompliance. Chapter 6 describes these models and their extensions in greater detail, as well as their implications for the design of civil tax penalties.

In general, sanctions can reduce the expected benefit to the taxpayer from noncompliance.[55] In the classic "Becker-Bentham fine" model, the deterrent effect of any legal sanction depends on the chance of detection and the magnitude of the sanction.[56] In principle, the expected cost of the sanction will depend not only on the chance of detection but also on the chance that the government will, in fact, impose the sanction in the event that the activity is detected.[57]

In the tax context, a taxpayer motivated exclusively to maximize their expected monetary outcome from either complying or not might similarly compare the expected tax savings from not complying with the expected cost of getting caught and being required to pay any penalties.[58] The decision of whether to comply or not may also depend on the taxpayers' level of risk aversion and how they respond to uncertainty.[59] All things being equal, however, a higher penalty amount would generally be necessary to deter noncompliance when a greater tax liability is at stake, and when the chance of detection is lower.

The deterrent effect of a civil tax penalty may also depend on exactly how, and at what level of detail, a taxing authority communicates the potential sanction to a delinquent taxpayer. A 2020 study conducted with the Colorado Department of Revenue found that delinquent taxpayers were more likely to comply after receiving a detailed notice explaining exactly how much they would be penalized, as compared to taxpayers who only received a general notice that they would be subject to a financial penalty.[60]

In the case of a nonmonetary sanction, in contrast, the deterrent effect will depend on its subjective cost to the taxpayer. In some cases, the same nonmonetary penalty could have an equal effect in deterring noncompliance, regardless of the taxpayer's income or the tax liability at stake. For example, the threat of imprisonment could have the same effect in deterring a lower-income taxpayer, even when a relatively small tax liability is at stake, or a higher-income taxpayer who is considering whether to avoid a larger potential tax liability. Similarly, taxpayers might place either the same or different subjective values on other nonmonetary sanctions, such as public shaming or losing their passport.

Benefits from Compliance

Taxpayers may also be motivated by benefits or incentives resulting from tax compliance. These benefits can offer tangible value to taxpayers, above and beyond those factoring into their intrinsic motivations to comply.

For one example, Professor Eric Posner argues that some taxpayers can benefit from tax compliance by using their compliance as a "signal" that they are a "good type" of person others will want to transact with.[61] Professor Posner argues that the government can leverage this motivation by increasing the stigma for tax noncompliance. By the same token, the government could also incentivize compliance by some taxpayers by publicizing that they voluntarily comply with their tax obligations. However, as tax scholars,[62] and even Posner himself,[63] have acknowledged, the privacy rules governing tax return information limit the signaling potential of tax compliance. Under current law, the IRS is generally prohibited from publicly disclosing any taxpayer's tax return or return information.[64]

In some cases, however, taxpayers may be motivated by signaling effects of compliance in cases where they are able to publicize this signal. For example, one independent nonprofit offers accreditation for businesses that follow standards for "responsible tax conduct."[65] Other examples of the value of signaling include individuals who disclose their own tax returns in the process of seeking loans from banks, applying for student financial aid, or running for national political office. Scholars have also proposed other positive incentives for compliant taxpayers, such as certifications or other forms of public recognition.[66]

Professor Emily Satterthwaite discovered evidence that positive signaling can encourage tax compliance in her study of small businesses in Canada deciding whether to voluntarily register and comply with their jurisdiction's Value-Added Tax systems.[67] Her research indicated that a significant number of small firms voluntarily complied with the VAT, even though they were legally exempt from these requirements because of their size. Despite the significant additional cost associated with this decision, many firms did so because of the positive benefits in the marketplace from signaling their compliance with applicable tax rules.

AN OVERVIEW OF THE TAX COMPLIANCE SYSTEM

These varied and sometimes conflicting factors in tax compliance help to explain the complex structure of the tax compliance system, the major components of which this section surveys briefly. Many of the statutory tax compliance rules are located in Subtitle F of the Internal Revenue Code ("Procedure and Administration").[68] Other tax compliance rules are found within statues providing for substantive tax rules, and are provided for not only in Treasury Regulations but also in formal and informal IRS guidance. As this section describes, these varied components leverage the different motivations in tax compliance, while also ensuring basic protections and fairness in the implementation of the tax laws.

IRS Administration and Enforcement

The IRS is the agency authorized by the Internal Revenue Code to administer the tax system and enforce compliance.[69] The IRS describes its core mission as follows: "The IRS role is to help the large majority of compliant taxpayers with the tax law, while ensuring that the minority who are unwilling to comply pay their fair share."[70]

The IRS performs three basic functions in executing this mission: (1) it processes returns and collects taxes paid; (2) it provides taxpayer assistance, services, and guidance; and (3) it enforces the tax law through audits, assessments, and legal proceedings with delinquent taxpayers. In addition to these basic functions, the IRS also participates in criminal investigations, sometimes in coordination with other federal agencies, and oversees certain types of entities, such as tax-exempt organizations and retirement plans.

The IRS's enforcement activities prevent noncompliance in two distinct ways. From an ex post (after the fact) perspective, IRS enforcement can recover the unpaid tax liabilities from taxpayers who have already underpaid their taxes. For example, the IRS's most recent tax gap study estimated that, through its enforcement and other actions, the IRS was able to recover $68 billion of the $498 billion gross tax gap for tax years 2014–2016, or nearly 14% of the total revenue lost from noncompliance.[71] From an ex ante (before the fact) perspective, IRS enforcement also prevents noncompliance from happening at all, chiefly by discouraging taxpayers from underpaying their taxes in the first place.[72]

The IRS has significant discretion in setting its enforcement priorities and methods, which are governed by the agency's public and internal policies and procedures. For example, the IRS's strategic plan for fiscal years 2023–2031 offers important insights into its current enforcement priorities. First, the plan describes how the IRS would prioritize efforts to "close the tax gap attributable to high-income and high wealth taxpayers" and expand enforcement for large corporations and partnerships.[73] The plan also describes the IRS's efforts to strategically use technology to optimize its enforcement efforts.[74] The IRS also recognizes that, in implementing these goals, it "has an obligation to administer the law in a fair manner" and that doing so "is central to the agency's mission and essential to fostering public trust."[75]

The IRS also preserves significant discretion in its audit selection methods and keeps these internal procedures confidential to prevent taxpayers from strategically gaming these methods to avoid detection. The IRS's confidential Discriminant Index Function (DIF) assigns numeric scores to tax returns based on the likelihood that the return reflects an underreported tax liability.[76] These DIF scores are then used by the agency to prioritize certain returns for audit review.[77]

Although the IRS has significant enforcement discretion, these activities are also often subject to extensive public scrutiny. For example, in the early 2010s, conservative groups claimed that the IRS improperly targeted certain nonprofit groups that had claimed tax-exempt status, resulting in a comprehensive investigation and report by the Senate Finance Committee.[78] More recently, researchers have investigated whether the IRS's audit selection methods can have the effect of causing Black households to be audited at a disproportionate rate, even after controlling for taxpayer income levels.[79]

The IRS also communicates its interpretation of the tax law and enforcement priorities to taxpayers through a variety of internal and external guidance documents and publications. These documents include the Internal Revenue Manual, Revenue Procedures, IRS Publication series, Revenue Rulings, Technical Advice Memoranda, Notices, and Announcements. Finally, the IRS also offers informal guidance, such as through IRS publications, online websites, and virtual assistants.[80]

Information Reporting and Disclosure

As described in greater detail in Chapter 9, the Internal Revenue Code imposes reporting obligations on both taxpayers and third parties. This information assists the IRS both in calculating tax liabilities and in identifying potential noncompliance.

The tax return itself is the most important form of information reporting, and the foundation of the taxpayer-initiated "voluntary compliance system." Every US taxpayer with sufficient gross income is obligated to file a Form 1040 (US Individual Income Tax Return), which includes detailed information on the taxpayer's sources of income, expenses and other deductions, and qualification for credits.[81] Taxpayers may also be obligated to file additional forms of "first-party" information reporting regarding their transactions. For example, in some cases taxpayers must also report information about their assets held abroad on the Form 8938 (Statement of Specified Foreign Financial Assets).[82]

For an example of first-party reporting, taxpayers who engage in certain "reportable" transactions that may indicate or enable compliance are also obligated to disclose these transactions to the IRS on Form 8886 (Reportable Transaction Disclosure Statement).[83] According to this requirement, transactions that must be reported include certain "listed transactions" that are designated by the IRS as potentially abusive.[84] Taxpayers and advisors must also disclose participation in any "transaction of interest" or any substantially similar transactions.[85] Unlike listed transactions – which the IRS explicitly describes as abusive – transactions of interest are potentially abusive but Treasury and the IRS "lack enough information" about the structure and purpose of these strategies.[86]

Importantly, the IRS also collects information from third parties, such as financial intermediaries and counterparties who transact with the taxpayer.[87] For example, employers are required to report the wages and salaries paid to employees on IRS Form W-2 (Wage and Tax Statement). Additionally, the IRS Form 1099 series requires payors to report a variety of payments to the IRS, including for interest, dividends, and non-employee compensation.

Withholding

The tax law also requires third parties in some cases to withhold taxes from payments to taxpayers and remit these amounts to the IRS. These rules can increase tax compliance through involuntary – rather than voluntary – measures. For example, employers are required to withhold from employee paychecks an amount equal to the employee's estimated income tax liabilities.[88] Third-party payors can also be required to withhold and remit taxes from other types of payments as "backup withholding" in some cases, such as when the taxpayer has not reported their income correctly or when they did not provide required information to the payor.[89]

Advisor Regulation

The tax compliance rules also impose reporting obligations and regulatory standards for tax advisors. For example, a "material advisor" to a reportable transaction must file Form 8918 (Material Advisor Disclosure Statement). Under these rules, a material advisor is a tax advisor who assists or advises on the transaction and is compensated for these services with income above a threshold amount.[90] Form 8918 requires the advisor to provide detailed information regarding the transaction and its anticipated tax consequences.

Tax advisors are also regulated by the IRS Office of Professional Responsibility (OPR). Among other functions, the OPR oversees the Treasury Department's Circular 230 Regulations Governing Practice before the Internal Revenue Service.[91] The Circular 230 rules prescribe standards for all written tax advice, including requirements that such advice reasonably considers all relevant facts and applicable law.

Civil Penalties and Interest

The Internal Revenue Code provides for a range of civil penalties designed to deter noncompliance.[92] For example, these include penalties for failure to file tax returns or pay taxes shown on the return,[93] for underpayments of tax,[94] and higher penalties for underpayments in certain circumstances, such as in the case of fraud or transactions lacking economic substance that are designed only to avoid taxes.[95] The law also provides for penalties designed to support other elements of the tax compliance system. For example, both taxpayers and third parties can be subject to penalties for failure to make necessary information disclosures.[96]

The tax law allows taxpayers to raise certain defenses to avoid the imposition of civil penalties. For example, a taxpayer can reduce the amount of an accuracy-related penalty on underpayments by showing a "substantial authority" in the law for the position claimed, or by claiming that they have a "reasonable basis" for their position and disclosing all relevant facts to the IRS.[97] The Internal Revenue Code also provides for a "reasonable cause and good faith" exception to the underpayment penalties, which can be satisfied when the taxpayer relies on the opinion of an advisor.[98]

Some civil penalties on both taxpayers and third-party advisors serve to reinforce other tax compliance rules and requirements. For example, the Internal Revenue Code imposes a penalty if a taxpayer participates in a "reportable transaction" and does not disclose the information on their tax return.[99] Material advisors on reportable transactions who fail to file necessary returns, or do not maintain proper records of clients participating in the transactions, can also be subject to penalties under the Internal Revenue Code.[100]

The Internal Revenue Code also specifies civil penalties for tax return preparers. If a tax advisor knowingly prepares a return with an understatement of tax liability resulting from an unreasonable position, the preparer can be subject to penalties based on the preparer's fees charged for the tax services.[101] Similarly, Circular 230 specifies potential penalties and sanctions for violation of its regulations, including censure, license suspension, or, in the cases of tax attorneys, disbarment.[102]

Finally, the Internal Revenue Code requires taxpayers to pay interest to the government in some cases, such as for late tax payments. These rules are designed to compensate the government for the delayed receipt of taxes owed, much like private party interest payments compensate a bank for the borrower's use of loan proceeds.[103] Accordingly, taxpayers must pay interest to the government on any taxes paid after their final due date, even if the taxpayer has received an extension of the time due for filing a return.[104] For individual taxpayers, the interest rate on underpayments is calculated by adding 3% to the federal short-term rate, which is published quarterly by the IRS.[105] The interest rules can also compensate the taxpayer for overpayments of taxes in some cases, such as when the government fails to issue a tax refund within a specified period.[106]

Criminal Penalties

Beyond the civil penalties and interest, the tax law also provides for potential federal criminal sanctions, particularly in cases of severe and deliberate tax abuse. For example, the Internal Revenue Code provides that an individual who "willfully attempts to evade or defeat any tax imposed ... or the payment thereof" may be guilty of a felony. If convicted, the person is subject to an additional criminal fine of up to $100,000 or imprisonment for up to five years.[107] The Internal Revenue Code also specifies criminal penalties in cases of less serious misdemeanors. For example, an individual can be subject to a criminal fine of up to $25,000 or imprisonment for up to one year for willful failure to make returns, pay estimated taxes, or keep required records.[108] Noncompliant taxpayers may also face criminal sanctions for violating other federal laws, such as conspiracy to defraud the government.[109]

Dispute Procedures

The tax compliance rules also govern the procedures in disputes between a taxpayer and the IRS. For example, as Chapter 8 describes in greater detail, the Internal Revenue Code specifies the procedures whereby the IRS can issue a notice of a tax deficiency[110] and limits the period during which the IRS can make tax assessments.[111] The Internal Revenue Code also describes the process and timing for filing a petition in the US Tax Court.[112]

Public and internal IRS policies and procedures also govern dispute procedures between taxpayers and the IRS. For example, the IRS prescribes the process for pursuing appeals through its Office of Appeals, which allows disputes to be settled before they would go to court.[113] The IRS also offers a host of procedures for resolving taxpayer issues, both before and after a dispute has arisen between a taxpayer and the IRS.[114] The Taxpayer Advocate Service, an independent organization within the IRS, represents taxpayer interests in the enforcement and administration of the tax law, as well as in disputes with the IRS.[115]

Finally, judicial rules govern many aspects of disputes between taxpayers and the IRS. For example, these rules can determine which legal precedents apply in the case of tax disputes arising in different jurisdictions.[116] General judicial principles govern tax litigation between taxpayers and the IRS, such as the principle of procedural due process, which ensures parties' basic rights in legal proceedings.[117] The different judicial venues for resolving tax disputes, including the US Tax Court, the US Court of Federal Claims, and the US district courts, also all have internal rules governing discovery and legal proceedings.[118]

The Taxpayer Bill of Rights

In addition to these general procedural protections, a federal statutory provision known as the "Taxpayer Bill of Rights" (or "TBOR") specifies taxpayers' basic rights and expectations in their interactions with the IRS. The TBOR provides that the IRS will execute its duties in accordance with ten taxpayer rights:

(A) the right to be informed; (B) the right to quality service; (C) the right to pay no more than the correct amount of tax; (D) the right to challenge the position of the IRS and be heard; (E) the right to appeal a decision of the IRS in an independent forum; (F) the right to finality; (G) the right to privacy; (H) the right to confidentiality; (I) the right to retain representation, and (J) the right to a fair and just tax system.[119]

The TBOR represents a set of core principles governing the IRS's administration of the tax system.[120] They can also offer guideposts for policymakers seeking ways to strengthen the tax compliance system while also, at the same time, maintaining a fundamental commitment to fairness and essential procedural rights.

TRADITIONAL RESPONSES TO HIGH-END NONCOMPLIANCE

After surveying the tax compliance rules and their purpose in the tax system, we can now turn to this book's core question: How can the tax compliance rules be improved to address high-end noncompliance more effectively?

Policymakers and academics have proposed many reforms to the tax compliance system designed to shrink the tax gap and to address the challenges of noncompliance. Subsequent chapters in the book detail many of these proposals, which include suggested reforms to different tax compliance rules. This section highlights two general and predominant approaches in current law and in reform proposals: (1) increasing IRS funding so it can more effectively enforce and administer the tax laws, and (2) what this book refers to as "activity-based rules" targeting specific taxpayer activities which can enable or indicate tax noncompliance.

Increasing IRS Funding

In recent years, policymakers and academics have argued that the IRS needs substantially increased funding to perform its mission and enforce the tax laws. This funding would allow the agency to modernize its technology, hire more agents, and audit more high-income taxpayers. For example, in 2016, Professor Leandra Lederman described an IRS "in crisis" and so hobbled by budget cuts that the agency was unable to perform essential taxpayer services and enforcement.[121] A 2019 Taxpayer Advocate Service report estimated that the IRS's budget was cut by more than 20% between 2010 and 2019, after adjusting for inflation, and identified the lack of sufficient funding as one of the agency's "most serious problems."[122] The Tax Policy Center reported that IRS employment also shrank in recent decades, from approximately 119,000 employees in 1989 to less than 74,000 in 2018.[123]

Increasing IRS funding can help shrink the tax gap through multiple effects. IRS enforcement can discourage taxpayers from choosing not to comply in the first instance. Giving the IRS additional enforcement resources can also increase not only the chance that the IRS will detect noncompliance, but also the IRS's chance of prevailing in a subsequent dispute with a noncompliant taxpayer. Further, increasing IRS funding can allow the agency to improve taxpayer services, which can foster public trust and encourage voluntary compliance.[124]

Prior academic work has highlighted the connection between IRS funding and progressive taxation. Professors Lily Batchelder and David Kamin have argued that "enforcement of the existing tax laws governing the wealthy is weak and getting weaker."[125] Professor Leandra Lederman has also raised alarms: She has argued that failing to adequately fund the IRS can undermine the progressivity of the tax system and increase income inequality.[126]

IRS funding constraints have contributed to a precipitous drop in audit rates of high-income taxpayers. Between 2012 and 2019, the total number of audits of individual returns dropped from approximately 1.2 million to under 400,000, even though the total number of returns filed actually increased during this period.[127] The decline in the rate of audits during this period was highest for taxpayers earning above $200,000, and is calculated to have been between 81% and 92% for taxpayers at the highest income levels.[128]

Increasing IRS funding can also improve the agency's ability to pursue cases of noncompliance once they have been detected. Even if the IRS identifies potential noncompliance, they often face a resource mismatch in subsequent disputes and proceedings with well-advised lawyers. The IRS's efforts to build a "Wealth Squad" that focused on sophisticated and complex tax evasion faced the challenge of unraveling complex tax structures defended by high-powered lawyers and accountants.[129] Increasing IRS funding can allow it to hire agents with the expertise necessary to confront these types of noncompliance.

In 2022, Congress answered the calls for increased IRS funding through the Inflation Reduction Act (IRA).[130] The IRA initially provided for an additional $79.6 billion in funding for the IRS (and related agencies) over ten years, as a supplement to its normal annual appropriations. To illustrate the magnitude of this investment, the IRS's actual expenditures were an estimated $14.3 billion in 2022.[131] The IRA allocated more than half of the additional funding – $45.6 billion – to support IRS enforcement capacity, allowing for the hiring of more agents and legal counsel, as well as for the acquisition and implementation of new enforcement technology.[132] The legislation increased total projected funding for enforcement by nearly 70%. The IRA also provided an additional $25.3 billion for IRS operations support (representing an increase of nearly 50%). Finally, the Act provided an additional $4.8 billion for updating the IRS's business systems and cybersecurity, and $3.2 billion for taxpayer services, including filing assistance and education.

Former IRS Commissioner Charles O. Rossotti characterized the IRA's investment a "once-in-a-century opportunity to restore a depleted IRS."[133] The IRS subsequently developed a strategic plan outlining how it would use the influx of resources.[134] Among other initiatives, the IRS stated that it would devote additional resources to enforcement of taxpayers with "complex tax filings" and "high-dollar noncompliance," by focusing on the returns of "large partnerships, large corporations, and high-income and high-wealth individuals."[135] This goal would be accomplished through, among other strategies, the use of advanced analytic processes and technology, as well as hiring new personnel with expertise in examining complex returns. At the same time, the strategic operating plan also evidenced a new focus on taxpayer services and building trust, rather than solely on enforcement efforts.[136]

As Chapter 3 describes, the promise of more funding by Congress does not guarantee that the IRS will see all of it, or that the agency will be able to devote the entire amount to its intended uses. Indeed, within a year after the passage of the IRA, Congress rescinded part of its new funding, and repurposed another 25% of the total amount, as part of legislation resolving a debt-ceiling crisis.[137] The IRS may be subject to future budget cuts and diminished political support in future years as well, which can all reduce the impact of the IRA funding or other measures to reinforce the tax compliance system.

Activity-Based Rules

As discussed throughout this book, current law and reform proposals generally adopt an "activity-based" approach to designing rules that address tax noncompliance. This activity-based approach adjusts specific tax compliance rules when taxpayers participate in certain activities identified by Congress or the IRS.

Activity-based rules can address noncompliance by targeting the specific activities that can enable or indicate tax noncompliance. As one example of an activity-based rule in current law, as described earlier, the reportable transaction rules specify increased reporting obligations for both taxpayers and material advisors, as well as potential additional penalties for undisclosed activities.[138] These reportable transaction rules can alert the IRS to specific taxpayer transactions that may be abusive, or that can hide improper tax reporting positions.

For another example, the 2021 Infrastructure Investment and Jobs Act introduced new information reporting obligations for brokers in cryptocurrencies, requiring these brokers, beginning in 2023, to start reporting their clients' trading activities to the IRS.[139] In the years leading up to this legislation, both policymakers and academics expressed alarm with the opportunities for tax avoidance enabled by cryptocurrency, since the IRS often has limited visibility into these investments.[140]

Some activity-based rules define the scope of the covered activities very narrowly, while others define the activities more broadly. For example, the categories of reportable transactions in the Treasury Regulations include both narrowly and broadly defined activity-based rules.[141] One narrowly defined category, "listed transactions," only applies to specific transactions or structures that the IRS has identified as potentially abusive through published guidance.[142] The listed transactions include specific tax-avoidance strategies, such as syndicated conservation easement transactions[143] or abusive trust arrangements using cash value life insurance policies.[144] The same Treasury Regulations also specify other broadly defined activities as reportable transactions. For example, the reportable transaction rules apply to any "confidential transaction," which is a transaction offered to a taxpayer under conditions of confidentiality and for a minimum specified fee,[145] or any "loss transaction," which applies to *any* transaction generating a large tax loss over a taxable year or a series of years.[146] For individuals and certain other entities, this category generally applies to any transaction generating a tax loss of $2 million in a single tax year or $4 million over a series of years.

Some activity-based rules depend on the degree of culpability of the taxpayer's activities. For example, the Internal Revenue Code specifies a higher penalty rate for underpayments resulting from fraud than that for underpayments resulting from negligence or "disregard of rules or regulations."[147] Other activity-based rules depend on the activity's role in enabling noncompliance. For example, taxpayers with assets held abroad may be subject to third-party reporting requirements under the Foreign Account Tax Compliance Act (FATCA).[148] Similarly, the additional disclosure requirements and potential penalties for taxpayers engaging in "listed" or "reportable" transactions reflect the fact that these transactions can indicate or enable noncompliance.

The discussions in the following chapters offer many additional examples of activity-based rules, both in current law and in reform proposals. In all these cases, these activity-based rules follow a simple logic: Policymakers can narrow the tax gap by targeting the specific activities that can indicate or enable noncompliance and subject these activities to heightened tax compliance requirements. These rules can also provide the IRS with greater visibility and information regarding activities where the agency cannot easily detect noncompliance.

Importantly, these activity-based rules do not explicitly take account of the characteristics of the taxpayer, such as their income or wealth, but only certain actions the taxpayer might take. Otherwise, these rules typically apply the same for all taxpayers engaging in the activity.

Many activities subject to heightened tax compliance rules will only be engaged in by higher-income taxpayers. Therefore, certain activities can partially indicate characteristics of the taxpayer as well. For example, very few, if any, taxpayers with low or moderate incomes participate in transactions generating a tax loss of $2 million or more in a single tax year. As a result, activity-based rules can also indirectly address the challenges of high-end noncompliance, especially when they focus on activities typically only engaged in by higher-income taxpayers. In a similar manner, the optimal taxation literature on "tagging" considers how observable taxpayer characteristics – such as their physical height or level of education – can correlate with (and therefore indicate) their income-earning potential and, thus, which may be a more efficient basis for taxation.[149] Certain observable activities of a taxpayer can similarly correlate with or indicate their economic circumstances, such as their income or wealth, which may make them appropriate bases for heightened tax compliance rules focused on high-end taxpayers. As we explain, however, using certain activities as imperfect proxies for a taxpayer's income can also cause a variety of design challenges when implementing activity-based rules.[150]

* * *

The tax compliance system serves a vital function in implementing the substantive tax rules. This function also sets the tax compliance rules apart as a distinct part of the tax system, with its own design considerations and policy objectives. The tax compliance system encompasses a broad scope of statutes, regulations, and formal and informal IRS policies and procedures. This system also typically focuses on IRS enforcement and activity-based rules as the primary responses to tax noncompliance. The following chapters begin to consider the limitations of this current approach, and how the tax compliance might be reimagined to address the challenges of high-end noncompliance more effectively.

NOTES

1 These rules are governed by I.R.C. Subtitle A (Income Taxes); Subtitle B (Estate and Gift Taxes).
2 For example, the progressive rate schedule on income in I.R.C. § 1(a)–(d), (j).
3 For example, the credits against the income tax provided in I.R.C. §§ 21–53.
4 I.R.C. § 11(a). This example assumes the corporation does not make the election described in I.R.C. § 1362(a) to be treated as an S corporation not subject to the corporate tax.
5 I.R.C. § 6707A (penalties for failing to include reportable transaction information with tax return); I.R.C. § 6707A(c) (definitions of "listed" and "reportable" transactions). For more discussion of the listed and reportable transaction penalties, see *infra*, section "An Overview of the Tax Compliance System."
6 For a survey of the literature on the topic, see Michael P. Keane, *Labor Supply and Taxes: A Survey*, 49 J. ECON. LIT. 961 (2011). Studies typically find that the labor supply response to taxation is relatively low, and particularly for working-age males. Studies have also found that in some cases the effect of taxation on reported labor income is predominantly caused by changes in tax reporting, rather than by real behavioral changes. *See, e.g.*, Joel Slemrod, *High-Income Families and the Tax Changes of the 1980s: The Anatomy of Behavioral Response*, in EMPIRICAL FOUNDATIONS OF HOUSEHOLD TAXATION 169 (Martin Feldstein & James Poterba, eds., 1996).
7 *See* Joel Slemrod & Shlomo Yitzhaki, *Tax Avoidance, Evasion and Administration*, in 3 HANDBOOK PUB. ECON. 1423, 1428 (Alan J. Auerbach & Martin Feldstein, eds., 2002).
8 *See* Johnathan H. Choi & Ariel Jurow Kleiman, *Subjective Costs of Tax Compliance*, 108 MINN. L. REV. 1255 (2024); Uwe Dulleck et al., *Tax Compliance and Psychic Costs: Behavioral Experimental Evidence Using a Physiological Marker*, 134 J. PUB. ECON. 9 (2016).

9 See Joram Mayshar, *Taxation with Costly Administration*, 93 SCANDINAVIAN J. ECON. 75 (1991).
10 Joel Slemrod & Shlomo Yitzhaki, *The Costs of Taxation and the Marginal Efficiency Cost of Funds*, 43 STAFF PAPERS (INTERNATIONAL MONETARY FUND) 172, 173 (1996).
11 Michael Keen & Joel Slemrod, *Optimal Tax Administration*, 152 J. PUB. ECON. 133 (2017).
12 See JANE G. GRAVELLE, CONG. RES. SERV., RL34229 CORPORATE TAX REFORM: ISSUES FOR CONGRESS 20–35 (2021) (reviewing evidence on the incidence and distributional effects of the corporate tax).
13 JOEL SLEMROD & CHRISTIAN GILLITZER, TAX SYSTEMS 6–7 (2014).
14 See Joel Slemrod, *Cheating Ourselves: The Economics of Tax Evasion*, 21 J. ECON. PERSP. 25, 44 (2007).
15 I.R.C. §§ 6671, 6601(e)(1).
16 See RICHARD A. MUSGRAVE, THE THEORY OF PUBLIC FINANCE: A STUDY IN PUBLIC ECONOMY 6–27 (1959).
17 Daniel N. Shaviro, *Rethinking Tax Expenditures and Fiscal Language*, 57 TAX L. REV. 187, 188 (2004).
18 *Id.* at 209 ("[T]he distributional branch ... as it is used to define the 'tax system' for tax expenditure purposes, should be thought of as limited to acting on the basis of broad equitable considerations, such as those involving inequality or ability to pay.").
19 I.R.C. § 1(a)–(d), (j).
20 *See, e.g.*, Shaviro, *supra* note 17, at 207 ("[A] Pigovian pollution tax is primarily allocative, designed to give polluters the right incentives with regard to pollution abatement.").
21 I.R.C. § 30D.
22 *See, e.g.*, JOINT COMM. ON TAX'N, JCX-38-21, DESCRIPTION OF SUBTITLE G – GREEN ENERGY: BUDGET RECONCILIATION LEGISLATIVE RECOMMENDATIONS 41 (2021) (describing the purpose of this provision and other green energy tax incentives).
23 *See* Joshua D. Blank & Ari Glogower, *Progressive Tax Procedure*, 96 N.Y.U. L. REV. 668, 671 (2021).
24 *See, e.g.*, Alec Schierenbeck, *The Constitutionality of Income-Based Fines*, 85 U. CHI. L. REV. 1869, 1879 (2018) (describing how income-adjusted fines can be used to progressively raise additional government revenue).
25 DEP'T OF TREASURY, OFF. OF TAX POL'Y, REPORT TO THE CONGRESS ON PENALTY AND INTEREST PROVISIONS OF THE INTERNAL REVENUE CODE 36 (1999).
26 I.R.C. § 30D(f)(10).
27 I.R.C. § 6662(a)–(b).
28 I.R.C. § 6662(d).
29 Similar critiques have been raised in the context of jurisdictions who regularly issue speeding tickets and other monetary sanctions for the purpose of raising revenue rather than promoting public safety. *See generally, e.g.*, April D. Fernandes et al., *Monetary Sanctions: A Review of Revenue Generation, Legal Challenges, and Reform*, 15 ANN. REV. L. SOC. SCI. 397 (2019); Mike McIntire & Michael H. Keller, *The Demand for Money behind Many Police Traffic Stops*, N.Y. TIMES (Oct. 31, 2021), https://www.nytimes.com/2021/10/31/us/police-ticket-quotas-money-funding.html.
30 IRS, INTERNAL REVENUE SERVICE INFLATION REDUCTION ACT STRATEGIC OPERATING PLAN FY 2023–2031 78 (2023).

31 For examples of such reforms, see *infra* section "Sanctions for Noncompliance."
32 *See* A. MITCHELL POLINSKY, AN INTRODUCTION TO LAW AND ECONOMICS 160–21 (4th ed. 2011) ("[R]edistribution through the legal system only may occur when a dispute arises, and not all members of a given income class will be involved in a dispute."); Louis Kaplow & Steven Shavell, *Why the Legal System Is Less Efficient Than the Income Tax in Redistributing Income*, 23 J. LEGAL STUD. 667, 674 (1994) ("[W]hen redistribution is possible, it tends to be limited to those few who become parties to lawsuits. And even then, redistribution may be haphazard.").
33 *See* POLINSKY, *supra* note 32, at 160–61.
34 IRS, PUB. 1415 (REV. 10-2022), FEDERAL TAX COMPLIANCE RESEARCH: TAX GAP ESTIMATES FOR TAX YEARS 2014–2016 (2022). For discussion, see also Chapter 1, section "How Big Is the 'Tax Gap'?".
35 IRS, PUB. 1415 (REV. 9-2019), FEDERAL TAX COMPLIANCE RESEARCH: TAX GAP ESTIMATES FOR TAX YEARS 2011–2013 (2019).
36 IRS, TAX GAP ESTIMATES FOR TAX YEARS 2008–2010 (2016).
37 IRS, TAX GAP "MAP" TAX YEAR 2006 ($ BILLIONS) (2011), https://www.irs.gov/pub/newsroom/tax_gap_map_2006.pdf.
38 IRS, TAX YEAR 2001 FEDERAL TAX GAP (2005), https://www.irs.gov/pub/irs-news/tax_gap_figures.pdf.
39 Compañia General de Tabacos v. Collector of Internal Revenue, 275 U.S. 87, 100 (1927) (Holmes, J., dissenting).
40 *See* TOM R. TYLER, WHY PEOPLE OBEY THE LAW (2006).
41 Michael Doran, *Tax Penalties and Tax Compliance*, 46 HARV. J. LEGIS. 111, 131–38 (2009) (describing the social norms model of taxpayer compliance).
42 *See* Erzo F. P. Luttmer & Monica Singhal, *Tax Morale*, 28 J. ECON. PERSP. 149, 155 (2014) (describing the motivations of civic duty and altruism).
43 Slemrod, *supra* note 14, at 40.
44 Marjorie E. Kornhauser, *A Tax Morale Approach to Compliance: Recommendations for the IRS*, 8 FLA. TAX REV. 599, 606–26 (2007).
45 TAXPAYER ADVOC. SERV., 2022 ANNUAL REPORT TO CONGRESS 29 (2023), https://www.taxpayeradvocate.irs.gov/wp-content/uploads/2023/02/2022-ARC_FullBook_02022023.pdf.
46 *See* Raj Chetty et al., *Salience and Taxation: Theory and Evidence*, 99 AM. ECON. REV. 1145 (2009).
47 *See, e.g.*, Mortgage Escrow Account Act, 765 ILL. COMP. STAT. 910 (2023) (Illinois statute requiring home loan borrowers to pay property taxes through an escrow account held by the mortgage lender).
48 *See, e.g.*, Slemrod, *supra* note 14, at 37; Anders Jensen, *Employment Structure and the Rise of the Modern Tax System*, 112 AM. ECON. REV. 213 (2022).
49 IRS, *supra* note 34, at 14.
50 *See, e.g.*, I.R.C. §§ 6651–6706 (civil penalties for tax noncompliance).
51 I.R.C. § 2714a; *see also* Joshua D. Blank, *Collateral Compliance*, 162 U. PA. L. REV. 719 (2014).
52 *See* Joshua D. Blank, *What's Wrong with Shaming Corporate Tax Abuse*, 62 TAX L. REV. 539 (2009).
53 *See* I.R.C. § 3406 (backup withholding).

54 See, e.g., I.R.C. §§ 7201–7206 (criminal sanctions for cases of severe tax noncompliance).
55 For further discussion, see Chapter 6, section "Tax Penalties and Deterrence."
56 See JEREMY BENTHAM, THE THEORY OF LEGISLATION 325 (C. K. Ogden ed., Richard Hildreth trans., 1931) (1802) (proposing that the "evil of the punishment must be made to exceed the advantage of the offence"); Gary S. Becker, *Crime and Punishment: An Economic Approach*, 76 J. POL. ECON. 169 (1968).
57 See Alex Raskolnikov, *Crime and Punishment in Taxation: Deceit, Deterrence, and the Self-Adjusting Penalty*, 106 COLUM. L. REV. 569, 581 (2006). For more discussion, see also Chapter 6, section "Underdeterrence at the Top."
58 See Michael G. Allingham & Agnar Sandmo, *Income Tax Evasion: A Theoretical Analysis*, 1 J. PUB. ECON. 323 (1972); Sarah B. Lawsky, *Modeling Uncertainty in Tax Law*, 65 STAN. L. REV. 241, 249–53 (2013).
59 See Lawsky, *supra* note 58, at 254–68.
60 Taylor Cranor et al., *Communicating Tax Penalties to Delinquent Taxpayers: Evidence from a Field Experiment*, 73 NAT'L TAX J. 331 (2020).
61 Eric Posner, *Law and Social Norms: The Case of Tax Compliance*, 86 VA. TAX. REV. 1781 (2000).
62 See, e.g., Blank, *supra* note 51, at 759; Dan M. Kahan, *Signaling or Reciprocating? A Response to Eric Posner's Law and Social Norms*, 36 U. RICH. L. REV. 367, 368–69 (2002) (proposing a theory of "moral and emotional" reciprocity as more accurate than Posner's economic signaling model); Leandra Lederman, *The Interplay between Norms and Enforcement in Tax Compliance*, 64 OHIO ST. L. J. 1453, 1476 n.122 (2003) ("[T]he signaling theory has fundamental problems.").
63 Eric A. Posner, *The Signaling Model of Social Norms: Further Thoughts*, 36 U. RICH. L. REV. 465, 468 (2002) (conceding that tax privacy limits signaling effects).
64 See I.R.C. § 6103 (confidentiality and disclosure of returns and return information).
65 Fair Tax Foundation (May 21, 2023) https://fairtaxmark.net/.
66 See Katharina Gangl & Benno Torgler, *How to Achieve Tax Compliance by the Wealthy: A Review of the Literature and Agenda for Policy*, 14 SOC. ISSUES & POL'Y REV. 108, 137 (2020).
67 Emily A. Satterthwaite, *Tax Signaling*, 74 TAX L. REV. 259 (2021).
68 I.R.C. §§ 6001–7874.
69 I.R.C. § 7801.
70 IRS, *The Agency, Its Mission and Statutory Authority* (Nov. 15, 2023), https://www.irs.gov/about-irs/the-agency-its-mission-and-statutory-authority.
71 IRS, *supra* note 34.
72 See, e.g., Sebastian Beer et al., *Do Audits Deter or Provoke Future Tax Noncompliance? Evidence on Self-employed Taxpayers* (Int'l Monetary Fund, Working Paper No. 2019/223, 2019).
73 IRS, INTERNAL REVENUE SERVICE INFLATION REDUCTION ACT STRATEGIC OPERATING PLAN FY 2023–2031 68–72. (2023).
74 *Id.* at 80–84.
75 *Id.* at 78.
76 TREASURY INSPECTOR GEN. FOR TAX ADMIN., REP. NO. 2020-30-056, INDIVIDUAL RETURNS WITH LARGE BUSINESS LOSSES AND NO INCOME POSE SIGNIFICANT COMPLIANCE RISK (2020).

77 IRS, FS-2006-10, Fact Sheet: The Examination (Audit) Process (2006), https://www.irs.gov/pub/irs-news/fs-06-10.pdf.
78 *See, e.g.*, S. Rep. No. 114-119, The Internal Revenue Service's Processing of 501(c)(3) and 501(c)(4) Applications for Tax-Exempt Status Submitted by "Political Advocacy" Organizations from 2010–2013 (2015).
79 Hadi Elzayn et al., *Measuring and Mitigating Racial Disparities in Tax Audits* (Stan. Inst. Pol'y Rsch., Working Paper, Jan. 30, 2023).
80 For discussion of these forms of informal guidance, see Joshua D. Blank & Leigh Osofsky, *The Inequity of Informal Guidance*, 75 Vand. L. Rev. 1093 (2022).
81 I.R.C. § 6012.
82 I.R.C. § 6038D (requiring first-party information reporting of specified foreign financial assets).
83 I.R.C. §§ 6011, 6707A. For more discussion, see *infra*, section "Activity-Based Rules."
84 Treas. Reg. § 1.6011-4(b)(2); IRS, *Recognized Abusive and Listed Transactions* (Jan. 17, 2023), https://www.irs.gov/businesses/corporations/listed-transactions.
85 Treas. Reg. § 1.6011-4(a), (b)(6).
86 T.D. 9350, 2007-38 I.R.B. 607, 608.
87 For example, the rules in I.R.C. §§ 6041-6050Y (third-party information reporting requirements).
88 I.R.C. § 3402.
89 I.R.C. § 3406.
90 Treas. Reg. § 301.6111-3.
91 Dep't of Treasury, Circular No. 230 (Rev. 6-2014), Regulations Governing Practice before the Internal Revenue Service (2014). For more discussion, see Chapter 7, section "Tax Advice as Tax Penalty Insurance."
92 For more discussion, see Chapter 6, section "Tax Penalties in Current Law."
93 I.R.C. § 6651.
94 I.R.C. § 6662.
95 I.R.C. § 6663 (fraud penalty); § 6662(i) (transactions lacking economic substance penalty).
96 *See, e.g.*, I.R.C. § 6721 (failure to file correct information returns).
97 I.R.C. § 6662(d)(2)(B).
98 I.R.C. § 6664(c) (reasonable cause exception for underpayments); Treas. Reg. § 1.6664-4. For more discussion, see Chapter 7, section "Tax Advice as Tax Penalty Insurance."
99 I.R.C. § 6707A. For a description of the different categories of reportable transactions, see *infra* notes 141–146 and accompanying text.
100 I.R.C. §§ 6707, 6708
101 I.R.C. § 6694.
102 Dep't of Treasury, *supra* note 91, at § 10.50.
103 Dep't of Treasury, *supra* note 25, at 40–42.
104 I.R.C. § 6601. The taxpayer can, however, prevent the accrual of interest by making a deposit to cover future taxes owed. I.R.C. § 6603.
105 I.R.C. § 6621
106 I.R.C. § 6611.
107 I.R.C. § 7201.

108 I.R.C. § 7203.
109 18 U.S.C. §§ 286, 371.
110 I.R.C. § 6212.
111 I.R.C. § 6501. For more discussion, see Chapter 8, section "The Ticking Tax Clock."
112 I.R.C. §§ 6213–6215.
113 IRS, Publication 5 (Rev. 4-2021), Your Appeal Rights and How to Prepare a Protest if You Disagree (2021).
114 For example, before filing a return or an IRS assessment, a taxpayer may seek an advanced resolution with the IRS through agreements such as a private letter ruling, determination letter, or prefiling agreement. Once a dispute has arisen with the IRS, a taxpayer may be able to seek closure through resolution processes such as the mutual agreement procedure, an accelerated issue resolution agreement, or post-appeals mediation. See, e.g., IRS, *Dispute Prevention and Resolution for Large Business and International Taxpayers* (Aug. 19, 2022), https://www.irs.gov/businesses/dispute-resolution.
115 Taxpayer Advoc. Serv., *About Us*, https://www.taxpayeradvocate.irs.gov/about-us/.
116 See, e.g., Golsen v. Comm'r of Internal Revenue, 54 T.C. 742 (1970) (holding that the Tax Court will generally apply precedent from the applicable federal Court of Appeals to which an appeal would be made).
117 For more discussion, see Chapter 4, section "Revisiting Constitutional Protections."
118 See, e.g., U.S. Tax Court, Rules of Practice and Procedure (2023), https://www.ustaxcourt.gov/resources/ropp/Complete_Rules_of_Practice_and_Procedure_Amended_03202023.pdf.
119 I.R.C. § 7803(a)(3); Taxpayer Advoc. Serv., *Taxpayer Bill of Rights* (Feb. 6, 2023), https://www.irs.gov/taxpayer-bill-of-rights.
120 See Alice G. Abreu & Richard K. Greenstein, *The U.S. Taxpayer Bill of Rights: Window Dressing or Expressions of Justice?* 4 J. Tax Admin. 25, 29 (2018) (arguing that the TBOR can align the administration of the tax system with principles of procedural justice).
121 Leandra Lederman, *The IRS, Politics, and Income Inequality*, 150 Tax Notes 1329 (Mar. 14, 2016).
122 Taxpayer Advoc. Serv., 2019 Annual Report to Congress 23 (2019), https://www.taxpayeradvocate.irs.gov/wp-content/uploads/2020/08/ARC19_Volume1.pdf.
123 Tax Policy Center, *Briefing Book: What Does the IRS Do and How Can It Be Improved?* (May 2020), https://www.taxpolicycenter.org/briefing-book/what-does-irs-do-and-how-can-it-be-improved.
124 See Taxpayer Advoc. Serv., *supra* note 122, at 23–26.
125 Lily Batchelder & David Kamin, *Policy Options for Taxing the Rich*, in Maintaining the Strength of American Capitalism 200, 205 (Melissa S. Kearney & Amy Ganz eds., 2019), https://economicstrategygroup.org/wp-content/uploads/2019/12/Maintaining-the-Strength-of-American-Capitalism-Policy-Options-for-Taxing-the-Rich.pdf.
126 Lederman, *supra* note 121, at 1333.
127 Gov't Accountability Off., GAO-22-104960, Tax Compliance: Trends of IRS Audit Rates and Results for Individual Taxpayers by Income 8 (2022).
128 *Id.*
129 See Chapter 1, section "How the Rich Avoid Taxes."

130 Inflation Reduction Act of 2022, H.R. 5376, 117th Cong., Pub. L. 117-169, 136 Stat. 1818.
131 IRS, Pub. 55-B (Rev. 3-2023), 2022 DATA BOOK 71, tbl. 30 (2021), https://www.irs.gov/pub/irs-prior/p55b–2022.pdf.
132 CONG. RES. SERV., IN11977, IRS-RELATED FUNDING IN THE INFLATION REDUCTION ACT (Oct. 20, 2022).
133 Charles O. Rossotti, *Success or Failure at the IRS: What Will Make the Difference?*, 177 TAX NOTES. FED. 1661, 1661 (2022).
134 IRS, *supra* note 73.
135 *Id.* at 62.
136 *See also* Jarod Facundo, *The Taxman Cometh: A New Plan from the IRS Lays Out How the Agency Intends to Revamp Itself*, AM. PROSPECT (Apr. 14, 2023), https://prospect.org/economy/2023-04-14-based-taxman-cometh-revamped-irs/.
137 Fiscal Responsibility Act of 2023, H.R. 3746, 118th Cong., Pub. L. 118-5, §§ 102, 251, 137 Stat. 10 (2023); *see also* CONG. RES. SERV., IN12172, CHANGES TO IRS FUNDING IN THE DEBT LIMIT DEAL (June 6, 2023).
138 *See* I.R.C. §§ 6707, 6707A; Treas. Reg. §§ 1.6011-4, 1.6111-3.
139 Infrastructure Investment and Jobs Act, H.R. 3684, 117th Cong., Pub. L. 117-58, § 80603, 135 Stat. 429 (codified at I.R.C. §§ 6045, 6045A).
140 *See, e.g.*, Omri Marian, *Are Cryptocurrencies Super Tax Havens?*, 112 MICH. L. REV. FIRST IMPRESSIONS 38 (2013); Jason Brett, *In 2021, Congress Has Introduced 35 Bills Focused On U.S. Crypto Policy*, FORBES (Dec. 27, 2021), https://www.forbes.com/sites/jasonbrett/2021/12/27/in-2021-congress-has-introduced-35-bills-focused-on-us-crypto-policy/?sh=20e4a053c9e8.
141 Treas. Reg. § 1.6011-4.
142 Treas. Reg. § 1.6011-4(b)(2).
143 IRS Notice 2017-10.
144 IRS Notice 2007-83
145 Treas. Reg. § 1.6011-4(b)(3).
146 Treas. Reg. § 1.6011-4(b)(5).
147 I.R.C. §§ 6662(a)–(b), 6663(a).
148 Hiring Incentives to Restore Employment Act, H.R. 2847, 111th Cong., Pub. L. No. 111-147, § 501, 124 Stat. 71, 97–99 (2010) (codified at I.R.C. §§ 1471–1474, 6038D).
149 *See* Matthew C. Weinzierl, *Why Do We Redistribute So Much but Tag So Little? The Principle of Equal Sacrifice and Optimal Taxation* 8-9 (Nat'l Bureau Econ. Rsch., Working Paper No. 18045, 2012). ("Tags carry information about ability but are hard to modify, so taxing them allows for redistributive gains without efficiency losses.").
150 For further discussion, see Chapter 3, section "Limitations of Activity-Based Rules."

3

Means-Adjusted Tax Compliance

A New Approach

What are the weaknesses of the current tax compliance rules, and how can these rules more effectively address the challenge of high-end tax noncompliance? This chapter first describes the limitations of the traditional responses to tax noncompliance in the law and in prominent reform proposals. It then introduces a new approach: a system of means-adjusted tax compliance rules. As we argue, this approach can both complement the traditional responses to noncompliance and counter their limitations to build a more robust and effective tax compliance system. The final section of this chapter describes how introducing means adjustments to the tax compliance rules would not be a radically new direction for tax reform, but rather an extension and rationalization of principles that are already embedded in the current tax law.

UNEQUAL EFFECTS OF GENERALLY APPLICABLE RULES

Before turning to the specific limitations of the traditional responses to tax noncompliance, this first section touches briefly on a central challenge in legal design: the potentially unequal effects of generally applicable rules.

Most tax compliance rules are generally applicable: They apply in the same way for all taxpayers without explicitly accounting for each taxpayer's economic circumstances. In many cases, however, these generally applicable rules can have unequal effects for higher- and lower-income taxpayers. As a result, these rules can often be less effective in deterring noncompliance by higher-income taxpayers.

For example, consider again the basic penalty deterrence model introduced in Chapter 2. Any given penalty amount – whether calculated as either a fixed amount or a percentage of the taxpayer's underpayment – will have less deterrent effect in situations where the IRS has a lower chance of detecting the tax avoidance and successfully imposing the penalty. As a result, generally applicable penalties can have a lower deterrent effect for higher-income taxpayers, to the extent that these taxpayers both have more expansive tax-avoidance opportunities and greater advantages in subsequent disputes with the IRS.

For another example of how generally applicable rules can have unequal effects, consider the rules governing the statutes of limitations. As Chapter 8 describes in greater detail, the IRS is subject to identical limitations periods for making assessments, regardless of the identity of the taxpayer.[1] This limitations period typically ranges from three to six years from the time the applicable tax return is deemed filed, although it remains open indefinitely in some cases, such as for fraud or when no return is filed.[2]

In many cases, however, higher-income taxpayers have more complex and less visible transactions and activities, which can take longer for the IRS to examine. As a result, a generally applicable rule, such as the uniform statute of limitations periods, can provide an unequal and disproportionate benefit to the highest-income taxpayers.

LIMITATIONS OF INCREASING IRS FUNDING

The IRS serves the critical role of executing and enforcing taxpayers' compliance obligations, which are essential to implementing the substantive tax rules. IRS administration and enforcement actions translate the tax rules from words on paper into the revenue that sustains the federal government. Without a well-funded IRS, the tax compliance rules would be empty words with no effect on tax revenues. As a result, any effort to narrow the tax gap must begin with adequately funding the IRS so it can perform its essential operations.

Investing in the IRS can also yield a significant positive return to the public, both by improving efficiency in tax administration and by narrowing the tax gap. For example, the Congressional Budget Office estimated that the $80 billion investment in the IRS through the 2022 Inflation Reduction Act would increase federal revenues by $180 billion or more over the following decade alone.[3] These official government estimates may be conservative. A study by Natasha Sarin and Mark Mazur argued that they were too low, and that the new funding would, in fact, yield a net revenue increase of $480 billion over the following decade, and possibly as much as $1 trillion.[4] At these levels, the substantial positive return to be raised from improving enforcement likely justifies the investment of additional resources in IRS operations, even if the monetary return from tax enforcement investments is not the only relevant criteria when determining the optimal level of enforcement.[5]

Adequately funding the IRS is a necessary precondition for giving effect to the tax laws. Simply giving the IRS more money, however, cannot fully solve the challenge of tax noncompliance. This section describes the different limitations of increasing IRS funding as a primary strategy to enforce the tax law. In light of these limitations, policymakers must also consider how the tax compliance rules themselves can be restructured to address the limitations the IRS encounters in its administration and enforcement operations.

A Political Football

Congressional budget allocations to the IRS can vary substantially from one legislative cycle to another, and IRS funding can be particularly vulnerable and variable when policymakers stoke public fears of the agency as overly intrusive and powerful. Questions of IRS funding are often treated as a political football, and policymakers use this debate to score political points and advance different views on the tax system and fiscal policy.

As recent history has shown, IRS funding can enter periods of decline in changing political environments. For example, a *ProPublica* report describes how in 2013, Republicans in Congress capitalized on claims that the IRS had targeted certain tax-exempt groups to justify significant budget cuts that starved the agency of needed revenue.[6] During that period, then Representative Ander Crenshaw (R-FL), who sat on the House Appropriation Committee, justified a $346 million budget cut to the IRS by claiming that the agency "targeted Americans based on their political beliefs" and "wasted millions of taxpayer dollars."[7] The impact of these cuts was stark, and relatively swift: A report by the National Taxpayer Advocate estimated that the IRS budget declined by nearly 20% in inflation-adjusted dollars in less than a decade, from $12.1 billion in 2010 to $10.1 billion in 2018.[8]

The $80 billion in increased IRS funding in the 2022 Inflation Reduction Act could be similarly exposed to shifts in political winds. For example, following the passage of the bill, the Republican Chair of the House Ways & Means Committee Representative, Jason Smith (R-MO), blasted the new reform in a letter to the IRS.[9] In his letter, Representative Smith argued that the reform would "raise audit rates on all Americans" and warned of the specter of "a more aggressive and assertive IRS conducting more and more audits of taxpayers at all income levels." Indeed, after the 2022 midterm elections, when Republicans assumed a majority in the House in January 2023, they immediately passed a bill attempting to rescind the new IRS funding in one of their first exercises of legislative power.[10] While the legislation was only symbolic at the time, since Democrats controlled both the Senate and the White House, the bill evidenced the political vulnerability of any significant increases in IRS funding.

The prospect of losing funding in the future in a different political climate also forces the IRS to conserve its current resources. For example, the IRS report detailing how the agency would allocate the $80 billion in additional funding offered two telling caveats. First, it noted that, even with this historic investment by Congress, the IRS would need "an ongoing investment on top of the allocated IRA funding to deliver all of the transformation objectives outlined in this Plan."[11] Second, the report explained that any future decline in Congress's regular annual appropriations for the IRS would require the agency to divert the resources it receives through the IRA to fund its daily operations.[12] In effect, the IRS would be obligated to set aside a portion of the funding as a precaution against changing political winds. Within less than a year, Congress proved just how uncertain the new funding measure was: It rescinded a portion of the promised funding and reduced the IRS's annual appropriations by $10 billion in each of the two succeeding fiscal years.[13]

The challenges with IRS funding long predate the IRA. Politicians have long capitalized on public fears of IRS power to undermine the agency. For example, Professor Leandra Lederman details how politicians throughout history have frequently exaggerated claims of the IRS's overreach and abuses of power to justify weakening the agency and subjecting it to excessive oversight.[14] To illustrate how politicians can capitalize on fears of the IRS to justify constraining the agency, Professor Lederman details how, in 1997, policymakers held hearings in which they focused on "horror stories of IRS abuse of taxpayers," which ultimately led to the passage of the Internal Revenue Service Restructuring and Reform Act of 1998. Professor Lederman argues that this legislation created unnecessary new constraints on IRS agents and oversight bodies, and ultimately precipitated a significant decline in IRS enforcement.[15]

Administrative Discretion

Even when the IRS does receive promised funding from Congress, the agency often retains significant discretion in how it uses its funds. Further, studies find that IRS enforcement efforts and resource allocations can also depend on the political priorities of the president in office.[16] As a result, IRS administrative and enforcement priorities can also change with the political climate. Merely increasing funding for the IRS will not necessarily ensure exactly how the IRS uses that funding in the future. As former IRS Commissioner Charles E. Rossotti cautioned soon after the IRA passed, "Only clear, regular improvements in the performance of the agency's mission will ... win the confidence of the public and Congress. Money alone will not make that happen."[17]

The IRS studiously seeks to maintain a significant degree of independence from the presidential administration, even more so than other executive agencies, to avoid the perception of political targeting. Studies suggest, however, that the IRS is often responsive to both the president and Congress regarding its overall policy priorities and, on balance, is understood to be an "effective bureaucratic agent of its presidential and congressional sponsors."[18] Indeed, the failure of the IRS to complete mandatory audits of President Trump's tax returns during the first two years of his presidency appears to amplify the findings that IRS policies can be influenced by changes in political power.[19]

The IRS does not have unlimited discretion in how it uses its budget. As in the case of the 2022 IRA funding, Congress may specify that certain amounts of funding are allocated for certain functions. Even for annual general IRS appropriations, Congress attaches administrative provisions, or "policy riders," which are designed to communicate to the IRS congressional priorities or expectations in the use of the appropriated funds.[20]

That said, the IRS nonetheless maintains significant discretion in setting not only its internal budget allocations but also its tax-enforcement priorities and methods.[21] Without explicit direction from Congress to focus on high-end noncompliance, a future IRS might use increased funding to target activities for which tax enforcement, including collection, is easier. The IRS also cannot always reallocate funding to different enforcement operations. For example, in 2019, then IRS Commissioner Charles Rettig addressed the disparity between relative audit rates of recipients of the EITC (who are low-income taxpayers) and high-end taxpayers, commenting that the "IRS cannot simply shift examination resources from single issue correspondence audits to more complex higher income audits because of employee experience and skillset."[22] This phenomenon has been observed in the literature as well. For example, a 2023 study found that the IRS allocated most of its audit resources designed to target international avoidance by high-income individuals to taxpayers earning $200,000 or less, even though these audits tended to yield less revenue relative to the enforcement dollars spent, as compared to those audits examining higher-income returns.[23]

The IRS has subsequently stated that it would prioritize using IRA funding to counter high-end noncompliance.[24] This shift, however, similarly evidences the discretion that the IRS retains in setting these priorities.

Following the passage of the IRA and the publication of the IRS strategic plan, organizations also urged the agency to use its discretion to reconsider how the additional resources should be allocated. The National Taxpayer Advocate argued for the reallocation of resources away from enforcement activities and toward investments in taxpayer services, reasoning that, "[t]he most efficient way to improve compliance is by encouraging and helping taxpayers to do the right thing on the front end" rather than "trying to audit our way out of the tax gap one taxpayer at a time on the back end."[25] Other commentators cautioned that the IRS could face challenges in reorganizing its structure in order to implement its new enforcement strategies.[26] Charles O. Rossotti cautioned that the IRS could be subject to even greater scrutiny as a result of the IRA funding, since "[t]his funding will increase expectations for improved IRS performance since it can no longer be cited as a major constraint."[27]

The IRS's broad enforcement discretion can also contribute to its perceptional challenges and political vulnerability. Because it exercises necessary discretion, the IRS often not only faces significant scrutiny, and even suspicion, but it can also find itself unduly vilified, even as it performs a vital mission that sustains the government and its citizenry.

Congress can help. As we explain, legislators can embed principles of equitable tax enforcement in statutes and in the structure of the tax compliance system, and thereby foster a perception that the IRS is executing policies and priorities supported by a public mandate.[28]

The Costs of Enforcement

Even if we set aside the IRS's changing political fortunes and shifting priorities, administrative enforcement will not always be the most cost-effective or efficient way to close the tax gap. Policymakers must take into account the various costs of enforcement, both to the IRS and to taxpayers, when considering how – and how much – the tax gap should be narrowed. These costs can include direct expenses for enforcement and compliance, behavioral changes, costs of tax planning, and even the psychic costs from enforcement.

For this reason, economists Michael Keen and Joel Slemrod argue that the IRS should not undertake any and all efforts to fully close the tax gap, since doing so could impose costs on both the IRS and taxpayers that would not be justified by the the additional revenue collected.[29] Similarly, Professors Norman Gemmell and John Hasseldine argue that conventional estimates of the tax gap are flawed by failing to account for behavioral responses that would reduce the revenue raised from efforts to close the tax gap.[30] As Joel Slemrod and Shlomo Yitzhaki have argued, policymakers should, in principle, always weigh whether it would be more costly to raise additional revenue through changes to the substantive tax rules or through increased enforcement.[31]

The IRA's new investments in the IRS will almost certainly assist in narrowing the tax gap. But policymakers should not always assume that increasing enforcement, despite its potential benefits, is necessarily the best way to close the tax gap. Even within the broad category of tax enforcement and administration measures, not all enforcement methods will be equally costly to taxpayers and the IRS. As a result, policymakers seeking to narrow the tax gap should consider the specific types of tax compliance rules or administrative policies that can narrow the tax gap in the most efficient manner.

To illustrate this point, let us return to the basic Becker-Bentham deterrence model, where policymakers can discourage an undesirable behavior by either increasing the sanction or increasing the chance of detection.[32] In many cases, higher sanctions can be much less costly to the government than steps taken to increase the chances of detecting noncompliant taxpayers. This is because increasing the potential sanction often requires only ex ante and relatively costless changes to the applicable tax compliance rules, whereas the latter requires active and more costly ex post investigations of taxpayers' transactions and activities.[33]

For instance, consider the case of a sophisticated taxpayer with a complex tax return that the IRS cannot easily examine before the applicable statute of limitations has expired. The IRS can devote resources to hiring additional highly skilled agents so that the return can be examined before this deadline. The IRS's 2023 strategic plan describes exactly this approach as one of the uses of the new IRA funding. Alternatively, policymakers can also make changes to the tax compliance rules, which can help lower the costs of examining the return and detecting noncompliance while increasing the deterrent effect to potentially noncompliant taxpayers. Such changes could include increasing the applicable penalties, extending the statute of limitations period, or requiring the taxpayer to report more information.

Joel Slemrod cautions against taking this rationale for increasing ex ante deterrence rather than ex post detection too far. Imposing excessively harsh sanctions could risk imposing disproportionate penalties for minor offenses, which could not only give too much power to administrators but also discourage courts from actually imposing the sanctions.[34] In this case, these deterrents must be designed in a way that ensures proportionality in punishments and basic procedural protections.

Further, ex ante changes to the compliance rules would not always be entirely costless. Additional information reporting requirements could increase the compliance costs for the taxpayer, and higher penalties could impose greater psychic costs if they fostered a fear of "getting caught" even among compliant taxpayers. In many cases, however, changes to the tax compliance rules can be a significantly less costly method of deterring compliance, as compared to exclusively devoting resources to ex post IRS enforcement. In other cases, changes to the tax compliance rules can also reduce the costs of necessary ex post enforcement actions.

For this reason, the IRS has recognized the limits of enforcement efforts, and has called on Congress to complement the agency's role through effective tax compliance legislation. In a 2020 letter on strategies to narrow the tax gap, then Commissioner Charles Rettig observed: "[E]nforcement alone will not narrow the Tax Gap, and the efforts necessary to raise compliance levels are resource intensive for the IRS and can be intrusive to taxpayers ... which is why we need legislation."[35]

The costs of additional IRS enforcement and detection are even greater in the case of measures designed to address high-end noncompliance. Wealthy taxpayers often enjoy the advantages of complexity, flexibility, reduced visibility, sophisticated legal counsel, and the ability to exploit ambiguities in the law, which can all escalate the costs of ex post IRS enforcement. Because of these higher enforcement costs, policymakers may achieve even greater efficiencies through changes to the tax compliance rules when seeking to close the tax gap at the top.

These considerations do not suggest that policymakers should not increase IRS funding significantly. To the contrary, increasing IRS funding from its current levels will likely yield a large positive benefit in terms of revenue, by enabling the IRS to modernize its technology and to target "low-hanging fruit": the most egregious and easily detectable forms of tax noncompliance.[36] Without a public perception that the IRS has in fact ramped up its enforcement efforts, and has made the investments necessary to increase enforcement capacity, even more stringent tax compliance rules will not have their intended deterrent effect. Rather, these considerations suggest that policymakers should also consider complementary, and potentially more cost-effective, reforms to the tax compliance rules as part of a comprehensive response to the tax gap.

THE LIMITATIONS OF ACTIVITY-BASED RULES

Policymakers and academics have long recognized that IRS funding alone cannot narrow the tax gap. They have also focused on the structure of the tax compliance rules and options for their reform. As Chapter 2 describes, the current statutory tax compliance rules and reform proposals mostly adopt an "activity-based" approach to addressing tax noncompliance. These activity-based rules impose more stringent requirements for taxpayers who engage in certain activities.

In many cases, these rules can help to target the specific activities that enable or indicate tax noncompliance. These rules also play an important role in addressing high-end noncompliance, especially when they target the activities that are disproportionately engaged in by high-end taxpayers.

However, these activity-based rules also face inherent limitations and design challenges. As a result, while they are a necessary part of a comprehensive response to tax noncompliance, they also do not offer a complete solution. The remainder of this section describes the limitations of activity-based rules as a response to high-end tax noncompliance and how policymakers have an even more difficult time defining effective activity-based rules when high-end taxpayers can take advantage of complexity, flexibility, reduced visibility, sophisticated legal counsel, and ambiguities in the law.

High-End Avoidance

High-end taxpayers often have significant flexibility in structuring their transactions and activities. This flexibility not only enables noncompliance – it also makes it harder for the IRS to enforce the tax law.[37] Such flexibility may also undermine the effectiveness of activity-based tax compliance rules. In many cases, high-income taxpayers can simply change the form of their activities to avoid those targeted by activity-based rules. This taxpayer flexibility leaves the IRS constantly playing catch-up and struggling to target the latest strategies while there is still time to recover lost tax revenues.

Well-advised high-income taxpayers can often avoid engaging in a specified activity that is subject to activity-based rules, such as those identified by the IRS as listed transactions or transactions of interest.[38] When the IRS announced its intention to challenge strategies such as BOSS (bond and option sales strategy),[39] CARDS (custom adjustable rate debt structure),[40] and contingent liability[41] tax shelter strategies in the early 2000s, taxpayers responded by shifting quickly to other tax-avoidance tactics.[42] Taxpayers can often adjust their activities in this way, by using tax structures and transactions that do not fall into the specific categories that would lead to additional tax shelter penalties.[43] Commentators have described the battle against tax shelters as similar to a game of "Whac-A-Mole." As soon as the IRS shuts down one strategy, another one emerges.[44]

Similarly, taxpayers may avoid offshore disclosure requirements by shifting their assets to other investments, such as cryptocurrency or other alternative asset classes. For example, FATCA and related offshore reporting rules address one activity taxpayers use to hide assets – holding them in foreign accounts – but these rules may simply encourage taxpayers to hide assets through other activities, such as holding cryptocurrency.[45] For this reason, Professor Omri Marian has argued that cryptocurrencies have the potential to "replace tax havens as the weapon-of-choice for tax-evaders."[46]

Policymakers often implement new activity-based rules in response to changes in taxpayer behavior and emerging avoidance strategies. In the case of cryptocurrencies, Congress introduced changes in 2021 to the information reporting rules that would require brokers of digital currencies to report information regarding digital asset transactions to the IRS.[47] By this time, however, taxpayers had already benefited from years of transactions that remained hard for the IRS to detect and identify and could have moved on to new strategies.

Because of transactional complexity, Congress and the IRS often require time to effectively implement new activity-based rules. For example, in the case of cryptocurrency legislation, policymakers have struggled to define the new information reporting requirements in the decentralized and technically complex digital asset sector.[48] Any delays in implementing activity-based rules allow more time for taxpayers to take advantage of abusive transactions before the IRS can stop them.

Reactive, Not Preemptive

Because of taxpayer flexibility, policymakers typically must implement activity-based rules reactively, based on emerging taxpayer behaviors, rather than preemptively. This approach leaves policymakers in the challenging position of constantly responding to new noncompliance strategies as they arise.

Policymakers cannot easily introduce activity-based rules preemptively. To do so, policymakers would have to anticipate the specific activities that taxpayers will engage in that will enable noncompliance. On the other hand, if policymakers try to impose preemptive rules that would apply to a broad range of possible activities, they risk imposing undue burdens on fully compliant taxpayers who are not the intended targets of these rules.

The reactive nature of most activity-based rules undermines their impact in two ways. First, as described earlier, reactive activity-based rules often invite taxpayers to simply shift their behavior to other activities which the rules do not cover. Because they are reactive rather than preemptive, activity-based rules can also encourage taxpayers to complete abusive transactions quickly before they are detected by the IRS. When the government targets specific abusive tax strategies through statutes or regulations, taxpayers may try to argue that their use of the strategies prior to enactment of these activity-based rules was permissible. For example, in *Compaq*

Computer v. Commissioner,⁴⁹ the taxpayer Compaq purchased $900 million of Royal Dutch American Depository Receipt (ADR) shares, received a dividend, claimed a corresponding foreign tax credit in the United States, and then quickly sold the ADRs.⁵⁰ The Fifth Circuit held that Compaq's tax-shelter strategy should have been allowed because Compaq completed all of its transactions before Congress enacted the activity-based rule that would have prohibited the practice.⁵¹

Finally, because activity-based rules react to specific developments in the tax planning industry, they generally necessitate administrative, rather than legislative, action. Congress usually cannot enact legislation that anticipates or targets specific abusive strategies quickly enough to control their spread. As a result, the IRS often implements activity-based rules targeting specific strategies through regulatory action.⁵² The rules for reportable and listed transactions offer one example of this inevitable division of labor.⁵³ However, because of developments in the field of administrative law, as we will discuss, the IRS now faces additional hurdles in implementing these rules through regulatory action.

Greater Burdens on Lower-Income Taxpayers

By focusing solely on activities rather than the actors, activity-based rules can also impose the highest burdens on lower- and middle-income taxpayers who engage in the identified activities. These taxpayers may bear proportionally higher compliance burdens or have less ability to contest penalties or other consequences. It may be easier for high-income taxpayers, on the other hand, to avoid or mitigate the effect of these activity-based rules. This upside-down effect of many activity-based rules results from the fact that differently situated taxpayers may engage in the same activities. Policymakers may not be able to effectively target these rules – and to isolate the cases of high-end noncompliance – by fine-tuning the definition of the covered activities.

Activities do not always serve as an effective indicator, or "tag," of the taxpayer's underlying income or earnings ability. The literature on tagging introduced in Chapter 2 observes that even effective tags may correlate with income "across the population in aggregate" but not with respect to any specific individual.⁵⁴ For the same reason, even if certain taxpayer activities may, in the aggregate, correlate with a taxpayer's income or wealth, these activities do not necessarily indicate that any specific taxpayer's income or wealth is, in fact, at a certain level.⁵⁵

For an example of this problem with activity-based rules, Professor Shu-Yi Oei has described the regressive consequences of the IRS's Offshore Voluntary Disclosure Program (OVDP). She argues that this program often resulted in the highest relative penalties for participating taxpayers with relatively small account balances.⁵⁶ She cites a 2014 National Taxpayer Advocate study that found that "in the 2009 OVDP, the median offshore penalty paid by those with the smallest accounts ... was almost six times the median unreported tax liability, while for those with the largest accounts, it was only about three times the unreported tax."[57] In contrast, higher-income taxpayers were often able to mitigate the burdens from these activity-based rules.[58]

More generally, any activity-based rule can have the effect of imposing the greatest relative burden on the lowest-income taxpayers engaging in the activity when it treats all participating taxpayers in the same way. This problem results from the imperfect correlation between certain activities and the income levels of actors who undertake them. However, if policymakers seek to define the activities more narrowly to avoid unintended burdens on lower-income taxpayers, they can also risk undermining the effectiveness of the activity-based rule.

A "Goldilocks" Problem

These various potential problems with activity-based rules present a design challenge for policymakers. Like Goldilocks seeking a chair that is just the right size, policymakers face different problems when they define activity-based rules too broadly or too narrowly.

Narrowly defined activity-based rules can allow sophisticated taxpayers to avoid them by simply changing their activities. On the other hand, policymakers encounter other problems if they define activity-based rules broadly, to cover a broader potential range of tax-avoidance strategies. When activity-based rules are broadly defined so that they can anticipate different forms of tax avoidance, they can also inadvertently penalize or unduly burden activities or taxpayers that should not be prioritized as targets for enforcement.[59]

One example of this problem is the introduction of the new broker reporting rules for digital assets in 2021. Policymakers faced a difficult challenge in appropriately defining the scope of activities subject to the new rules. Defining brokers too narrowly, to cover only a small range of actors engaged in only some cryptocurrency trading activities, could limit the rule's impact in reducing tax avoidance through cryptocurrency. On the other hand, a broader definition could impose new obligations on many compliant taxpayers, or it could create compliance burdens out of proportion to the potential tax revenues to be recovered.[60]

Defining activity-based rules too broadly can also simply shift the discretion to the courts or the IRS, which must then decide how to apply the rule so that it avoids inadvertent burdens on the wrong taxpayers. Consider what happened when, in 2010, Congress introduced new penalties for taxpayers with underpayments resulting from transactions lacking economic substance. Commentators argued that this broad doctrine could be applied to penalize many non-abusive transactions.[61] In this case, tax administrators and courts sometimes react to an overbroad activity-based rule by simply declining to apply the rule or by preserving their own discretion, which can undermine the impact of implementing the rule in the first instance. In the case of the economic substance doctrine, commentators have argued that the codification did not change the ability of courts to engage in their own style of tax-shelter analysis.[62]

Chapter 10 similarly describes how the Goldilocks problem poses a basic design challenge for information reporting requirements, such as in the case of FATCA and the Biden Administration's 2021 bank account information reporting proposal.[63] In these cases, defining the activities subject to broader information reporting too broadly can impose onerous new compliance burdens, while defining the activities too narrowly can enable taxpayer avoidance and undermine the effect of the reforms.

ADMINISTRATIVE CONSTRAINTS ON THE IRS

Activity-based rules encounter inherent limitations, regardless of which branch of government implements them. When the IRS introduces these activity-based rules as administrative actions, they face additional constraints that Congress does not encounter when it enacts these rules through legislation.

Implementing activity-based tax compliance rules often necessitates administrative rulemaking by an executive agency such as the IRS, instead of legislative action by Congress. Because of taxpayers' flexibility in structuring their activities, Congress cannot easily anticipate the specific activities taxpayers will engage in to avoid paying taxes. As a result, in many cases Congress defines general principles in the Internal Revenue Code, and then authorizes the Treasury (and ultimately the IRS) to define the specific activities subject to the statutory rules.

For an example of this division of labor between Congress and Treasury, consider the structure of the reportable transaction rules introduced in Chapter 2. Congress cannot easily enact legislation that anticipates or targets specific abusive strategies quickly enough to control their spread.[64] As a result, the IRS implements these rules by designating specific tax strategies as potentially abusive tax shelters when it issues notices of listed transactions and transactions of interest.[65]

Because the IRS often needs to act quickly through agency action, however, it can also face administrative law challenges to these actions by taxpayers and their advisors. Congress has broad, though certainly not unlimited, powers under the Constitution to enact tax law through the legislative process. As an executive agency, in contrast, the IRS is subject to additional substantive and procedural restrictions. These restrictions limit the scope of the IRS's rulemaking authority and impose additional procedural requirements on its administrative actions.

Recent developments in administrative law have made it even harder for Congress and the IRS to maintain this division of labor in defining activity-based rules. In recent years, the courts have further constrained the IRS's ability to perform its basic mission to administer the tax laws, in what scholars have described as a "systematic 'tilt' of administrative law against revenue."[66]

To back up for a moment, consider first the different constitutional powers granted to Congress and the IRS. Article I Section 8 of the Constitution grants Congress the broad power to "lay and collect taxes" and "to provide for the common Defense and general Welfare of the United States."[67] This section also grants Congress authority to enact any laws "necessary and proper" in exercising its constitutional powers.[68] The Sixteenth Amendment also provides that Congress can impose an income tax without having to apportion the tax among the states relative to their population.[69]

The Courts have generally recognized Congress's broad powers to enact tax legislation, as long as it does not violate other constitutional limitations. Under the "direct tax clauses," Congress cannot enact a direct tax, such as a capitation tax, without apportionment.[70] Among other limitations, Congress also cannot use its taxing powers to enact rules that are, in substance, regulations rather than taxes, and which would otherwise exceed Congress's regulatory powers.[71]

Any tax laws introduced by Congress must be properly enacted through legislative procedures. Tax legislation originates in the House of Representatives, but it can be delayed indefinitely by a "filibuster" in the Senate, unless sixty senators vote for cloture to end debate on the legislation.[72] The Congressional Budget Act of 1974 offered an alternative method for Congress to pass tax legislation when they lack the requisite supermajority in the Senate. Through the budget reconciliation process, Congress can pass tax legislation by a simple majority, if the legislation conforms to previously specified "reconciliation instructions" passed by the House and the Senate.[73] To reign in potential abuse of this alternative legislative procedure, Congress also enacted the "Byrd rule" in 1990, which allows a senator to challenge a provision passed through this procedure that is "extraneous" to the reconciliation process.[74]

As parts of the executive branch of government, the Department of the Treasury, together with its tax administration agency, the IRS, have much more limited authority to make law, and no separately enumerated constitutional powers. Congress established the Treasury in 1789 for the purpose of managing the government's revenue collection and finances,[75] and it established the IRS within the Treasury in 1862, with the specific purpose of managing the collection of tax revenues and the administration of the tax system.[76]

As part of the executive branch of government, Treasury and the IRS are formally tasked with executing laws enacted by Congress, rather than making the law through legislation. As such, IRS regulatory actions are subject to basic statutory and judicial constraints. Under the "*Chevron* Doctrine," courts will often defer to an executive agency's statutory interpretation that is a "permissible construction" of the statute, as long as Congress has not directly spoken to the question at issue.[77] Congressional delegations of rulemaking power to agencies such as the IRS are limited, however, by the "nondelegation doctrine." Under this rule, Congress can only assign the IRS the role of interpreting or implementing "intelligible principles" specified in the statute.[78]

The Administrative Procedure Act (APA) imposes additional procedural requirements for regulatory actions by administrative agencies,[79] including the specification of a "notice-and-comment" process for informal agency rulemaking.[80] Under notice-and-comment rulemaking, the agency must generally provide the public with notice, typically through the publication of proposed rules in the Federal Register, and allow the public an opportunity to comment on them.[81]

In recent years, Treasury Regulations and IRS actions have come under increased scrutiny for their compliance with APA procedures. A debate in the academic literature offers differing views on the questions of whether prior IRS regulations have fully complied with the APA requirements and whether applying a uniform model for all administrative procedures is appropriate in the case of tax regulations.[82] What is indisputable, however, is that recent court decisions have decidedly turned toward a more stringent application of APA requirements to tax regulations, in a manner that will often constrain the IRS's ability to develop the rules necessary to appropriately enforce the tax law and address noncompliance.[83]

The following section describes how the legal dispute between the IRS and CIC Services, a tax advisor who assisted in the structuring of "micro-captive" insurance strategies, illustrates the many challenges the IRS encounters when it seeks to challenge abusive tax strategies through activity-based tax compliance rules.

CIC Services, LLC v. IRS

The Supreme Court's 2021 holding in the case *CIC Services, LLC v. IRS* has made it easier for taxpayers to challenge IRS actions as violating the rulemaking requirements outlined in the APA.[84] The aftermath of this case illustrates the increasingly stringent application of APA requirements to IRS rulemaking and how these restrictions can hinder the implementation of activity-based tax compliance rules.

The plaintiff in the case, a Tennessee firm named CIC Services, advised clients regarding micro-captive insurance strategies. In these transactions, a taxpayer makes deductible insurance premium payments to a related "captive" insurer, which then makes an election under Section 831(b) of the Internal Revenue Code to exclude the premiums from taxable income.[85] The transaction can improperly erode the parties' total taxable income if the arrangement is not a bona fide insurance contract.[86] The complex strategy exploits ambiguities in the law to synthesize an improper tax benefit that Congress never contemplated when enacting these provisions.

In 2016, the IRS issued Notice 2016-66, which designated these strategies as transactions of interest.[87] In doing so, it imposed reporting obligations on taxpayers participating in these transactions and their material advisors, as well as potential penalties if they did not comply.[88]

Prior to Notice 2016-66's first reporting deadline, CIC Services filed a complaint claiming that the notice was invalid under the APA.[89] The petitioner argued that the issuance of the notice was subject to the APA's notice-and-comment procedures for legislative rulemaking.[90] The government countered by arguing that the APA challenge was premature, since the Anti-Injunction Act (AIA) bars any "suit for the purpose of restraining the assessment or collection of any tax."[91] Under this Act, plaintiffs must instead pay the tax liability due and then seek a refund from the IRS.[92] The lower courts rejected CIC Services' argument, finding that the AIA applied to the tax law at issue.[93]

On May 17, 2021, the US Supreme Court reversed the appellate court's holding and issued a unanimous decision in favor of CIC Services.[94] The Court held that the petitioner's pre-enforcement suit, the purpose of which was to enjoin the IRS from designating a transaction as a reportable transaction through the issuance of Notice 2016-66, was not barred by the AIA, even though noncompliance with the Notice could result in a tax penalty.[95]

The Court reached its conclusion by relying on a number of tenuous arguments that attempted to distinguish between the reporting requirements and penalties at issue, on the one hand, and standard taxes subject to the AIA, on the other. In trying to draw this distinction, the Court focused on the additional compliance costs and reporting obligations on third-party advisors, as well as the potential for criminal penalties, to reach the conclusion that these rules were not "taxes" for purposes of the AIA.[96] Because it draws tenuous distinctions among different elements of the tax compliance system when applying the AIA, the holding in *CIC Services* can have unpredictable implications for future IRS actions.

The *CIC Services* Court interpreted the scope of the AIA, but not the petitioner's underlying claim that the IRS violated the APA in issuing Notice 2016-66.[97] At the time, commentators disagreed on whether CIC Services or the IRS would prevail on this substantive question. Some argued that the IRS's process was already compliant with the APA,[98] while others suggested that the APA required a more complete notice-and-comment process for reportable transactions notices.[99]

In the wake of the Supreme Court's ruling in *CIC Services* that the APA challenge was not barred by the AIA, taxpayers proceeded to challenge the IRS's authority to designate listed transactions without notice-and-comment rulemaking. In the wake of the Court's holding, CIC Services sought a preliminary injunction in District Court for the Eastern District of Tennessee to prohibit enforcement of Notice 2016-66 pending a trial on the merits.[100] The Court subsequently ruled for the taxpayer on the merits and vacated Notice 2016-66, on the ground that the IRS did not comply with the APA notice and comment procedures and acted "arbitrarily and capriciously."[101]

Around this time, courts similarly invalidated other IRS actions addressing abusive strategies. In *Mann Construction v. United States*, the Sixth Circuit Court of Appeals invalidated IRS Notice 2007-83, which identified as a listed transaction certain abusive employee trust arrangements, on the same grounds that the notice did not comply with APA procedures.[102] Soon thereafter, the Tax Court similarly held that another IRS notice identifying another abusive tax strategy – syndicated conservation easements – as a listed transaction[103] was also invalid for the same reason of insufficient compliance with the APA.[104]

The IRS has stated that it disagrees with the substance of these holdings, all of which held that the agency cannot identify listed transactions through its process for promulgating these notices.[105] Nonetheless, in recognition of the new reality, or perhaps because it has no alternatives in light of these aggressive judicial interpretations, the IRS has begun to reidentify listed transactions and transactions of interest through a comprehensive notice-and-comment process.[106] For example, the IRS subsequently issued new notices of proposed rulemaking targeting the syndicated conservation easements and micro-captive transactions.[107]

Implications for Activity-Based Rules

These developments in administrative law present additional legal hurdles and risks for the IRS in its efforts to implement activity-based rules such as the reportable transaction disclosure requirements. First, after *CIC Services*, taxpayers and their advisors may be able to bring APA challenges to a broader range of IRS actions that implement activity-based rules before they have to pay any applicable taxes or penalties. The lifting of the AIA bar is significant because, when it applies, taxpayers or advisors would have to first incur taxes or penalties for noncompliance before bringing a legal challenge. As in the case of *CIC Services*, taxpayers and tax advisors may now seek preliminary injunctions to prevent notices from going into effect even before a trial on the merits of the claim.[108] If petitioners are successful in enjoining the IRS from enforcing reportable transaction notices, the IRS may be unable to effectively detect and deter abusive tax strategies by designating them as reportable transactions through its current procedures. Further, because the *CIC Services* holding rests on tenuous distinctions among different tax compliance rules, the case can increase uncertainty as to when a court will find that the AIA does or does not apply.

Second, the recent cases invalidating IRS notices implementing the reportable transaction rules indicate the shift in some jurisdictions towards stringent application of the APA procedural requirements to IRS regulatory actions. As a result of this shift, courts may continue to require the more time-consuming and comprehensive notice-and-comment process for more IRS actions implementing activity-based rules.

These judicial developments do not prevent the IRS from implementing activity-based rules, such as the reportable transaction notices, through regulatory action. Instead, as discussed earlier, the IRS has taken the step of reidentifying abusive transactions as listed transactions and transactions of interest through notice-and-comment rulemaking. The IRS has also argued that it will continue to defend the validity of other listing notices when the facts are different than those in the cases where courts invalidated certain notices.[109] Other sub-regulatory IRS guidance may also continue to be exempt from notice-and-comment rulemaking requirements.[110]

These additional procedural hurdles and legal risks to IRS regulatory actions can nonetheless hinder the effectiveness of activity-based rules, particularly when these actions target avoidance by high-end taxpayers. Because high-end taxpayers have the greatest flexibility to restructure their activities, the IRS often must act quickly to combat new strategies before it is too late. Even the risk of litigation or preemptive challenges can slow the IRS's ability to collect information from taxpayers and advisors about emerging avoidance strategies, and wealthy parties with vested interests may be encouraged to challenge IRS actions.[111] The IRS will also face greater legal uncertainty regarding the outcomes of these challenges. At the same time, if the IRS changes its procedures to reduce legal exposure, it risks taking additional measures beyond what the APA requires, which can further impair its efforts to challenge emerging tax-shelter transactions. Finally, the IRS may also hesitate to issue new listed transaction and transaction of interest notices if these additional obstacles would make notices more burdensome and less effective.[112]

Interest Group Influence on Regulatory Process

In addition to their legal hurdles and risks, activity-based rules implemented through agency actions can also be susceptible to significant influence from interest groups seeking to undermine or challenge these rules. Scholars have documented how special interests can obstruct agency rulemaking and take advantage of the notice-and-comment process. These interests often have a disproportionate stake in the outcome, especially in cases when the narrow issue is less salient to the public.

These effects may be more pronounced in the context of tax regulation. Professor Clinton Wallace's research shows the "lopsided" nature of the "notice-and-comment" process in tax rulemaking, where, in many cases, private special interest groups have accounted for a disproportionate share of all comments on IRS regulatory actions during the three-year period from 2013 through 2015.[113] Wallace attributes this phenomenon to a number of factors that are more pronounced in the context of tax rulemaking, including the low salience of narrow and technical issues, and the potential for "concentrated costs" on particular actors but "diffuse benefits" to the public.

Scholars have identified a similar impact of interest groups on nontax agency rulemaking as well.[114] As Professor Wallace and others have argued, however, many tax rules may be even more vulnerable to industry group lobbying, because these rules are purely "zero-sum," in that "[a] failure to raise revenue currently implies a tax increase on future taxpayers" who "are particularly poorly positioned to have organized groups representing their interests."[115]

The specific activities targeted through activity-based rules may impose even greater concentrated costs on a few industry actors who have much to lose from even small technical changes to the tax compliance rules. *CIC Services* illustrates how this dynamic can affect IRS implementation of activity-based rules through regulatory action. CIC Services is a firm that specializes in advising taxpayers on the specific captive insurance transactions targeted by the IRS. Therefore, it had a disproportionate interest in challenging the IRS's efforts to stop these specific abusive tax transactions and was able to concentrate opposition to the IRS regulatory actions.[116] Legal victories can also be a springboard for such taxpayers to mount further challenges. Industry news sources reported that, following their Supreme Court victory, CIC Services announced plans to establish a lobbying group dedicated to challenging future IRS actions.[117]

A NEW APPROACH: MEANS-ADJUSTED TAX COMPLIANCE RULES

Policymakers should not rely exclusively on IRS funding and activity-based rules to address the challenges of high-end tax noncompliance. In contrast, we propose that they should also adopt a new approach – means adjustments to the tax compliance rules. Under our approach, taxpayers with greater economic resources would be subject to means-adjusted tax compliance rules, which could better address the challenges of high-end tax noncompliance. Unlike the activity-based responses in current law and in reform proposals, this approach would account for characteristics of the taxpayers when designing the tax compliance rules, and not just their specific activities.

Later chapters in this book describe exactly how these adjustments could operate in different areas of the tax compliance system. For instance, high-end taxpayers could be subject to higher civil tax penalty rates, more stringent standards for using tax advice as a "penalty shield," longer statutes of limitations on assessment, and additional information reporting requirements.

Before we consider how policymakers should design these means adjustments, however, the remainder of this chapter describes the general advantages of this new approach. Means adjustments to the tax compliance rules can counter many of the limitations in the traditional responses to tax noncompliance and can build a more robust and effective tax compliance system. Introducing these adjustments would not radically change the structure of the tax compliance system but would rather offer a more systematic and consistent approach to principles already embedded in current law.

THE ADVANTAGES OF MEANS-ADJUSTED TAX COMPLIANCE RULES

Means-adjusted tax compliance rules could fill in many of the holes in the current tax compliance system and complement the traditional responses of activity-based rules and IRS enforcement. This section describes, in broad terms, the general advantages of means adjustments as a new approach to tax compliance.

Equalizing Effects

Rules that apply the same for all taxpayers can have unequal effects for taxpayers in different economic circumstances. As a result, these rules can be less effective in deterring noncompliance by high-end taxpayers. This basic limitation helps to explain why the current tax compliance rules often do such a poor job in countering high-end noncompliance.

Policymakers can tailor means adjustments to the tax compliance rules so they can equalize the effects of these rules and address the specific advantages of higher-income taxpayers under generally applicable rules. The following chapters describe in detail how higher civil penalty rates can account for high-end taxpayers' greater chances of avoiding detection and enforcement. Similarly, a longer statute of limitations period can account for the higher complexity and lower visibility of their transactions and activities.

From a policy perspective, the tax compliance rules do not necessarily need to operate in the same way for all taxpayers. Chapter 4 offers reasons, however, as to why equalizing the effects of the tax compliance rules should be a priority for the tax system. Further, as Chapter 1 described, the IRS has articulated that it is an important goal to treat all taxpayers equally in the administration of the tax system.

Minimizing Costs

Congress also cannot rely exclusively on IRS enforcement to solve the problem of high-end noncompliance. IRS funding can be variable and subject to political reversals in Congress, and, in any event, increasing enforcement is not always the most cost-effective response to noncompliance.

Means adjustments to the tax compliance rules can narrow the tax gap while minimizing the costs to both the taxpayers and the government. The government can deter taxpayers from deciding not to comply with the tax laws by increasing either sanctions or the chance of detection. As in the case of the basic Becker-Bentham deterrence model, policymakers can, in principle, minimize the costs of deterrence by increasing the potential sanction, which can be done at a lower administrative cost rather than by increasing the chance of detection, which often requires significant administrative expenses. Policymakers are most likely to effectively raise additional revenue through compliance and enforcement efforts, as compared to increasing the substantive tax rates, in cases where these administrative measures do not entail significant additional costs.[118]

In this way, means adjustments could more effectively deter high-end noncompliance while minimizing additional costs. For example, the following chapters describe how higher penalty rates or additional disclosure obligations for high-income taxpayers can reduce the ex ante expected value from noncompliance without the need for more government expenditures on administration and enforcement. These adjustments could also discourage noncompliance without imposing excessive new costs or burdens on taxpayers.

Preemptive, Not Reactive

Means-adjusted tax compliance rules can be implemented preemptively and would not depend on a taxpayer's particular activities. As a result, taxpayers could not avoid these tax compliance rules by restructuring their transactions and activities. Means adjustments would also not incentivize taxpayers to rush to use specific tax-avoidance strategies before the government acts to shut them down or to argue that they had completed their transactions before the application of the new rules, such as in the *Compaq* case described earlier in this chapter.

In this way, preemptive means-adjusted tax compliance rules could allow the IRS to address the challenges of high-end tax noncompliance more broadly, rather than by constantly reacting to the latest tax-avoidance strategies. As a result, the IRS could more effectively target enforcement resources to counter a broader range of avoidance strategies.

Avoiding Administrative Law Challenges

The judicial developments in administrative law described earlier in this chapter can make it even more difficult for the IRS to enforce activity-based rules through regulatory action. IRS regulatory actions can face additional legal obstacles and uncertainty, as well as the increased risk of preemptive challenge by taxpayers. These developments raise the stakes for the tax compliance system and increase the need to build a robust system of tax compliance rules capable of withstanding administrative law challenges.

Means adjustments to the tax compliance rules could avoid many of the administrative constraints on activity-based rules. As the later chapters describe, Congress can enact most means adjustments to the tax compliance rules as statutory legislation, which it often cannot do in the case of activity-based rules. A means-adjusted approach can be implemented generally and preemptively across multiple areas of the tax compliance rules. In contrast, activity-based rules are often implemented on a transaction-by-transaction basis through agency rulemaking, and often under time constraints.

As a result, statutory means adjustments can also avoid the administrative law challenges the IRS faces when it seeks to implement activity-based rules through regulation. Statutory changes enacted by Congress would not be subject to legal challenge, as long as they were enacted according to legislative procedures and within Congress's broad constitutional taxing power. Because means-adjusted rules can be applied generally and preemptively, the Treasury can also implement certain adjustments with less legal risk and with time for notice-and-comment when required by the APA.[119]

Of course, any means adjustments enacted by Congress would have to overcome the many hurdles in the legislative process. We argue that legislators in Congress should embrace this challenge as an important step for tax reform. Further, as we explain, means adjustments would not encounter the same obstacles that the IRS faces in implementing activity-based rules.

Addressing the Social Costs of Noncompliance

Means adjustments to the tax compliance rules can address the greater social costs of tax noncompliance at the top of the income distribution. These rules can also rebalance the IRS's economic incentive to focus on the tax gap at the bottom of the income distribution, where the monetary returns to increased enforcement can potentially be higher, when measured in additional revenues collected for every dollar investment in enforcement.

Policymakers should not implement any and all measures to eliminate the tax gap, and particularly not measures that impose costs on the government and taxpayers that are not justified by the additional revenue raised. This framework suggests a ceiling to the additional compliance burdens and deterrents that may be desirable to introduce to the tax compliance rules.

At the same time, each dollar of noncompliance at the top of the income distribution also entails a greater social welfare cost than does a dollar of noncompliance by a lower-income taxpayer.[120] For the same reason, higher costs of taxation at the top of the income distribution may be justified by the higher social welfare gains when revenue is collected from higher-income taxpayers. If these costs borne by high-income taxpayers are negligible compared to the welfare gains from redistribution of the tax revenue raised, then the optimal tax rate on these taxpayers would be the revenue-maximizing rate.[121]

This same framework has similar implications for balancing the costs and benefits from enforcement rules and noncompliance. Enforcement rules can impose additional costs on high-end taxpayers, such as those resulting from additional compliance obligations, behavioral changes, or the psychic disutility from higher potential penalties or sanctions. In this case, means adjustments to the tax compliance rules can be similarly warranted, even when they impose greater burdens on high-income taxpayers, on account of the greater social benefit from reducing noncompliance at the top of the income distribution.

Two additional considerations, however, mitigate the concern that means adjustments to tax compliance rules would, in fact, impose significant additional costs on high-income taxpayers. First, the current tax compliance rules likely impose minimal costs on these taxpayers, as compared to their social benefits in raising additional revenue. As many have argued, significant additional revenue could be raised from the wealthiest taxpayers through even modest increases in enforcement that would not impose significant additional costs on these taxpayers.[122] Indeed, a

2023 study finds that tax enforcement against high-end taxpayers can raise revenue at a lower welfare cost, as compared to increases in their substantive tax rates.[123]

Finally, many of the tax compliance adjustments designed to deter taxpayers from choosing not to comply ex ante, such as higher penalties or a longer statute of limitations period, can be designed to impose almost no additional costs for either taxpayers or the IRS. Some adjustments to the tax compliance rules that we propose, such as the increased information reporting requirements discussed in Chapter 10, could impose new compliance costs on high-end taxpayers. In this case, however, these taxpayers can take advantage of their economies of scale and more frequent ongoing interactions with tax advisors to minimize the additional cost of new compliance obligations. Low-income taxpayers, in contrast, would have to incur higher proportional costs to similarly comply with new information reporting rules.

Effect on Tax Morale

Tax morale, which is the intrinsic motivation to pay taxes, serves an essential role in both voluntary tax compliance and public support for the tax system.[124] The tax compliance rules – and the substantive values and norms these rules express – also serve a broader function in influencing tax morale and public perceptions of the tax system.

Scholars and policymakers have examined how the administration of the tax system affects taxpayer morale and, in turn, how taxpayer morale affects compliance with the substantive tax rules. For example, the 2018 National Taxpayer Advocate Report suggested that voluntary compliance depends not only on the traditional deterrence models but also on taxpayers' "faith and trust in the fairness of the tax system."[125] Public perceptions of tax noncompliance by other taxpayers, and particularly by the rich, can also depress tax morale, while both progressive taxation and perceptions that the tax system is administered fairly can improve morale.[126]

Means-adjusted tax compliance rules would foster public faith and trust in the fairness of the tax system, which could serve to improve tax morale. Adjustments designed to rebalance the effect of the tax compliance rules can counter the perception that high-income taxpayers have unfair or undue advantages that enable tax evasion.

Means-adjusted tax compliance rules would provide a salient and easily comprehensible assurance that high-income taxpayers do not enjoy special advantages in tax compliance.[127] These adjustments could have a more significant effect on tax morale if they can yield observable evidence that high-income taxpayers are, in fact, affected by the means adjustments.[128] In this case, means-adjusted tax compliance rules could strengthen tax morale by positively affecting taxpayer perceptions of the government's tax-enforcement capabilities and priorities.

Enabling Structural Reforms

The possibility of tax avoidance can reduce the revenue-raising potential of potential tax reforms, which can pose further political challenge for these reforms. It can be even more difficult for policymakers to implement progressive reforms designed to raise revenue from the richest taxpayers when these taxpayers can avoid the effect of the new reforms.

Means adjustments to the tax compliance rules can help to counter this effect, and thereby also enable structural reforms. By reducing opportunities for tax avoidance, these adjustments can lower the elasticity of the tax base, which, in turn, can enable politicians to implement reforms that will have their intended revenue effects. These broad adjustments to the tax compliance system can also reduce the need for policymakers to enact specific anti-avoidance measures in connection with proposed substantive reforms, which, as we have seen, can be both costly and ineffective.

Political Feasibility

Like any tax reform designed to progressively raise additional tax revenues, statutory means adjustments to the tax compliance rules would undoubtedly face political opposition. As a result, Congress could only enact this kind of system during a period of sufficient political support for it in both the House and the Senate, as well as from the White House.

Enacting means adjustments to the tax compliance rules would undoubtedly be a challenge for policymakers, as would any major tax reform. For the reasons presented throughout this book, we argue that policymakers should focus on this new direction to build a more effective and fair tax system by embedding principles of fairness in the structure of the tax compliance rules.

Unlike many activity-based rules, means adjustments to the tax compliance rules would also face less risk of opposition by special interest groups that hold disproportionate stakes in relation to specific activity-based rules. For example, because activity-based tax-shelter rules are, by necessity, often implemented on a transaction-by-transaction basis, certain tax advisors and promoters specializing in particular transactions – such as CIC Services in the case of micro-captive insurance transactions – may have a greater incentive to challenge agency actions targeting those transactions.

A means-adjusted approach, in contrast, does not encounter this same special interest problem, even when specific adjustments are implemented through administrative rulemaking rather than through legislation. Since means adjustments are applied generally, without targeting specific transactions or industries, they avoid a potential disparity in the salience of these rules between the public and affected parties. Specifically, they incorporate general principles of fair taxation that would be applied across the tax compliance system, rather than on a case-by-case basis with respect to specific tax-avoidance strategies.

Stability

Once enacted, statutory means adjustments can offer more durable and stable improvements to the tax compliance system than either increasing IRS funding or implementing activity-based rules through administrative rulemaking. While statutory changes are never irreversible or permanent, they are often more durable than other elements of the tax compliance system relying on agency action or discretion.

Means adjustments to the tax compliance rules would not require annual appropriations from Congress, unlike changes to IRS funding. Similarly, statutory reforms would not depend on shifting IRS priorities through changes in power, nor would they be subject to the same legal risks and challenges as would some activity-based rules implemented through IRS regulatory action.[129]

Of course, Congress periodically modifies the Internal Revenue Code, through both smaller legislative adjustments and significant tax reform. A future Congress could always repeal or dilute any statutory means adjustments to the tax compliance rules. Many statutory tax rules have proven remarkably durable, however, once introduced to the Internal Revenue Code. For example, the several means adjustments already in the tax compliance rules that we discuss later in this chapter were introduced decades ago and have not been subject to the same changes and reversals as the IRS's annual budget allocation.[130]

Means adjustments to the tax compliance rules can also be applied across multiple areas of the tax law, to advance a similarly broad principle of fairness in taxation. Throughout waves of tax reform and turnovers in Congress, the basic principle of progressivity in the substantive tax system has proven remarkably durable.[131] Once introduced, the concept of means-adjusted tax compliance rules can similarly embed a basic structural principle, the foundation of which can endure even as future legislators negotiate and renegotiate the design of particular provisions.

A COMPLEMENTARY APPROACH

Robust IRS enforcement and activity-based rules, despite their limitations, are essential and necessary pillars of the tax compliance system. Policymakers should not interpret their limitations as reasons to abandon these responses, but rather as reasons to reinforce them through a comprehensive and multifaceted approach to tax noncompliance.

Means adjustments to the tax compliance rules would operate most effectively as a complement to – rather than a replacement for – activity-based rules and increased IRS enforcement. Each of these three responses in isolation is unlikely to offer a complete solution to the complex challenge of high-end tax noncompliance. When employed together, however, these tools offer a more comprehensive approach and a more versatile mix of responses available to tax administrators. An intersecting system comprised of these different elements can also more effectively fine-tune the tax compliance rules to target the specific challenges posed by high-end noncompliance.

Chapters 6–10 offer many examples of how means adjustments to the tax compliance rules can also improve the effect of both IRS enforcement and activity-based rules to build a more robust tax compliance system. In some cases, means adjustments can directly improve the effect of IRS enforcement and magnify the impact of reforms that increase IRS funding. For example, increasing the statute of limitations period for high-end taxpayers can amplify the impact of the IRS's 2023 plan to devote more resources and agents to uncovering complex forms of tax avoidance, which can often take longer to detect.

Means adjustments can also help activity-based rules to operate more effectively while redressing their limitations. For example, consider again the limitations of the current activity-based reportable transaction rules implemented by the IRS. If the default statute of limitations for a taxpayer has already expired by the time the IRS designates a tax strategy as a listed transaction or a transaction of interest, the limitations period cannot, under the current system, be reopened or extended.[132] In this case, the issuance of the notice would have no effect in improving compliance. A statutory means adjustment that extended the statute of limitations period for high-end taxpayers would allow notices of a listed transaction or a transaction of interest to remain in effect for a longer period. As a result, the IRS would also face less pressure to issue notices quickly and would have more time to comply with requirements under the APA.[133]

Finally, a layered approach that combines activity-based rules, means adjustments, and IRS enforcement can most effectively target an area of particular concern to the tax system: when high-end taxpayers engage in activities that can enable noncompliance. We describe how policymakers can incorporate both activity-based and means adjustments to the civil tax penalties, to provide for the highest penalties in cases where high-end taxpayers engage in certain known activities that can enable or indicate noncompliance. This layered approach can realize the advantages of activity-based rules while also avoiding problems that occur when these rules disproportionately burden the lowest-income taxpayers who happen to engage in the targeted activities.

MEANS ADJUSTMENTS IN CURRENT TAX COMPLIANCE RULES

Introducing means adjustments to the tax compliance rules might seem to be a radical new direction for the tax system. To the contrary, current law already contains many instances of means adjustments in the tax compliance rules, albeit through a haphazard and inconsistent set of provisions. This book introduces a more systematic and consistent approach to principles already embedded in current law.

Of course, the substantive progressive tax rules themselves are explicitly means adjusted: They impose different tax rates, exclusions, deductions, and credits for taxpayers in different economic circumstances. The current tax compliance rules, in contrast, typically do not distinguish between taxpayers depending on their economic circumstances. For example, all taxpayers face the same penalty rates on underpayments and failures to file returns,[134] the same interest rates on underpayments,[135] and the same statute of limitations for IRS assessments.[136]

In certain cases, however, the tax compliance rules do already incorporate means adjustments, often by following the same principles motivating the adjustments introduced in this book. Typically, these means adjustments in the current tax compliance system explicitly provide more favorable treatment benefiting lower-income taxpayers. In other cases, however, the rules already impose additional requirements or burdens on higher-income taxpayers to account for their advantages under generally applicable tax compliance rules.

As this section also illustrates, the current tax compliance rules only implement means adjustments narrowly and in particular cases, rather than systematically and consistently. Some current tax compliance rules also have the effect of imposing *additional* burdens on lower-income taxpayers – as regressive and backward applications of the same principles motivating the adjustments introduced in this book.

High-End Adjustments in Current Law

One group of statutory tax compliance rules explicitly imposes additional burdens on wealthier taxpayers. These provisions all refer to the same net wealth test used for a general fee-shifting provision in the 1980 Equal Access to Justice Act.[137] This fee-shifting rule can allow some litigants to recover their attorney's fees if they are successful in litigation against the government. In order to qualify for fee-shifting as a "party" under this rule, the individual must – in addition to satisfying other requirements – have net assets of $2 million or less.[138] Congress introduced the fee-shifting provision in order to lower the economic barriers for individuals when they are in disputes with the government, but included the net asset test in order to ensure that the rule would apply only "to those persons and small businesses for whom costs may be a deterrent to vindicating their rights."[139]

A series of statutory tax compliance rules consequently incorporate this same net asset test in order to determine eligibility for fee-shifting in certain tax disputes,[140] judicial review of a failure by the IRS to abate interest charges,[141] award of attorney's fees in cases of unauthorized inspection or disclosure of taxpayer information,[142] burden of proof shifting in tax proceedings,[143] and waiver of a penalty for failure to deposit employment taxes.[144] All these examples follow the same principles of underlying the adjustments introduced in this book: adjustments to the tax compliance rules that impose different consequences for high-end taxpayers.

Lower-Income Adjustments in Current Law

The tax compliance rules also provide some benefits for lower-income taxpayers. From one perspective, adjustments benefiting lower-income taxpayers and adjustments imposing more requirements on higher-income taxpayers can have the same effect, with only a semantic distinction in how the rules are framed. Both types of adjustments have the same effect of varying the tax compliance rules based on the taxpayer's economic circumstances. A rule advantaging lower-income taxpayers can also be characterized as a rule disadvantaging higher-income taxpayers who are denied the favorable treatment.

For an example of an adjustment that offers a proportionally greater benefit to lower-income taxpayers, the Internal Revenue Code provides for special informal Tax Court proceedings for what are known as "S cases," which involve disputes of $50,000 or less.[145] These informal proceedings are not explicitly limited to lower-income taxpayers. As such, this program may be understood as an adjustment based on factors that closely correlate with a taxpayer's means, rather than an explicit means adjustment to the applicable rules based on the taxpayer's economic circumstances. Nonetheless, the availability of these proceedings will tend to benefit lower-income taxpayers to the extent they are more likely to have smaller amounts in dispute with the IRS. For example, one commentator observes that "S cases do not always involve poor or middle-class people and are not always brought pro se, but probably the vast majority of S cases fall into those categories."[146]

Other tax compliance rules, however, can explicitly impose *greater* burdens on lower-income taxpayers. In a backward application of the principles motivating this book, these rules regressively treat lower-income taxpayers worse – rather than more favorably – than higher-income taxpayers.

For example, a low-income taxpayer who improperly claims the EITC can be disqualified from claiming the credit for the following two years, and a taxpayer who fraudulently claims the credit can be disqualified for the following decade.[147] These harsh consequences will only impact lower-income taxpayers who could otherwise claim the credit in those subsequent years and can result in penalty amounts – expressed as a percentage of the amount of underpayment – far in excess of those imposed on reckless or fraudulent activity by higher-income taxpayers.

For example, in 2023, the maximum amount of the EITC that could be claimed was $7,430, which could be claimed by a joint filing taxpayer with more than two qualifying children and earned income of up to $28,120.[148] If a taxpayer with this profile is found to have recklessly claimed the EITC in Year 1, they cannot claim the credit in Years 2 and 3. In this case, the effective penalty amount would be 200% of the amount improperly claimed (and more than 50% of the taxpayer's entire annual earned income for Year 1).[149] In contrast, the highest explicit penalty rate in the Internal Revenue Code applicable to higher-income taxpayers is the 75% penalty for fraud.[150]

Even tax compliance rules ostensibly designed to benefit lower-income taxpayers can also entail procedural disadvantages. For example, a taxpayer cannot appeal a decision from an S case in the United States Tax Court.[151] Low-income taxpayers may also encounter other procedural disadvantages in S cases. One commentator has argued that the *Golsen* rule – whereby the applicable circuit court precedent applies in Tax Court cases in the jurisdiction – could disadvantage low-income taxpayers in S cases, since it can limit the consideration of precedents that are favorable to these taxpayers.[152]

Inconsistent Application

Many of the means adjustments in the current tax compliance rules reflect the same principles behind the adjustments introduced in this book. These adjustments can account for taxpayers' varying economic circumstances and can equalize the effect of the tax compliance rules for different groups of taxpayers. The current tax compliance rules only include these adjustments in narrow circumstances, however, and not as part of a systematic and consistent approach. Some of these rules have the precisely opposite effect of imposing even greater burdens on the lowest-income taxpayers.

In this respect, the adjustments introduced in this book may be understood as an extension and rationalization of rules currently in the tax law, rather than as a fundamentally new direction. The adjustments introduced in this book offer a more methodical and systematic application of these principles already embedded in current law.

* * *

Means adjustments to the tax compliance rules can complement the traditional responses of increasing IRS enforcement and activity-based rules. These means adjustments can enable a more robust and effective tax compliance system, which can better address the challenges of high-end noncompliance.

Means adjustments would also not be new to the tax compliance system. Subjecting higher-income taxpayers to different tax compliance rules, however, might strike some readers as unfair, or perhaps violating principles of equality in the law. Chapter 4 takes a deeper look at this question and considers how these adjustments can conform with legal principles favoring equal treatment and generally applicable legal rules.

NOTES

1 *See* Chapter 8, section "The Ticking Tax Clock."
2 I.R.C. § 6501.
3 *See* Cong. Budget Off., Estimated Budgetary Effects of H.R. 5376, the Inflation Reduction Act of 2022 (2022), https://www.cbo.gov/system/files/2022-08/hr5376_IR_Act_8-3-22.pdf; Letter from Phillip L. Swagel, Dir., Cong. Budget Off., to Reps. Kevin Brady (R-TX) and Jason Smith (R-MO), *Re: Additional Information about Increased Enforcement by the Internal Revenue Service* (Aug. 25, 2022), https://www.cbo.gov/system/files/2022-08/58390-IRS.pdf.

4 Natasha Sarin & Mark J. Mazur, *The Inflation Reduction Act's Impact on Tax Compliance – and Fiscal Sustainability* (Working Paper, 2023).
5 Joel Slemrod and Shlomo Yitzhaki argue, for example, that policymakers should instead increase tax-enforcement efforts up to the point that the marginal enforcement costs equal their marginal social benefit. Joel Slemrod & Shlomo Yitzhaki, *The Optimal Size of a Tax Collection Agency*, 89 SCANDINAVIAN J. ECON. 183 (1987).
6 Paul Kiel & Jesse Eisinger, *Gutting the IRS: How the IRS Was Gutted*, PROPUBLICA (Dec. 11, 2018), https://www.propublica.org/article/how-the-irs-was-gutted. For more discussion, see also Chapter 5, section "Public Perceptions of the IRS."
7 Rep. Ander Crenshaw (R-FL), *Rep. Crenshaw: Keep the Reins Tight on the IRS*, USA TODAY (Dec. 21, 2014), https://www.usatoday.com/story/opinion/2014/12/21/irs-rep-ander-crenshaw-house-subcommittee-editorials-debates/20741177/.
8 TAXPAYER ADVOC. SERV., SPECIAL REPORT TO CONGRESS: EARNED INCOME TAX CREDIT: MAKING THE EITC WORK FOR TAXPAYERS AND THE GOVERNMENT 9 n.37 (2019), https://www.taxpayeradvocate.irs.gov/wp-content/uploads/2020/08/JRC20_Volume3.pdf; *see also* Chapter 2, section "Increasing IRS Funding."
9 Letter from Rep. Jason Smith (R-MO), Chairman, Comm. on Ways and Means, to Douglas O'Donnell, Acting Comm'r, IRS (Feb. 7, 2023).
10 Family and Small Business Taxpayer Protection Act, H.R. 23, 118th Cong (2023); *see also* Jeff Carlson, *House Passes Measure Clawing Back Nearly $80 Billion from IRS*, THOMSON REUTERS (Jan. 11, 2023), https://tax.thomsonreuters.com/news/house-passes-measure-clawing-back-nearly-80-billion-from-irs/.
11 IRS, INTERNAL REVENUE SERVICE INFLATION REDUCTION ACT STRATEGIC OPERATING PLAN FY 2023–2031, at 129 (2023).
12 *Id.* at 128.
13 Fiscal Responsibility Act of 2023, H.R. 3746, 118th Cong., Pub. L. No. 118-5, §§ 102, 251 (2023); *see also* CONG. RES. SERV., IN12172, CHANGES TO IRS FUNDING IN THE DEBT LIMIT DEAL (June 6, 2023).
14 Leandra Lederman, *IRS Reform: Politics as Usual?*, 7 COLUM. J. TAX L. 36 (2016).
15 *Id.* at 64; *see also* Keith Fogg, *Revisiting the Ten Deadly Sins Created in the IRS Restructuring and Reform Act*, 20 PITT. TAX REV. 241 (2022) (arguing that restrictions on IRS employees in the bill offered "symbolic legislation rather than passing a law seeking to meaningfully influence behavior in a way that would positively influence compliance").
16 *See* Sutirtha Bagchi, *The Political Economy of Tax Enforcement: A Look at the Internal Revenue Service from 1978 to 2010*, 36 J. PUB. POL'Y 335 (2016).
17 Charles O. Rossotti, *Success or Failure at the IRS: What Will Make the Difference?*, 177 TAX NOTES. FED. 1661, 1661 (Dec. 19, 2022).
18 Marilyn Young et al., *The Political Economy of the IRS*, 13 ECON. & POL. 201 (2001); *see also* Bagchi, *supra* note 16 (finding that the president has a "pronounced influence on the allocation" of IRS resources).
19 Dustin Jones, *The IRS Did Not Audit Trump during His Presidency's First 2 Years*, NATIONAL PUB. RADIO (Dec. 21, 2022), https://www.npr.org/2022/12/20/1144472882/a-house-panel-voted-to-publicly-release-a-report-on-trumps-tax-returns. The House Ways & Means Committee's report on this matter indicated that the IRS only began one audit on President Trump's tax returns during this period, which it did not complete, and which, as

the article points out, "is in violation of standing IRS policy." *Id*. Several media reports attributed the IRS's failure in this matter directly to Trump's perceived influence over the agency. *See, e.g.*, Noah Bookbinder, *The IRS Really, Really Should Have Audited Trump*, THE ATLANTIC (Dec. 30, 2022), https://www.theatlantic.com/ideas/archive/2022/12/trump-tax-returns-released-house-committee-irs-audit/672582/.

20 *See, e.g.*, CONGRESS RES. SERV., INTERNAL REVENUE SERVICE APPROPRIATIONS, FY2023 (Apr. 10, 2023).
21 *See* Chapter 2, section "IRS Administration and Enforcement."
22 Letter from Charles P. Rettig, Comm'r, IRS, to Sen. Ron Wyden (D-OR) 2 (Sept. 6, 2019), https://www.documentcloud.org/documents/6430680-Document-2019-9-6-Treasury-Letter-to-Wyden-RE.html.
23 TREASURY INSPECTOR GEN. FOR TAX ADMIN., REP. NO. 2023-30-019, THE IRS LARGE BUSINESS AND INTERNATIONAL DIVISION SHOULD CONSIDER SHIFTING INDIVIDUAL EXAMINATION RESOURCES TO MORE PRODUCTIVE EXAMINATIONS, at 4–6 (2023).
24 *See* IRS, *supra* note 11, at 72.
25 TAXPAYER ADVOC. SERV., NTA BLOG, NATIONAL TAXPAYER ADVOCATE URGES CONGRESS TO MAINTAIN IRS APPROPRIATIONS BUT RE-DIRECT SOME FUNDS TOWARD TAXPAYER SERVICE AND INFORMATION TECHNOLOGY MODERNIZATION (Mar. 16, 2023), https://www.taxpayeradvocate.irs.gov/news/nta-blog-nta-urges-congress-to-maintain-irs-appropriations-but-re-direct-some-funds-toward-taxpayer-service-and-it-modernization/.
26 Jonathan Curry, *IRS Compliance Restructuring Plan Faces Steep Road to Reality*, 179 TAX NOTES FED. 693 (Apr. 24, 2023).
27 *See* Rossotti, *supra* note 17, at 1668; *see also* Jarod Facundo, *Reanimating the Tax Man*, AM. PROSPECT (Jan. 26, 2023), https://prospect.org/economy/2023-01-26-reanimating-taxman-internal-revenue-service/.
28 For more discussion, see also Chapter 5, section "Public Perceptions of the IRS."
29 Michael Keen & Joel Slemrod, *Optimal Tax Administration*, 152 J. PUB. ECON. 133, 134 (2017). There may be additional social benefits from not enforcing the tax laws in some cases. For example, if taxpayers with lower-earning ability engage in certain forms of tax evasion, then it may be optimal to achieve distributive aims by reducing enforcement targeting these activities. *See* Wojciech Kopczuk, *Tax Simplification and Tax Compliance: An Economic Perspective*, *in* BRIDGING THE TAX GAP: ADDRESSING THE CRISIS IN FEDERAL TAX ADMINISTRATION 111, 127–28 (Max B. Sawicky ed., 2005).
30 Norman Gemmell & John Hasseldine, *Taxpayers' Behavioural Responses and Measures of Tax Compliance "Gaps": A Critique and a New Measure*, 35 FISC. STUD. 275 (2014).
31 Keen & Slemrod, *supra* note 29.
32 *See* Chapter 2, section "Factors in Tax Compliance."
33 *See* A. MITCHELL POLINSKY, AN INTRODUCTION TO LAW AND ECONOMICS 82–83 (4th ed. 2011) (observing that policymakers can minimize administrative costs of deterrence by increasing the sanction rather than the chance of detection, since the latter requires additional government spending, and the former does not).
34 Joel Slemrod, *Cheating Ourselves: The Economics of Tax Evasion*, 21 J. ECON. PERSP. 25, 43 (2007).

35 See Charles Rettig, IRS, A Closer Look: Implementing the Tax Gap 15 (Dec. 3, 2020).
36 See Cong. Budget Off., supra note 3.
37 See Chapter 1, section "How the Rich Avoid Taxes."
38 See Joshua D. Blank, *Overcoming Overdisclosure: Toward Tax Shelter Detection*, 56 UCLA L. Rev. 1629, 1638 (2009); Marvin A. Chirelstein & Lawrence A. Zelenak, *Tax Shelters and the Search for a Silver Bullet*, 105 Colum. L. Rev. 1939, 1950 (2005) (describing the problem with "prospective" legislative fixes, as "taxpayers merely move on to new types of shelters not yet legislated against").
39 IRS Notice 99-59, 1999-52 I.R.B. 761.
40 IRS Notice 2002-21, 2002-1 C.B. 730.
41 IRS Notice 2001-17, 2001-1 C.B. 730.
42 For discussion, see Chirelstein & Zelenak, supra note 38.
43 See id.; Dep't of Treasury, The Problem of Corporate Tax Shelters: Discussion, Analysis and Legislative Proposals 5 (1999); Joseph Bankman, *The New Market in U.S. Corporate Tax Shelters*, 83 Tax Notes 1775 (1999).
44 See, e.g., Press Release, Dep't of Treasury, Treasury Acting Assistant Secretary for Tax Policy Jonathan Talisman Remarks to the Tax Executives Institute Midyear Conference, Washington, DC (Mar. 21, 2000), https://home.treasury.gov/news/press-releases/ls485; see also Del Wright Jr., *Financial Alchemy: How Tax Shelter Promoters Use Financial Products to Bedevil the IRS (And How the IRS Helps Them)*, 45 Ariz. St. L. J. 611, 653 (2013).
45 See Omri Marian, *Are Cryptocurrencies Super Tax Havens?*, 112 Mich. L. Rev. First Impressions 38, 38 (2013).
46 See id.; see also Katherine Baer et al., *Taxing Cryptocurrencies*, 39 Oxford Rev. Econ. Pol'y 478 (2023); Omri Marian, *Blockchain Havens and the Need for Their Internationally-Coordinated Regulation*, 20 N.C. J.L. & Tech. 529, 529 (2019) ("[T]he unique nature of blockchain-based technology – most importantly, decentralization and temper resistance – makes such traditional anti-tax haven policies ineffective in the blockchain context.").
47 Infrastructure Investment and Jobs Act, H.R. 3684, 117th Cong., Pub. L. 117-58, § 80603 (codified at I.R.C. §§ 6045, 6045A).
48 See, e.g., IRS, Announcement 2023-2, Transitional Guidance under Sections 6045 and 6045A with Respect to the Reporting of Information on Digital Assets by Brokers (2022); Morgan Lewis, *Digital Asset Brokers: Proceed with Caution* (Dec. 28, 2022), https://www.morganlewis.com/pubs/2022/12/digital-asset-brokers-proceed-with-caution (describing IRS delay in implementing the new rules).
49 Compaq Computer Corp. Subsidiaries v. Comm'r, 277 F.3d 778 (5th Cir. 2001).
50 Id.
51 Id. For criticism of this decision, see Daniel N. Shaviro & David A. Weisbach, *The U.S. Fifth Circuit Gets It Wrong in Compaq v. Commissioner*, 94 Tax Notes 511, 514 (2002); David P. Hariton, *The Compaq Case, Notice 98–5, and Tax Shelters: The Theory Is All Wrong*, 94 Tax Notes 501 (2002); Shannon Weeks McCormack, *Tax Shelters and Statutory Interpretation: A Much Needed Purposive Approach*, 2009 U. Ill. L. Rev. 697 (2009).
52 See Joshua D. Blank & Ari Glogower, *The Trouble with Targeting Tax Shelters*, 74 Admin L. Rev. 69, 77–78 (2022).

53 See Tax Section, N.Y. State Bar Ass'n, Rep. No. 1126, Report on Proposed Regulations Amending the Reportable Transaction Disclosure and List Maintenance Rules 6 (2007).
54 Matthew C. Weinzierl, *Why Do We Redistribute So Much but Tag So Little? The Principle of Equal Sacrifice and Optimal Taxation* 6 (Nat'l Bureau Econ. Rsch., Working Paper No. 18045, 2012). For discussion, see also Chapter 2, section "Traditional Responses to High-End Noncompliance."
55 *See* Weinzierl, *supra* note 54, at 5.
56 Shu-Yi Oei, *The Offshore Tax Enforcement Dragnet*, 67 Emory L.J. 655, 702–03 (2018).
57 *Id.* at 703 (citing Taxpayer Advoc. Serv., 2014 Annual Report to Congress 86 (2014)).
58 *See, e.g., id.* at 708–9 (describing how "major offenders" may not have been "sufficiently sanctioned" under the OVDPs, even as the programs imposed significant costs on other actors).
59 *See, e.g.,* Amy S. Elliott, *Practitioners Blast Economic Substance Guidance with No Angel List*, 128 Tax Notes 1212 (2010) (describing practitioner concerns that the codified economic substance doctrine and related penalty could be applied too broadly to penalize non-abusive transactions).
60 *See, e.g.,* Letter from Sen. Rob Portman (R-OH) et al. to Janet Yellen, Sec'y, Dep't of Treasury (Dec. 14, 2021) (cautioning against the unintended costs of an overly broad interpretation of the provision's definition of "broker"), https://waysandmeans.house.gov/wp-content/uploads/2022/12/sfc-sfrc-wm-r_letter_to_secretary_yellen-1.pdf; *see also* Morgan Lewis, *supra* note 48.
61 I.R.C. § 6662(i).
62 *See, e.g.,* Joshua D. Blank & Nancy C. Staudt, *Corporate Shams*, 87 N.Y.U. L. Rev. 1641, 1656–57 (2012); David Hariton, *Has Codification Changed the Economic Substance Doctrine?*, 2 Colum. J. Tax L. Tax Matters 1, 3 (2019) ("[C]odification has almost no substantive effect."); Richard M. Lipton, *'Codification' of the Economic Substance Doctrine – Much Ado about Nothing?*, 112 J. Tax'n 325, 333 (2010) ("[I]t would seem that little has changed concerning the manner in which the economic substance doctrine will be applied to transactions.").
63 *See* Chapter 10.
64 *See, e.g.,* IRS, *Recognized Abusive and Listed Transactions* (Jan. 17, 2023), https://www.irs.gov/businesses/corporations/listed-transactions.
65 For a discussion of this feature of the reportable transaction rules, see Tax Section, N.Y. State Bar Ass'n, *supra* note 53.
66 Brian Galle & Stephen Shay, *Admin Law and the Crisis of Tax Administration*, 101 N.C. L. Rev. 1645 (2023).
67 U.S. Const. art. I, § 8, cl 1.
68 U.S. Const. art. I, § 8, cl 18.
69 U.S. Const. amend. XVI. For a discussion of the consequences of apportionment and why it would make a progressive tax scheme impracticable, see Ari Glogower, *A Constitutional Wealth Tax*, 118 Mich. L. Rev. 717, 724 (2020).
70 U.S. Const. art. I, § 2, cl 3; U.S. Const. art. I, § 9, cl 4. For a discussion of the debates in the literature regarding the definition of a direct tax, see Glogower, *supra* note 69, at 725–28.

71 See, e.g., the distinction articulated in Nat'l Fed'n of Indep. Bus. v. Sebelius, 567 U.S. 519, 574 (2012).
72 See Ellen Aprill & Daniel Hemel, *The Tax Legislative Process: A Byrd's Eye View*, 81 L. & CONTEMP. PROBS. 99 (2018).
73 Congressional Budget Act of 1974, H.R. 7130, 93rd Cong., Pub. L. No. 94-344, §§ 300–311.
74 A provision is extraneous if, among other factors, it does not affect outlays or revenues, or does so in a way that does not follow the reconciliation instructions, or if the changes in outlays or revenues are incidental to the nonbudgetary elements of the provision. 2 U.S.C. § 644(b)(1).
75 An act to establish the Treasury department, 1st Cong., Sept. 2, 1789.
76 Revenue Act of 1862, 37th Cong., 12 Stat. 432.
77 Chevron U.S.A., Inc. v. Natural Resources Defense Council, Inc., 467 U.S. 837 (1984). For a summary of Chevron's legacy in the following decades, see Peter M. Shane & Christopher J. Walker, *Foreword: Chevron at 30: Looking Back and Looking Forward*, 83 FORDHAM L. REV. 475 (2014).
78 See, e.g., J. W. Hampton, Jr., & Co. v. United States, 276 U.S. 394 (1928). For a critical assessment of this doctrine's practical import, see Keith E. Whittington & Jason Iuliano, *The Myth of the Nondelegation Doctrine*, 165 U. PA. L. REV. 379 (2017).
79 Administrative Procedure Act, Pub. L. 79-404, 60 Stat. 237 (enacted June 11, 1946 at 5 U.S.C. § 551 et seq).
80 Administrative Procedure Act, 5 U.S.C. § 553. These requirements do not apply to merely "interpretative" rules or, in some cases, where the agency finds notice-and-comment rulemaking would be impracticable or against the public interest. Administrative Procedure Act, 5 U.S.C. § 553(b).
81 Administrative Procedure Act, 5. U.S.C. § 553.
82 See, e.g., Galle & Shay, supra note 66; Kristin E. Hickman, *Coloring Outside the Lines: Examining Treasury's (Lack Of) Compliance with Administrative Procedure Act Rulemaking Requirements*, 82 NOTRE DAME L. REV. 1727 (2006); Clint Wallace, *Congressional Control of Tax Rulemaking*, 71 TAX L. REV. 179 (2017); David A. Weisbach, *Against Anti-tax Exceptionalism*, 77 TAX. L. REV. (forthcoming, 2024).
83 See Galle & Shay, supra note 66.
84 CIC Servs., LLC v. IRS, 141 S. Ct. 1582, 1586–88 (2021).
85 Id. at 1586–87.
86 For further discussion, see Charlene D. Luke, *Captivating Deductions*, 46 HOFSTRA L. REV. 855, 866–68 (2018) (discussing micro-captive insurance strategies).
87 IRS Notice 2016–66, 47 I.R.B. 745.
88 For a discussion of the consequences from characterizing these strategies as transactions of interest, see Chapter 2, section "An Overview of the Tax Compliance System."
89 Complaint at 9-11, CIC Servs., LLC v. IRS, No. 3:17-cv-110, 2017 WL 5015510 (E.D. Tenn. Mar. 27, 2017).
90 Id., applying Administrative Procedure Act, 5 U.S.C. §§ 551–559, 561–570a, 701–706, at 553.
91 Memorandum in Support of the Defendant's Motion to Dismiss at 12, CIC Servs., LLC v. IRS, No. 3:17-cv-110, 2017 WL 5015510 (E.D. Tenn. May 30, 2017) (quoting Anti-Injunction Act, I.R.C. § 7421).

92 I.R.C. § 7421(a).
93 CIC Servs., LLC v. IRS, No. 3:17-cv-110, 2017 WL 5015510, at *4 (E.D. Tenn. Nov. 2, 2017), aff'd, 925 F. 3d 247 (6th Cir. 2019), rev'd, 141 S. Ct. 1582 (2021).
94 CIC Servs., LLC, 141 S. Ct. 1582 (2021). For further discussion of the case and its consequences, see Kristen A. Parillo, *Supreme Court's CIC Services Opinion Clarifies Scope of AIA*, TAX NOTES TODAY FED., https://www.taxnotes.com/tax-notes-today-fed eral/litigation-and-appeals/supreme-courts-cic-services-opinion-clarifies-scope-aia/2021/05/ 18/6olcw (May 18, 2021); Daniel Hemel, *Treasury Needs to Act Fast to Save the Tax-Shelter Disclosure Regime*, SUBSTANCE OVER FORM (May 18, 2021), https:// substanceoverform.substack.com/p/treasury-needs-to-act-fast-to-save; Lee A. Sheppard, *Successful Challenges to IRS Guidance After CIC Services?*, 171 TAX NOTES 1349 (2021).
95 CIC Servs., LLC, 141 S. Ct. at 1593–94.
96 Id. at 1591–92.
97 Id. at 1586.
98 See Sheppard, *supra* note 94, at 1353–55 (arguing that Congress has endorsed current IRS procedures for issuing notices, as provided in section 559 of the APA and citing Mann Construction Inc. v. United States. No. 1:20-cv-11307, 2021 WL 1923412 (E.D. Mich. May 13, 2021)). For further discussion, see also Clinton G. Wallace & Jeffrey M. Blaylock, *Administering Taxes Democratically*, 94 TEMPLE L. REV. 49 (2022).
99 See Sheppard, *supra* note 94, at 1355 (quoting Professor Kristin Hickman as expressing skepticism of the congressional endorsement argument).
100 CIC Servs., LLC v. IRS, No. 3:17-cv-00110, 2021 WL 4481008, at *1 (E.D. Tenn. Sept. 21, 2021); see also Kristen A. Parillo, *CIC Services Dispute Returns to Court*, 172 TAX NOTES FED. 843 (Aug. 2, 2021).
101 CIC Servs., LLC v. IRS, 2022 WL 985619 (E.D. Tenn. Mar. 21, 2022), as modified by 2022 WL 2078036 (E.D. Tenn. June 2, 2022).
102 Mann Construction v. United States, 27 F.4th 1138, 1147 (6th Cir. 2022).
103 IRS Notice 2017-10, 2017-4 I.R.B. 544.
104 Green Valley Investors, LLC v. Comm'r, 159 T.C. No. 5 (2022).
105 IRS, ANNOUNCEMENT 2023-11, LISTED TRANSACTIONS AND TRANSACTIONS OF INTEREST.
106 See id. at 2 ("The Department of the Treasury ... and the IRS disagree with the recent court decisions holding that listed transactions cannot be identified by notice or other subregulatory guidance. However, the Treasury Department and IRS will no longer take the position that transactions of interest can be identified without complying with APA notice-and-comment procedures.").
107 See Syndicated Conservation Easement Transactions as Listed Transactions, 87 Fed. Reg. 75,185 (proposed Dec. 8, 2022), Prop Reg. §§ 1.6011-9; Micro-Captive Listed Transactions and Micro-Captive Transactions of Interest, 88 Fed. Reg. 21,547 (proposed Apr. 11, 2023), Prop. Reg. §§ 1.6011-10, 1.6011-11; see also Chandra Wallace, *Government Hardens Stance on Microcaptives in Proposed Regs*, TAX NOTES TODAY FED. (Apr. 11, 2023), https://www.taxnotes.com/tax-notes-today-federal/tax-system-administration/govern ment-hardens-stance-microcaptives-proposed-regs/2023/04/11/7ggv4.
108 For a discussion of value of pre-enforcement litigation to taxpayers, see Kristin E. Hickman & Gerald Kerska, *Restoring the Lost Anti-Injunction Act*, 103 VA. L. REV.

1683, 1765 (2017); Stephanie Hunter McMahon, *Pre-enforcement Litigation Needed for Taxing Procedures*, 92 WASH. L. REV. 1317, 1362–91 (2017).
109 IRS, *supra* note 105, at 3.
110 *Id.*
111 For discussion, see, e.g., James M. Puckett, *Structural Tax Exceptionalism*, 49 GA. L. REV. 1067, 1109–18 (2015).
112 For example, following Congress's enactment of significant penalties for noncompliance with the reportable transaction rules, the IRS appears to have designated fewer tax strategies as listed transactions. See Hemel, *supra* note 94 (observing that the IRS has only designated two transactions as listed transactions since 2015).
113 Wallace, *supra* note 82, at 216–30.
114 Wendy Wagner et al., *Rulemaking in the Shade: An Empirical Study of EPA's Air Toxic Emission Standards*, 63 ADMIN. L. REV. 99 (2011); Jason Webb Yackee & Susan Webb Yackee, *A Bias towards Business? Assessing Interest Group Influence on the U.S. Bureaucracy*, 68 J. POL. 128 (2006).
115 Wallace, *supra* note 82, at 222; *see also* Daniel Shaviro, *Beyond Public Choice and Public Interest: A Study of the Legislative Process as Illustrated by Tax Legislation in the 1980s*, 139 U. PENN. L. REV. 1 (1990).
116 *See CIC Servs., LLC*, 141 S. Ct. 1588.
117 *CIC Services Backs Lobbying Group to Tackle IRS "Abuse" on Micro Captives*, CAPTIVE INTERNATIONAL (July 7, 2022), https://www.captiveinternational.com/news/cic-services-backs-lobbying-group-to-tackle-irs-abuse-on-micro-captives-4781.
118 Keen & Slemrod, *supra* note 29, at 137.
119 *See* DEP'T OF TREASURY, POLICY STATEMENT ON THE TAX REGULATORY PROCESS 2–3 (2019) (describing the Treasury Department's commitment to public participation and transparency in tax regulatory process).
120 *See* Chapter 1, section "Why the Distribution of Noncompliance Matters."
121 *See* Emmanuel Saez & Gabriel Zucman, *Progressive Wealth Taxation*, BPEA CONFERENCE DRAFTS 47–48 (Sept. 5–6, 2019)
122 *See, e.g.*, Natasha Sarin & Lawrence H. Summers, *Shrinking the Tax Gap: Approaches and Revenue Potential*, 165 TAX NOTES FED. 1099, 1104–05 (2019) (describing how increasing audits of high-income individuals could "substantially increase tax collections" notwithstanding the higher cost of conducting these audits); *see also* Keen & Slemrod, *supra* note 29, at 137 (arguing that a higher "enforcement elasticity" can "strengthen[] the case for raising additional revenue by spending additional resources on enforcement rather . . . because administrative measures are then more productive of revenue").
123 William C. Boning et al., *A Welfare Analysis of Tax Audits Across the Income Distribution* (NBER Working Paper No. 31376, June 2023).
124 *See* Chapter 2, section "Factors in Tax Compliance."
125 TAXPAYER ADVOC. SERV., 2018 ANNUAL REPORT TO CONGRESS 117 (2019), https://www.taxpayeradvocate.irs.gov/wp-content/uploads/2020/07/ARC18_Volume1.pdf.
126 *See* Chapter 1, section "Why the Distribution of Noncompliance Matters."
127 For discussions of the role of salience and perceptions of fairness in tax compliance, see Slemrod, *supra* note 34 at 25, 39; Susan Cleary Morse, *Using Salience and Influence to Narrow the Tax Gap*, 40 LOY. U. CHI. L.J. 483, 507 n.114 (2009) ("There is a positive

correlation between tax compliance and the perceived fairness of the tax system."); Jan-Emmanuel De Neve et al., *How to Improve Compliance? Evidence from Population-Wide Experiments in Belgium* 28 (Said Bus. Sch., Working Paper No. 2019-07, 2019) ("Simplifying communication by the tax administration consistently improves tax compliance.").
128 For a discussion of the role of evidence on public perceptions of tax administration, see Joshua D. Blank, *In Defense of Individual Tax Privacy*, 61 EMORY L.J. 265, 288–90 (2011) (discussing the power of specific tax-enforcement examples on taxpayers' perceptions); ALAN H. PLUMLEY, IRS, THE DETERMINANTS OF INDIVIDUAL INCOME TAX COMPLIANCE 36 (1996) ("[T]he most important influence that these [tax-evasion] convictions have on the general population may be to satisfy the typical taxpayer that criminals are not going scott-free, thus encouraging him to pay his 'fair share.'"); *see also, e.g.*, Jeffrey A. Dubin, *Criminal Investigation Enforcement Activities and Taxpayer Noncompliance*, 35 PUB. FIN. REV. 500, 502 (2007) (finding that IRS criminal investigations measurably increase voluntary tax compliance).
129 Scholars have argued, however, that agencies can strategically enact regulations that can be "stickier" and cannot be easily changed by subsequent administrations. *See* Aaron L. Nielson, *Sticky Regulations*, 85 U. CHI. L. REV. 85 (2018).
130 *See, e.g.*, I.R.C. §§ 7430(c)(4)(A)(ii), 7491(a)(2), 6404(h).
131 For a discussion of the broad ideological consensus supporting the basic principle of progressive taxation, *see* Jeremy Bearer-Friend et al., *Taxation and Law and Political Economy*, 83 OHIO ST. L.J. 471, 495–96 (2022).
132 Rev. Proc. 2005-26, 2005-1 C.B. 965; Treas. Reg. § 301.6501(c)-1(g)(2) (providing that the rule extending the period until a year after disclosure "does not apply to any period of limitations on assessment that expired before the date on which the failure to disclose the listed transaction under Section 6011 occurred").
133 For more discussion, see Chapter 8, section "Advantages over Current Law."
134 *See* I.R.C. § 6651 (delinquency penalties); § 6662 (accuracy-related penalties); § 6663 (civil fraud penalties).
135 *See* I.R.C. § 6601.
136 *See* I.R.C. § 6501.
137 28 U.S.C. § 2412. For a discussion of these provisions, see also Steve R. Johnson, *A Modest Proposal to Improve Tax Compliance: Curbing Penalty-Protection Opinions* 53–59 (July 18, 2013) (unpublished manuscript), https://papers.ssrn.com/sol3/papers.cfm?abstract_id=1285282.
138 28 U.S.C. § 2412(d)(2)(B).
139 S. Rep. No. 96-235, Equal Access to Justice Act (1979).
140 I.R.C. § 7430(c)(4)(A)(ii).
141 I.R.C. § 6404(e)(1).
142 I.R.C. § 7431(c)(3).
143 I.R.C. § 7491(a)(2)(C).
144 I.R.C. § 6656(c)(1).
145 I.R.C. § 7463; *see also* U.S. TAX COURT, TAX COURT RULES (Feb. 8, 2021), https://www.ustaxcourt.gov/rules.html (providing "Small Tax Case Rules" for disputes involving amounts of $50,000 or less).

146 Carlton M. Smith, *Does the Tax Court's Use of Its Golsen Rule in Unappealable Small Tax Cases Hurt the Poor?*, 11 J. TAX PRAC. & PROC. 35, 35 (2009).
147 I.R.C. § 32(k)(1).
148 I.R.C. § 32(a)–(c); JOINT COMM. ON TAX'N, JCX-9R-23, OVERVIEW OF THE FEDERAL TAX SYSTEM AS IN EFFECT FOR 2023, at 10 (2023).
149 The effective penalty amount would be nearly $15,000, or more than half of the taxpayer's $28,120 of income.
150 I.R.C. § 6663(a).
151 I.R.C. § 7463(b).
152 *See* Smith, *supra* note 146, at 36.

4

When Are Means Adjustments Fair and Efficient?

Means adjustments could enable the tax compliance rules to address the challenges of high-end noncompliance more effectively. Treating some taxpayers differently based solely on their income or wealth, however, might strike some readers as fundamentally objectionable, or violating a principle that the law should apply in the same way to everyone.

This chapter takes a step back and considers principles in the law favoring generally applicable legal rules – which would treat all individuals the same – and explains how means adjustments to the tax compliance rules can align with these principles. This chapter's investigation of these principles also yields important practical insights for how these means adjustments should be designed.

In this chapter, we explain three principles in the law that may favor generally applicable or uniform legal rules. First, principles and norms that are grounded in the "rule of law" favor rules that apply generally, in contrast to rules that target certain individuals or groups. Second, in many cases, the US Constitution requires the law to treat individuals equally and to ensure everyone basic protections, regardless of their circumstances. Finally, in some cases, economic theory also favors generally applicable legal rules that do not vary based on an individual's income or wealth. According to the "double distortion" principle in the law and economics literature, policymakers should pursue distributional goals through means adjustments only in the case of tax rules. While the tax system is well suited to advance distributional goals, extending these adjustments to other legal rules could inefficiently disincentivize otherwise desirable behavior.

The progressive federal tax system represents a prominent exception to these principles favoring generally applicable legal rules. The tax rules, such as those governing the federal income tax, explicitly account for individuals' economic means when determining tax liabilities and impose proportionally higher burdens on higher-income taxpayers.

With these considerations in mind, how should we evaluate means adjustments to the tax compliance rules? This chapter argues that these rules represent a unique category of legal rules because of their role in implementing the substantive tax system and its core distributive function. As a result, means adjustments in the tax compliance system should be evaluated differently under the principles favoring generally applicable legal rules.

The desirability of means-adjusted tax compliance rules under these principles depends, critically, on their design and purpose. When properly designed, these adjustments could advance, rather than violate, rule of law principles. Further, they would not violate constitutional protections. In fact, means adjustments would, in some cases, be desirable, or even necessary, under these principles, particularly when these adjustments are necessary to implement the distributive function of the tax system.

PRINCIPLES FAVORING GENERALLY APPLICABLE LEGAL RULES

Generality and the Rule of Law

The "rule of law" refers to a set of basic legal protections to which every individual should be entitled. Professor Lawrence Solum describes the rule of law as a "set of ideals" rather than a "single concept," which can, broadly speaking, "curb abuses of the powerless by the powerful."[1] Legal theorists have defined the content of the rule of law differently, and they have offered various views of how it might be reconciled with principles of justice and fairness.

Professor Solum identifies seven basic elements in rule of law principles: (1) the absence of obligatory "extralegal commands," (2) rule-based regulation of public officials, (3) publicity of the legal system, (4) that laws should be "general in statement" and "not aimed at particular individuals," (5) the regularity of the legal system, (6) fair and orderly procedures, and (7) a reasonable expectation that persons can comply with the law.[2] These definitions all look to the content of the law itself. Alternatively, "court-focused" understandings of the rule of law instead focus on the role of judges in policymaking and a hypothesized distinction between law and politics.[3]

Professor Solum's fourth principle, on generality, prescribes that the laws should be uniform and generally applicable, and should not be designed to penalize or target certain individuals or groups. Philosopher Lon L. Fuller identifies generality as the "first desideratum of a system for subjecting human conduct to the governance of rules."[4] Similarly, philosopher John Rawls argues that the condition of regularity requires that rules express "general properties and relations" that do "not require a knowledge of contingent particulars" and are "capable of serving as a public charter of a well-ordered society."[5]

As Professor Robin West describes, this generality principle also informs the concept of "formal equality."[6] The concept of formal equality traces back to Aristotle's famous principle that the law should treat "like cases alike" and that equal persons should be treated equally.[7] This principle invites challenging and familiar questions: What does it mean for two cases to be alike? And when should policymakers account for differences among individuals, which may justify their different treatment under the law?[8]

To apply the rule of law's generality principle, policymakers must therefore decide which attributes *should* be taken into account in legal design, and which attributes should not. Legal design faces an essential tension between the generality principle, which seems to require treating individuals equally, and the need for sufficient specificity in the law so it can account for meaningful differences between individuals and their actions.[9] For example, it would not make sense for policymakers to impose equal penalties for speeding on all drivers who exceed the speed limit, regardless of whether they only slightly exceeded the limit on an empty highway or whether they were racing on a residential street.

A very narrow interpretation of the generality principle would simply require that laws not target specified individuals without regard to their actions.[10] Conversely, a very broad interpretation might require the law to always treat everyone the same and with formal equality, even when there are meaningful differences between individuals that might justify their different treatment. Between these two extremes, a balanced interpretation might say that the law should not treat individuals differently based on *arbitrary* or *irrelevant* factors. Professor David Strauss consequently argues that Aristotle's principle might be better understood as requiring that any differences in legal treatment among individuals must be justified, and that "if people are treated differently, there has to be a (legitimate) reason for the difference in treatment."[11]

With these considerations in mind, when should policymakers consider an individual's economic means under the generality principle? A very broad or formal interpretation of the generality principle might suggest that policymakers should *never* take account of an individual's economic means when designing legal rules. Any rule that imposed higher penalties for high-end individuals could appear to target them on account of their economic circumstances and unfairly subject them to more burdensome legal consequences.

For example, consider the case of an income-based fine, such as a rule imposing higher-fine speeding tickets on higher-income individuals. Such a rule may be perceived as improperly targeting these individuals and subjecting them to more burdensome legal consequences solely based on their economic circumstances, while lower-income individuals who engage in the same behaviors, with the same social costs, would face less severe legal consequences.[12] On the other hand, if lower- and higher-income speeders are different in some meaningful way, then the law should rightfully treat them differently under Aristotle's principle. For example, the different speeding fines may be necessary to account for the different effects of the fine on the utility of drivers at different income levels, so that they can achieve an equal deterrent effect.[13]

Scholars have criticized overly formal and simplistic understandings of the rule of law's generality principle for conflicting with principles of justice and fairness. When applied too broadly or simplistically, a principle of formal equality can reinforce structural inequality and unequal effects of the law. Under this view, the rule of law's generality principle can lead to unjust outcomes. Professor Robin West describes the critiques of formal equality as a concept that is backward-looking, indeterminate, and "politically regressive" by "reifying and then valorizing the status quo."[14] Professor Martha Minow similarly outlines a distinction between "equal policies" and "policies that lead to equality." Specifically, Minow argues that "formal equality" – which "insists on general rules and practices without reference to group or individual characteristics"[15] – "can be critiqued as lacking any substantive content, failing to specify or even understand what should be the same across people, and focusing on group classifications rather than on social hierarchies."[16]

Scholars also propose different approaches to interpreting principles of generality and formal equality in a way that they can achieve just outcomes. Professor West, for example, argues that, despite its potential abuses, the concept of formal equality nonetheless reflects a "sound moral intuition about law."[17] She introduces a "humanistic" interpretation of the rule of law, which is grounded in "mutual recognition and sympathy."[18] This conception would recognize "shared human traits[,]" while also embracing a "complex rather than reductionist account of humanity" that would account for meaningful differences among individuals in legal design.[19]

According to Professor Paul Gowder, the rule of law's generality principle, when properly understood, can *require*, rather than preclude, attention to the unequal effects of formally equal laws. Gowder argues that to assess a law under this principle, policymakers must first assess the "public reason" for the law and how it interacts with underlying social circumstances.[20] He offers the example of literacy tests for voting in the Jim Crow South.[21] While these laws may have satisfied a requirement of formal equality, since – at least in principle – the literacy requirement applied the same to all prospective voters, they failed to satisfy rule of law principles, because of their public reason of disenfranchising Black voters, who as a group had lower rates of literacy at the time.[22]

Gowder argues further that this same understanding of the rule of law can require policymakers to enact formally *unequal* laws or policies in some cases, particularly when doing so would be necessary to remediate unequal social circumstances.[23] He offers the example of a law against theft, which, while necessary for a legal system, will also impose greater burdens on the poor. If society has no choice but to preserve a law against theft, then the only alternative is to also implement policies remediating economic injustice, and, consequently, the conditions resulting in the unequal effect of the law.[24]

Constitutional Protections

The US Constitution enshrines certain rule of law principles through both substantive and procedural protections. Both the Constitution's Equal Protection and Due Process Clauses formally require the law to be generally applicable in certain circumstances.[25] Where the Equal Protection Clause prohibits state laws from discriminating on the basis of certain group classifications without a sufficient justification,[26] the Fifth Amendment's Due Process Clause extends this equal protection restriction to the federal government.[27]

Many public policies routinely and deliberately differentiate among individuals. In many cases, this type of differentiation is a basic function of the law, rather than a violation of its central tenets. For example, an occupational licensing requirement, when used as a means to protect the public from the unsafe provision of services by untrained people, necessarily disadvantages unlicensed practitioners.[28] Another way in which the law similarly discriminates between individuals is through the rules used to determine whether individuals are qualified to receive certain government benefits. By definition, means-tested government benefits intentionally advantage beneficiaries based on their income. One example of this approach is the USDA's Supplemental Nutrition Assistance Program (SNAP), which provides food benefits only to individuals who meet certain income and resource criteria.[29]

For this reason, the US Supreme Court has held that only rules discriminating on the basis of certain suspect classifications, such as race, religion, or national origin, are subject to heightened scrutiny under the Equal Protection Clause, such as the standards of "intermediate scrutiny" or "strict scrutiny."[30] Otherwise, the Court has only applied heightened scrutiny to rules that deprive certain individuals of fundamental rights, such as the right to vote or to travel.[31] Aside from these heightened scrutiny standards on the basis of suspect classifications and for fundamental rights, the Court has generally deferred to Congress in the sphere of economic legislation and policy.[32] As a result, those rules that do not discriminate on the basis of suspect classifications, and that do not violate fundamental rights, are typically subject to rational basis review. This lower standard for scrutiny[33] only requires a legitimate state purpose in enacting the law, and "generally results in the validation of state action."[34]

In addition to these substantive guarantees against discrimination and unequal treatment, the Constitution also ensures every individual the right to basic procedural protections in their interactions with the government. The Due Process Clauses in the Fifth and Fourteenth Amendments provide that the federal and state governments cannot deprive an individual of "life, liberty, or property, without due process of law."[35] Procedural due process ensures that every individual is entitled to certain prerequisites of procedural fairness when the government deprives them of their protected interests.[36] Among other factors, courts have held that procedural due process requires notice and an opportunity to be heard, which are essential to protecting individuals against arbitrary deprivations by the government.[37]

These procedural due process protections also reflect some of the other rule of law elements described earlier in this chapter. Most importantly, these protections ensure publicity and regularity of the legal system, as well as fair and orderly procedures.[38]

Due process generally requires greater procedural protections when individuals face deprivation of what is considered to be a more important interest.[39] For this reason, an individual facing a serious deprivation of liberty, such as incarceration, will generally be entitled to greater procedural protections than a person the government is depriving of a purely economic interest. For example, as the Supreme Court famously held in its 1976 decision in *Mathews* v. *Eldridge*, an individual is not entitled to an evidentiary hearing for the termination of Social Security disability benefits, in part because the potential deprivation was found to be less severe than in other cases requiring greater procedural protections.[40] In contrast, an individual facing a criminal sanction like a prison sentence will be entitled to significant and more extensive procedural protections prior to being convicted.[41]

The Double Distortion Principle

Under certain conditions, economic theory also favors generally applicable legal rules that do not vary based on an individual's income. The "double distortion" principle in the law and economics literature provides that legal rules designed to affect the distribution of income should be reserved for the tax and transfer system, while other legal rules should instead be optimized for efficiency.[42] For these purposes, efficiency refers to the maximization of the net aggregate benefits to society, but without regard to how these benefits are distributed among individuals.[43] Under this principle, the tax and transfer system is the preferred locus for redistribution, because doing so through other legal rules can compound the distortive effects of the redistributive policy.[44]

Within this framework, means adjustments to legal rules may not be desirable, particularly if the purpose of these adjustments is to redistribute from a higher-income offender to the government or to lower-income victims. For example, consider again the case of speeding drivers. Professors Louis Kaplow and Steven Shavell argue that to optimize a speeding fine for efficiency alone, the expected cost of the fine should be set at the amount of the expected harm to others from the speeding.[45] This analysis reflects the same factors in the "Becker-Bentham" deterrent model, where the deterrent effect of any sanction depends upon both the size of the sanction and the chance of detection and enforcement.[46]

If policymakers set the speeding fine equal to the expected harm to others, then individuals would only drive at high speeds when their benefits from speeding – such as in a medical emergency – exceed the expected harm. In this scenario, the speeding driver could compensate any victim for the harm caused, and still realize a net increase to aggregate welfare. For example, assume the expected harm caused from driving ten miles above the speed limit is $100. If a driver would realize a $120 benefit from speeding, the driver could pay the $100 fine to compensate for the harm caused, and still realize a net $20. Importantly, this benefit would not exist if policymakers set the fine at $120 or more, and as a result the driver did not speed.

Now consider the behavioral incentives if policymakers introduce a means adjustment to this fine, to raise more speeding-ticket revenue from higher-income drivers.[47] Assume, for example, that taxpayers with income above $200,000 who drive ten miles above the speed limit instead pay a $150 fine. This means adjustment to the fine can affect two behavioral margins – the choice to speed and the choice to earn additional income.[48] In this case, the driver who could realize a $120 benefit from speeding will not drive over the limit, and the $20 of social surplus (the excess of their $120 benefit from speeding over the $100 of expected harm) would be lost. That is, this rule would over-deter the behavior subject to the fine. This rule would impose an additional burden on those whose income is above $200,000 (in the form of a higher potential speeding fine) in the same manner as would an explicit tax on that income.

In principle, the same distributive goal of this means-adjusted speeding fine could instead be achieved at a lower efficiency cost by adjusting the rate of tax on the offender's income instead.[49] For example, policymakers could set the fine at the efficient level of $100, and instead impose an additional income tax on taxpayers earning income above $200,000. In this case, the driver could still face the same disincentive to earn additional income, but would no longer face the additional disincentive to speed when doing so would increase aggregate welfare.

Importantly, this analysis would not change if the individual had a greater propensity to commit the offense, or could do so at a lower personal cost or with a greater personal benefit. For example, in principle this analysis would not change if some drivers enjoyed speeding more or had faster cars that accelerated more effortlessly.[50] In all events, this frame would imply setting the fine at the level of the expected social cost, regardless of the offender's wealth, so that any driver may speed as long as they are willing to bear the cost of their offense.

Even when accepted on its own terms, this framework might still allow for means adjustments to legal rules under certain conditions. First, to set the expected fine amount equal to the expected harm from the offending behavior, policymakers must also account for the chance that the behavior will be detected and that the fine will be successfully enforced.[51] As a result, if certain drivers systematically had a lower chance of being caught and facing the penalties, this framework would therefore imply that different fine levels would be required for these drivers to achieve the same deterrent effect.

For example, assume that the expected social cost from speeding is $100. Also assume, however, that the drivers at different income levels have different chances that their speeding will be detected and that a fine will be imposed, even though the expected harm from their speeding behavior is the same. Assume Driver A, with $50,000 of income, has a 50% chance of detection. In the basic deterrence model, Driver A's speeding fine should be set equal to $200, for an expected sanction of $100 equal to the social cost of the offense. Assume Driver B, with $100,000 of income, can afford to have sophisticated radar detection equipment that reduces the chance of detection. If Driver B's chance of detection is only 25%, then Driver B's fine should instead be set equal to $400, so that both drivers face the same expected sanction from the offense. Importantly, in this case, the higher fine is not warranted solely because Driver B has a higher income, but because this higher income enables Driver B to lower the chance that speeding will be detected.

The double distortion framework also assumes that policymakers only want individuals to engage in harmful behaviors when it would be efficient to do so, and when the benefits to the offender could offset the social costs. In fact, policymakers may, alternatively, seek to discourage a certain activity altogether, or to deter, to the same extent, all individuals from participating in that activity. For example, assume that the policymakers' goal is to deter all individuals from engaging in criminal behavior equally. In this case, means adjustments to monetary fines or penalties for higher-income taxpayers may be necessary to equalize their deterrent effect for taxpayers at different income levels.

For example, policymakers have sought ways to design monetary fines that equalize the subjective cost of those fines – and therefore their deterrent effect – for taxpayers at different income levels. A higher-income offender may be less deterred by a monetary sanction of any fixed amount if they face a lower expected utility loss from paying the penalty, as compared to a lower-income taxpayer paying the same penalty.

A number of jurisdictions have consequently experimented with "variable fines" or "day fines" for criminal and civil offenses that vary with the offenders' income.[52] Finland's penal code, for example, provides for a system of day fines that are calculated as a fraction of the offender's average annual income, reduced by an exemption amount for basic consumption needs.[53] This system garnered public attention for resulting in large speeding tickets on high-income drivers, in some cases exceeding the equivalent of $100,000.[54] In principle, adjusting these monetary sanctions based on the offender's income can equalize their deterrent effect, to the extent a higher-value fine would be necessary to impose the same cost in utility terms to a high-income offender.[55]

Scholars have also observed that the double distortion framework would only lead to the conclusion that legal rules should not be means-adjusted under simplified and potentially unrealistic conditions. As a result, scholars have offered additional reasons why it may still be desirable to advance distributive policy through nontax legal rules. First, the double distortion principle presumes a "first-best" world in which policymakers can, in fact, achieve the optimal degree of efficient redistribution through income taxation alone.[56] In a "second-best" world, it may be more desirable to redistribute through a combination of legal rules and tax rules, if the aggregate costs resulting from these adjustments would be less than the costs resulting from redistribution through an income tax alone.[57] Similarly, this framework does not account for other possible costs of redistribution through the tax system, such as the high administrative costs that would be required to enforce increasingly high levels of taxation.[58]

Policymakers may also face greater political constraints when they are limited to redistributing through the tax system alone.[59] One possible constraint on progressive taxation is that political opponents may be able to more effectively concentrate their challenges on a single legal instrument with substantial redistributive effects. For example, Michael Graetz and Ian Shapiro chronicle the largely successful political campaign by anti-tax advocates to vitiate the estate tax in the 1990s, which the protesters accomplished by concentrating their lobbying efforts against one explicitly redistributive tax instrument.[60]

Finally, scholars have also argued that nontax legal rules may be able to account for non-income characteristics, which the tax system cannot do as easily, and that a broader system of means adjustments to legal rules can promote substantive values of distributional equity throughout the legal system.[61] For example, Professor Zachary Liscow has argued that individuals may have "category-by-category" moral commitments that would necessitate incorporating distributional considerations across the legal system.[62] Professors Tomer Blumkin and Yoram Margalioth have similarly argued that legal rules should account for distribution when the form of redistribution has "intrinsic value," or where the "efficient" legal rule would itself generate the inequity.[63]

Notwithstanding these qualifications and limitations, the double distortion principle poses a basic question for policymakers: When would means adjustments to nontax legal rules be desirable, especially if policymakers could redistribute through taxes and transfers instead? This principle highlights the potential costs and reasons for caution when introducing these distributional adjustments more broadly throughout the legal system.

AN EXCEPTION: THE PROGRESSIVE TAX SYSTEM

The progressive federal tax system occupies a special role within all these principles that favor generally applicable legal rules. Unlike many other areas of law, the progressive tax system explicitly subjects taxpayers to different legal consequences based on their economic circumstances. For example, a taxpayer's average federal income tax liability increases with a measure of their relative "ability to pay."[64] In the progressive federal income tax system, higher-income taxpayers generally pay taxes at higher average rates.[65]

The public finance literature distinguishes among the core functions of fiscal policy. One of these functions, the distributive function, determines how economic resources are distributed across individuals and businesses.[66] The government primarily executes this distributive function through tax and transfer policies,[67] and most prominently through the progressive tax system.[68] In that case, it may come as no surprise that treating taxpayers differently based on their economic circumstances operates as a "central organizing principle"[69] for the tax system. As early economist and tax theorist Henry C. Simons observes, the case for progressive taxation "must be rested on the case against inequality."[70]

It may appear that the progressive tax system violates the rule of law's generality principle, as it subjects higher-income individuals to higher rates of taxation. A broad consensus from across the ideological spectrum, however, embraces the central premise that the tax system should account for differences in taxpayers' abilities to pay, and that these adjustments do not violate the principles of generality and the rule of law.[71] Although some theorists within the classical liberal tradition may consider any progressive taxation to violate rule of law principles,[72] even most libertarian or entitlement-based views typically embrace some degree of progressivity as a necessary prerequisite for distributive fairness.[73]

The differential treatment through progressive taxation can also be reconciled with the rule of law's generality principle. The analysis depends again on the question of when individuals should be treated differently under the law, and what attributes the law should account for.[74] In this case, a progressive tax system that treats taxpayers differently based on their income can also treat taxpayers more equally in other more relevant respects.

Progressive taxation is commonly justified under a principle of declining marginal utility, in which additional dollars of income provide less marginal utility to the taxpayer.[75] Under this theory, the first dollars that a taxpayer earns and uses to buy essential items (such as food and clothing) results in greater increases in marginal utility than the last dollars a taxpayer earns (such as the millionth dollar earned by a high-income taxpayer).[76] For this reason, treating taxpayers differently, as measured by their income, can result in more equal treatment, as measured by the utility that this income represents.[77]

Courts have similarly held that differentiating among taxpayers through progressive taxation does not violate the Due Process and Equal Protection Clauses. Soon after adoption of the modern income tax in 1913, petitioners challenged the law on the grounds that progressive taxation violated these clauses, by subjecting taxpayers to different rates of tax depending on their income.[78] In the 1916 case of *Brushaber v. Union Pacific Railroad Co.*,[79] the Supreme Court held that a progressive tax structure does not violate the Due Process or Equal Protection Clauses, and dismissed the "mistaken theory" that "although there be differences between the subjects taxed, to differently tax them transcends the limits of taxation."[80]

Finally, the progressive tax rules serve as the preferred situs for redistribution under the double distortion argument in the law and economics literature. This framework explicitly embraces the distributive function of fiscal policy and its implementation through progressive taxation. In principle, distributional adjustments to the tax rules can avoid distortions to other behavioral margins, and thereby implement social preferences for redistribution while minimizing efficiency costs.

EVALUATING MEANS-ADJUSTED TAX COMPLIANCE RULES

What do these principles favoring generally applicable legal rules – and their exceptions – imply for designing means-adjusted tax compliance rules? To apply these principles in the context of the tax compliance rules, we must first reconsider the unique role of these rules within the legal system. As Chapter 2 describes, the tax compliance rules serve a unique "implementing" function, which is integral to, but is also conceptually distinct from, the functions of substantive tax rules. Unlike other nontax legal rules, the tax compliance rules serve an essential role in implementing the substantive tax rules and, therefore, their distributive function. Unlike the substantive tax rules, however, the tax compliance rules do not have an ex ante primary purpose of affecting the allocation and distribution of resources.

Because of their unique function, the tax compliance rules should also be evaluated differently under the principles favoring generally applicable legal rules. Their analysis under these principles, however, will depend on the purpose and the design of these adjustments. Most importantly, these principles would justify, or even require, means adjustments to the tax compliance rules, if they are designed to equalize the effect of the tax compliance rules for all taxpayers and to improve its implementing function. On the other hand, these adjustments may not be justified when they are designed to target or improperly burden a certain group of taxpayers solely on account of their economic circumstances.

A consistent theme emerges across these different areas of legal theory: Policymakers should design the tax compliance rules to ensure their equal effect across taxpayers. This principle also helps to explain the IRS policy that it should enforce the tax law consistently for all taxpayers and address all "areas with significant perceived noncompliance," while not singling out any particular group of taxpayers for particularly beneficial or harsh treatment.[81]

Revisiting Generality and the Rule of Law

Means adjustments to the tax compliance rules could appear to contravene the rule of law principle favoring generally applicable rules. These rules might be perceived as unfairly "targeting" the wealthy as a class and imposing more burdensome legal rules on them based solely on their economic circumstances. The analysis of means adjustments to the tax compliance rules under the rule of law's generality principle depends, however, on their design and intended function within the tax system.

Means adjustments may be necessary to equalize the effects of the tax compliance rules. Further, means-adjusted tax compliance rules can be uniquely important when they are necessary to implement the essential distributive function of the tax and transfer system. On the other hand, means adjustments designed instead to impose new or additional burdens on a subset of taxpayers could raise the same concerns addressed by the rule of law's generality principle.

Although the rule of law's generality principle can be best understood as requiring laws to have a legitimate reason for treating individuals differently, a more searching conception of this principle would also account for how generally applicable laws can generate unequal outcomes. In the latter case, treating individuals differently would be necessary to achieve equal treatment in situations where generally applicable laws would have unequal effects.

In the case of the tax compliance rules, means adjustments could similarly account for the specific advantages of high-end taxpayers under the current system of generally applicable tax compliance rules. High-end taxpayers can often take advantage of more, and more effective, tax-avoidance opportunities, which can result in unequal effects from uniform tax compliance rules.[82] Means adjustments could account for these social circumstances, and thereby equalize the effect of these rules for taxpayers at varying income and wealth levels.

Importantly, this justification would depend on the design and function of the means adjustments. Most importantly, policymakers should only make these adjustments when there is, in fact, a legitimate reason for them, such as to counteract the specific advantages of high-end taxpayers under the current tax compliance system. If, instead, these adjustments were designed to impose additional burdens on high-end taxpayers in the absence of any specific and legitimate purpose, then they may not be justified.

The discussion thus far evaluates means adjustments to the tax compliance rules similarly to other laws that treat individuals differently. The tax compliance rules, however, also represent a special case because of their role in implementing the substantive tax rules. The tax system serves an essential and unique distributive function, which represents a widely accepted exception to the rule of law's generality principle. The tax compliance system, in turn, sustains the tax system and this distributive function. In this case, means adjustments to the tax compliance system can serve a uniquely important role: By allowing the tax compliance system to function properly, they implement this widely accepted distributive function.

Revisiting Constitutional Protections

Properly tailored means adjustments to the tax compliance rules would also not violate the Constitution's Equal Protection and Due Process Clauses. Regarding equal protection, the Supreme Court has not treated different income groups as suspect classes with heightened protections.[83] As a result, rules that differentiate among individuals based on their economic circumstances are only subject to the lower standard of rational basis review, rather than the heightened scrutiny required of laws that discriminate on the basis of suspect classifications.[84] Alec Schierenbeck observes that, in fact, the Equal Protection Clause has been interpreted to require courts to take income into account in some cases, "rather than to prohibit attention to income."[85]

Means adjustments to the tax compliance rules, such as higher accuracy-related tax penalties for high-end taxpayers, would align with the Equal Protection Clause, provided that these rules satisfied the standard for rational basis review, which is that the rule must "rationally further[] a legitimate state purpose or interest."[86] Adjustments properly tailored to address the specific tax-avoidance opportunities of high-end taxpayers under the tax compliance rules would not face a risk of challenge under this standard. In contrast, rules designed solely for the purpose of burdening high-end taxpayers that do not even have a rational basis could face constitutional challenge.

Policymakers should also design means adjustments to the tax compliance rules so that they do not violate the procedural protections in the Due Process Clauses. Policymakers should never deny taxpayers any of their basic procedural protections, such as the rights to notice and opportunity to a fair hearing.[87] Further, policymakers should be especially cautious when introducing any means adjustments to the criminal tax procedure rules, under which taxpayers face the risk of incarceration or other criminal sanctions, and for which the Due Process Clauses consequently require greater procedural protections.

Importantly, the current tax compliance rules regime already adopts many of the same means adjustments described in the later chapters in this book, specifically through its system of activity-based rules. For example, taxpayers who engage in certain activities are already subject to a longer statute of limitations, higher civil penalties, more limited penalty defenses, or greater information reporting requirements. These current adjustments do not violate the Due Process Clauses, and the adjustments contemplated in this book would only make similar adjustments in additional circumstances as well.

Finally, the federal Taxpayer Bill of Rights (TBOR), discussed in Chapter 2, articulates a series of basic protections for taxpayers and expectations in their interactions with the IRS.[88] Scholars have considered the degree to which the TBOR offers meaningful protections for taxpayers, or merely amounts to "window-dressing."[89] The TBOR does, however, provide guidance to policymakers seeking to strengthen the tax compliance system, by affirming a fundamental commitment to fairness and core procedural rights. Importantly, some elements of the TBOR reflect constitutional due process protections. For example, the TBOR provides for the "right to be informed," the "right to challenge the position of the IRS and be heard," and the "right to appeal a decision of the IRS in an independent forum."[90] Policymakers implementing means adjustments to the tax compliance rules can thereby reinforce core procedural protections when they design these adjustments in coordination with the TBOR requirements.

Revisiting the Double Distortion Principle

Means adjustments to the tax compliance rules would also be evaluated differently under the double distortion principle, as compared to the analysis of both the substantive tax rules and nontax legal rules. Here as well, the evaluation of means adjustments to the tax compliance rules will depend on the design and the intended function of these adjustments.

It might appear that means adjustments to both nontax legal rules and tax compliance rules would be evaluated similarly under the double distortion principle. From an ex post perspective, means adjustments to both types of rules can have the effect of imposing greater burdens on high-end individuals, based on both their means *and* an activity in which they engage. For example, just as a means-adjusted speeding ticket can affect the decisions to earn income and to speed, a means-adjusted tax compliance rule can affect the decisions to earn income and to engage in tax-avoidance behavior.

In the case of means-adjusted tax compliance rules, however, the behavior subject to the distortion is essentially different than in the case of behaviors encouraged or discouraged through nontax legal rules. In the paradigmatic double distortion scenario, policymakers should seek to encourage the behavior at the efficient or socially optimal level, because, in doing so, they will not discourage the production of social surplus, such as in a case where a driver speeds during an emergency. In the case of the tax compliance rules, the behavior to be discouraged – tax noncompliance – will not yield social surplus, but rather a reallocation of money from the government to the taxpayer.[91]

This consideration does not imply, however, that the government should consequently take any possible measures to eliminate all noncompliance. Enforcement measures can entail additional costs to taxpayers and the government, and in some cases can outweigh the benefits of collecting revenue lost from noncompliance.[92] In the case of tax noncompliance, the lost tax revenue is also not wasted or destroyed. Rather, the lost revenue is merely retained by the taxpayer, instead of being used for public purposes.[93] For this reason, Joel Slemrod and Shlomo Yitzhaki argue that tax-enforcement efforts should only be increased up to the point that the marginal enforcement costs equal their marginal social benefit, and not necessarily whenever the marginal tax revenues collected exceed the marginal enforcement costs.[94]

The different nature of the behavior to be discouraged in the tax-enforcement context – the act of tax noncompliance – does have one important implication: When determining the optimal level of tax administration, policymakers would not need to also account for additional social welfare that could have been generated by the tax-avoidance activities themselves, in contrast to those benefits that could result from behaviors such as speeding during an emergency.[95]

Because of this difference, the double distortion principle would allow for means adjustments to the tax compliance rules when they would not be justified for other legal rules. Further, in some cases, this principle would even *require* such adjustments. Because of their implementing role, the tax compliance rules enable the operation of the substantive tax rules, which is the most efficient instrument for distribution policy under the double distortion framework. As a result, if means adjustments could enable the tax compliance rules to implement the substantive tax rules – and their distributive function – more effectively, then these adjustments could improve efficiency within the double distortion framework.

This analysis of means-adjusted tax compliance rules within the double distortion framework depends, again, on their implementing function. Consider, in contrast, the case where policymakers designed means adjustments to the tax compliance rules for the purpose of raising additional revenue from a subset of taxpayers beyond what is prescribed by the substantive tax rules. In this case, these adjustments could distort, rather than help implement, the distributive function of the tax system.

* * *

The principles favoring generally applicable legal rules offer helpful guidance for policymakers when designing means adjustments to the tax compliance rules. With these insights in mind, Chapter 5 begins this book's turn from the theory to the implementation of means-adjusted tax compliance.

NOTES

1 See Lawrence Solum, *The Rule of Law*, LEGAL THEORY LEXICON (Apr. 23, 2023), https://lsolum.typepad.com/legal_theory_lexicon/2004/01/legal_theory_le_3.html.
2 Lawrence B. Solum, *Equity and the Rule of Law*, in THE RULE OF LAW 120, 121–22 (Ian Shapiro ed., 1994).
3 *See* ROBIN WEST, RE-IMAGINING JUSTICE: PROGRESSIVE INTERPRETATIONS OF FORMAL EQUALITY, RIGHTS, AND THE RULE OF LAW 13–15, 18–26 (2003).
4 *See* LON L. FULLER, THE MORALITY OF LAW 46–49 (rev. ed. 1969). Fuller includes generality in a list of features he considers essential to the "internal morality of the law," including that the law must be "general, public, prospective, understandable, noncontradictory, stable, and practicable." *Id.* at 39, 45.
5 JOHN RAWLS, A THEORY OF JUSTICE 113–14 (1971).
6 *See* WEST, *supra* note 3, at 107.
7 ARISTOTLE, NICOMACHEAN ETHICS Book V 1131a-b (Roger Crisp trans., Cambridge University Press, 2d ed. 2014); *see also* David A. Strauss, *Must Like Cases Be Treated Alike?* (U Chicago Pub. L. & Leg. Theory Working Paper No. 24, 2002); *see also* H. L. A. HART, THE CONCEPT OF LAW 157–66 (3d ed. 2012).
8 *See* Strauss, *supra* note 7, at 2 ("How do we decide what cases are alike, in the relevant sense? Similarly, how do we decide what constitutes treating cases alike?").

9 *See* Paul Gowder, The Rule of Law in the Real World 28, 33 (2016) (describing the general challenge of defining a "relevant distinction" when assessing whether a law complies with the generality principle).
10 *See* Fuller, *supra* note 4, at 47.
11 Strauss, *supra* note 7, at 2.
12 *See* Alec Schierenbeck, *The Constitutionality of Income-Based Fines*, 85 U. Chi. L. Rev. 1869, 1883 (2018) (noting the "objection [] that income-based fines could lead to discriminatory enforcement against the wealthy").
13 *See* Chapter 2, section "Factors in Tax Compliance."
14 West, *supra* note 3, at 109; *see also id.* at 119–29 (describing critiques of formal equality in the literature).
15 Martha Minow, *Equality vs. Equity*, 1 Am. J.L. & Equal. 167, 179, 182 (2021).
16 *Id.* at 188. Minow notes that rules prioritizing "equity" instead of "equality" by tailoring the law to individual needs and circumstances face a similar challenge, by requiring policymakers to decide "which individual differences deserve what kinds of treatment." *Id.*
17 West, *supra* note 3, at 130.
18 *Id.* at 149–55.
19 *Id.* at 154.
20 *See* Gowder, *supra* note 9, at 45 ("[B]ecause generality is an expressive ideal, and because the expressive content of any legal act... depends on social meanings that themselves depend on social facts, our evaluation of whether a law is subject to criticism will depend in part on prevailing social conditions....").
21 *Id.* at 42–45.
22 *Id.* at 42–44.
23 *See* Paul Gowder, *Equal Law in an Unequal World*, 99 Iowa L. Rev. 1021, 1061–62 (2014).
24 *Id.*
25 U.S. Const. amend. V; amend. XIV, § 1.
26 *See* Kenji Yoshino, *The New Equal Protection*, 124 Harv. L. Rev. 747, 755–63 (2011).
27 Bolling v. Sharpe, 347 U.S. 497 (1954).
28 *See, e.g.*, Williamson v. Lee Optical, Inc., 348 U.S. 483 (1955) (upholding state licensing requirements restricting the business activities of persons not licensed as optometrists or ophthalmologists). For discussion of this principle, see also Yoshino, *supra* note 26, at 759–60.
29 *See* Dep't of Agriculture, Snap Eligibility (July 13, 2022), https://www.fns.usda.gov/snap/recipient/eligibility.
30 This doctrine originates in the famous "footnote four" in United States v. Carolene Prods. Co., 304 U.S. 144, 152 n.4 (1938).
31 *See, e.g.*, Skinner v. Oklahoma, 316 U.S. 535 (1942) (right to avoid forced sterilization); Shapiro v. Thompson, 394 U.S. 618 (1969) (right to travel); Dunn v. Blumstein, 405 U.S. 330 (1972) (right to vote and travel).
32 This absence of constitutional protections for socioeconomic rights has also been critiqued on account of its consequences for lower-income groups. *See* Mario L. Barnes & Erwin Chemerinsky, *The Disparate Treatment of Race and Class in Constitutional Jurisprudence*, 72 Law & Contemp. Probs. 109, 110 (2009) (observing that "wealth, as a classification,

and the poor, as a group, have only rarely commanded the full breadth of the Court's attention"); Ganesh Sitaraman, *The Puzzling Absence of Economic Power in Constitutional Theory*, 101 CORNELL L. REV. 1445 (2016) (describing the general lack of concern with economic difference in constitutional theory).

33 *See, e.g.,* the standard of review applied in *Williamson*, 348 U.S. 483 (1955).
34 Yoshino, *supra* note 26, at 755–56.
35 U.S. CONST. amend. V; amend. XIV, § 1
36 *See generally* Erwin Chemerinsky, *Procedural Due Process Claims*, 16 TOURO L. REV. 871 (2016) (describing the constitutional requirements of procedural due process).
37 *See, e.g.,* Fuentes v. Shevin, 407 U.S. 67, 81 (1972) ("The requirement of notice and an opportunity to be heard raises no impenetrable barrier to the taking of a person's possessions. But the fair process of decisionmaking that it guarantees works, by itself, to protect against arbitrary deprivation of property.").
38 *See* Solum, *supra* note 2, and accompanying text.
39 *See* Morrissey v. Brewer, 408 U.S. 471, 481 (1972) ("[D]ue process is flexible and calls for such procedural protections as the particular situation demands.").
40 424 U.S. 319, 341 (1976).
41 *See* Niki Kuckes, *Civil Due Process, Criminal Due Process*, 25 YALE L. & POL'Y. REV. 1, 18–20 (2006) (describing the extensive due process protections for criminal defendants at the trial and sentencing stages). In some cases, criminal defendants may be entitled to fewer procedural protections at the pretrial stage, as compared to civil defendants. *See id.* at 34–42.
42 *See generally* Louis Kaplow & Steven Shavell, *Why the Legal System Is Less Efficient Than the Income Tax in Redistributing Income*, 23 J. LEGAL STUD. 667, 667 (1994); A. MITCHELL POLINSKY, AN INTRODUCTION TO LAW AND ECONOMICS 158–59 (4th ed. 2011) ("The tax and transfer system is a *much* less expensive way to redistribute income than is the legal system.") (emphasis in original). Polinsky argues that redistribution through nontax legal rules may be "costly" because of both greater administrative costs and because "inefficient rules may have to be chosen in order to achieve the desired distributional effect." *Id.*
43 *See* POLINSKY, *supra* note 42, at 165.
44 Kaplow & Shavell, *supra* note 42, at 667–68. Under some views, this same double distortion logic would imply limiting the tax base to a tax on labor income alone, since a tax on the return to savings can similarly distort behavior across two margins – the choice to earn income and the choice to save the income for consumption in future periods. *See generally, e.g.,* Joseph A. Bankman & David Weisbach, *The Superiority of an Ideal Consumption Tax over an Ideal Income Tax*, 58 STAN. L. REV. 1413 (2006); *but see* Peter Diamond & Emmanuel Saez, *The Case for a Progressive Tax: From Basic Research to Policy Recommendations*, 25 J. ECON. PERSP. 165, 177–83 (2011) (offering arguments for the positive taxation of capital income).
45 Kaplow & Shavell, *supra* note 42, at 669–70 (evaluating an efficient sanction set at an amount equal to the "net expected accident costs").
46 *See* JEREMY BENTHAM, THE THEORY OF LEGISLATION 325 (C. K. Ogden ed., Richard Hildreth trans., Routledge & Kegan Paul Ltd. 1931) (1802) (presenting a basic deterrence model where the sanction must exceed the benefit to the offender); Gary S. Becker, *Crime*

and Punishment: An Economic Approach, 76 J. POL. ECON. 169, 190–98 (1968) (describing a model for setting optimal fines where the penalty is set equal to the marginal harm from the offense); see also Chapter 2, section "Factors in Tax Compliance."

47 Finland and other jurisdictions have experimented with similar forms of income-based fines.

48 Kaplow & Shavell, supra note 42, at 669–71.

49 Id. at 671–74.

50 Id. at 675–76. Kaplow and Shavell note that an individual's risk aversion should also not factor into the calculation, on the assumption that private insurance is available. Id. at 675–76.

51 See POLINSKY, supra note 42, at 81.

52 See Beth A. Colgan, Graduating Economic Sanctions According to Ability to Pay, 103 IOWA L. REV. 53 (2017); Gary M. Friedman, The West German Day-Fine System: A Possibility for the United States?, 50 U. CHI. L. REV. 281 (1983); Sally T. Hillsman, Fines and Day Fines, 12 CRIME & JUST. 49 (1990); Schierenbeck, supra note 12, at 1876–79.

53 Sakosta, muuntorangaistuksesta ja rikesakosta [Fine, Conversion Sentence and Summary Penal Fee] (Apr. 30, 1999/550), https://finlex.fi/fi/laki/ajantasa/1889/18890039001, translated in Criminal Code of Finland Ch. 2a (Fin. Ministry of Just.), https://finlex.fi/en/laki/kaannokset/1889/en18890039_20150766.pdf.

54 See SUZANNE DALEY, Speeding in Finland Can Cost a Fortune, If You Already Have One, N.Y. TIMES (Apr. 25, 2015), https://www.nytimes.com/2015/04/26/world/europe/speeding-in-finland-can-cost-a-fortune-if-you-already-have-one.html; JOE PINSKER, Finland, Home of the $103,000 Speeding Ticket, ATLANTIC (Mar. 12, 2015), https://www.theatlantic.com/business/archive/2015/03/finland-home-of-the-103000-speeding-ticket/387484. As one high-income speeder in Finland found out the hard way, understating your income is not a good option for getting out of this situation, as it can result in the assessment of additional monetary penalties. JARED CLINTON, Report: Leo Komarov Slapped with $40,000 Fine for Speeding in Finland, THE HOCKEY NEWS (Aug. 21, 2015), https://thehockeynews.com/news/report-leo-komarov-slapped-with-40000-fine-in-finland-for-speeding (reporting that when the speeder, professional hockey player Leo Komarov, faced monetary fines for committing fraud, on top of those he had already been assessed for speeding, after reporting that he had "no income").

55 See Elena Kantorowicz-Reznichenko, Theoretical Perspectives on Day Fines, in DAY FINES IN EUROPE: ASSESSING INCOME-BASED SANCTIONS IN CRIMINAL JUSTICE SYSTEMS 8, 15–16 (Elena Kantorowicz-Reznichenko & Michael Faure eds., 2021) ("From a deterrence perspective, a (fixed) fine ... can never equally deter all types of offenders.... [T]hey merely create a pricing system for wealthier offenders, who can decide the offence is worth paying for."); see also Joshua D. Blank & Ari Glogower, Progressive Tax Procedure, 96 N.Y.U.L. REV. 668, 710–11 (2021); Friedman, supra note 52, at 286 (describing how the West German day-fine system was designed "to effect an equal impact on all offenders").

56 See generally R. G. Lipsey & Kelvin Lancaster, The General Theory of Second Best, 24 REV. ECON. STUD. 11 (1956).

57 Cf. David Gamage, The Case for Taxing (All of) Labor Income, Consumption, Capital Income, and Wealth, 68 TAX L. REV. 355 (2015) (arguing that redistribution through

multiple tax instruments may be desirable to minimize the distortions and costs of redistribution through any one instrument).
58 *But see* POLINSKY, *supra* note 42, at 159 (arguing that "the tax and transfer system is a *much* less expensive way to redistribute income than is the legal system") (emphasis in original).
59 For a discussion of challenges the federal tax system faces in realizing its progressive potential, *see* Jeremy Bearer-Friend et al., *Taxation and Law and Political Economy*, 83 OHIO ST. L.J. 471, 516–17 (2022).
60 *See generally* MICHAEL J. GRAETZ & IAN SHAPIRO, DEATH BY A THOUSAND CUTS: THE FIGHT OVER TAXING INHERITED WEALTH (2005). Kaplow and Shavell similarly note there may be political constraints on redistribution through the tax and transfer system, but also observe that there may be similar political constraints to redistribution through other legal rules. Kaplow & Shavell, *supra* note 42, at 675.
61 *See* Zachary Liscow, *Reducing Inequality on the Cheap: When Legal Rule Design Should Incorporate Equity as Well as Efficiency*, 123 YALE L.J. 2478 (2014); *see also* Tomer Blumkin & Yoram Margalioth, *On the Limits of Redistributive Taxation: Establishing a Case for Equity-Informed Legal Rules*, 25 VA. TAX REV. 1, 18 (2005) (arguing that nontax legal rules can account for "non-income-based measures of equality").
62 *See* Zachary Liscow, *Redistribution for Realists*, 107 IOWA L. REV. 495, 512 (2022) (arguing that "attitudes about redistribution apply differently across [policy] silos").
63 Blumkin & Margalioth, *supra* note 61, at 15, 19–20 ("For example, in certain cases people might find redistribution through the tax and transfer system distasteful and have a preference for redistribution through legal rules.").
64 *See, e.g.*, the definition of progressivity in MICHAEL J. GRAETZ & ANNE L. ALSTOTT, FEDERAL INCOME TAXATION: PRINCIPLES AND POLICIES 21 (9th ed. 2022) ("The income tax is progressive in that the rate of tax applied to an individual's income increases as income increases.") (emphasis deleted). For purposes of the definition, progressivity is measured by reference to average, rather than marginal, rates of tax. *Id.*
65 *See, e.g.*, the progressive rate schedule in I.R.C. § 1(a)-(d), (j).
66 For a discussion, see also Chapter 2, section "The Function of Tax Compliance Rules."
67 *See* RICHARD A. MUSGRAVE, THE THEORY OF PUBLIC FINANCE: A STUDY IN PUBLIC ECONOMY 17–27 (1959) (describing the central role of the tax and transfer system in the "distribution branch" of fiscal policy).
68 *See id.* at 18 (arguing that the tax and transfer system is the "easiest and most direct way" of implementing distributional adjustments).
69 Bearer-Friend et al., *supra* note 59, at 495.
70 HENRY C. SIMONS, PERSONAL INCOME TAXATION: THE DEFINITION OF INCOME AS A PROBLEM OF FISCAL POLICY 18–19 (1938).
71 For a discussion of these views, see Bearer-Friend, *supra* note 59, at 495–96.
72 For a description of these views, *see* Åsbjørn Melkevik, *No Progressive Taxation without Discrimination? On the Generality of the Law in the Classical Liberal Tradition*, 27 CONST. POL. ECON. 418, 419–21 (2016).
73 *See, e.g.*, MILTON FRIEDMAN, CAPITALISM AND FREEDOM 176, 190–95 (40th anniversary ed. 2022) (advocating for a minimal degree of redistribution through a negative

income tax); Daniel Hemel & Miranda Fleischer, *Atlas Nods: The Libertarian Case for a Basic Income*, 2017 WIS. L. REV. 1189 (2017).

74 For an argument that progressive taxation may be reconciled in this manner with the rule of law's generality principle, *see generally* Melkevik, *supra* note 23.

75 *See, e.g.*, LOUIS KAPLOW, THE THEORY OF TAXATION AND PUBLIC ECONOMICS 43 (2010); *see also* Chapter 1, section "Tax Noncompliance and Progressivity."

76 *Id.* at 42–43.

77 *See id.* at 44–47 (explaining how redistribution through progressive taxation can increase equality of utility); *see also* Joseph Bankman & Thomas Griffith, *Social Welfare and the Rate Structure: A New Look at Progressive Taxation*, 75 CAL. L. REV. 1905, 1914 (1987).

78 *See, e.g.*, Brushaber v. Union Pac. R.R. Co., 240 U.S. 1, 3 (1916) (appellant's argument that the 1913 Income Tax "involves unreasonable discrimination and arbitrary classifications").

79 *Id.*

80 *Id.* at 26. In *Brushaber* the Court observed that a tax would only be invalid if it was "so arbitrary ... that it was not the exertion of taxation but the confiscation of property ... or ... so wanting in basis for classification ... as to produce such a gross and patent inequality." *Id.* at 24–25. *See also* Bell's Gap R.R. Co. v. Pennsylvania, 134 U.S. 232, 237 (1890) ("The ... fourteenth amendment ... was not intended to prevent a state from adjusting its system of taxation in all proper and reasonable ways. ... But clear and hostile discriminations against particular persons and classes ... might be obnoxious to the constitutional prohibition.").

81 *See* CHARLES RETTIG, IRS, A CLOSER LOOK: IMPLEMENTING THE TAX GAP 9–10 (Dec. 3, 2020).

82 *See* Chapter 1, section "How the Rich Avoid Taxes" and Chapter 3, section "Unequal Effects of Generally Applicable Rules."

83 *See supra* note 32 and accompanying text.

84 *See* Schierenbeck, *supra* note 12, at 1886 (citing Harris v. McRae, 448 U.S. 297, 323 (1980); San Antonio Indep. Sch. Dist. v. Rodriguez, 411 U.S. 1, 29 (1973)); *see also* Barnes & Chemerinsky, *supra* note 32, at 111–14.

85 Schierenbeck, *supra* note 12, at 1887 (citing Williamson v. Illinois, 399 U.S. 235 (1970) and other cases where the Court has considered a defendant's low income when applying the Equal Protection Clause).

86 San Antonio Indep. Sch. Dist. v. Rodriguez, 411 U.S. 1, 55 (1973) (quoting McGinnis v. Royster, 410 U.S. 263, 273 (1973)).

87 *See also* Blank & Glogower, *supra* note 55, at 715.

88 *See* Chapter 2, section "The Taxpayer Bill of Rights."

89 *See* Alice G. Abreau & Richard K. Greenstein, *The U.S. Taxpayer Bill of Rights: Window Dressing or Expressions of Justice?* 4 J. TAX ADMIN. 25, 29 (2018) (arguing that the TBOR can align the administration of the tax system with principles of procedural justice).

90 I.R.C. § 7803(a)(3)(A), (D), (E).

91 *See* Alex Raskolnikov, *Accepting the Limits of Tax Law and Economics*, 98 CORNELL L. REV. 523, 531–36 (2013).

92 *See* Chapter 3, section "The Costs of Enforcement."

93 For an analysis of this difference, see Joel Slemrod, *Cheating Ourselves: The Economics of Tax Evasion*, 21 J. ECON. PERSP. 25, 43 (2007). Joel Slemrod and Shlomo Yitzhaki argue,

for example, that policymakers should instead increase tax-enforcement efforts up to the point that the marginal enforcement costs equal their marginal social benefit. Joel Slemrod & Shlomo Yitzhaki, *The Optimal Size of a Tax Collection Agency*, 89 SCANDINAVIAN J. ECON. 183 (1987).

94 Slemrod & Yitzhaki, *supra* note 93.
95 Of course, a taxpayer may also derive satisfaction from avoiding their tax obligations. Policymakers may not wish, however, to account for personal utility that derives from illegal behavior.

5

From Theory to Legal Design

Means-adjusted tax compliance rules can promote a more equitable and effective tax system. By modifying tax compliance rules to account for a taxpayer's economic circumstances, policymakers can more effectively deter high-end tax avoidance and abuse, as well as address resource imbalances between these taxpayers and the IRS. More generally, these adjustments can promote basic fairness by increasing the potential for high-end taxpayers to pay their required share of taxes.

Policymakers face many design possibilities when implementing these adjustments. Should a means-adjusted tax compliance rule be based on a taxpayer's income or wealth, or some combination of the two? Or, alternatively, should means adjustments only apply if some other factor is present? What are the threshold amounts of income or wealth that should cause means-adjusted tax compliance rules to apply? Should means adjustments apply to all tax compliance rules or to only a subset of them? These are just a few of the questions that policymakers would encounter when introducing means adjustments as legislative and regulatory reforms.

This chapter serves as the bridge from theory to legal design. We begin this transition by identifying some of the key design considerations that policymakers should take into account when introducing means adjustments to the tax compliance rules. In general, we propose means adjustments to certain tax compliance rules that favor high-end taxpayers when they are applied the same to everyone. These adjustments should also be designed to preserve core prerequisites of procedural fairness, and should also include an underpayment-based threshold to exempt less consequential tax offenses from these heightened tax compliance rules.

DESIGN CONSIDERATIONS

Means adjustments are not appropriate in all cases and policymakers should consider their limitations when introducing them. In particular, policymakers should consider several factors when designing means-adjusted tax compliance rules, including (1) the specific tax compliance rules to be adjusted and the types of affected taxpayers; (2) the base, such as income or wealth, that should determine the amount, form, and timing of the adjustments; (3) the monetary thresholds that would trigger the adjustments; (4) the avoidance of undue adjustments for low-value underpayments by high-end taxpayers; and (5) the effect of means-adjusted tax compliance rules on public perceptions of the taxing authority. We discuss each of these design considerations in the sections that follow.

Choice of Tax Compliance Rules and Affected Taxpayers

Policymakers should first determine the specific tax compliance rules that will be subject to means adjustments. These adjustments would be most appropriate for generally applicable rules that have different effects for taxpayers in varying economic circumstances, and where means adjustments would operate to counteract these effects. In each case, policymakers should assess how the proposed adjustments would be likely to affect high-end taxpayers' behavior and improve their level of tax compliance.

For the reasons described in Chapters 1–4, policymakers should focus on adjustments to tax compliance rules that serve an implementing function in the tax system.[1] Rules that seek to bolster deterrence and IRS detection of tax noncompliance, such as civil tax penalties, serve this function by implementing the substantive tax law. Means adjustments to these tax compliance rules could enhance their ability to achieve this implementing function more effectively, and particularly in the context of high-end tax noncompliance. In contrast, generally applicable tax compliance rules are often less effective for high-end taxpayers, when these taxpayers enjoy distinct advantages, including but not limited to increased opportunities to engage in sophisticated tax structuring based on third-party advice, as well as the means to not only pursue complex investment and business strategies but also to assert civil tax penalty defenses during negotiations with the IRS.[2] On the other hand, policymakers should not apply means adjustments to tax compliance rules that do not primarily serve an implementing function. For instance, means-based adjustments would not be warranted in the case of the rules governing interest charges on underpayments of tax liability by taxpayers.[3] In this example, the tax compliance rules primarily serve a compensatory function, as they impose a charge upon taxpayers who retain funds that they should have remitted to the IRS as tax payments.

Attention should also be focused on means adjustments to the tax compliance rules as they apply to individual taxpayers, even though the principles in this book could also have implications for rules governing tax entities such as corporations. At first glance, some of our analysis could appear to be similarly relevant in cases of tax avoidance by entities. Large multinational corporations frequently engage high-priced lawyers to advise on complex structuring and to provide opinions that can shield the firms from tax penalties. For example, in 2022, the *New York Times* reported on the accidental disclosure of a tax dispute between the IRS and the pharmaceutical giant Bristol Meyers Squibb over an aggressive tax structure that would save the company around $1.4 billion in taxes.[4] Key details from the report were the company's receipt of tax opinion letters from PricewaterhouseCoopers and White & Case LLP, which the company could have used to defend against certain civil tax penalties.[5]

Although portions of our argument could be applicable to entities as well, the analysis of means-adjusted tax compliance rules for entities differs from the analysis for individual taxpayers in important respects. First, individual tax noncompliance is a much larger factor in the overall federal tax gap than is corporate tax noncompliance. For the 2014–2016 tax years, the IRS estimates that the gross federal tax gap was $496 billion.[6] Of this amount, the IRS estimates that noncompliance with the individual income tax (before accounting for avoidance of employment taxes) contributed $357 billion to the tax gap, more than 70% of the total amount, while noncompliance with the corporate income tax only accounted for about 8%, or $41 billion.[7] The relative decline in the significance of the corporate income tax as a percentage of total tax revenues in recent decades has resulted from a number of factors, including taxpayer avoidance of the corporate form,[8] the reduction in the corporate tax rate,[9] and tax preferences for foreign-sourced global income.[10]

The social costs of noncompliance also differ in the case of corporations. Corporate tax avoidance ultimately benefits individuals proportionately to how they bear the incidence of the corporate income tax. Although a significant proportion of the total corporate income tax is borne by higher-income taxpayers,[11] the relative size of the corporation itself will not necessarily correlate with how its taxes are borne by individual taxpayers at different income levels.

Further, the income of any single corporation may not indicate its total economic resources, nor its access to sophisticated legal counsel and complex tax planning. Larger firms, in particular, often organize corporate entities within tiers of affiliated corporate subsidiaries. Inferring a corporation's total economic resources for the purposes of means-adjusted tax compliance rules would, therefore, require complex and necessarily imprecise aggregation rules.

Means adjustments are also not necessary where tax compliance rules create expected costs that are already high enough to deter tax noncompliance, or where further adjustments would not serve a significant additional deterrent effect that justifies their potential costs to taxpayers. In the case of criminal tax sanctions, for instance, the potential loss of liberty and related consequences likely deter many taxpayers from pursuing criminal forms of tax evasion. As an example, for high-end taxpayers, the consequences of being convicted for willfully failing to file tax returns could include a monetary sanction, imprisonment, and public disclosure. In addition to a potential prison sentence, a criminal sanction for tax noncompliance may prevent a high-end taxpayer from engaging in a professional trade, such as the practice of law, or may hinder the individual's ability to engage in future business ventures and partnerships. In these cases, the expected cost of noncompliance is often high, even when the chances of IRS detection are low, and policymakers cannot easily impose more severe criminal tax sanctions without unduly restricting the liberty of offenders.

For similar reasons, policymakers should not apply means adjustments to rules that implicate core principles of access to justice. For example, they should not prevent high-end taxpayers from pursuing appeals of adverse judicial decisions, nor should they exempt the IRS from providing taxpayers with notice of their tax deficiencies. In accordance with foundational principles of our legal system described in Chapter 4, every taxpayer should have equal and full access to these procedural opportunities, irrespective of their income or wealth. These rights are enshrined in the Constitution: The Equal Protection Clause would require a rational basis for any law that operates differently for rich taxpayers, while the Due Process Clause ensures basic procedural protections, including notice and an opportunity to be heard, in any dispute with the IRS.[12] Additionally, the statutory Taxpayer Bill of Rights (TBOR)[13] ensures taxpayers' basic procedural protections, including the right to be informed, the right to pay no more than the correct amount of tax, the right to be heard and to challenge the position of the IRS, and the right to appeal an IRS decision in an independent forum.[14] As we will demonstrate in Chapters 6–10, policymakers can introduce means adjustments to certain tax compliance rules without violating these provisions or otherwise implicating core safeguards of access to justice.

Base for Means Adjustments

Policymakers must also determine the base that will be used to determine whether a means adjustment applies. Such adjustments could be linked to different base options, including the taxpayer's income, the taxpayer's wealth, or a combination thereof. Of course, no measure will offer an objectively superior and accurate base to use for making the adjustments. However, policymakers can use available information to design an effective system that would also minimize new administrative and compliance costs, both for the government and for taxpayers.

As previously stated, one option is to consider a taxpayer's income when determining whether a means adjustment should be made to a tax compliance rule. For instance, if a tax penalty relates to an underpayment of income tax liability,[15] then a means-based adjustment to this tax penalty could be triggered when a taxpayer's income meets a threshold amount.

In this case, policymakers must also decide on the definition of income that would be used for the threshold. The classic Haig–Simons formulation – a comprehensive income measure that includes both consumption and changes in wealth – would account for all forms of economic income, including asset appreciation prior to a disposition or "realization" event.[16] In principle, using a comprehensive income tax base would most accurately identify those taxpayers with the greatest economic resources and who, therefore, are often best able to take advantage of the current tax compliance rules.

The US federal income tax, in contrast, uses a narrower concept of income that accounts for the privacy, liquidity, and administrability problems that are inherent in taxing a comprehensive income base. First, individual taxpayers calculate their "adjusted gross income," which reflects some deductions for items that should not be included in a net income base, such as non-employee business expenses, and which does not include some forms of economic income, such as unrealized capital gains.[17] Next, individual taxpayers calculate their "taxable income" by subtracting either the standard deduction (a flat dollar amount, indexed for inflation) or itemized deductions (such as for charitable contributions and medical expenses) from their adjusted gross income.[18]

The measure of adjusted gross income more closely measures a comprehensive income tax base, since the measure of taxable income also accounts for certain policy choices that are not designed to accurately measure income. Further, current law provisions that are designed to take into account taxpayers' means – such as the EITC,[19] child and dependent care credit,[20] and education credits,[21] among many others – all begin to phase out as a taxpayer's adjusted gross income increases. Policymakers could create a simple and administrable system of means-adjusted tax compliance rules by using adjusted gross income as the base, which is already calculated by taxpayers when they prepare and file their tax return.

Income-based adjustments may also be more desirable than adjustments based on the size of a taxpayer's delinquency or tax underpayment. A taxpayer's annual adjusted gross income can provide a more accurate reflection of a taxpayer's economic circumstances than the amount of any delinquency or underpayment in a single tax year. A low-income taxpayer can also become delinquent in paying a large outstanding tax liability, especially after accounting for late-payment and late-filing penalties and interest on underpayments.[22] Similarly, a taxpayer could report a large tax liability in a single tax year, even though the taxpayer typically has lower taxable income from wages and other sources.[23]

Of course, by hiding a portion of their income from the tax authorities, non-compliant taxpayers may also appear to have less income for the purposes of these adjustments. To prevent taxpayers from avoiding such adjustments, and to smooth out the effects of irregular income, policymakers could base the adjustment on an average of an individual's income over a period of prior years. Chapter 10 also describes why taxpayers would not face the same incentives to underreport their income for purposes of these adjustments as they do when they hide income to reduce their substantive tax liabilities.[24] Further, these thresholds can be administered more effectively in connection with reforms we propose to the information reporting rules.[25]

In some cases, the IRS could only ascertain that a taxpayer meets the threshold – and is therefore subject to means-adjusted tax compliance rules – after conducting an examination. Current adjustments to the tax compliance rules operate in the same way, however, and therefore face this same problem. For example, the IRS can only establish that a taxpayer is subject to the longer statute of limitations period in a case of a "substantial omission" from gross income or fraud after determining that the taxpayer has engaged in these activities.[26]

Income is not the only possible base that could trigger means adjustments. Another approach could be to adjust tax compliance rules, such as tax penalties, based on the taxpayer's wealth. Scholars have argued that a taxpayer's wealth – or a combination of income and wealth – may yield a more accurate measure of relative economic circumstances than income alone.[27] In this case, means adjustments to the tax compliance rules could apply if the taxpayer holds assets that have aggregate value in excess of a set threshold.

The possibility of using a taxpayer's wealth to trigger means adjustments may appear to be impractical under current law. First, high-end taxpayers could respond to the possibility of means adjustments to tax compliance rules by challenging the IRS's valuation of their assets. Disputes over valuation of assets, such as land, closely held corporate stock, and artwork, often consume significant time and resources from the IRS.[28] In estate and gift tax disputes, the core issues frequently involve questions of valuation.[29] Second, policymakers would also need to decide whether the measurement of asset value should reflect liabilities, or not. If so, many wealthy individuals may be able to avoid application of the means adjustments by encumbering their assets with debt (including debt owed to entities owned by the taxpayer). Last, unlike taxable income, taxpayers do not currently report their total net wealth to the IRS in order to calculate tax liabilities.

Despite these apparent limitations, policymakers may nonetheless be able to use wealth as the base for means adjustments if they introduce other changes to the law. For example, a wealth-based adjustment would be more feasible if policymakers were to implement a federal wealth tax.[30] In this case, a wealth-based adjustment could rely upon the infrastructure and methods developed to implement and administer the substantive wealth tax. A federal wealth tax, however, is not a necessity for implementing wealth-based adjustments to the tax compliance rules. As we discuss in greater detail in Chapter 10, policymakers could instead require high-end taxpayers to submit annual reports of their net wealth to the IRS. The chapter proposes an annual reporting requirement that would require taxpayers with net assets that meet or exceed specific thresholds to file a form with the IRS that reports their assets and their approximate value.[31] This proposal builds on other types of asset reporting obligations in the Internal Revenue Code today, such as those involving certain foreign financial assets. If Congress were to introduce a federal wealth tax or, as we propose, a net asset information reporting requirement, then the possibility of using net wealth as a base for determining means adjustments to tax compliance rules would be much more feasible than it would be under the current system.

Thresholds for Means Adjustments

Policymakers must also set the monetary thresholds that will trigger means adjustments to the tax compliance rules. In other words, what is the amount of annual income or wealth that individual taxpayers must meet in order to be subject to means-adjusted rules? No single threshold, of course, can perfectly address all the different concerns with high-end noncompliance.[32] As a result, policymakers must strike a balance with threshold levels that substantially address these concerns, while also minimizing additional burdens on taxpayers that would be neither justified nor necessary.

Tax avoidance opportunities are very different for taxpayers at the very top of the income distribution. Taxpayers in the top 1% of the income scale, or even in the top 0.1%, typically have different noncompliance opportunities than even other high-income taxpayers, such as those in the top 10%. For example, a doctor or a lawyer earning $400,000 of labor income will have relatively fewer opportunities to avoid taxes through aggressive and abusive tax-planning opportunities. If these individuals are employees, they are subject to third-party information reporting and withholding, features that allow the IRS to identify underreporting of wage income quickly. On the other hand, the founder and owner of a hedge fund who has $40 million of income each year, from both labor and investment activity, may take advantage of many more tax-avoidance strategies. For a simple example, the 2022 report of the Joint Committee on Taxation on President Trump's tax returns highlights a variety of possible tax-avoidance strategies that are simply unavailable to taxpayers who are "merely" at the 90th percentile of the income distribution, even though the latter group would be deemed to earn a high income when they are compared to most other taxpayers.[33]

For the reasons explained in Chapter 1, tax noncompliance at the very top is often the most challenging type for the IRS to detect, let alone challenge. Some of the most common tax-avoidance techniques of high-end taxpayers involve the use of offshore bank accounts, virtual currency, tax shelters, subchapter S corporations, the qualified business income deduction, among many others. Unlike individuals who earn the bulk of their annual income from wages that are subject to third-party information reporting and withholding, taxpayers at the very top earn more of their income through capital, including businesses operated through entities, and are not subject to similar reporting and withholding. While the IRS estimates the current gross federal tax gap to be approximately $500 billion, commentators have observed that, as a result of tax noncompliance at the very top, "the rich have hidden away far more than that offshore and in business activity the IRS can't easily track."[34] In Chapter 9, we illustrate the many ways in which high-end taxpayers take advantage of these gaps in the tax-enforcement infrastructure to avoid scrutiny by the IRS.

Further, only individuals at the very top of the income distribution can afford tax lawyers and advisors necessary to pursue sophisticated tax-avoidance strategies. According to a 2023 report, several major law firms in New York charge clients at least $1,000 per hour for work done by junior associates.[35] The price for partners and other experienced attorneys is often even higher.[36] As sophisticated tax planning and advice can result in significant billable hours, especially where formal written tax opinions are involved, only individual taxpayers who are in the highest income percentiles can rely on these advisors to pursue sophisticated tax-avoidance strategies.

Other aspects of the social costs from high-end tax noncompliance might imply different threshold levels for these adjustments. For example, in a progressive tax system, noncompliance by higher-income taxpayers entails a greater social welfare cost than noncompliance by lower- or middle-income taxpayers, due to the declining marginal utility of income earned by high-end taxpayers. This consideration might suggest that different threshold levels would be needed if policymakers were accounting primarily for these varying social welfare costs of noncompliance at different points on the income distribution. In this case, choice of certain threshold levels will also depend on understandings of what the marginal utility of income is for individuals at different points on the income distribution scale.

The chosen threshold levels for the adjustments will also affect how much additional revenue is raised by these reforms. Using lower threshold levels would affect a broader range of taxpayers, and would therefore have a greater revenue effect, but at the potential cost of imposing additional compliance rules on a broader set of taxpayers.

In light of these considerations, how should policymakers determine the monetary threshold at which to institute means adjustments to the tax compliance rules? One approach could be to attempt to tailor means adjustments to individual taxpayers based on their income or wealth at a granular level. For example, when designing these adjustments, they could seek more empirical research that provides relevant data to aid in their decision-making, including (1) the type of individual taxpayers engaged in specific tax-avoidance activities, (2) the income necessary to hire tax lawyers and accountants who engage in aggressive tax planning, and (3) the income and wealth of individual taxpayers who are engaged in the highest-value tax controversies with the IRS. While this type of analysis would certainly be helpful, because there are so many relevant factors, it is unlikely to produce a clear answer or a single numerical threshold that would consistently address all the concerns with high-end tax noncompliance.

Another, more practical, approach would be to use broad income cutoffs as proxies for tax-avoidance opportunities. Policymakers have several helpful sources of data regarding individuals' income and, to some extent, wealth, which they can use for these thresholds. For example, each year, the IRS publicly reports statistical information regarding taxpayers' income.[37] While these reports do not include information regarding the normative, or economic, concept of income, they do provide percentile statistics showing adjusted gross income reported on individual income tax returns. As an example, the IRS reported that, in 2020, the cutoffs for adjusted gross income at the top were $548,336 for the top 1% of returns, $2,614,565 for the top 0.1%, and $14,757,246 for the top 0.01%.[38]

Our focus in this book is on taxpayers at the very top of the income distribution, especially the top 0.1% and above. As a result, throughout the remaining chapters of this book, we provide examples of thresholds of annual adjusted gross income of $2 million and annual aggregate net assets of $10 million. These thresholds are illustrative examples that would limit the applicability of the proposed adjustments to within roughly the top 0.1% of taxpayers. Policymakers, of course, can introduce different thresholds that not only focus on other income thresholds at the very top but also incorporate new research insights that help fine-tune the adjustment levels.

An Exception for Low-Value Underpayments

Means-adjusted tax compliance rules could result in disproportionate targeting by the IRS, even when doing so would not be warranted. If means-adjusted tax compliance rules apply whenever individuals meet the income or asset thresholds, then IRS agents might focus disproportionately on the tax returns of these taxpayers. Under our system, critics might argue, IRS agents would have an incentive to focus on high-end taxpayers' returns because these investigations could potentially allow them to take more time to conduct their review and could, eventually, result in greater tax penalties than in the case of other taxpayers.

If policymakers do not take this possible effect into account, means-adjusted tax compliance rules could subject high-end taxpayers to unduly burdensome tax compliance rules, even when they only commit minor offenses. For instance, a high-end taxpayer who omits a small amount of income from their tax return, or who fails to report a small part of a larger item of income, could face increased tax penalties or other changes to tax compliance rules simply because they meet the income or asset threshold for means adjustments.

Our goal is not to subject high-end taxpayers to excessive IRS scrutiny and increased compliance burdens in all cases. Instead, our proposed approach focuses on an area of unique concern for the tax system: the cases of significant tax noncompliance by high-end taxpayers. Minor or low-value tax offenses simply do not create the same risks to the tax system as high-value tax noncompliance. Unduly burdening minor acts of tax noncompliance, even by high-end taxpayers, would not meaningfully narrow the tax gap. Additionally, heightened tax compliance rules for minor offenses could create traps for the unwary and impose burdens on taxpayers that outweigh the benefits from collecting the limited tax revenue at stake.

For example, imagine a group of business executives who work at the same financial advisory firm and who gather for lunch at an expensive restaurant once a year, where they do not conduct or discuss any business or engage with clients. At this annual event, a member of the firm uses the firm credit card to pay for everyone's lunch. The employer pays for the nonbusiness lunch, which is attended only by employees of the same firm. Even though individuals in this example should include the value of the lunch as ordinary income, in many cases, they do not.

Aside from the relatively low dollar value of the tax noncompliance in this example, the IRS may also receive information about the event if the firm attempts to deduct the cost as an ordinary and necessary business expense. The economic consequences from this type of noncompliance to the tax system, in terms of lost revenue and the spread of tax noncompliance, are far lower than when individuals avoid substantial tax liabilities by using strategies such as offshore bank accounts or virtual currency to escape IRS detection. Such acts of low-value tax noncompliance, even by high-end taxpayers, do not necessarily warrant the introduction of means-adjusted tax compliance rules.

Policymakers could address the potential for overburdening high-end taxpayers who commit minor tax offenses by creating an exception for low-value understatements of income or underpayments of income tax. For example, many of the civil tax penalty rules calculate the amount of the penalty by applying a rate to the taxpayer's underpayment of income tax.[39] Policymakers could include an exception from means-adjusted tax penalty rules when the amount of a taxpayer's underpayments for the year falls below a particular dollar value.

An exemption for low-value underpayment amounts would reduce the IRS's incentive to scrutinize the tax returns of high-end taxpayers excessively because of those taxpayers' elevated economic status. It would allow high-end taxpayers who commit minor tax offenses to be subject to the same tax compliance rules that apply to all other taxpayers. Such minor offenses might include failure to report income, or improperly deducting expenses, when doing so does not result in a significant amount of underpaid tax liability. By including an exemption for such low-value underpayments, Congress would allow the IRS to reserve the use of means-adjusted tax compliance rules for situations where high-end taxpayers engage in significant and costly acts of tax noncompliance.

Public Perceptions of the IRS

Finally, policymakers should consider how means-adjusted tax compliance rules would affect public perceptions of the taxing authority – the IRS. Would means adjustments diminish the willingness of high-end taxpayers, and their advisors, to cooperate with the agency? Would they have adverse effects on overall voluntary compliance, including by taxpayers other than those at the top? And how would such a system impact Congress's oversight and funding of the IRS?

Congress can help to improve public perceptions of the IRS by embedding principles of fair tax administration in the structure of the Internal Revenue Code. Means-adjusted tax compliance rules could help to reinforce a principle that the tax law should be administered fairly and equally for all taxpayers, and that the decisions regarding tax-enforcement priorities are not made by the IRS alone.

Our proposal implicates important perceptions of the legitimacy and fairness of the taxing authority in the eyes of the public. The concept of "sociological legitimacy" is a primary objective for every government agency, including the IRS.[40] Compared to other forms of legitimacy that depend on legal authority, the sociological legitimacy of an action or institution of the government centers on whether "the relevant public regards it as justified, appropriate, or otherwise deserving of support for reasons beyond fear of sanctions or mere hope for personal reward."[41] If individuals view the tax law, or the institution that administers it, as illegitimate, they may fail to comply with their own taxpaying obligations.[42] Further, a perception of illegitimacy may hamper the IRS's attempts to propose new rules and regulations[43] or obtain necessary budgetary allocations from Congress.

One important factor that can affect the sociological legitimacy of the IRS is whether the public views the IRS as unfairly targeting certain taxpayers. Consider some recent examples of the targeting concern. The first example is the 2013 controversy regarding the IRS's review of tax-exempt organization applications, notoriously described by some as the "IRS scandal."[44] In May 2013, the head of the IRS's Tax Exempt and Government Entities Division stated that in reviewing applications by organizations to receive Section 501(c)(4) tax-exempt status as "social welfare" organizations – which only permits organizations to engage in limited political activities – her division had especially scrutinized organizations with terms such as "Tea Party" or "Patriot" in their title.[45]

Days later, a report issued by the Treasury Inspector General for Tax Administration found that the IRS used "inappropriate criteria" based on applicants' political affiliation, not only to screen Section 501(c)(4) applicants but also to delay processing of applications and to submit "unnecessary information requests" to applicants.[46] This statement was followed, in that same year, by a wave of accusations by critics that the IRS discriminated against conservative organizations due to their political ideology.[47]

While a subsequent 2017 review determined that the IRS had scrutinized tax-exempt applications from both conservative and liberal groups,[48] surveys showed that, immediately following the initial controversy, less than a third of taxpayers reported that they trusted the IRS to fairly enforce the tax law.[49] In an attempt to quell outrage over alleged IRS targeting, the then president Barack Obama reaffirmed that "you want to make sure everybody is being treated fairly."[50]

Similar concerns arose following the 2022 enactment of the Inflation Reduction Act, in which Congress allocated an additional $80 billion of funding to the IRS. In the months that followed, high-level officials at the IRS, including the

Commissioner, pledged to use some of these new resources to increase audits of wealthy taxpayers. Fearing the potential for the IRS to target certain high-end individuals, in 2023, the *Wall Street Journal* Editorial Board warned that "[t]he fear of many Americans is that, flush with its new $80 billion in funding from Congress, the IRS will unleash its fearsome power against political opponents."[51]

Several adverse consequences could occur if a sizeable segment of the public comes to believe that the IRS is arbitrarily targeting high-end taxpayers. The most direct effect is that, if affected taxpayers view means-adjusted tax compliance rules as excessive, they may choose to litigate rather than enter into settlement agreements with the IRS.[52] An increase in tax litigation with high-end taxpayers could consume valuable tax-enforcement resources and, from the perspective of the IRS, introduce the risk that a court could side with the taxpayer in high-profile, publicly visible litigation.[53]

More generally, if members of the public perceive that the IRS is unilaterally attempting to exercise its audit and tax penalty powers against certain taxpayers based solely on their economic status, they could view the agency as acting illegitimately. A potential consequence of this perception is that other taxpayers, and not just those directly affected, could reduce their own tax compliance in response. Legislators may also respond to such concerns, whether they would be justified in doing so or not, by increasing scrutiny of the IRS or by refusing to provide promised or requested operational funding.

To address concerns regarding the public's perception of the IRS, Congress should make it clear that it is introducing a new approach to tax compliance by enacting statutes that include rules such as means-adjusted tax penalties, statutes of limitations, and information reporting rules. This approach would be consistent with Congress's enactment of progressive features of current law: not only graduated tax rates but also numerous deductions and credits that vary depending upon taxpayers' adjusted gross income. Through the legislative history and public statements, and perhaps even in "sense of Congress" statements in the legislation itself,[54] Congress must make it clear to the public that it is directing the IRS to carry out these reforms to create a level playing field between high-end taxpayers and the agency.

In the end, Congress should not rely solely on the IRS to develop means-adjusted approaches to tax enforcement, including by focusing exclusively on increased audits of certain taxpayers. Aside from the fact that the IRS and Treasury do not have the legal authority to institute changes to tax penalty rates and the statute of limitations by themselves, the agencies cannot, working alone, implement this new approach to tax compliance in a way that would preserve the agencies' sociological legitimacy. Instead, Congress must lead the way to this new approach to tax compliance.

* * *

The purpose of means-adjusted tax compliance is not to generate additional tax revenue beyond that required by substantive tax rules. Nor is it to impose different overall tax burdens on groups of taxpayers based on their economic circumstances. Rather, the objective is to prevent high-end abusive tax avoidance and tax evasion by helping to level the playing field between the IRS and this group of taxpayers. This chapter has outlined some of the key considerations that should influence policymakers' decisions when they implement the theory of means-adjusted tax compliance through the design of new legal rules. In Chapters 6–10, we will propose several concrete applications of means-adjusted tax compliance: civil tax penalties; tax advice and its relevance to the "reasonable cause" defenses to certain civil tax penalties; the statute of limitations on assessment; and tax information reporting rules.

NOTES

1 *See* Chapter 2, section "The Role of the Tax Compliance Rules"; *see also* Joshua D. Blank & Ari Glogower, *When Should Means Matter? The Case of Tax Compliance*, 42 VA. TAX REV. 243, 257 (2022).
2 *See* Chapter 1, section "How the Rich Avoid Taxes."
3 *See* I.R.C. § 6601.
4 Jesse Drucker, *An Accidental Disclosure Exposes a $1 Billion Tax Fight with Bristol Myers*, N.Y. TIMES (Apr. 1, 2021), https://www.nytimes.com/2021/04/01/business/bristol-myers-taxes-irs.html?smid=url-share.
5 *See id.*
6 IRS, PUB. 1415 (REV. 10-2022), FEDERAL TAX COMPLIANCE RESEARCH: TAX GAP ESTIMATES FOR TAX YEARS 2014–2016 (2022).
7 *Id.*
8 *See* JOINT COMM. ON TAX'N, JCX-14-22, OVERVIEW OF THE FEDERAL TAX SYSTEM AS IN EFFECT FOR 2022 34 tbl. A-4 (2022) (measuring the decline in the number of total C corporation returns filed since the mid-1980s).
9 I.R.C. § 11; Tax Cuts and Jobs Act, H.R. 1, 115th Cong., Pub. L. 115-97, 131 Stat. 2054, 2096, at § 13,001 (2017).
10 *E.g.*, I.R.C. § 245A (exemption of foreign-sourced dividends).
11 *See* JANE G. GRAVELLE, CONG. RSCH. SERV., RL34229, CORPORATE TAX REFORM: ISSUES FOR CONGRESS 20–35 (2021).
12 *See* Chapter 4, section "Constitutional Protections."
13 *See* I.R.C. § 7803(a)(3).
14 *See id.*
15 *See* I.R.C. § 6662(a).
16 *See* ROBERT M. HAIG, THE CONCEPT OF INCOME–ECONOMIC AND LEGAL ASPECTS (1921); HENRY C. SIMONS, PERSONAL INCOME TAXATION: THE DEFINITION OF INCOME AS A PROBLEM OF FISCAL POLICY (1938).
17 *See* I.R.C. § 62(a).
18 *See* I.R.C. § 63(a).

19 *See* I.R.C. § 32.
20 *See* I.R.C. § 21.
21 *See* I.R.C. § 25A.
22 *See, e.g.*, TAXPAYER ADVOC. SERV., *I Can't Pay My Taxes* (Dec. 1, 2022), https://www.taxpayeradvocate.irs.gov/get-help/paying-taxes/cant-pay-my-taxes.
23 For example, a lower-income taxpayer may receive a large taxable payment from settling a lawsuit. *See* I.R.C. § 104(a) (flush language) (providing that emotional distress does not constitute a physical injury, such that damages for emotional distress may be subject to tax).
24 *See* Chapter 10.
25 *See id.*
26 I.R.C. § 6501. For more discussion, see Chapter 8, section "The Ticking Tax Clock."
27 *See, e.g.*, Ari Glogower, *Taxing Inequality*, 93 N.Y.U. L. REV. 1421, 1467–83 (2018) (describing how wealth and income can be incorporated into a combined tax base measuring relative economic spending power); David Shakow & Reed Shuldiner, *A Comprehensive Wealth Tax*, 53 TAX L. REV. 499 (2000).
28 *See* IRS, IRM 4.25.12 VALUATION ASSISTANCE (Apr. 21, 2023), https://www.irs.gov/irm/part4/irm_04-025-012 (describing asset valuation challenges).
29 *See, e.g.*, Michael Cohn, *Whitney Houston's Estate Strikes $2M Tax Deal with IRS*, ACCT. TODAY (Jan. 5, 2018), https://www.accountingtoday.com/news/whitney-houstons-estate-strikes-2m-tax-settlement-with-irs (describing a valuation dispute between the IRS and the estate of Whitney Houston); Kelly Phillips Erb, *Michael Jackson's Estate to IRS: Beat It*, FORBES (Aug. 21, 2013), https://www.forbes.com/sites/kellyphillipserb/2013/08/21/michael-jacksons-estate-to-irs-beat-it (describing a valuation dispute between the IRS and the estate of Michael Jackson); *see also* Mitchell M. Gans et al., *The Estate Tax Fundamentals of Celebrity and Control*, 118 YALE L.J. POCKET PART 50 (2008).
30 *See, e.g.*, Press Release, Elizabeth Warren, Senator (D-MA), Senator Warren Unveils Proposal to Tax Wealth of Ultra-Rich Americans (Jan. 24, 2019). For a discussion of possible constitutional constraints on a federal wealth tax, and why a court could find it to be constitutional, see generally Ari Glogower, *A Constitutional Wealth Tax*, 118 MICH. L. REV. 717 (2020).
31 *See* Chapter 10, section "Reform Proposal: An Annual Net Asset Statement."
32 *See* Chapter 1, section "Why the Distribution of Noncompliance Matters."
33 *See* JOINT COMM. ON TAX'N, REPORT TO THE HOUSE COMMITTEE ON WAYS AND MEANS TO CHAIRMAN RICHARD NEAL (2022).
34 Ben Steverman, *Inside the IRS's Shrinking Band of Wealth Hunters*, BLOOMBERG (Apr. 12, 2023), https://www.bloomberg.com/news/features/2023-04-12/irs-funding-bill-will-add-agents-but-won-t-fix-all-problems.
35 *See* Debra Cassens Weiss, *Nearly $1,000 an Hour Is Rate for Second-Year Associates at These BigLaw Firms*, ABAJOURNAL (Apr. 3, 2023), https://www.abajournal.com/news/article/nearly-1000-an-hour-is-rate-for-second-year-associate-at-these-biglaw-firms.
36 *See, e.g.*, *How Much Does a Tax Attorney Cost*, CROSS L. GRP. (Jan. 16, 2017), https://www.crosslawgroup.com/blog/hiring-tax-attorney-worth-cost; *What Is the Average Cost of Hiring a Tax Attorney?*, SUPERMONEY (Oct. 31, 2022), https://www.supermoney.com/what-average-cost-hiring-tax-attorney.

37 See IRS, *SOI Tax Stats – Individual Income Tax Rates and Tax Shares* (Nov. 3, 2022), https://www.irs.gov/statistics/soi-tax-stats-individual-income-tax-rates-and-tax-shares.
38 IRS, *Number of Returns, Shares of AGI, Selected Income Items, Credits, Total Income Tax, AGI Floor on Percentiles, and Average Tax Rates, Tax Year 2020*, https://www.irs.gov/statistics/soi-tax-stats-individual-income-tax-rates-and-tax-shares (Apr. 21, 2023).
39 *See, e.g.*, I.R.C. § 6662(a) (20% of accuracy-related underpayments); § 6663(a) (75% of fraud-related underpayments).
40 Richard H. Fallon Jr., *Legitimacy and the Constitution*, 118 HARV. L. REV. 1787, 1795 (2005); *see also* JAMES O. FREEDMAN, CRISIS AND LEGITIMACY: THE ADMINISTRATIVE PROCESS AND AMERICAN GOVERNMENT 10–11 (1978); Michael L. Wells, "Sociological Legitimacy" in Supreme Court Opinions, 64 WASH. & LEE L. REV. 1011, 1017–22 (2007).
41 *See* Fallon, *supra* note 40.
42 *See, e.g.*, Karyl A. Kinsey, *Deterrence and Alienation Effects of IRS Enforcement: An Analysis of Survey Data*, *in* WHY PEOPLE PAY TAXES: TAX COMPLIANCE AND ENFORCEMENT 259, 259 (Joel Slemrod ed., 1992); John T. Scholz & Mark Lubell, *Trust and Taxpaying: Testing the Heuristic Approach to Collective Action*, 42 AM. J. POL. SCI. 398, 408 (1998).
43 *See* Darryl K. Brown, *Criminal Law's Unfortunate Triumph over Administrative Law*, 7 J.L. ECON. & POL'Y 657, 668 (2011).
44 *See, e.g.*, Marc A. Thiessen, *How Obama's IRS Scandal Harms National Security*, WASH. POST (Aug. 5, 2013), https://www.washingtonpost.com/opinions/marc-thiessen-how-obamas-irs-scandal-harms-national-security/2013/08/05/9fea9616-fde1-11e2-96a8-d3b921c0924a_story.html.
45 *See* Fred Stokeld, *IRS Sparks Outrage with Admission It Mistreated Tea Party Groups*, TAX NOTES TODAY FED. (May 13, 2013), https://www.taxnotes.com/tax-notes-today-federal/exempt-organizations/irs-sparks-outrage-admission-it-mistreated-tea-party-groups/2013/05/13/f319?highlight=Fred%20Stokeld%2C%20IRS%20Sparks%20Outrage%20with%20Admission%20It%20Mistreated%20Tea%20Party%20Groups%2C%20TAX%20NOTES%20TODAY%20May%2013%2C%202013%20.
46 *See* TREASURY INSPECTOR GEN. FOR TAX ADMIN., INAPPROPRIATE CRITERIA WERE USED TO IDENTIFY TAX-EXEMPT APPLICATIONS FOR REVIEW 3 (2013).
47 *See, e.g.*, Molly Wharton, *Issa to IRS Commissioner: 'You Have a Problem Maintaining Credibility'*, NAT'L. REV. (June 24, 2014), https://www.nationalreview.com/corner/issa-irs-commissioner-you-have-problem-maintaining-credibility-molly-wharton (quoting Rep. Darrell Issa); Thiessen, *supra* note 44.
48 *See* TREASURY INSPECTOR GEN. FOR TAX ADMIN., REVIEW OF SELECTED CRITERIA USED TO IDENTIFY TAX-EXEMPT APPLICATIONS FOR REVIEW (2017); Press Release, US Treasury Inspector General for Tax Administration, Agency Statement on Audit Report: "Review of Selected Criteria Used to Identify Tax-Exempt Applications for Review" (Oct. 5, 2017), https://www.tigta.gov/articles/press-releases/agency-statement-audit-report-review-selected-criteria-used-identify-tax.
49 *Just 31% Trust the IRS*, RASMUSSEN REPS. (Mar. 27, 2015), http://www.rasmussenreports.com/public_content/business/taxes/march_2015/just_31_trust_the_irs.

50 *The Daily Show* (Comedy Central broadcast July 22, 2015), https://www.youtube.com/watch?v=L88H2HWEXrw (interviewing President Barack Obama).
51 Editorial Board, *The IRS Makes a Strange House Call on Matt Taibbi*, WALL ST. J. (Mar. 27, 2023), https://www.wsj.com/articles/irs-matt-taibbi-twitter-files-jim-jordan-daniel-werfel-lina-khan-84ee518.
52 For a general overview of dispute procedures, see I.R.C. §§ 6213 (procedures for Tax Court litigation), 7422 (procedures for civil actions for tax refund).
53 *See, e.g.*, Compaq Comput. Corp. v. Comm'r, 277 F.3d 778, 780, 788 (5th Cir. 2001) (overturning a Tax Court judgment that penalized the taxpayer for violating § 6662 through deficiencies and accuracy-related negligence); IES Industries, Inc. v. United States, 253 F.3d 350, 351, 356 (8th Cir. 2001) (reversing in part a lower-court judgment against the taxpayer asserting a sham transaction); UPS of Am., Inc. v. Comm'r, 254 F.3d 1014, 1017, 1020 (11th Cir. 2001) (reversing a tax court decision and finding economic substance in the challenged transaction).
54 *See* PAUL S. RUNDQUIST, CONG. RSCH. SERV., "SENSE OF" RESOLUTIONS AND PROVISIONS (2019).

6

Tax Penalties

Many high-end taxpayers engage in sophisticated tax-avoidance and evasion strategies because the potential adverse consequences from pursuing them are often much lower than their potential tax benefits. Compared to the typical taxpayer, whose income consists of wages and interest subject to third-party information reporting, high-end taxpayers can often avoid or evade tax liabilities by using strategies that are more difficult for the IRS to detect.[1] As Chapter 1 explained, these strategies include the use of tax haven entities, closely held corporations, pass-through entities such as partnerships and subchapter S corporations, in-kind wealth transfers, and cryptocurrency, among many others.[2] Given the obstacles that the IRS faces in detecting and challenging these strategies, current tax penalties are too low to deter high-end taxpayers under either the expected value model or the expected utility model.

This chapter addresses the weaknesses of tax penalties in current law as deterrents of high-end tax noncompliance and describes how Congress could introduce tax penalties that vary depending upon taxpayers' means. The chapter begins with a discussion of the possible motivations for individual tax compliance, including potential adverse consequences of noncompliance and, specifically, civil tax penalties. It then considers why current civil tax penalties often fail to deter high-end tax noncompliance. Finally, the chapter presents means-adjusted tax penalties as a new approach to the design of civil tax penalties, illustrates this approach with several examples, and addresses additional concerns.

TAX PENALTIES AND DETERRENCE

Why do most individuals comply with the tax law, while some do not? There is no single answer to this question. As Chapter 2 describes, individual taxpayers are motivated to comply with the tax law for a variety of reasons.[3] The most common explanation is that many individual taxpayers are subject to third-party information reporting and withholding.[4] However, as we will discuss in Chapter 9, this explanation is far less persuasive in the case of many high-end taxpayers. Aside from information reporting and withholding, some of the most prominent explanations of motivations of tax compliance include the expected costs of tax noncompliance,[5] including monetary and non-monetary penalties; the belief that because others are complying with the tax law, they should reciprocate and comply as well;[6] concerns regarding the negative signal of tax noncompliance;[7] and the view that it is a civic duty to pay one's taxes.[8] Scholars have also argued that cognitive biases, such as the availability bias, can also influence individuals' tax compliance.[9] Policymakers can also encourage tax morale, or the intrinsic motivation of taxes, by fostering perceptions of fairness in the design and administration of the tax system.

Many taxpayers are certainly motivated by the expected monetary returns associated with tax compliance or noncompliance. Under a simple expected return model of tax compliance, a taxpayer will comply with the tax law where the taxpayer's expected after-tax outcome from complying exceeds the expected financial outcome that would result from not complying.[10] The expected outcome includes the possibility that the tax authority will detect and challenge the taxpayer's position, and that the taxpayer will be forced to pay not only the unpaid tax liability but also a tax penalty and interest. The consequences of not complying, in turn, depend upon both the chance that the taxing authority will detect the tax noncompliance, as well as the magnitude of the potential tax penalty.[11] That is, in this simple model, the taxpayer will comply when $I - T > p(I - T - F) + (1 - p)(I)$, where (I) is the taxpayer's pretax income, (T) is the potential tax liability the taxpayer is considering whether to avoid through noncompliance, (p) is the probability that noncompliance will be detected, and (F) is the amount of the additional fine if the noncompliance is detected.

For example, imagine an individual taxpayer, Ethan, who is only concerned with the financial outcome when determining whether to comply with the tax law or not. Let us assume that Ethan has $2,000 of pretax income and is taxed on this income at a rate of 20%, resulting in a $400 tax liability.[12] If Ethan complies with the tax law, Ethan will have $1,600 of after-tax income ($2,000 pretax income minus $400 tax liability). However, if the chance that the IRS detects noncompliance and successfully imposes a penalty is 10% and the penalty rate is 50% of the tax underpayment, the expected value of tax noncompliance would be $1,940 (this can be calculated as follows: 0.1(2,000 − 400 − 200) + 0.9(2,000)). In Ethan's case, the expected outcome from not complying with the tax law exceeds the expected outcome from complying ($1,940 is greater than $1,600). This simple example illustrates that a combination of high penalty rates and a significant chance of detection would be necessary to induce compliance for a taxpayer making the decision on this basis alone.[13]

This basic model of tax compliance mirrors the "Becker-Bentham fine" model introduced in Chapter 2. Under this model, the deterrent effect of any legal sanction depends on the chance of detection and the size of the sanction if (1) the offense is detected and (2) the sanction is, in fact, imposed.[14] For reasons explained in Chapter 4, nontax legal offenses present a different situation than tax noncompliance: In principle, the deterrent effect from sanctions and the detection rate would be set to preserve only efficient offenses, where the benefit to the offender exceeds the social costs resulting from the activity.[15] In the case of tax noncompliance, however, any degree of noncompliance can instead be understood to result in a net revenue loss.[16]

However, improving tax compliance through deterrence and enforcement can also impose additional costs on both the government and taxpayers. These costs may include additional administrative burdens on the government, as well as a variety of possible costs imposed on taxpayers, including the costs of compliance, behavioral changes, or even the psychic costs from enforcement and penalties.[17] As a result, adjustments to tax penalties (as well as other tax compliance rules) may not be desirable, if such rules would impose costs on the government and taxpayers that would outweigh the social benefit that would result from raising additional revenue and narrowing the tax gap.[18] Further, at a certain point, policymakers may be able to raise more revenue from high-end taxpayers – at a lower social cost – by increasing rates in the substantive tax law rather than through increased enforcement and administration.[19]

Scholars have also described extensions of the basic model of taxpayer compliance. One extension would account for taxpayers' risk aversion by evaluating the expected utility from compliance or noncompliance, rather than the expected dollar return. In this case, under an assumption of declining marginal utility of income, a taxpayer may experience utility loss from monetary losses and less corresponding utility gains from additional income. Adjusting the formula described earlier to reflect expected utility rather than the expected dollar return, the taxpayer will comply when $U(I - T) > pU(I - T - F) + (1 - p)U(I)$, where $U(x)$ represents the taxpayer's utility function.[20]

Consider again the same example we described earlier involving Ethan. A common assumption in the literature would represent Ethan's utility function as the natural log of Ethan's income.[21] In this case, Ethan's expected utility from compliance would be approximately 6.68[22] and the expected utility from noncompliance would be approximately 6.87.[23] The effect of risk aversion in the expected utility model would generally induce taxpayers to comply at lower penalty and detection rates than under the simple expected value model. This example also illustrates, however, that the detection and penalty rates would still need to be significant to effectively deter noncompliance under the expected utility model. If making a decision on this basis alone, Ethan would still not comply, notwithstanding the fact that risk aversion would lead Ethan to value potential losses more heavily than potential gains of equal value.

Some scholars argue that the basic model does not accurately predict levels of taxpayer compliance, and that taxpayers do not necessarily make compliance decisions based on the penalty rate and chance of detection.[24] Economists Joel Slemrod and Christian Gillitzer observe, however, that this "dismissive" approach to the basic model understates the "varying rates of the chance of detection" in the model.[25] They argue that, once chances of detection are taken into account, levels of compliance for different forms of income are "absolutely consistent with the deterrent model."[26] This important insight highlights the critical role of IRS detection as an ex ante deterrent against tax noncompliance, and not just as an ex post method of collecting unpaid taxes.

As Chapter 2 discussed, this expected return model only offers a partial explanation for why taxpayers may comply with tax obligations.[27] For this reason, policymakers must account for the complex and varied motivations for tax compliance in their efforts to narrow the tax gap. To do this, policymakers must look beyond the prescriptions of the expected return model alone, while also designing sufficient deterrents to reduce the potential rewards from tax noncompliance.

WHY TAX PENALTIES FAIL TO DETER THE RICH

Despite the potential consequences, many high-end taxpayers continue to pursue abusive tax-avoidance and evasion strategies. For these taxpayers, the threat of the civil tax penalties appears to be too weak to deter many forms of tax noncompliance. This section reviews the structure of federal tax penalties under current law, considers reasons why they appear to under-deter high-end tax noncompliance, and describes some of the tax penalty reforms that have been proposed in the literature.

Tax Penalties in Current Law

Two of the main factors in tax noncompliance are "underreporting" and "underpayment." Most of the current gross tax gap (an estimated $496 billion according to the IRS's most recent tax gap study for the years 2014–2016) is attributable to taxpayers failing to report their full tax liability on a timely filed return (an estimated $398 billion of the gross tax gap).[28] This type of tax noncompliance is described as "underreporting," which is typically the primary focus of tax scholars and policymakers. In other cases, taxpayers fail to pay their tax even though there is an established tax liability. "Underpayment" – or "tax delinquency" – represents a substantial portion of the annual federal gross tax gap (an estimated $59 billion).[29] For these noncompliant taxpayers, there is no dispute that they owe a certain amount of tax liability; they just do not pay. Additionally, every year, hundreds of thousands of taxpayers, owing an estimated $39 billion in federal taxes in the aggregate, simply fail to file federal tax returns at all.[30]

Tax penalties play a central role in the tax compliance system as prominent tools for discouraging tax noncompliance. Tax penalties promote voluntary compliance with the tax law in two ways: (1) by deterring noncompliant taxpayers, and (2) by bolstering confidence in compliant taxpayers that the government punishes tax abuse. For example, civil penalties for failing to report or pay taxes reduce the expected benefit from noncompliance. In most cases, governments turn to civil tax penalties, which require taxpayers to pay additional money to the taxing authority, as a way to prevent and reduce tax noncompliance. Governments also threaten to subject taxpayers to criminal tax penalties in the case of tax fraud, but they rarely impose extreme penalties such as imprisonment on noncompliant taxpayers.

At the federal level, the Internal Revenue Code contains over 100 separate civil monetary tax penalties.[31] These penalties can be grouped into several categories: failure to file and failure to pay penalties; estimated tax penalties; the failure to deposit penalty; return-related penalties; preparer, promoter, and material advisor penalties; information return penalties; exempt organization penalties; international tax penalties; excise tax and estate and gift tax penalties; penalties applicable to incorrect appraisals; and reportable transaction penalties.[32] Some of these penalties are imposed as fixed amounts, while others are calculated as a percentage of the applicable tax liability.

For one example of a "percentage-based" penalty, taxpayers who do not pay their taxes on time are subject to a delinquency penalty of up to 25% of their tax liability.[33] Accuracy-related tax penalties, similarly, require individuals who underpay their taxes through particular types of misconduct – such as negligence or disregard of rules and regulations – to pay an additional tax penalty equal to 20% of the underpayment of tax liability.[34] And civil fraud penalties, which apply when taxpayers intentionally underpay their taxes, apply an additional penalty equal to 75% of the underpayment of tax liability.[35] At the federal level, percentage-based tax penalties are those that the IRS applies most frequently.[36]

The alternative form of monetary tax penalties that appears regularly in the tax law are "fixed-amount" tax penalties, which specify a single dollar amount that all taxpayers must pay for every occurrence of a specified offense. Individuals are subject to fixed-amount tax penalties, for instance, when they file frivolous tax returns[37] or false statements regarding tax withholdings.[38] For example, the federal tax law includes fixed-amount tax penalties such as $50,000 for every instance of failing to file a return or submit required information relating to "reportable transactions";[39] $1 per day for each day that a taxpayer fails to file a notification of change of status of a pension plan;[40] and $500 for every instance of providing a false statement regarding tax withholdings.[41] These fixed-amount penalties reflect the basic logic that, in some cases, certain actions should be discouraged regardless of the amount of the tax underpayments that result from them.

Underdeterrence at the Top

Even when the IRS can detect noncompliance by high-income taxpayers, it may not be able to recover the applicable tax liabilities and penalties due. These taxpayers have greater resources to spend on sophisticated tax advisors and representation in disputes with the IRS, as well as in negotiations and appeals,[42] and these procedural advantages reduce the amount of taxes and penalties that the IRS ultimately recovers as a result of enforcement actions against them.[43]

Recent reports illustrate the uphill battle that the IRS faces when attempting to audit and challenge the tax positions of high-income taxpayers. In 2018, *ProPublica* interviewed over fifty current and former IRS employees and issued a series of reports describing the agency's attempts to increase enforcement of the tax laws against the ultra-wealthy.[44] As the report details, the IRS's Wealth Squad, discussed earlier in Chapter 1, reduced the scale of its audits following lobbying by targeted taxpayers.[45] According to one report, the IRS only audited twelve to eighteen wealthy taxpayers in the group's first year.[46] Even in this limited number of audits, the Treasury Inspector General for Tax Administration (TIGTA) found that in over 40% of the cases, the IRS did not assess any additional tax liability.[47] A subsequent report by TIGTA found that the IRS's audits of wealthy taxpayers had become less comprehensive and that, in several cases, the IRS allowed their delinquent outstanding tax liabilities to expire.[48] As Richard Schickel, a former IRS agent, commented in 2019, "this is a great time for not being compliant with paying taxes."[49] Despite the IRS's 2023 pledge that it will use a portion of the increased IRA funding to address high-end tax noncompliance in particular, the agency will encounter ongoing challenges in its efforts to close the tax gap at the top.

Publicly available data shows that IRS rarely enforces some of the most significant civil tax penalties. Each year, the IRS publishes its annual *Data Book*, which includes statistics related to many aspects of the tax compliance rules, such as the number of individual and business tax returns filed, among many other items. In the IRS *Data Book* that presented the results of fiscal year 2021, the IRS stated that it assessed approximately 33.4 million separate civil tax penalties against individual taxpayers.[50] Within this figure, however, the IRS only assessed the tax penalties that most directly address underreporting, which the IRS describes broadly as "accuracy" penalties, approximately 788,000 times – which is about 2.3% of the total number of assessed individual civil tax penalties in that year.[51] These penalties, according to the IRS *Data Book*, represent penalties for: negligence; substantial understatements of income tax; substantial valuation misstatements; substantial understatements of pension liabilities; substantial estate or gift tax valuation understatements; understatements of reportable transactions; and underpayment of stamp tax.[52] Further, the IRS stated that in 2021, it only assessed the civil fraud penalty, which imposes a penalty equal to 75% of the underpayment of tax, 1,296 times – or about 0.003% of the total number of assessed civil tax penalties.[53]

While the IRS does not publish the distribution of the assessed tax penalties among taxpayers based upon their income, there are several features of current civil tax penalties that cause them to fail to deter high-end taxpayers from engaging in abusive tax avoidance and tax evasion.

First, because of the relatively low probability that the IRS will successfully detect noncompliance and impose the penalties, the dollar values of current civil tax penalties under current law are far too low to be effective deterrents for many high-end taxpayers. Under the basic model of tax compliance, rational taxpayers consider the probability that they will face IRS audit and challenge when deciding whether to claim a questionable tax position.

For the fiscal year 2022, the IRS audited only 0.38% of all individual income tax returns, and only 2.38% of all tax returns of individual taxpayers with an income of $1 million or more.[54] A low chance of audit by the IRS, of course, also reduces the chance that the IRS will apply a civil tax penalty. Therefore, this low audit rate for high-end taxpayers, which has dropped to historic lows in recent years,[55] causes current civil tax penalties, by themselves, to be weak deterrents against tax noncompliance for high-end taxpayers who adhere to the basic model of tax compliance. Further, these monetary tax penalties are typically set at relatively low rates, and, except in cases of specific highly publicized threats, Congress has rarely raised them.[56]

Second, many of the penalties depend on subjective, rather than objective, factors, which means that high-end taxpayers often have greater advantages when it comes to avoiding them. For example, to assess the 20% accuracy-related tax penalty for underpayments of tax attributable to negligence, the IRS must show that the taxpayer failed to make a "reasonable" attempt to comply with the tax law.[57] For another accuracy-related penalty example, the tax penalty for disregard of rules and regulations, which is also 20%, requires the IRS to show that a taxpayer acted with "careless, reckless, or intentional disregard" of tax rules and regulations.[58] And the 75% fraud tax penalty requires the IRS to prove, by clear and convincing evidence, that a taxpayer intentionally attempted to defraud the government.[59]

In each of these examples, high-end taxpayers can plan ahead to avoid tax penalties in many ways, such as by hiring lawyers and accountants who may suggest plausible statutory and regulatory support for their tax positions. As described in Chapter 1, these taxpayers can often take the best advantage of sophisticated tax structuring and legal counsel to exploit ambiguities in the tax law. For these reasons, high-end taxpayers are often better situated to produce evidence that prevents the IRS from establishing the subjective, intent-based elements of many civil tax penalties.

Third, many of the statutes and regulations regarding current civil tax penalties allow taxpayers to apply formal defenses in order to prevent the IRS from applying these penalties. For example, taxpayers who have access to sophisticated tax advisors can take advantage of the "reasonable cause" defense to certain penalties by obtaining written tax advice from these advisors prior to claiming tax positions.[60] As described in greater detail in Chapter 7, high-end taxpayers are also more likely than others to derive the greatest benefit from these defenses, which in turn can reduce their chances of paying additional tax liability and tax penalties, even if the IRS does detect potential tax noncompliance.

Unequal Deterrent Effects

In many cases, generally applicable penalties, which apply the same to all taxpayers, can have a lower deterrent effect for high-end taxpayers. This section describes the unequal deterrent effects of both fixed-amount penalties and fixed-percentage penalties.

To start, consider the case of a fixed-amount penalty, which will generally have a lower deterrent effect for high-income taxpayers who face a larger expected tax savings from noncompliance. This effect can be compounded in an expected utility model, where a rational taxpayer would account for the expected utility they will derive from complying and not complying, rather than simply the expected monetary outcome of their decision.[61]

In general, penalties have a modestly higher deterrent effect in an expected utility model than they do in an expected monetary outcome model. This is because a taxpayer with declining marginal utility experiences lesser utility gains from an additional dollar of income, as compared to the utility loss they would experience from losing the same dollar amount of income.

This deterrent effect from risk aversion can have less effect, however, for taxpayers at the top of the income distribution, depending on the shape of the assumed utility curve.[62] Under the assumption of declining marginal utility of income, a taxpayer with lower income will experience steep utility losses as their income declines, whereas a higher-income taxpayer will not experience the same utility loss from a commensurate decline in their income.[63]

To illustrate the unequal deterrent effects of a fixed-amount penalty for taxpayers at different points on the income distribution, assume an individual taxpayer, Sophia, has $1,000 of income, and another individual taxpayer, Charlotte, has $100,000 of income. Also assume that each underreports 10% of their incomes, each of their utility curves is represented by the natural log of income, each faces a fixed-amount $250 penalty if the noncompliance is detected, and the chance that the IRS successfully detects the noncompliance and imposes the penalty is 40%. Also assume again that under the applicable rate schedule, the first $1,000 of income is taxed at a 20% rate, and any additional income is taxed at a 40% rate.

In this case, Sophia would have greater expected utility from compliance than from noncompliance.[64] Charlotte, in contrast, would still have a greater expected utility from noncompliance than from compliance, when facing the same penalty amount and chances of detection as Sophia faces.[65] This different outcome results from two effects: (1) the fact that the fixed-amount penalty represents a proportionally smaller amount as compared to Charlotte's potential savings from noncompliance, and (2) the fact that Charlotte is at a higher location on the utility curve than Sophia, and therefore experiences a lower disincentive effect from risk aversion for local changes in income. In this case, a significantly higher fixed-amount penalty would be necessary to equalize the deterrent effect of the penalty between the two taxpayers.

The analysis changes slightly for percentage-based tax penalties that depend on the amount of the tax underpayment, such as the accuracy and fraud penalties under the current law. Of course, a percentage-based penalty applied to a taxpayer's underpayment can already impose a higher burden on higher-income taxpayers in the presence of a progressive rate schedule. For illustration, assume again that Sophia and Charlotte underreport the same proportion of their actual incomes, and assume a simplified progressive tax schedule that taxes the first $1,000 of income at a 20% rate and additional income at a 40% rate. Also assume that they both face the same 20% accuracy-related penalty for underreporting of income.[66]

Assume that Sophia – with $1,000 of pretax income and a potential $200 tax liability – underreports income by $100, or 10% of total pretax income, resulting in a $20 tax underpayment.[67] If Sophia is caught and subject to an accuracy-related tax penalty, Sophia will pay an additional $4 penalty,[68] which is 0.4% of total income.

Now assume Charlotte has $100,000 of pretax income and underreports $10,000 (also 10%) of income, for a tax underpayment of $4,000.[69] If Charlotte is caught and subject to an accuracy-related penalty, Charlotte will pay an additional $800 penalty,[70] which is 0.8% of total income. Both in absolute dollar terms and when measured as a percentage of each taxpayer's total income, the higher-income taxpayer Charlotte would pay a penalty that is twice the amount paid by the lower-income taxpayer Sophia.

Notwithstanding the higher proportional penalty for a higher-income taxpayer, a fixed-percentage penalty can still have a reduced deterrent effect for taxpayers at the top. Most critically, as described in Chapter 2, the design of tax compliance rules such as penalties should not be assessed ex post in the case where they end up being applied (as in the example in the preceding paragraph), but ex ante, with respect to their effect in deterring noncompliance in the first place.[71]

From an ex ante perspective, the deterrent effect of penalty rates for lower- and higher-income taxpayers will depend on the interaction of the varying rates and income levels in the progressive rate schedule, and on changes in taxpayers' risk aversion at these varying levels. Professors Joel Slemrod and Shlomo Yitzhaki observe that, in principle, higher tax rates – such as in a progressive rate schedule – can increase the deterrent effect of underpayment-based penalties.[72] Other scholars have also observed that although "an increase in the tax rate has a theoretically ambiguous effect in most models ... both experimental, as well as econometric, research consistently finds that higher tax rates are associated with greater evasion."[73]

In the case of all civil tax penalties, whether fixed-amount or percentage-based, means adjustments for higher-end taxpayers would also be justified in the basic model to the extent that the other variable in the model – the chance of detection and enforcement – is lower for high-end taxpayers. The chance of detection will depend on a range of factors, including the nature of the taxpayer's income and income-generating activities. As we have discussed, however, many high-end taxpayers can take advantage of sophisticated tax-avoidance strategies that reduce their chance of detection that are not available to lower-income taxpayers.

The penalty deterrence model would not only take account of the chance of detection, but also the chance that the IRS would succeed in enforcing a penalty even if the noncompliance is detected. High-end taxpayers have more resources and procedural advantages that can allow them to avoid or reduce the imposition of penalties in a subsequent dispute with the IRS, even if the agency does successfully detect the noncompliance.[74] For example, consider again Sophia with $1,000 of pretax income and Charlotte with $100,000 in pretax income, facing the same fixed-amount or underpayment base penalty. In each case, if Charlotte has a lower risk that the IRS will detect the noncompliance and enforce the penalty (as compared to Sophia's risk), then a higher penalty would be required for Charlotte to achieve the same deterrent effect between the two taxpayers.

PRIOR REFORM PROPOSALS

Scholars and policymakers have proposed a variety of reforms to the rules governing civil tax penalties to enable these rules to serve a more effective role in encouraging tax compliance. Prior works in the literature have recognized that higher penalties could more effectively deter noncompliance,[75] but also that the rates of both penalties and noncompliance detection would need to be significantly higher than under current law and practice in order to realize this benefit.

As an alternative to simply increasing penalty rates, Professor Alex Raskolnikov has proposed a "self-adjusting" tax penalty, where taxpayers who report an illegitimate deduction on the same line on the tax return as a legitimate deduction would be subject to a tax penalty that is based not on the amount of the illegitimate deduction item, but instead on the amount of the legitimate deduction item.[76] The objective of this proposal is to increase the expected cost of noncompliance for taxpayers who attempt to avoid tax liability by concealing abusive tax positions from the IRS.[77] Similarly, Professor Kyle Logue has offered another extrapolation of the Bentham-Becker fine by proposing strict liability tax penalties equal to the taxpayer's underpaid tax divided by the probability that the IRS would detect the taxpayer's noncompliance ex ante.[78]

Other tax scholars have offered additional proposals for increasing or reforming civil tax penalties.[79] As discussed earlier, the IRS publishes limited information regarding its assessment of civil tax penalties against any specific groups of taxpayers, including high-end taxpayers. As an alternative to adjusting the magnitude of monetary tax penalties themselves, scholars such as Professor Eric Zolt have argued that Congress should subject its enactment of tax penalties to the same type of IRS statistical reporting procedures that apply to tax expenditures, in order to ensure that tax penalties do not have undesirable effects on taxpayer behavior.[80] Under this type of proposal, the IRS would be required to increase the specificity of its published aggregate tax enforcement statistics.

Consider several examples from the 2021 IRS *Data Book*. While the IRS reports that it assessed 788,243 "accuracy penalties,"[81] it could distill this figure into the multiple tax penalties that the IRS considers to fall under this broad category, such as tax penalties for negligence, substantial understatement of income tax, substantial valuation misstatements, substantial overstatement of pension liabilities, and understatement of reportable transactions, among others. It could also provide more granular information regarding the economic, and other characteristics of taxpayers subject to these penalties.

These proposals have expanded debate and understanding among tax scholars and economists, but they have not been implemented by the federal or state governments.[82] Despite the potential appeal of these proposals under different models of compliance, legislators face political economy and other constraints in implementing the steep penalty increases necessary to effectively discourage non-compliance by all taxpayers. Professor Michael Doran argues that it is unlikely that sufficiently large penalties would "be acceptable on political ... grounds[,]" and that significantly increasing audit rates and enforcement would face similar resistance to what could be viewed as "government intrusiveness."[83] Professor Joel Slemrod similarly cautions that "the harsher the penalty, the more damage a corrupt administrator could inflict and, in the case of an honest mistake, the more capricious the system."[84] He also cautions that "with harsher penalties, courts may be more reluctant to find the taxpayer guilty of evasion, so that one practical consequence may be fewer penalties imposed."[85]

REDESIGNING CIVIL TAX PENALTIES

Under current law, civil tax penalties apply at the same rate to everyone, even though wealthy taxpayers can often engage in transactions that are harder for the IRS to detect and challenge. In order to equalize the effect of tax penalties for taxpayers in different economic circumstances, Congress could instead adjust these general tax penalties depending on a taxpayer's means, such as income and wealth. In the following section, we illustrate how Congress could introduce means-adjusted tax penalties, describe advantages of this penalty model over current law, address potential objections and responses, and discuss how policymakers can coordinate the use of means-adjusted tax penalties with other sanctions.

Incorporating Means Adjustments

Let us begin by reviewing how civil tax penalties apply under current law. Consider a hypothetical private equity fund manager, Oliver, who reported $11 million of income for the 2023 tax year on Oliver's federal tax return. Imagine that the IRS audited Oliver's 2023 tax return and determined that Oliver's $2 million deduction for "consulting fees" did not qualify as ordinary and necessary business expenses. Further, because the fees related to personal financial matters, imagine that the IRS determined that Oliver failed to make a reasonable attempt to comply with the law and, as a result, was subject to an accuracy-related civil tax penalty due to negligence.[86] If the illegitimate $2 million business expense deduction allows Oliver to underpay 2023 federal income tax by $740,000,[87] Oliver owes, in addition to the amount of tax that was not paid, a civil tax penalty of 20% of the underpayment, or $148,000.[88] The rate of this civil tax penalty, 20%, is the same rate that would apply to any taxpayer whom the IRS determined had underpaid tax due to negligence.

Congress could instead introduce civil tax percentage-based penalties that are means-adjusted and would vary based on the taxpayer's income or wealth. For a simple illustration, instead of the 20% civil tax penalty on underpayments for negligence and other acts specified in the applicable tax provision,[89] Congress could revise this statute to provide that:

- taxpayers with adjusted gross income below $2 million would still incur accuracy-related tax penalties at a rate of 20% of the underpayment;
- taxpayers with adjusted gross income of $2 million or more, but below $5 million, would incur these penalties at a rate of 30%; and
- taxpayers with adjusted gross income of $5 million or more would incur these penalties at a rate of 40%.

Returning to the example earlier, under this new penalty structure, Oliver would pay a 40% tax penalty, $296,000, rather than the 20% penalty of $148,000.[90]

Similarly, Congress could enact means-adjusted civil tax penalties that would apply when taxpayers' aggregate net assets reach certain thresholds, such as $10 million. This alternative wealth-based threshold could be implemented in connection with our wealth-reporting reform proposal, which is discussed in Chapter 10.

Congress could also increase fixed-amount tax penalties based on a taxpayer's adjusted gross income or net assets. For example, under current law, all individuals who fail to file a reportable transaction form,[91] a form that may alert the IRS to potential tax-shelter activity, are required to pay a fixed-amount tax penalty of $10,000 for each occurrence. Congress could revise this tax penalty so that taxpayers with an adjusted gross income of $2 million or more, or who hold assets with an aggregate value of $10 million or more, could be subject to a $50,000 tax penalty, rather than the current $10,000 penalty, for each failure to file a reportable transaction form. Similarly, for taxpayers who meet the same adjusted gross income or net asset threshold, Congress could increase the tax penalty for filing a frivolous tax return[92] from $5,000 to $25,000.

In this way, means adjustments could preserve the advantages of fixed-amount penalties while avoiding their undesirable effects. Means-adjusted fixed-amount penalties could still serve the role of deterring noncompliance activities, regardless of their resulting underpayments, without having a reduced deterrent effect for high-end taxpayers.

Choosing the Penalties for Adjustment. Which types of tax penalties should policymakers adjust for high-end taxpayers? There are many types of sanctions for tax noncompliance under current law. These include the types of federal civil tax penalties that we have described, such as the accuracy-related tax penalties.[93] There are many other federal civil tax penalties that may apply, such as those levied when taxpayers engage in transactions that lack economic substance, or when they fail to file tax returns and pay tax on time.[94] Beyond federal civil tax penalties, the Internal Revenue Code also provides for criminal tax penalties, such as those that apply when taxpayers attempt to evade tax, which can result in monetary sanctions and prison sentences of varying length.[95] These types of civil and criminal sanctions for tax noncompliance also may apply at the state level.

We do not propose that policymakers should apply means adjustments to all possible tax penalties. Instead, they should focus on those penalties where (1) the expected cost of the tax penalty is too low to deter high-end taxpayers from engaging in noncompliance, and (2) this low expected cost tends to correlate with the income or wealth of the taxpayer.

For example, means adjustments could improve the effect of the accuracy-related tax penalties for underpayments that are attributable to negligence, disregard of rules and regulations, and substantial understatements. When high-end taxpayers pursue tax-avoidance strategies, such as tax shelters, these strategies are harder for the IRS to detect than more basic forms of tax avoidance and evasion, such as underreporting of wage income. The sophistication and complexity of tax-avoidance strategies pursued by many high-end taxpayers limit the ability of the IRS to detect these tax positions and assert accuracy-related tax penalties. Further, if the IRS detects the transactions, high-end taxpayers may avoid application of the tax penalties by engaging sophisticated legal counsel, and potentially relying on tax advice to assert a reasonable cause defense. In Chapter 7, we address the unique advantages that the reasonable cause defense provides to high-end taxpayers in penalty disputes with the IRS. In all these cases, means adjustments to the applicable penalties can counteract their reduced deterrent effect for high-end taxpayers.

Low-Value Underpayment Exception. To prevent the possibility of excessive scrutiny of small items on high-end taxpayers' returns, Congress could incorporate into its means-adjusted tax penalties exemptions for low-dollar value underpayments. For instance, in the means-adjusted tax penalty that applies to Oliver in our example earlier, Congress could include an exemption for taxpayers who have an aggregate underpayment of less than $50,000 for the year. The law already uses this amount as the threshold for a low-value underpayment in other contexts.[96] This exemption could apply for both percentage-based and fixed-amount tax penalties.

The examples we describe in this chapter are not exhaustive. Congress could apply means adjustments to any or all of the dozens of civil tax penalties under current law.⁹⁷ Further, if policymakers prefer to implement a more tailored application of means adjustments, they could refine the simple examples presented in this chapter by introducing graduated fixed-amount or percentage-based penalty schedules, similar to the schedule that applies to the calculation of tax liability for dividends and net capital gains under the current law.⁹⁸

Interaction with Activity-Based Rules. Rather than focusing solely on a specific activity, these means-adjusted calculations of civil tax penalties would apply to all high-end taxpayers with underpayments above the threshold amount. As we have shown, current law frequently deploys an activity-based approach to tax enforcement by increasing the tax penalty for certain types of tax-shelter transactions and other tax offenses. For instance, the civil tax penalty rules include tax-shelter penalties that apply when taxpayers participate in an abusive tax strategy that is designated as a "listed transaction" or "reportable transaction"⁹⁹ or fail to file a required reportable transaction form.¹⁰⁰

With these means adjustments, high-end taxpayers would still be subject to increased tax penalties¹⁰¹ even if they were able to circumvent tax-shelter tax penalties, such as the reportable transaction¹⁰² or nondisclosed listed transaction penalties.¹⁰³ However, if desired, policymakers could apply means adjustments to *both* the activity and the taxpayer by introducing even greater increases to the tax-shelter penalties for high-end taxpayers. For example, in the case of high-end taxpayers, Congress could increase the nondisclosed noneconomic substance transaction penalty from 40% to 50%.¹⁰⁴

Advantages

Carefully designed means adjustments to the civil tax penalties could help to equalize their effect for taxpayers at different income levels, and counteract high-end taxpayers' greater opportunities to avoid detection and enforcement. Means-adjusted civil tax penalties would serve to counterbalance the IRS's resource challenges that hinder its ability to detect tax noncompliance by high-end taxpayers, which has declined over the last decade due to significant budget reductions and the complexity of the tax positions of high-end taxpayers.¹⁰⁵

Through means adjustments to civil tax penalties, Congress could signal to all high-end taxpayers that their costs of tax noncompliance have increased. Means-adjusted civil tax penalties could also bolster tax morale among all taxpayers by providing salient signals that the government is treating high-end taxpayers differently when necessary to deter tax noncompliance. Under current law, there are subtle variances between the treatment of high-income and low-income taxpayers, such as how the IRS views an individual's education and professional background when determining whether to allow the reasonable cause defense to civil tax penalties. For example, the Treasury Regulations state that a taxpayer's reasonable cause defense must be evaluated in light of the taxpayer's "experience, knowledge, and education."[106] These exceptions are not generally apparent to the public and are easily overshadowed by vivid news reports of the IRS's meager tax enforcement against the richest taxpayers, such as *ProPublica's* 2018 exposé on this topic.[107] Means-adjusted civil tax penalties, on the other hand, would allow the government to make its renewed focus on high-end taxpayers both prominent and explicit. Such a change in the structure of tax penalties could enhance taxpayers' confidence in the government's ability to enforce the tax law effectively by deterring those with the greatest resources and access to sophisticated advisors from avoiding and evading their tax liabilities.

Additional Considerations

Unfair Targeting. One possible concern with a means-adjusted penalty structure is that it could create too much of an incentive for the IRS to audit high-end taxpayers compared to others, which may allow tax noncompliance by middle- and low-income taxpayers to flourish. Under the example of means-adjusted tax penalties we described earlier in this chapter, an IRS agent could assess a 30% or even 40% accuracy tax penalty by auditing and challenging the tax positions of a high-end taxpayer, compared to a 20% accuracy tax penalty for all other taxpayers. The higher penalty percentages would also likely apply to larger underpayment amounts than those that appear on the tax returns of other individual taxpayers, resulting in greater payments of tax penalties to the IRS.

While means adjustments to the civil tax penalty rules could induce some shift in IRS focus away from lower-income noncompliance, it is not likely the IRS would dramatically shift its resource allocations. The IRS assigns its agents to different audit units based on the complexity of the returns.[108] Revenue agents, the most experienced IRS examiners, are assigned to examine complex tax returns of high-end taxpayers, which often involve partnerships and other pass-through entities, offshore transactions, and cryptocurrency.[109] Revenue agents undergo rigorous training and must have several years of work experience before they are assigned to review these returns.[110] Further, if high-end taxpayers or their advisors perceive that the IRS may increase scrutiny of their tax positions in order to collect additional revenue, this perception (even if inaccurate) would only serve to increase deterrence of high-end tax noncompliance. More generally, these means adjustments would not be designed to unduly burden a subset of taxpayers, but rather to advance the IRS's stated goal of administering the tax law equally and consistently for all taxpayers.

Resource Constraints. Another possible concern is that even if the IRS wanted to focus and apply these penalties, it lacks the resources to review the tax positions and strategies of high-end taxpayers. Penalty reforms alone cannot narrow the tax gap without robust IRS enforcement. For instance, as the Joint Committee on Taxation's investigation of the IRS audits of President Donald Trump's tax returns illustrated,[111] IRS agents are often overwhelmed by the complexity of the tax returns of high-end taxpayers, which can involve tiers of partnerships and other entities owned directly and indirectly by these individuals. Historically, the IRS has lacked the enforcement resources to investigate high-end taxpayers, electing instead to pursue correspondence examinations involving relatively simple deficiencies, such as reported income that does not match information reports.[112] Without being able to identify the potential abuse underlying certain tax positions of high-end taxpayers, it would be difficult for the IRS to assert means-adjusted tax penalties.

One response to this concern is that the IRS has recently received funding that will enable it to increase its focus on high-end taxpayers, which can allow the agency to effectively utilize means-adjusted tax compliance rules to narrow the tax gap. In August 2022, President Biden signed the Inflation Reduction Act of 2022, which, among other provisions, allocated an additional $80 billion of funding to the IRS through the end of fiscal year 2031.[113] Under the legislation, the IRS must use $45.6 billion for tax-enforcement activities, which may include hiring additional agents and lawyers.[114]

Following the signing of the legislation, the White House,[115] the Commissioner of Internal Revenue,[116] and the Secretary of the Treasury[117] all issued press releases that stated that the IRS would use this new funding to "go after wealthy tax cheats" rather than middle-class and small business taxpayers. In a specific example of how this would play out, Treasury Secretary Janet Yellen directed the IRS to not use the new funding to "raise audit rates for households making less than $400,000, relative to historical levels."[118] If the IRS is able to follow through on these enforcement promises, then means-adjusted tax penalties may indeed become powerful deterrents against abusive tax planning by high-end taxpayers.

Further, the allocation of increased funding to the IRS, despite the historic allocation from the Inflation Reduction Act, is not enough to prevent high-end tax noncompliance. To deter tax noncompliance by high-end taxpayers, Congress should also provide the IRS with new tax enforcement tools in the form of means-adjusted tax penalties. In this case, means adjustments can complement increased IRS enforcement efforts and enable the agency to use its increased resources more effectively and efficiently.

Constitutionality. Opponents of means-adjusted tax penalties may argue that Congress should reject them on fairness and even constitutional grounds. As discussed earlier, the Constitution's Equal Protection and Due Process Clauses mandate that the law should be generally applicable in certain circumstances. The Equal Protection Clause prohibits laws that discriminate on the basis of certain group classifications without a sufficient justification, while the Due Process Clauses in the Fifth and Fourteenth Amendments also ensure the equal right to basic procedural protections, including notice, the opportunity to be heard, and the right to a neutral decision-maker. Opponents could characterize means-adjusted tax penalties as violating one or both of these constitutional protections because these tax penalties would impose higher penalty rates on high-end taxpayers than others.

There are several responses to this objection. First, according to the Supreme Court's Equal Protection jurisprudence, socioeconomic status, such as that of high-end taxpayers, is not a suspect classification that is subject to heightened constitutional scrutiny.[119] As long as Congress has a rational basis for enacting means-adjusted tax penalties, and they are not only tailored to address specific tax-avoidance opportunities of high-end taxpayers under generally applicable tax compliance rules, but also do not otherwise affect other procedural due process protections, these sanctions would satisfy constitutional requirements. Further, Congress can implement means adjustments that stay well within the bounds of the current penalty rates, which reach up to 40% of an underpayment for certain accuracy-related penalties and 75% in the case of fraud, and still not raise any constitutional problems.

More generally, by introducing means-adjusted tax penalties, Congress could address the inequality that currently exists in the tax system, where high-end taxpayers, in comparison to others, enjoy disproportionate opportunities to engage in tax noncompliance. When wealthy individuals engage in these types of activities, it undermines the progressive tax system and its core distributive function. Rather than unfairly targeting high-end taxpayers, means-adjusted tax penalties would instead serve as a counterbalance to these advantages, and help implement the substantive tax law more evenly and equally.

Limited Agency Authority. A final possible concern is that Treasury and the IRS cannot implement means adjustments to the civil tax penalty rules alone. Treasury can propose and issue regulations that interpret existing tax penalties, subject to the notice-and-comment procedures and other requirements of the Administrative Procedure Act, and the IRS can issue guidance regarding how it will determine whether a particular tax position merits application of a tax penalty. Yet neither possesses the legal authority to make many of the types of changes that we have proposed, which, in the case of tax penalties, would require adjustments to the applicable tax penalty rates.

In response to this concern, we agree that Congress must assume the primary responsibility for introducing means-adjusted tax penalties. One of the motivations underlying this book is our desire to highlight for Congress the reality that it cannot address tax noncompliance by high-end taxpayers effectively through its traditional approaches. By delegating responsibility for tax enforcement against high-end taxpayers to Treasury and the IRS, Congress encourages these agencies to develop rules that target specific activities, such as the use of certain abusive tax-shelter strategies. The implementation of these types of activity-based rules falls within agencies' rulemaking authority. Once Congress enacts means-adjusted tax penalties, Treasury and the IRS can similarly address how these statutes are interpreted and implemented. For instance, following enactment of legislation, Treasury can issue guidance regarding the methods that taxpayers should use to calculate the value of net assets in consideration of the potential means-adjusted tax penalties that would apply on the basis of taxpayers' wealth.

NOTES

1 *See, e.g.*, Press Release, Richard Neal, Chairman, US House Committee on Ways & Means, Neal Opening Statement at Hearing on Understanding the Tax Gap and Taxpayer Noncompliance (May 9, 2019), https://neal.house.gov/news/documentsingle.aspx?DocumentID=1614 ("[H]igh-income taxpayers have the most opportunity to engage in tax avoidance planning."). For a discussion, see also Chapter 1, section "How the Rich Avoid Taxes."
2 *See,* for instance, the strategies described in David Kamin et al., *The Games They Will Play: Tax Games, Roadblocks, and Glitches under the 2017 Tax Legislation*, 103 MINN. L. REV. 1439, 1451–52 (2019).
3 *See* Chapter 2, section "Factors in Tax Compliance."
4 IRC §§ 6041–6050Y (Information Concerning Transactions with Other Persons). *See* IRS, PUB. 1415 (REV. 9-2019), FEDERAL TAX COMPLIANCE RESEARCH: TAX GAP ESTIMATES FOR TAX YEARS 2011–2013 3 (2019).
5 *See, e.g.*, Gary S. Becker, *Crime and Punishment: An Economic Approach*, 76 J. POL. ECON. 169, 209 (1968); Alex Raskolnikov, *Crime and Punishment in Taxation: Deceit, Deterrence, and the Self-Adjusting Penalty*, 106 COLUM. L. REV. 569, 571 (2006).
6 *See* Ernst Fehr & Simon Gächter, *Reciprocity and Economics: The Economic Implications of Homo Reciprocans*, 42 EUR. ECON. REV. 845, 845–46 (1998); Dan M. Kahan, *The Logic of Reciprocity: Trust, Collective Action, and Law*, 102 MICH. L. REV. 71, 71 (2003).
7 *See* Eric A. Posner, *Law and Social Norms: The Case of Tax Compliance*, 86 VA. L. REV. 1781, 1789 (2000) (applying signaling model to tax compliance).
8 *See, e.g.*, John T. Scholz, *Contractual Compliance and the Federal Income Tax System*, 13 WASH. U. J.L. & POL'Y 139, 189 (2003) (describing the empirical support for the duty of citizenship model of tax compliance).
9 *See, e.g.*, Joshua D. Blank, *In Defense of Individual Tax Privacy*, 61 EMORY L.J. 265, 287–322 (2011) (exploring how various cognitive biases affect taxpayer decisions); Edward J. McCaffery, *Cognitive Theory and Tax*, 41 UCLA L. REV. 1861, 1876 (1994); Deborah H. Schenk, *Exploiting the Salience Bias in Designing Taxes*, 28 YALE J. REGUL. 253, 261–63 (2011).
10 *See* Sarah B. Lawsky, *Modeling Uncertainty in Tax Law*, 65 STAN. L. REV. 241, 249–53 (2013) (detailing a general model of tax-evasion factoring in audit probabilities).
11 *Id.* at 249–50.
12 Assume, for this example, that Ethan's income would be taxed at a 20% rate.
13 *See* Lawsky, *supra* note 10, at 252. Taxpayers may decide to comply for other reasons that are not reflected in this simple model. *See id.* For a discussion of other explanations of why taxpayers may comply with the tax law, see *supra* notes 3–9 and accompanying text.
14 *See* JEREMY BENTHAM, THE THEORY OF LEGISLATION 325 (C. K. Ogden ed., Richard Hildreth trans., Routledge & Kegan Paul Ltd. 1931) (1802) (proposing that the "evil of the punishment must be made to exceed the advantage of the offence"); Becker, *supra* note 5;

see also A. MITCHELL POLINSKY, AN INTRODUCTION TO LAW AND ECONOMICS 79–90 (4th ed. 2011) (providing a broad analysis of optimal deterrence and fines). In this case, policymakers can minimize administrative costs by increasing the sanction rather than the chance of detection, since the latter requires additional government spending and the former does not.
15 See POLINSKY, *supra* note 14, at 80.
16 Alex Raskolnikov, *Accepting the Limits of Tax Law and Economics*, 98 CORNELL L. REV. 523, 531–36 (2013); *see also id.* at 536 ("[T]he basic law and economics approach ... is well suited for activities that are socially desirable at some level.... The optimal response to taxation is no response."). Raskolnikov argues that the case of tax noncompliance may be more appropriately analogized to the case of nonconsensual transfers or theft, which results in a gain to one party and a loss to the other, plus socially wasteful transfer costs. *Id.* at 534. This framework assumes, critically, that the substantive tax rules (and all the compliance rules they entail) in fact represent the socially desirable or optimal tax system. *Id.* at 574–75 ("If corporate tax is not part of the optimal tax system ... the optimal taxpayer response to corporate tax is to evade it."). For a discussion, see also Chapter 4, section "Revisiting the Double Distortion Principle."
17 See Joel Slemrod & Shlomo Yitzhaki, *The Costs of Taxation and the Marginal Efficiency Cost of Funds*, 43 STAFF PAPERS (INT'L MONETARY FUND) 172, 173 (1996).
18 See Michael Keen & Joel Slemrod, *Optimal Tax Administration*, 152 J. PUB. ECON. 133, 134 (2017).
19 *See id.* at 133 (posing a basic choice for policymakers, of whether it is better "to raise an additional dollar of revenue by increasing statutory tax rates or by strengthening tax administration so as to improve compliance").
20 See Lawsky, *supra* note 10, at 254–57.
21 *See id.* at 255 ("[A] taxpayer's utility function is often taken to be the natural log of the taxpayer's income, probably because natural log is an easy function to work with and represents a person who has declining marginal utility, a popular assumption.").
22 $\ln(1{,}000 - 200)$.
23 $0.1 \ln(1{,}000 - 200 - 100) + 0.9 \ln(1{,}000)$.
24 See Lars P. Feld & Bruno S. Frey, *Trust Breeds Trust: How Taxpayers Are Treated*, 3 ECON. GOVERNANCE 87, 88 (2002) (arguing that "expected punishment is rarely statistically significant and, if it is, the effect is of quite a small magnitude").
25 JOEL SLEMROD & CHRISTIAN GILLITZER, TAX SYSTEMS 43 (2013); *see also* Joel Slemrod, *Cheating Ourselves: The Economics of Tax Evasion*, 21 J. ECON. PERSP. 25, 39 (2007) ("[T]he low average audit coverage rate vastly understates the chances that the average dollar of unreported net income would be detected.").
26 SLEMROD & GILLITZER, *supra* note 25, at 43.
27 Slemrod and Gillitzer argue that these other taxpayer motivations should be understood as additional factors in compliance, rather than as alternatives to the basic model. *Id.*
28 IRS, PUB. 1415 (REV. 10-2022), FEDERAL TAX COMPLIANCE RESEARCH: TAX GAP ESTIMATES FOR TAX YEARS 2014–2016, at 8, fig. 1 (2022).
29 *Id.*
30 *Id.*
31 *See generally* I.R.C. §§ 6651–6702.

32 See id.
33 See I.R.C. § 6651 (delinquency penalties).
34 See I.R.C. § 6662 (accuracy-related penalties).
35 See I.R.C. § 6663 (civil fraud penalties).
36 See IRS, PUB. 55-B (REV. 5-2022), 2021 DATA BOOK 60, tbl. 26 (2021), https://www.irs.gov/pub/irs-prior/p55b–2022.pdf.).
37 I.R.C. § 6702(a) ($5,000 penalty).
38 I.R.C. § 6682 ($500 penalty).
39 I.R.C. § 6707A.
40 I.R.C. § 6652(d)(2).
41 I.R.C. § 6682.
42 See Raskolnikov, *supra* note 5, at 581 ("The probability of punishment is a cumulative probability: that an offense will be detected; that it will be selected for prosecution; that the government will prevail at trial on the substantive issue, decide to seek a penalty and convince a court to impose it; that the judgments favoring the government will survive appeals; and, finally, that the government will actually collect the penalty from a taxpayer."). For a discussion, see Chapter 1, section "How the Rich Avoid Taxes."
43 See Michael Doran, *Tax Penalties and Tax Compliance*, 46 HARV. J. LEGIS. 111, 157 (2009) (describing the insufficient standards for legal advisors in fostering taxpayer compliance).
44 See, e.g., Jesse Eisinger & Paul Kiel, *Gutting the IRS: The IRS Tried to Take on the Ultrawealthy. It Didn't Go Well*, PROPUBLICA (Apr. 5, 2019), https://www.propublica.org/article/ultrawealthy-taxes-irs-internal-revenue-service-global-high-wealth-audits.
45 Id.
46 See *Few Millionaires Audited by IRS Global High Wealth Group*, TRANSACTIONAL RECORDS ACCESS CLEARINGHOUSE (Apr. 10, 2012), https://trac.syr.edu/tracirs/newfindings/v17.
47 TREASURY INSPECTOR GEN. FOR TAX ADMIN., REP. NO. 2015-30-078, IMPROVEMENTS ARE NEEDED IN RESOURCE ALLOCATION AND MANAGEMENT CONTROLS FOR AUDITS OF HIGH-INCOME TAXPAYERS, at 15 (2015), https://www.tigta.gov/sites/default/files/reports/2022-02/201530078fr.pdf.
48 See TREASURY INSPECTOR GEN. FOR TAX ADMIN., REP. NO. 2017-30-069, PRIORITIZATION OF COLLECTION CASES IS INCONSISTENT AND SYSTEMATIC ENFORCEMENT ACTIONS ARE LIMITED FOR INACTIVE CASES, at 7, 19 (2017), https://www.tigta.gov/sites/default/files/reports/2022-02/201730069fr.pdf.
49 Paul Kiel et al., *The Golden Age of Rich People Not Paying Their Taxes*, ATLANTIC (Dec. 11, 2018), https://www.theatlantic.com/politics/archive/2018/12/rich-people-are-getting-away-not-paying-their-taxes/577798.
50 See IRS, *supra* note 36.
51 Id.
52 Id. at 61 n. 4.
53 See id. at 60, tbl. 26 .
54 See *IRS Audits Few Millionaires but Targeted Many Low-Income Families in FY 2022*, TRANSACTIONAL RECORDS ACCESS CLEARINGHOUSE (Jan. 4, 2023), https://trac.syr.edu/reports/706/.

55 *See id.; see also* Richard Rubin, *IRS Audit Rate Drops Again as It Examines Fewer High-Income Households*, WALL ST. J. (May 20, 2019), https://www.wsj.com/articles/irs-audit-rate-drops-again-as-it-examines-fewer-high-income-households-11558363990. Rachel Sandler, *Why Are the Superrich Getting Audited Less?*, FORBES (May 21, 2019), https://www.forbes.com/sites/rachelsandler/2019/05/21/why-are-the-super-rich-getting-audited-less/?sh=3089505b57d7.
56 *See generally* 1 JOINT COMM. ON TAXATION, JCS-3-99, STUDY OF PRESENT-LAW PENALTY AND INTEREST PROVISIONS AS REQUIRED BY SECTION 3801 OF THE INTERNAL REVENUE SERVICE RESTRUCTURING AND REFORM ACT OF 1998 37 (1999).
57 I.R.C. § 6662(c).
58 *Id.*
59 *See* I.R.C. § 7454; DiLeo v. Comm'r, 96 T.C. 858, 873 (1991); US Tax Court Rule 142(b).
60 I.R.C. § 6664(c).
61 As described in Chapter 1, the basic model likely provides only a partial explanation for why taxpayers comply with tax obligations.
62 *See* Joel Slemrod & Shlomo Yitzhaki, *Tax Avoidance, Evasion, and Administration*, in 3 HANDBOOK OF PUBLIC ECONOMICS 1423, 1431 (Alan J. Auerbach & Martin Feldstein eds., 2002) ("Regardless of whether the penalty depends on the tax understatement or income understatement, more risk-averse individuals will, *ceteris paribus*, evade less. Individuals with higher income will evade more as long as absolute risk aversion is decreasing; whether higher-income individuals will evade more, as a fraction of income, depends on relative risk aversion.").
63 *See* HARVEY S. ROSEN & TED GAYER, PUBLIC FINANCE 179–80 (10th ed. 2014).
64 Sophia would have an expected after-tax return of $800 from compliance, for an expected utility of approximately 6.68. Sophia would have an expected utility of only approximately 6.67 from noncompliance, calculated as 0.4 ln(1,000 − 200 − 250) + 0.6 ln(1,000).
65 Charlotte would have an expected after-tax return of $60,200 from compliance, for an expected utility of approximately 11. Charlotte would have an expected utility of approximately 11.31 from noncompliance, calculated as 0.4 ln(100,000 − 39,800 − 250) + 0.6 ln (1,000).
66 *Cf.* I.R.C. § 6662(a) (applying a penalty equal to 20% of the portion of the underpayment to which the section applies).
67 The $100 of income underreported that would have been taxed at a 20% rate.
68 20% of the $20 underpayment.
69 The $10,000 of income underreported that would have been taxed at a 40% rate, since Charlotte is in the higher 40% tax bracket.
70 20% of the $4,000 underpayment.
71 *See* Chapter 2, section "The Function of Tax Compliance Rules."
72 *See* Slemrod & Yitzhaki, *supra* note 17, at 1430 ("This is an important change, because it means that the tax rate has no effect on the terms of the tax evasion gamble; as t rises, the reward from a successful understatement of a dollar rises, but the cost of a detected understatement rises proportionally.").
73 Feld & Frey, *supra* note 24, at 88; *see also* Fabrizio Balassone & Philip Jones, *Tax Evasion and Tax Rate: Properties of a Penalty Structure*, 26 PUB. FIN. REV. 270, 274 (1998).
74 *See* Chapter 1, section "How the Rich Avoid Taxes."

75 See, e.g., Lawsky, *supra* note 10, at 248–56 (describing models of how penalties could deter taxpayers from underpaying taxes and the potential limitations of more modest penalties in achieving this desired deterrence effect).
76 See Raskolnikov, *supra* note 5, at 599–605.
77 See *id.*
78 Kyle D. Logue, *Tax Law Uncertainty and the Role of Tax Insurance*, 25 VA. TAX REV. 339, 351–52 (2005).
79 See, e.g., Michael Asimow, *Civil Penalties for Inaccurate and Delinquent Tax Returns*, 23 UCLA L. REV. 637 (1976) (arguing for the adoption of the Administrative Conference of the United States' proposals in Recommendation 75–77); William A. Drennan, *Strict Liability and Tax Penalties*, 62 OKLA. L. REV. 1 (2009) (proposing a strict-liability penalty system); Mark P. Gergen, *Uncertainty and Tax Enforcement: A Case for Moderate Fault-Based Penalties*, 64 TAX L. REV. 453 (2011) (proposing a fault-based penalty); Jay A. Soled, *Third-Party Civil Tax Penalties and Professional Standards*, 2004 WIS. L. REV. 1611 (2004) (proposing reforms for professional standards and third-party civil tax penalties); Eric M. Zolt, *Deterrence via Taxation: A Critical Analysis of Tax Penalty Provisions*, 37 UCLA L. REV. 343 (1989) (arguing that Congress should only enact new tax penalties when it can demonstrate the advantages of such penalty provisions over direct sanctions).
80 Zolt, *supra* note 79.
81 See IRS, *supra* note 36.
82 See Raskolnikov, *supra* note 16, at 573–80 (discussing "[t]he disconnect between the optimal tax theory and the actual tax system").
83 See Doran, *supra* note 43, at 130.
84 Slemrod, *supra* note 25, at 43 (2007).
85 *Id.*
86 I.R.C. § 6662(b)(1).
87 This assumes the $2 million deduction offsets taxable income taxed at a rate of 37%. I.R.C. § 1(j)(2)(C).
88 0.2 * $740,000 = $148,000.
89 I.R.C. § 6662(b) (imposing a penalty for negligence, substantial understatement of income tax, and other acts).
90 0.4 * $740,000 = $296,000.
91 I.R.C. § 6707A(b)(2)(B).
92 I.R.C. § 6702(a).
93 See I.R.C. § 6662 (accuracy-related penalties).
94 See generally I.R.C. §§ 6651–6702.
95 See generally I.R.C. §§ 7201–7217.
96 See, e.g., I.R.C. § 7345 (passport revocation for tax delinquencies above $50,000, among other conditions); § 7463 (codifying separate dispute procedures involving delinquencies not exceeding $50,000).
97 See generally I.R.C. §§ 6651–6702.
98 I.R.C. § 1(h)(1), (11) (tax rates on net capital gain and qualified dividend income).
99 I.R.C. § 6662A(a) (20% tax penalty).
100 I.R.C. § 6707A(b)(2)(B) (additional $10,000 tax penalty).

101 For example, they would be subject to a 30% penalty instead of 20% penalty in the case of accuracy-related penalties, as described in the example earlier in this chapter.
102 I.R.C. § 6662A(a).
103 I.R.C. § 6707A(b)(2)(B).
104 I.R.C. § 6662(i)(1).
105 *See* Eisinger & Kiel, *supra* note 44; Taxpayer Advoc. Serv., Special Report to Congress: Earned Income Tax Credit: Making the EITC Work for Taxpayers and the Government 9 n.37 (2019) (describing $2 billion IRS budget decline, in inflation-adjusted dollars, from 2010 to 2018).
106 Treas. Reg. § 1.6664-4(b)(1).
107 Eisinger & Kiel, *supra* note 44.
108 Letter from Charles P. Rettig, IRS Comm'r, to Sen. Ron Wyden (D-OR) 2 (Sept. 6, 2019), https://www.documentcloud.org/documents/6430680-Document-2019-9-6-Treasury-Letter-to-Wyden-RE.html IRS, IRM 4.1.1 Planning, Monitoring, and Coordination (Sept. 25, 2020), https://www.irs.gov/irm/part4/irm_04-001-001 (instructing IRS employees about the factors the agency considers in assigning staff).
109 *See* Rettig IRS Letter, *supra* note 108, at 2.
110 *See id.*
111 Joint Comm. on Tax'n, Report to the House Committee on Ways and Means Chairman Richard Neal (2022).
112 *See id.* at 4.
113 Inflation Reduction Act of 2022, H.R. 5376, 117th Congress, Pub. L. No. 117-169, 136 Stat. 1818 (2022).
114 *See id.*
115 The White House, *Fact Sheet: The Inflation Reduction Act Supports Workers and Families* (Aug. 19, 2022) ("The Inflation Reduction Act will make our tax code fairer by cracking down on millionaires, billionaires, and corporations that evade their obligations.").
116 Charles Rettig, *Rettig Praises Signing of the Inflation Reduction Act*, Tax Notes (2022) ("A Message from Chuck Rettig IRS Commissioner").
117 Wally Adeyemo, Deputy Secretary of the Treasury, *Taxpayers Will See Improved Service This Filing Season Thanks to Inflation Reduction Act* (Jan. 23, 2023), https://home.treasury.gov/news/featured-stories/taxpayers-will-see-improved-service-this-filing-season-thanks-to-inflation-reduction-act.
118 *Id.*
119 *See* United States v. Carolene Prods. Co., 304 U.S. 144, 152 n. 4 (1938); *see also* Kenji Yoshino, *The New Equal Protection*, 124 Harv. L. Rev. 747, 755–63 (2011).

7

Tax Advice

The problems with the civil tax penalties described in Chapter 6 – low chances of detection, low tax penalty rates, and subjective legal requirements – are not the only reasons why these tax penalties often fail to deter high-end tax noncompliance. At first glance, many tax penalties appear to apply whenever taxpayers engage in certain types of behaviors, such as underpaying taxes due to negligence or by disregarding rules and regulations.

However, taxpayers can avoid the application of many common civil tax penalties by asserting formal defenses that are provided by tax statutes and regulations. Especially when potential penalties involve subjective factors, such as reasonableness or nontax business purpose, high-end taxpayers can hire lawyers who can argue that statutory and regulatory exceptions should prevent the IRS from asserting these penalties. For example, the "reasonable cause and good faith" defense requires taxpayers to establish that they acted reasonably in attempting to assess their proper tax liability.[1] Under current law, sophisticated taxpayers can often prepare ahead of time to satisfy this subjective standard by obtaining a written tax opinion from an advisor before pursuing an aggressive tax strategy.[2]

The option of using written tax advice to avoid the application of certain civil tax penalties disproportionately benefits high-end taxpayers, who have the economic resources necessary to pay for sophisticated tax advice regarding complex transactions. As described later in this chapter, Congress has limited the penalty defense for certain types of transactions to prevent taxpayers from using this kind of advice when they engage in certain abusive activities. However, high-end taxpayers can often avoid engaging in these specific tax-avoidance activities.[3] As a result, they may continue to use written tax advice to assert tax penalty defenses in many other cases.

This chapter addresses the role of tax advice in encouraging aggressive and abusive tax planning by high-end taxpayers. It begins with a discussion of the different roles of tax advice, one of which is its use as a form of tax penalty insurance. The chapter then shows how the rich can benefit disproportionately from the ability to avoid penalties through tax advice. After describing these effects, we offer a proposal for incorporating means adjustments into the tax-penalty-defense rules, focusing specifically on tax advice, and we respond to potential objections and concerns.

TAX ADVICE AS TAX PENALTY INSURANCE

Taxpayers seek tax advice for different reasons. Some may seek it because they need guidance regarding ambiguous applicable law. Others seek a written tax opinion from an advisor to satisfy a contractual condition, such as the requirement of another party to a merger transaction or a loan. Finally, in some cases, taxpayers rely on tax opinions as a form of tax penalty insurance.

This section reviews some of the common motivations of taxpayers for seeking tax advice, explains how it can enable a taxpayer to defend against some of the most common civil tax penalties, and highlights the limitations of the current requirements governing it.

Motivations for Seeking Tax Advice

Tax advice can occur in a variety of forms. A tax lawyer or accountant may provide a taxpayer with oral advice regarding the tax consequences of a transaction in an in-person meeting or a telephone conversation. Tax advisors may also provide tax advice through more informal means, such as email. And in situations involving complex tax planning, especially when there is a high amount of tax at stake, tax lawyers often provide clients with a formal written tax opinion. What are some of the primary motivations of taxpayers to seek advice from tax advisors?

Legal Analysis. Taxpayers often request tax advice from lawyers and accountants because they want to understand the likely tax treatment and potential legal ambiguities of a transaction before they pursue it. Especially when a transaction involves complicated or newly enacted tax statutes and regulations, taxpayers may want to make sure that they understand the possible tax treatment and potential tax risks before agreeing to participate in the transaction.

For example, shortly after the enactment of the Tax Cuts and Jobs Act of 2017, one law firm announced to potential clients:

> Why are tax opinions especially relevant today? Recent changes in the tax laws have left taxpayers and return preparers grappling with challenging tax planning and return position issues. In particular, we are seeing business owners and investors struggling with the intricacies of IRC § 199A's 20% deduction for qualified business income, the functioning of IRC § 1202's exclusion of income from the sale of qualified small business stock (QSBS), and IRC § 1061's new three year holding period requirement for carried interests.[4]

As Professor Linda Galler has written, "when a client is risk averse or wishes to minimize the risk that a tax return position will be successfully challenged, a thoughtful analysis by the client's tax professional provides reassurance."[5]

Contractual Condition. Taxpayers may also seek tax advice in the form of written tax opinions because the terms of a contract require one before the transaction closes. Contracts involving business transactions that may present significant tax law issues, such as whether a transaction receives taxable or tax-deferred treatment, frequently require a written opinion of legal counsel stating that the transaction should or will qualify for the tax treatment that the parties desire.

For instance, imagine that a wealthy individual is the sole owner of a family business, which is operated through a subchapter C corporation, and that the individual is entertaining an offer to sell all of the individual's stock in the corporation to an acquiror corporation. This individual may demand, as a condition to closing, that the parties obtain a written tax opinion from a law firm that the transaction will qualify as a tax-deferred reorganization under Section 368 of the Internal Revenue Code.[6] A similar situation would be the case of individuals who desire to swap two valuable parcels of real estate and desire to treat the transaction as a tax-deferred like-kind exchange under IRC Section 1031.[7]

As some commentators have noted, parties may also include tax opinion conditions in contracts in order to create options for delaying, or even exiting, agreements before the closing.[8]

Tax Penalty Insurance. When taxpayers engage in more aggressive tax strategies with uncertain legal consequences, they may also seek a written tax opinion to protect themselves from the imposition of certain civil tax penalties. According to one tax practitioner, "[t]he most commonly stated reason to get a tax opinion is to avoid penalties."[9]

This motivation is common when the potential tax penalties involve subjective factors regarding state of mind or nontax-related business purpose. Taxpayers are often successful in avoiding civil tax penalties by informing the IRS that they have obtained a written tax opinion from a law or accounting firm, especially if the opinion expresses a significant degree of confidence that the taxpayer's claimed treatment is correct. In many cases where this has happened, judges have denied IRS efforts to assess civil tax penalties, even when courts have rejected taxpayers' substantive tax positions.[10]

As we will discuss in the following section, an array of statutes and regulations create multiple opportunities for taxpayers to avoid civil tax penalties by obtaining written tax advice from counsel.

Tax Advice as Tax Penalty Defense

If a taxpayer has received tax advice from a tax professional before claiming a tax position, the taxpayer may be able to use the taxpayer's personal reliance upon the tax advice to argue that certain civil tax penalties should not apply.

The law currently adopts an activity-based approach in these rules, restricting taxpayers from relying upon statutory and regulatory defenses, such as the "reasonable cause and good faith" defense, when they have engaged in certain potentially abusive transactions.[11] For example, if a transaction lacks "economic substance" as defined in the Internal Revenue Code, a taxpayer may not assert the defense against accuracy-related tax penalties resulting from that transaction.[12] Similarly, in some cases a taxpayer may not assert the reasonable cause defense for certain tax-shelter penalties if they fail to disclose participation in an abusive tax strategy, such as a listed transaction, to the IRS.[13]

As we described earlier, the accuracy-related tax penalties apply to underpayments attributable to negligence, disregard of rules or regulations, substantial understatements, and other categories of tax avoidance. In the following subsections, we briefly review how taxpayers may use tax advice to defend against each of these tax penalties under the current law.

Negligence. The negligence tax penalty applies where a taxpayer has failed to make a "reasonable attempt to comply" with the tax law.[14] Current law allows all taxpayers to rely on the statutory "reasonable cause and good faith" defense to defend against the application of this tax penalty.[15] Taxpayers can satisfy the reasonable cause standard by showing that they reasonably relied in good faith on advice – whether oral or written – from professional tax advisors regarding the treatment of tax positions.[16]

Rather than focusing solely on the specific tax laws at issue in the tax controversy, this defense allows taxpayers to present information about their personal attributes, including "experience, knowledge, and education," in order to show that the claimed tax position was reasonable.[17] Therefore, in response to a negligence defense, the IRS will apply a facts-and-circumstances analysis, focusing on whether the taxpayer's position was reasonable in light of the taxpayer's personal characteristics and background.[18]

In addition, a taxpayer may obtain tax advice in order to claim a "reasonable basis" defense against the negligence tax penalty.[19] A reasonable basis exists if it is based upon one or more of the specific authorities described in the regulations, such as provisions of the Internal Revenue Code, Treasury Regulations, and tax treaties, among others.[20] Many practitioners have described reasonable basis as a tax position that has at least a 20–30% chance of prevailing.[21]

Under current law, a taxpayer may seek a written tax opinion that explicitly states that there is a "reasonable basis for the conclusion that. . . ." In the event of a subsequent audit by the IRS, the taxpayer can point to the legal authorities described in the written opinion in order to assert this defense. When filing a tax return with the IRS, a taxpayer does not currently need to disclose the taxpayer's belief that there is a reasonable basis for a tax position, or any of the specific sources that support this belief, in order to use this reasoning later to defend against a negligence tax penalty.[22]

Disregard of Rules and Regulations. The disregard of rules and regulation tax penalty applies where a taxpayer has demonstrated "careless, reckless or intentional disregard" of provisions of the Internal Revenue Code and Treasury Regulations.[23] Taxpayers can use tax advice as a defense against this tax penalty in two ways. First, in response to this penalty, taxpayers can offer a "reasonable cause and good faith" defense by showing reasonable reliance on tax advice.[24] Second, taxpayers may seek written tax advice from tax lawyers in order to obtain opinions stating that they had a reasonable basis for claiming the positions.

To avoid this penalty, however, taxpayers must also disclose the specifics of the reasonable basis claim by filing an additional form with the IRS together with their tax return.[25] IRS Form 8275 must be filed if the return position has a reasonable basis (but does not involve a position in conflict with a Treasury Regulation), while IRS Form 8275-R is used for tax positions that are contrary to Treasury Regulations.[26] These forms require taxpayers to include detailed explanations and describe the specific authorities upon which they are relying, although they do not require the taxpayers to submit any written advice.

Unlike the reasonable basis defense that applies to the negligence tax penalty, this rule essentially requires taxpayers to raise a red flag for the IRS that a particular transaction may be questionable.

Substantial Understatements. Under current law, taxpayers are subject to the "substantial understatement" penalty if they understate the gross tax on their returns by the greater of $5,000 or 10% of the gross amount of tax required to be shown for the year.[27] Taxpayers have three options for using tax advice to defend against this penalty.

One option is that taxpayers who are subject to a substantial understatement tax penalty, but who have received tax advice, can show reliance on this tax advice to assert a reasonable cause and good faith defense.[28] A second option is that taxpayers may use tax advice to show the necessary analysis to assert a reasonable basis defense. However, taxpayers may only use this defense against this penalty if they had disclosed the reasonable basis claim, using the appropriate IRS form, when they filed their initial returns.[29]

As a third option, a taxpayer may be able to assert the "substantial authority" defense as the basis of an argument that the substantial understatement tax penalty should not apply.[30] To assert this defense, the taxpayer must show that, on balance, the weight of authorities (of the type specified in the Treasury Regulations) supporting the taxpayer's tax treatment is "substantial" in relation to the authorities that support contrary positions. Many tax practitioners consider a 40–50% chance of prevailing on this argument as sufficient to satisfy this standard.[31]

Unlike the reasonable basis defense in response to a disregard of rules and regulations tax penalty and a substantial understatement tax penalty, taxpayers are not required to disclose to the IRS in advance that they believe their tax positions are supported by substantial authority.[32] In order to prepare for an eventual controversy with the IRS, a taxpayer who plans in advance can seek a written tax opinion that uses the phrase "substantial authority" when reaching its conclusions regarding the taxpayer's actions.[33]

For taxpayers who expect to use written tax advice for tax penalty protection, the words and confidence levels in the written advice matter. Most law firms preface their written tax opinions with a phrase such as "Based on and subject to the foregoing, we are of the opinion that . . ." and then offer their legal conclusions.[34] The tax opinions are generally signed with the name of the law firm rather than any particular individual attorney, which signals to the client that the entire law firm is responsible for the opinion.

The confidence level expressed in the opinion matters as well. An opinion's legal conclusion may range from "not frivolous," which is the weakest confidence level, to "reasonable basis" (20–30%) to "substantial authority" (40–50%) to "more likely than not" (51% or more) to "should" (60–80%) to "will" (95–100%), the highest confidence level.[35] The confidence level contained in the written tax opinion may be relevant to the taxpayer's ability to assert one of the specific tax penalty defenses described earlier in this chapter.

In order to assert the reasonable cause defense, the taxpayer only needs to show that the taxpayer reasonably relied upon the advice when claiming a tax position. While some commentators have suggested that reasonable reliance requires a confidence level in the tax opinion of at least a reasonable basis (20–30%),[36] others have stated that taxpayers who show reasonable reliance on a tax opinion "can satisfy the reasonable cause and good faith defense without having any particular level of confidence."[37]

Requirements of Tax Advice

While written tax advice, such as a formal tax opinion, may enable taxpayers to avoid each of the accuracy-related tax penalties, this reliance is conditioned upon several requirements, including having a reasonable basis for factual and legal assumptions, not having a conflict of interest, and having followed the rules outlined in Circular 230.

No Unreasonable Factual or Legal Assumptions. Under the applicable regulations, to qualify for the reasonable cause and good faith defense, the tax advice must consider all pertinent facts and circumstances. It cannot be based on unreasonable factual or legal assumptions, nor can it be based on unreasonable reliance on representations and statements by the taxpayer.[38]

The United States Tax Court, in a 2001 decision, *Neonatology Associates, P.A.*, explained that in order for a taxpayer to use reliance on tax advice to assert the reasonable cause and good faith defense, the taxpayer must show that: (1) the advisor was a competent tax professional; (2) the taxpayer provided necessary and accurate information to the advisor; and (3) the taxpayer actually relied in good faith on the tax advice.[39] In cases where taxpayers have failed to show that they have met these requirements, courts have applied accuracy-related tax penalties, despite any professed reliance on tax advice made by the taxpayer.

No Conflicts of Interest. A court may reject a taxpayer's attempt to assert the reasonable cause and good faith defense if the tax advisor who provided the tax advice had a conflict of interest. Further, if a court finds that the tax advisor is also the promoter of the tax-avoidance scheme that is the focus of the tax controversy, then the court may not accept the taxpayer's defense against the tax penalties.

For example, in its 2010 decision in the case of *Stobie Creek Investments LLC v. United States*,[40] which involved the "Son of BOSS" tax shelter,[41] the Federal Circuit Court of Appeals found that the taxpayer's law firm had a conflict of interest arising from its role in "promoting, implementing, and receiving fees from" the tax-shelter strategy.[42] The court held that the taxpayer's reliance on the law firm's advice was not reasonable because of this conflict, about which the taxpayer was aware. Several other courts have similarly rejected taxpayers' reasonable cause defenses in cases where their advisors held financial interests in the promotion of the tax-avoidance strategies at issue.[43]

Circular 230. Finally, tax advisors who practice before the IRS must follow specific rules in providing written tax advice to clients. These rules are contained in Circular 230, discussed earlier in Chapter 2, and apply not only to tax lawyers and accountants but also to any individuals who represent taxpayers before the IRS.[44] Under Circular 230, as revised in 2014, when providing written advice, a practitioner must: (1) base the advice on reasonable factual and legal assumptions; (2) reasonably consider all relevant facts and circumstances; (3) use reasonable efforts to ascertain the facts relevant to written advice on each federal tax matter; (4) not rely upon representations of the taxpayer if reliance on them would be unreasonable; (5) relate applicable law to facts; and (6) not take into account tax audit risk.[45] If a practitioner fails to comply with these rules, the consequences may include censure (a public reprimand), suspension of the privilege to practice before the IRS and, potentially, disbarment.[46]

HOW TAX ADVICE HELPS THE RICH

Tax opinions provided by law and accounting firms have long played a central role in tax planning by high-end taxpayers.[47] In the late 1970s and early 1980s, high-income taxpayers actively sought written tax opinions as a means of avoiding tax penalties in thousands of cases involving tax-shelter strategies.[48] During this time, wealthy business owners, politicians, and high-profile celebrities engaged in tax shelters where a written tax opinion played a pivotal role.

Twenty years later, throughout the corporate tax shelter boom of the late 1990s, corporate taxpayers paid hefty sums for standard form written opinions, many of which included questionable legal conclusions.[49] Professors Marvin Chirelstein and Lawrence Zelenak have described the role of tax opinions in these transactions, concluding that tax-shelter promoters have sought tax opinions from law and accounting firms not only "to immunize the taxpayer from the danger of civil penalties" but also, consequently, to encourage those taxpayers to invest in the strategies.[50]

While these prior eras of mass-marketed tax shelters have subsided,[51] high-end individual taxpayers continue to seek written opinions from professional tax advisors, which present varying levels of confidence, in order to take advantage of the reasonable cause and other tax penalty defenses described earlier in this chapter.[52]

Compared to most people, high-end taxpayers benefit disproportionately from written tax advice. This section discusses some of the major reasons why written tax advice especially helps high-end taxpayers, not only as they engage in aggressive tax planning but also as they prepare for potential tax controversies, including disputes over tax penalties.

Access to Tax Advisors

High-end taxpayers benefit from the economies of scale that enable them to hire sophisticated tax advisors. When a taxpayer has the possibility of a significant tax payment at stake, it can be more cost-effective for them to hire an expensive tax advisor.

People who can afford to hire professional tax advisors can also purchase written tax advice before pursuing any transaction with uncertain tax consequences.[53] Major law firms in legal markets such as New York and Chicago, among others, charge hefty fees to provide clients with written tax opinions for two reasons. First, the firm must conduct the legal research and analysis regarding the taxpayers' proposed transactions in order to provide an opinion that reaches any degree of confidence regarding the proper tax treatment. Second, tax opinions expose the firm to malpractice liability suits if the IRS or state taxing authority disagrees with the firm's analysis. Indeed, malpractice litigation between taxpayers and their professional advisors regarding tax opinions issued during the mass-marketed tax-shelter boom of the early 2000s is still ongoing in 2024, over twenty years later.[54]

Whether the firm charges an hourly rate or a flat fee, the price of written tax advice usually is so expensive that only high-end individual and business taxpayers can pay it. As one commentator has observed, "tax advisors need to charge fees for their services, and rich taxpayers with big tax dollars at stake are more likely than the working class or the poor to purchase tax opinions to provide penalty immunity."[55]

Many of the reforms that the government has enacted regarding written tax advice have indirectly made the advice more expensive. For example, as discussed earlier, Circular 230 requires practitioners to use all reasonable efforts to identify and ascertain facts regarding the taxpayer's transaction, and to reasonably consider all facts and circumstances when providing written tax advice.[56] Tax practitioners who follow these requirements and others that are similar must engage in comprehensive inquiries into their clients' transactions, analyze their clients' motivations through the receipt of written representations, and, often, deliver lengthy written legal analysis. These requirements are designed to halt the type of short-form and superficial tax opinions that some tax practitioners issued during the tax-shelter boom of the early 2000s.[57] At the same time, these requirements also ensure that tax practitioners who follow the rules when providing written tax advice will also have to bill their clients for many hours of services. This means that, while typical taxpayers may be able to seek oral advice from their accountants or, more likely, refer to TurboTax or a government-hosted website, they likely will not be able to afford formal written tax opinions that meet the Circular 230 requirements.

Resource Imbalance Between Taxpayer and IRS

High-end taxpayers also benefit from written tax opinions by using them to prepare in advance for the possibility of a tax controversy with the IRS. Obtaining a written tax opinion from experienced tax advisors before engaging in a transaction or filing a tax return can help the taxpayer feel prepared to respond to the IRS in the event of a challenge. As one practitioner has commented, "[t]ax opinions are of enormous value as a resource for cutting and pasting."[58]

Written tax advice, which contains detailed legal analysis and arguments, can exacerbate the resource imbalance between taxpayers and the IRS. If a high-end taxpayer has consulted with a professional tax advisor, such as a lawyer or accountant, the taxpayer often has an additional advantage in subsequent negotiations with the IRS, and this advice can often help them exploit ambiguities in the tax law, which can allow the taxpayer to engage in more aggressive tax planning.

For example, as the public reports on the IRS's interactions with President Donald Trump reveal, when IRS agents determined that Trump had received tax advice from an accounting firm, the agents concluded that the returns merited only a "limited examination" because "the taxpayer hires a professional accounting firm and counsel to prepare and file his tax returns, and those parties perform the necessary activities to ensure the taxpayer properly reports all income and deduction items correctly."[59] Similarly, according to public reports, in 2016 the IRS claimed that an auto-parts magnate, Georg Schaeffler, owed taxes and tax penalties of approximately $1.2 billion as a result of the restructuring of billions of dollars in debt.[60] In 2019, news reports noted that the IRS ultimately withdrew its tax penalty assertions and accepted a payment of tens of millions rather than the original $1.2 billion deficiency.[61]

Many tax advisors have noted that written tax opinions can provide similar benefits during the early phases of IRS audits. Not only can they enable a taxpayer to provide "a strong rationale for a tax position or a strategy[;]" but they can also, at the very least, convince the IRS to decline to assert accuracy-related tax penalties.[62] Even if the IRS is able to increase its audits of high-end taxpayers as a result of funding provided by the Inflation Reduction Act of 2022, its agents and lawyers will still face these taxpayers' high-priced private sector advisors during subsequent tax controversies.

Subjective Factors

Another feature of the rules regarding tax advice that especially benefits high-end taxpayers is that these rules involve subjective factors. Under current law, taxpayers who can show that they reasonably relied upon tax advice can then claim the reasonable cause and good faith defense as a shield against each of the accuracy-related tax penalties.[63]

In addition to the taxpayer's act of seeking a written tax opinion, several other factors count heavily in the analysis of whether the taxpayer meets the reasonable reliance standard, including the quality of the tax advisor involved, the apparent thoroughness of the tax opinion, and the taxpayer's knowledge of the tax law.[64] For instance, by hiring a law firm to issue a lengthy written tax opinion that analyzes the taxpayer's proposed tax strategy and relies upon taxpayer-provided representations, a high-end taxpayer can quickly show that the advisor was a "competent tax professional" to whom the taxpayer provided all "necessary and accurate information." As long as the taxpayer can show that they reasonably relied upon this opinion in pursuing the transaction or tax position at issue, they can avoid most accuracy-related tax penalties. Further, as we discuss in the following section, the level of confidence expressed in the tax opinion does not necessarily need to be high, or even correct.

Low Chance of Success or Incorrect Analysis

The reasonable cause defense is often possible even in cases where the written tax advice received by these taxpayers does not offer conclusions with high degrees of confidence. Many courts have accepted taxpayers' claims of reasonable reliance upon tax opinions where the opinions have reached, at a minimum, a "reasonable basis" level of confidence.[65] This result has been criticized for allowing high-end taxpayers to "achieve penalty immunity if the taxpayer can find a tax advisor who will say that the position has at least a twenty percent chance."[66] Indeed, if a high-end taxpayer wishes to engage in a highly aggressive or abusive tax strategy, it may even be possible for them to use the reasonable reliance defense when a written tax opinion expresses a level of confidence even lower than 20%.

The reasonable reliance defense does not even require that the legal analysis and conclusions underlying the written tax advice be correct. Instead, under current law, the reasonable cause defense is available as long as a taxpayer can show that they reasonably relied upon the advice in good faith when claiming tax benefits. Each of these features benefits high-end taxpayers in particular because they are typically the only taxpayers who can afford to purchase written tax advice to protect themselves against accuracy-related tax penalties.

Lack of Disclosure

When high-end taxpayers obtain written tax opinions, they are not required to disclose any of the legal analysis in these opinions to the IRS at the time they file their tax returns.

First, the reasonable cause and good faith defense, which applies to all of the accuracy-related tax penalties discussed earlier in this chapter, does not require disclosure of any legal analysis to the IRS. While the exception focuses on the taxpayer's reliance on the opinion, it does not require disclosure to the IRS of the receipt of an opinion. As other tax scholars have noted, the reasonable cause defense that applies to the more general accuracy-related tax penalties is more lenient than other tax penalty defense rules because disclosure of the legal analysis regarding the transaction at issue is not required.[67]

Second, in the case of the negligence tax penalty, a high-end taxpayer may claim a "reasonable basis" defense, meaning that the taxpayer relied on a specific authority in the Internal Revenue Code or Treasury Regulations. However, in this case as well, the taxpayer is not required to disclose to the IRS that reliance, or the specific authority, at the time of filing their tax return.[68]

Further, if a taxpayer receives a tax opinion that finds at least "substantial authority" (40–50% confidence) for the taxpayer's position, the taxpayer may use this conclusion to defend against accuracy-related tax penalties without disclosing the legal analysis to the IRS. As one law firm has informed clients, this type of opinion "substitutes for the need to disclose the position on Schedule 8275," which a taxpayer must file when asserting only a reasonable basis defense (20% confidence) to the accuracy-related tax penalties attributable to disregard of rules and regulations or substantial understatements of income tax.[69]

These rules regarding disclosure also provide advantages to high-end taxpayers. Most significantly, these disclosure rules enable high-end taxpayers to use written tax advice as a shield against tax penalties without requiring them to tip off the IRS regarding questionable transactions or legal analysis. The lack of required disclosure makes it harder for the IRS to determine whether a taxpayer has engaged in a transaction or tax strategy that merits scrutiny. When the IRS does challenge a high-end taxpayer's abusive tax position, the taxpayer can defend against tax penalties by using the act of relying on the tax opinion and, if necessary, the legal analysis contained in the opinion. In the end, the secrecy surrounding written tax opinions further hinders the IRS's ability to detect and deter tax avoidance and abuse by high-end taxpayers.

Type of Transactions

Finally, high-end taxpayers are much more likely than most other individuals to engage in complex transactions and to exploit ambiguities in the tax law. It is in these cases where a written tax opinion would be most helpful. For example, when wealthy taxpayers consider ways to reduce or avoid tax liability, they have a number of options to choose from, including but not limited to transactions involving offshore entities; tax-deferred exchanges of property; pass-through entities, such as partnerships and subchapter S corporations; and conservation easement charitable contributions. In these situations, a written tax opinion may offer several benefits, including providing a means of avoiding tax penalties.

Instead of labor-based wages and salaries, high-end taxpayers are more likely to earn capital and business income, which can often allow for greater structuring flexibility and complexity. Wage and salary earners are typically subject to automatic third-party information reporting and withholding, which further reduces the tax-avoidance opportunities for many lower- and middle-income taxpayers. In this way, the benefits of receiving written tax advice can compound the advantages of earning capital and business income.

Compared to high-end taxpayers who purchase written tax opinions, most individuals who receive informal tax advice cannot rely upon it, as a legal matter, to defend against civil tax penalties or to bind the IRS. For instance, when a low-income taxpayer reviews the IRS website to determine eligibility to claim the EITC, that taxpayer is receiving an informal type of guidance. Even though they are receiving advice from the government, they cannot use that advice to assert certain tax penalty defenses, including the reasonable basis or substantial authority defenses. To compound the problem, some courts have refused to allow taxpayers to assert reasonable cause and good faith penalty defenses when they have relied upon advice from third-party software, such as Intuit's TurboTax, as opposed to that from a law or accounting firm.[70]

These striking contrasts regarding the treatment of written tax opinions issued by law and accounting firms highlight how the tax penalty defenses related to tax advice disproportionately help the rich.

REDESIGNING THE TAX PENALTY DEFENSES

While the current tax penalty defenses involving tax advice provide significant benefits to the rich, policymakers could better tailor these defenses to account for the economic characteristics of the taxpayer. As we have shown, high-end taxpayers can use tax opinions as forms of tax penalty insurance, as long as they ensure that their advisors and the form of advice provided meet the applicable regulatory requirements. Rather than continuing to allow tax opinions to serve this purpose, policymakers should instead reform the tax penalty defenses to eliminate some of their features that provide disproportionate advantages to high-end taxpayers.

Policymakers should seek to accomplish three interrelated objectives when revising the rules related to tax penalty defenses. First, they should revise current law to prevent high-end taxpayers from exploiting subjective factors regarding their state of mind in relying upon written tax advice. Second, they should, instead, increase the focus on the substance of the legal analysis and arguments in written tax advice, rather than on the taxpayer's state of mind. Third, they should find ways to reconfigure internal IRS procedures to ensure that high-end taxpayers who (1) engage in aggressive tax planning and (2) have received tax advice raise red flags at the time they file their tax returns. In the following section, we offer examples of how Congress, the Treasury, and the IRS could implement reform of the tax penalty defenses that achieve these goals.

Incorporating Means Adjustments

The most important step that policymakers could take to remove some of the strategic advantages that tax penalty defenses under current law provide to high-end taxpayers is to reform the reasonable cause and good faith defense. Rather than allowing all taxpayers to show that they acted reasonably and in good faith in claiming tax positions, policymakers could revise current law to prevent taxpayers whose income or wealth exceed specified thresholds from using this defense.

For instance, policymakers could revise the law to provide that in the case of individual taxpayers with adjusted gross incomes of $2 million or more, or aggregate net assets of $10 million or more, the reasonable cause and good faith defense would not be available to prevent the application of accuracy-related tax penalties.[71] Policymakers could adjust these illustrative income and asset thresholds upward or downward, in order to further tailor the effects of the adjustments.

Additionally, policymakers could allow exceptions to this adjustment for taxpayers with low-value underpayments. For example, as in the case of our earlier proposal involving civil tax penalties, there could be an exception to this rule for taxpayers with an aggregate underpayment for the year of less than $50,000. While it is unlikely that the types of transactions where high-end taxpayers seek to avoid tax would involve such low amounts, this exception could counter the possible motivation of IRS agents to challenge low-value tax positions of high-end taxpayers, or to unduly burden minor offenses.

Importantly, these means adjustments would apply only to the reasonable cause and good faith defense. That is, these adjustments would not create a "strict liability" regime where high-end taxpayers could not claim any defenses at all against civil tax penalties. As we will discuss further, high-end taxpayers could still assert other types of defenses, which focus more squarely on the substance of the legal analysis rather than on the taxpayer's state of mind or other subjective factors.

Advantages

Today, all taxpayers, regardless of their economic resources or sophistication, can use the reasonable cause and good faith defense to argue that accuracy-related tax penalties should not apply. Removing this specific tax penalty defense for high-end taxpayers offers several advantages over current law.

Subjective Reliance. Most importantly, our proposed means adjustments to current law would take away from those taxpayers with the greatest economic resources the most subjective of the tax penalty defenses: the reasonable cause and good faith defense, which focuses most intently on the taxpayer's state of mind. By eliminating this defense for high-end taxpayers, policymakers would prevent them from using their reliance on any form of tax advice, such as written tax opinions, as a defense against the accuracy-related tax penalties.[72] More generally, this adjustment would allow the IRS to avoid the obligation to consider more general facts and circumstances when applying accuracy-related tax penalties.[73] For instance, it would also prevent high-end taxpayers from arguing that their ignorance or unfamiliarity with complex tax statutes and regulations, in addition to other subjective characteristics, are enough to show reasonable cause and good faith.

Deterrence. Means-based adjustments to the reasonable cause defense would also enhance deterrence by increasing the expected value of tax penalties. As we have discussed, while the dollar value of the IRS's initial asserted tax penalties against high-end individuals can be substantial, the IRS often settles these cases without imposing the tax penalties.[74] Under our approach, high-end taxpayers would not be entitled to claim the reasonable cause and good faith defense to contest any accuracy-related tax penalty, including when they rely on a written tax opinion. This change to the structure of tax controversies would not only increase the ex ante risk that high-end taxpayers could face penalties, but it would also strengthen the IRS's bargaining power in settlement negotiations.

Perceptions of the IRS and Tax Morale. As a result of the tax penalty insurance function of written tax advice, many high-end taxpayers do not expect to, and often do not, pay civil tax penalties. Our proposal could combat perceptions by taxpayers that due to weaknesses in tax enforcement, the IRS does not apply effective sanctions against high-end taxpayers.

By reforming the reasonable cause and good faith defense according to the taxpayer's income or aggregate net assets, policymakers, including members of Congress, could frame the change as closing a loophole that disproportionately helps high-end taxpayers. This framing could facilitate a credible argument that the IRS may no longer permit high-end taxpayers, who can afford to pay for a written tax opinion from a lawyer or accountant, to use this advice as a penalty waiver. Further, those policymakers could also make known that one of the most common tax penalty defenses, the reasonable cause and good faith defense, would now be available only to middle- and low-income taxpayers. These adjustments could thus improve taxpayers' perceptions of the fairness of the tax system and the IRS, a shift that could enhance tax morale and tax compliance.

Focus on Legal Arguments and Taxpayer Disclosure. Under our proposal, high-end taxpayers could still defend against certain accuracy-related tax penalties, as long as they did so using defenses other than the reasonable cause and good faith defense. By retaining and elevating other tax penalty defenses, including the reasonable basis and substantial authority defenses, our proposal offers two significant advantages over current law in the case of high-end tax avoidance and abuse.

First, the reasonable basis and the substantial authority defenses require the taxpayer to make arguments based upon the substance of the law rather than the taxpayer's reliance on written advice regarding the law. For example, imagine a wealthy taxpayer who owns a subchapter C corporation and is engaged in a dispute with the IRS over whether payments made by the corporation for a luxury limousine car rental served personal or business purposes. If the IRS has asserted that the disregard of rules and regulations tax penalty applies, the taxpayer in this case could attempt a "reasonable basis" defense by showing the IRS that specific judicial decisions held that this type of expense was deductible. Remember, this defense requires the taxpayer to have reasonably relied upon a specific authority from a list of sources described by the Treasury. Compared to arguments over whether the taxpayer reasonably relied upon their tax advisor's written tax opinion regarding the tax treatment of limousine car rental expenses, the reasonable basis defense would instead require the taxpayer to convince the IRS (or a court) that the tax position is justified under substantive law.

Second, high-end taxpayers who would attempt to assert the reasonable basis defense against certain tax penalties, such as the disregard of rules and regulations and the substantial understatement tax penalties, would be required to raise a red flag for the IRS regarding this argument. In the example involving the limousine car expenses described earlier, in order to claim the reasonable basis defense, the taxpayer must have also filed the appropriate form, such as IRS Form 8275, at the same time that they filed the tax return.[75]

A significant benefit of our proposal is that it would require high-end taxpayers who wish to assert the reasonable basis defense to disclose this intention to the IRS in advance of any tax controversy. The increased advance disclosure of these positions, along with detailed explanations that cite specific legal authorities, would enhance the IRS's ability to detect potentially abusive tax positions. Additionally, the Treasury could increase the potential for advance disclosure of aggressive tax positions by requiring taxpayers to file such disclosure forms in order to claim the reasonable basis defense in response to other types of accuracy-related tax penalties, such as those attributable to negligence.

More Tailored than Current Law. Our proposal suggests a broader, but also more properly tailored, approach to the reasonable cause and good faith defense than under current law. Today, taxpayers are prevented from asserting this defense against accuracy-related tax penalties only when they engage in specific activities, such as when they participate in listed transactions and fail to file the required disclosure forms.[76] That is, current law adopts an "activity-based" approach when denying the availability of this penalty defense.

However, because many high-end taxpayers can avoid participating in these designated transactions, tax advice is still relevant to the question of whether a taxpayer can assert a defense against one of the more general accuracy-related tax penalties. Our proposal would prevent high-end taxpayers from asserting the reasonable cause and good faith defenses, irrespective of whether their tax position is a nondisclosed listed transaction or one that is more general, such as a tax position attributable to negligence or disregard of rules and regulations.[77]

At the same time, our proposed means adjustments would still allow taxpayers other than high-end taxpayers to assert the reasonable cause and good faith defense. By restricting our reform to taxpayers with significant income or wealth, policymakers would not prevent other taxpayers from using their reliance on statements made by advisors or government officials to claim the reasonable cause and good faith defense.

For example, in October 2021, the IRS announced that it would allow taxpayers who had relied upon certain significant Frequently Asked Questions (FAQs) posted to the IRS website to assert the reasonable cause and good faith defense against accuracy-related tax penalties, such as the negligence tax penalty.[78] While average taxpayers lack access to tax lawyers and other sophisticated advisors, and the IRS policy regarding FAQs is limited, they would still be able to defend against accuracy-related tax penalties by arguing that the facts and circumstances of their specific situations showed reasonable cause and good faith. Policymakers could even expand the availability of these defenses, when appropriate, for lower- and middle-income taxpayers, without the risk that high-end taxpayers could take unfair advantage of any reforms that broaden access to penalty defenses.

More Comprehensive than Prior Proposals. Our proposed reform of the reasonable cause and good faith penalty defense would also be more comprehensive, and more accurately tailored, than other reform approaches in the tax law literature. Professor Steve Johnson, for example, has argued that Congress should not allow wealthy taxpayers to assert the "reliance on opinion or advice" exception to defend against accuracy-related tax penalties.[79] Our approach, in contrast, is simultaneously broader and more tailored than this prior proposal.

First, the adjustment would prevent high-end taxpayers from asserting the entire reasonable cause and good faith defense against tax penalties, rather than just the reliance on opinion or advice exception. That is, our proposal would also prevent high-end taxpayers from arguing general facts and circumstances, including the taxpayer's knowledge and an honest misunderstanding of fact or law, as a tax penalty defense. Further, the exception for low-value underpayments could preserve a high-end taxpayer's ability to raise the defense in cases of more minor offenses. Finally, the adjustment to the reasonable cause and good faith defense that we have proposed would, ideally, be implemented as part of a systematic program of means adjustments designed to comprehensively address high-end noncompliance, rather than as a unique and isolated rule change.

Additional Considerations

Chilling Effects. One possible concern with this approach is that without the reasonable cause defense, high-end taxpayers could be subject to tax penalties in situations where the tax treatment was uncertain at the time they filed their tax returns. That is, sometimes taxpayers utilize tax advice to evaluate ambiguities in the law, even when they are not seeking to reduce their tax liabilities through aggressive transactions.

For example, consider a wealthy taxpayer who desires to participate in a debt modification and who would like to take the legal position that the modification does not result in taxable cancellation of indebtedness income because there are conflicting authorities on this particular issue.[80] Under our proposed framework, the taxpayer could be concerned that if they were to claim the tax position, they could be subject to an accuracy-related tax penalty without being able to assert the reasonable cause and good faith defense. In this case, some might argue that the denial of the reasonable cause and good faith defense leaves the taxpayer in a no-win situation, either by imposing excessive tax penalties on the taxpayer – if they were to pursue the restructuring and were subject to a penalty – or by creating excessive opportunity costs, which could induce the taxpayer not to pursue it because of the increased penalty risk.

A response to this concern is that, under our proposal, this taxpayer would not be without any penalty defenses. If the IRS asserted an accuracy-related tax penalty due to a "substantial understatement," for example, the taxpayer could still present a "substantial authority" defense, arguing that the weight of supporting authorities is substantial compared to the weight of contrary authorities.[81] If the taxpayer had obtained a written tax opinion that concluded there was substantial authority for the position, the taxpayer could articulate the legal arguments – or even share the opinion with the IRS – during the audit and penalty discussions. Further, as we discussed, the taxpayer could also assert a reasonable basis defense by describing legal authorities that justified the position. In fact, in some cases, the taxpayer would be required to disclose the reasonable basis in advance.

By heightening the importance of these defenses, other than the reasonable cause and good faith defense, policymakers would effectively require high-end taxpayers to articulate the legal arguments for the claimed tax position directly.

Regulation of Tax Advisors. Some might also question whether our focus on high-end taxpayers is appropriate. Why not just increase the regulation of tax advisors and tax advice? After all, these professionals often play an important role in aggressive and abusive tax planning.

We agree that the government should monitor and address the role of tax advisors in tax planning by enforcing measures such as Circular 230, discussed earlier. That said, policymakers face a number of significant challenges in enforcing tax compliance through the regulation of third-party tax advisors. First, these advisors face a different set of incentives and legal obligations and are not necessarily culpable in a taxpayer's noncompliance in same manner as the taxpayer. Second, excessive regulation of advisors can interfere with other priorities for the legal system, such as preserving the attorney–client relationship. Finally, not all advisors can be made subject to the jurisdiction of US laws, and some advisors may only have incomplete knowledge of the taxpayer's overall tax circumstances.

For an illustration of these challenges, in 2004 the Treasury attempted to strengthen the Circular 230 rules governing "covered opinions,"[82] but ultimately found these rules to be overly complex, costly, and intrusive, while only providing minimal benefits to taxpayers. Within a decade, in 2014, the Treasury replaced the detailed covered opinion rules with the more general reasonableness standard for tax advisors.[83]

One lesson from this experience is that attempting to rein in abuse by those tax advisors in particular who, on behalf of their clients, exploit broad tax penalty defenses, such as reasonable cause and good faith, often introduces new challenges to tax administration and enforcement. Professional and ethical standards that apply to third-party advisors are, thus, not sufficient on their own to deter abusive tax strategies.

Attorney–Client Relationship. Some might also argue that disallowing a reasonable cause and good faith defense could invade the attorney–client relationship between high-end taxpayers and their advisors. Some may argue that the change would disincentivize high-end taxpayers from seeking legal advice regarding transactions and strategies in cases where the tax treatment is ambiguous. Critics of the tax penalty for non-economic substance transactions,[84] which applies on a strict liability basis,[85] made similar arguments when Congress enacted the law in 2010.[86]

Means adjustments, however, would not prevent taxpayers from seeking legal counsel regarding any tax issue or the tax treatment of any proposed transaction. The only restriction created by means-based adjustments is that high-end taxpayers could not rely on legal advice to avoid accuracy-related tax penalties. If taxpayers have questions regarding whether a tax position is consistent with the tax law, they could still seek advice from a tax lawyer or accountant before claiming the tax position. The absence of the reliance on opinion and advice exception may alter taxpayers' willingness to engage in abusive tax strategies, but that result would be a socially desirable outcome.

NOTES

1 I.R.C. § 6664(c).
2 Treas. Reg. § 1.6664-4(c)(1).
3 *See* Chapter 3, section "The Limitations of Activity-Based Rules."
4 Scott W. Dolson, *A Taxpayer's Consumer Guide to "Substantial Authority" Tax Opinions*, Frost Brown Todd (May 24, 2019), https://frostbrowntodd.com/a-taxpayers-consumer-guide-to-substantial-authority-tax-opinions/.

5 Linda Galler, *Tax Opinion Policies and Procedures*, 75 TAX LAW. 443, 445 (2022).
6 *See, e.g.*, Robert P. Rothman, *Tax Opinion Practice*, 64 TAX LAW. 301 (2011); I.R.C. § 368.
7 I.R.C. § 1031.
8 *See* Galler, *supra* note 5; Rothman, *supra* note 6.
9 Robert W. Wood, *Seven Reasons to Get a Tax Opinion before You File with the IRS*, FORBES (Nov. 16, 2022), https://www.forbes.com/sites/robertwood/2022/11/16/seven-reasons-to-get-a-tax-opinion-before-you-file-with-irs/?sh=58a7c652124b.
10 *See, e.g.*, Klamath Strategic Inv. Fund, LLC v. United States, 472 F. Supp. 2d 885 (E.D. Tex. 2007); Litman v. United States, 78 Fed. Cl. 90 (2007); Southgate Master Fund, L.L.C. ex rel. Montgomery Capital Advisors, LLC v. United States, 659 F.3d 466 (5th Cir. 2011); Romanowski v. Comm'r, T.C.M. 2013-55 (2013).
11 I.R.C. § 6664(c).
12 I.R.C. § 6664(c)(2).
13 I.R.C. § 6664(d)(3).
14 I.R.C. §§ 6662(b)(1), 6662(c).
15 I.R.C. § 6664(c).
16 Treas. Reg. § 1.6664-4(c).
17 Treas. Reg. § 1.6664-4(b).
18 Treas. Reg. § 1.6664-4(c)(1).
19 Treas. Reg. § 1.6662-3(b)(1).
20 Treas. Reg. § 1.6662-3(b)(3).
21 *See, e.g.*, Galler, *supra* note 5.
22 Treas. Reg. § 1.6662-3(b)(3).
23 I.R.C. §§ 6662(b)(1), 6662(c).
24 I.R.C. § 6664(c)(1).
25 Treas. Reg. § 1.6662-3(c)(1).
26 Treas. Reg. § 1.6662-3(c)(2).
27 I.R.C. §§ 6662(d)(1).
28 I.R.C. § 6664(c)(1).
29 I.R.C. § 6662(d)(2)(B)(ii).
30 I.R.C. § 6662(d)(2)(B)(i).
31 *See, e.g.*, Galler, *supra* note 5; Rothman, *supra* note 6.
32 I.R.C. § 6662(d)(2)(B)(i).
33 *See* Dolson, *supra* note 4.
34 *See* Rothman, *supra* note 6.
35 *See* Galler, *supra* note 5.
36 *See, e.g.*, Heather M. Field, *Tax Lawyers as Tax Insurance*, 60 WM. & MARY L. REV. 2111, 2124 (2019).
37 *See, e.g.*, Michelle Kwon, *Dysfunction Junction: Reasonable Cause and Good Faith Reliance on Tax Advisors with Conflicts of Interest*, 67 TAX LAW. 403, 409 (2014).
38 Treas. Reg. § 1.6664-4(c)(1)(i), (ii).
39 Neonatology Assocs., P.A. v. Comm'r, 115 T.C. 43 (2000).
40 608 F.3d 1366 (Fed. Cir. 2010).
41 The "Son of BOSS" tax avoidance scheme used "a series of contrived steps (in this case involving interests in a partnership) to generate artificial tax losses designed to offset

income from other transactions." Press Release LS-831, U.S. Dept. of the Treasury, Treasury Shuts Down "Son of BOSS" Abusive Tax Shelter (Aug. 11, 2000), https://home.treasury.gov/news/press-releases/ls831.

42 *Stobie Creek Investments LLC*, 608 F.3d, at 1366.
43 *Id.*
44 31 C.F.R. § 10 (Practice before the Internal Revenue Service).
45 31 C.F.R. § 10.37(a)(2).
46 31 C.F.R. § 10.50-53 (Sanctions for Violation of Regulations).
47 *See* Michael Doran, *Tax Penalties and Tax Compliance*, 46 HARV. J. LEGIS. 111, 117 (2009); William A. Drennan, *Strict Liability and Tax Penalties*, 62 OKLA. L. REV. 1, 17–18 (2009); Rachelle Y. Holmes, *The Tax Lawyer as Gatekeeper*, 49 U. LOUISVILLE L. REV. 185, 204–05 (2010); Leigh Osofsky, *The Case Against Strategic Tax Law Uncertainty*, 64 TAX L. REV. 489, 510–11 (2010).
48 *See generally* Tanina Rostain, *Sheltering Lawyers: The Organized Tax Bar and the Tax Shelter Industry*, 23 YALE J. ON REGUL. 77 (2006); Jay A. Soled, *Tax Shelter Malpractice Cases and Their Implications for Tax Compliance*, 58 AM. U. L. REV. 267, 272 (2008); Dennis J. Ventry, Jr., *Raising the Ethical Bar for Tax Lawyers: Why We Need Circular 230*, 111 TAX NOTES 823, 825 n. 18 (2006).
49 *See* TANINA ROSTAIN & MILTON C. REGAN, JR., CONFIDENCE GAMES: LAWYERS, ACCOUNTANTS, AND THE TAX SHELTER INDUSTRY 218–36 (2014); Joseph Bankman, *The New Market in Corporate Tax Shelters*, 83 TAX NOTES 1775, 1782 (1999); DEP'T OF TREASURY, THE PROBLEM OF CORPORATE TAX SHELTERS: DISCUSSION, ANALYSIS AND LEGISLATIVE PROPOSALS x (1999).
50 Marvin A. Chirelstein & Lawrence A. Zelenak, *Tax Shelters and the Search for a Silver Bullet*, 105 COLUM. L. REV. 1939 (2005).
51 *See* Joshua Blank & Ari Glogower, Corporate Tax Shelters, *in* RESEARCH HANDBOOK ON CORPORATE TAXATION (Reuven Avi-Yonah, ed., Edward Elgar Publishing, 2023).
52 *See* Emily Cauble, *Accessible Reliable Tax Advice*, 51 U. MICH. J.L. REFORM 589, 591 (2018); Field, *supra* note 36; Robert W. Wood, *Why Tax Opinions Are Valuable*, FORBES (Jan. 18, 2011), https://www.forbes.com/sites/robertwood/2011/01/18/why-tax-opinions-are-valuable/?sh=2560a87b2536.
53 *See, e.g., What Is the Average Cost of Hiring a Tax Attorney?*, SUPERMONEY (Oct. 31, 2022), https://www.supermoney.com/what-average-cost-hiring-tax-attorney/; Joshua D. Blank & Leigh Osofsky, *The Inequity of Informal Guidance*, 75 VAND. L. REV. 1093, 1125 (2022).
54 *See, e.g.,* Soled, *supra* note 48.
55 Drennan, *supra* note 47, at 28.
56 31 C.F.R. § 10.37(a)(2).
57 *See* Ventry, *supra* note 48.
58 Wood, *supra* note 9.
59 JOINT COMM. ON TAX'N, REPORT TO THE HOUSE COMMITTEE ON WAYS AND MEANS CHAIRMAN RICHARD NEAL 5 (2022).
60 *Id.*
61 *Id.*

62 See, e.g., Galler, *supra* note 5; Wood, *supra* note 9.
63 I.R.C. § 6664(c).
64 See Treas. Reg. § 1.6664-4(c)(1)(i), (ii).
65 See *supra* note 10.
66 Drennan, *supra* note 47, at 27.
67 See, e.g., Kwon, *supra* note 37.
68 Treas. Reg. § 1.6662-3(b)(3).
69 Dolson, *supra* note 4.
70 See, e.g., Reynolds v. Comm'r, 296 F.3d 607 (7th Cir. 2002).
71 Of course, any income threshold will create a "cliff effect," where taxpayers with income close to the threshold may be subject to significantly different treatment, depending upon whether their income reaches the threshold. For discussion, see Manoj Viswanathan, *The Hidden Costs of Cliff Effects in the Internal Revenue Code*, 164 U. PA. L. REV. 931 (2016). These effects are not relevant for high-end taxpayers with income or wealth significantly higher than the thresholds.
72 Treas. Reg. § 1.6664-4(c).
73 Treas. Reg. § 1.6664-4(c)(1).
74 See, e.g., Jesse Eisinger & Paul Kiel, *Gutting the IRS: The IRS Tried to Take on the Ultrawealthy. It Didn't Go Well*, PROPUBLICA (Apr. 5, 2019), https://www.propublica.org/article/ultrawealthy-taxes-irs-internal-revenue-service-global-high-wealth-audits.
75 Treas. Reg. §§ 1.6662-3(c)(1), (2).
76 *Id.*
77 *Id.*
78 IRS News Release IR-2021-202 (Oct. 15, 2021).
79 Steve R. Johnson, *A Modest Proposal to Improve Tax Compliance: Curbing Penalty-Protection Opinions*, 53–59 (July 18, 2013) (unpublished manuscript), https://papers.ssrn.com/sol3/papers.cfm?abstract_id=1285282. For other proposed reforms to this defense that do not explicitly adjust on the basis of a taxpayer's wealth, see Linda M. Beale, *Putting SEC Heat on Audit Firms and Corporate Tax Shelters: Responding to Tax Risk with Sunshine, Shame and Strict Liability*, 29 J. CORP. L. 219, 264 (2004); Jeremiah Coder, *Achieving Meaningful Civil Tax Penalty Reform and Making It Stick*, 27 AKRON TAX J. 153, 178 (2012); Drennan, *supra* note 47, at 35; Calvin H. Johnson, *Ending Reliance on Tax Opinions of the Taxpayer's Own Lawyer*, 141 TAX NOTES 947, 961 (2013); Kwon, *supra* note 37, at 443–49.
80 See Treas. Reg. § 1.1001-3 (detailing the complex rules regarding the modification of debt instruments).
81 I.R.C. § 6662(d)(2)(B)(i).
82 69 Fed. Reg. 75839–75845 (Dec. 20, 2004).
83 79 Fed. Reg. 33685 (June 12, 2014) (seeking to "eliminate the complex rules governing covered opinions").
84 I.R.C. § 6662(b)(6).
85 See I.R.C. § 6664(c)(2).
86 See, e.g., Clinton Stretch et al., *Economic Substance and Strict Liability Do Not Mix*, 113 TAX NOTES 1357, 1361 (2009); AM. INST. OF CERTIFIED PUB. ACCTS., REPORT ON

CIVIL TAX PENALTIES: THE NEED FOR REFORM 9–11 (2009) ("The lack of a reasonable cause or waiver provision in penalties involving complex determinations is particularly troubling."). For additional criticism of the codified economic substance doctrine, see Kathleen DeLaney Thomas, *The Case against a Strict Liability Economic Substance Penalty*, 13 U. PA. J. BUS. L. 445 (2011); *see also* Leandra Lederman, *W(h)ither Economic Substance?*, 95 IOWA L. REV. 389 (2010).

8

The Statute of Limitations

The statute of limitations governing the timing of when the IRS may assess a tax liability can further hinder the agency's ability to challenge and deter tax noncompliance. Under current law, the IRS must assess additional tax or, at a minimum, issue a notice of deficiency, before the statute of limitations that applies to the tax return in question expires.[1] While the statute of limitations can provide closure and repose for old offenses, high-end taxpayers can often take advantage of these rules to enable tax noncompliance.

Consider, for example, the first major investigative report on the tax returns of President Donald Trump, his family, and the Trump Organization by the *New York Times* in 2018.[2] The report alleged that Trump and several of his family members had engaged in aggressive tax-avoidance strategies, including claiming low property valuations in order to avoid hundreds of millions of dollars of estate and gift taxes, and deducting inflated business expenses to avoid federal income tax.[3] The reporters characterized several of the tax positions, including those involving property valuations and transactions between related parties, as "dubious tax schemes," "tax dodges," and "overt fraud."[4] In addition, the reporters noted that the IRS would be unlikely to be able to review the returns for the years covered in the story, some dating to the 1960s and 1970s, because "the acts happened too long ago and are past the statute of limitations."[5]

Similarly, following further public reporting on President Trump's tax returns, together with the 2022 public disclosure of the returns themselves by the House Committee on Ways & Means, one commentator noted that "if you go back to those big losses in the 1990s, the statute of limitations ran out. It looks as if the IRS just never adjusted any taxes for the positions Trump took."[6] In the end, while the investigations into Trump's tax returns leave many unanswered questions, one common takeaway is that it is likely that the statute of limitations prevents the IRS from assessing additional tax liability for many years of these returns.

This chapter considers how the statute of limitations can enable high-end tax noncompliance and prevent the IRS from challenging tax positions of high-end taxpayers. The chapter begins by describing the statute of limitations on tax assessment and the rationale underlying its design, which is followed by an explanation of how it encourages and facilitates abusive tax avoidance by high-end taxpayers. Following this discussion, we present a proposal for incorporating means adjustments into the statute of limitations in order to level the playing field between high-end taxpayers and the IRS.

THE TICKING TAX CLOCK

The statute of limitations limits the amount of time that the IRS has to assess additional tax liability. It plays the same role as the shot clock in basketball: A clock begins to count down from the moment the offensive team gains possession of the ball, and that team must attempt a shot on the basket before the clock runs out. Likewise, in tax enforcement, once the statutory time period runs out, the IRS loses the ability to "assess" additional tax liability (formally record additional tax liability) for the tax year in question.[7] The exact timing of the running of the statute of limitations clock depends upon the circumstances surrounding the taxpayer's tax return, which are discussed in the following section.

When the Clock Starts, Stops, and Pauses

The tax clock begins to tick from the date that a taxpayer files their tax return with the IRS.[8] For purposes of the start of the statute of limitations period, the tax law provides detailed rules for determining when a taxpayer's tax return is deemed to be filed. If a taxpayer files a return *before* the due date for the return (ignoring extensions), then the taxpayer's return is "deemed filed" on the last day "prescribed by law," which is generally April 15 for individual income tax returns.[9] Therefore, if a taxpayer files their individual tax return with the IRS on March 5, then the statute of limitations still runs from April 15, the due date for filing this return. On the other hand, if a taxpayer files a tax return with the IRS *after* the due date for the return, then the statute of limitations begins to run from that date.[10] Therefore, if a taxpayer files their tax return with the IRS on June 10, and it was due on April 15, then the statute of limitations would run from June 10 rather than the original due date, April 15. Each of these examples assumes that the taxpayer files the return by delivering it to the IRS in person or electronically; the tax law contains additional rules and requirements regarding tax returns delivered by mail and other means.[11]

When does the tax clock stop ticking? By default, the statute of limitations runs for three years from the date that a taxpayer files a tax return.[12] Basically, once the clock starts ticking, the IRS typically has three years from the deemed filing of the taxpayer's return to assess additional tax liability.[13] While the three-year time limit is the default rule, if the taxpayer engages in certain specific activities when claiming tax positions on the original return, this time limit may be longer or in some cases indefinite.

In addition, the tax law also contains detailed rules that require the running of the statutory period to pause during certain events. For example, if the IRS mails the taxpayer a statutory notice of deficiency regarding a specific tax return, the taxpayer has ninety days from this letter to petition to the US Tax Court to hear the case (the "90-day letter").[14] Once the IRS mails the 90-day letter, the IRS may not assess any additional tax with respect to the deficiency while the taxpayer takes up to ninety days to decide whether or not to petition the US Tax Court (the "prohibited period").[15] If the taxpayer decides to file a petition, this prohibited period on assessment extends until the US Tax Court reaches a final decision.[16] Further, the law provides that if the IRS can mail the statutory notice of deficiency before the expiration of the statute of limitations, the ticking clock will pause during the prohibited period, plus an additional sixty days, and the IRS challenge can proceed.[17]

Activity-Based Statute of Limitations Extensions

The current law provides activity-based adjustments to these rules as well, which provide for an extension of the IRS's statute of limitations period when taxpayers commit specific acts or abuses. As with other activity-based tax compliance rules, these adjustments can aid the IRS when a taxpayer engages in certain actions that can enable or indicate noncompliance.

Substantial Omissions. If a taxpayer's return reflects a "substantial omission," meaning that the taxpayer improperly omits an amount of income that is greater than 25% of the gross income stated on the return, then the statute of limitations period is doubled from three years to six years.[18] The reason for this rule is that Congress wanted to give the IRS additional time to challenge the taxpayer's position in situations where the taxpayer has failed to report a large amount of income.

This adjustment only applies, however, in narrow circumstances identified in the statute. In most cases, the taxpayer must omit the *entire amount* of income in order to trigger the substantial omission exception.[19] For example, if a taxpayer received shares of stock of a start-up corporation in exchange for services, and then underreported the value of those shares as gross income while still reporting some of its value to the IRS, the six-year statute of limitations would not apply.[20]

Fraud or No Return Filed. If a taxpayer files a fraudulent return, the IRS may not be able to identify the abusive tax positions on the return easily, if ever. Similarly, if a taxpayer fails to file returns at all, the IRS will not be able to determine the taxpayer's proper tax liability without creating a "substitute" return for the taxpayer.[21] In each of these types of cases, the statute of limitations never expires.[22] However, as we explain later in this chapter, these limitation period extensions can be difficult for the IRS to obtain and relatively easy for taxpayers to avoid.

Listed Transactions. Last, if a taxpayer fails to disclose participation in a listed transaction to the IRS, the statute of limitations does not expire until one year after the taxpayer (or the taxpayer's material advisor) discloses participation in the transaction to the IRS.[23] If, however, the default statute of limitations for a taxpayer has already expired by the time the IRS designates a tax strategy that the taxpayer has used as a listed transaction, the limitations period cannot be reopened or extended.[24] This special extension similarly adopts a narrowly defined activity-based approach, as taxpayers must engage in a specified listed transaction for the rule to apply.

Why Limit the Time for Assessment?

The statute of limitations on tax assessments serves several important functions, many of which are similar to the reasons for time limits in civil and criminal actions outside of the tax context. Specifically, these functions operate to facilitate fairness and repose, administrability, and voluntary compliance.

Fairness and Repose. The most common justification for the statute of limitations on tax assessments is fairness. The federal US income tax system is based on voluntary compliance, which means that taxpayers are responsible for calculating their own tax liability on their tax returns, paying taxes owed in a timely manner, and keeping records to substantiate their tax positions.

If the IRS were able to challenge items on returns filed decades ago, taxpayers would be forced to search for supporting documents and other information in order to respond to the IRS's deficiency assertions, and might not be able to retrieve such information or consult with the advisors who may have assisted with the filing of the initial return. The tax clock is designed to ensure that the IRS reviews taxpayers' returns in a timely manner in order to ensure that tax audits and potential tax controversies are fair.

Administrability. Another important justification for restricting the time that the IRS has to review tax returns is administrability. In 2022, the IRS received more than 262 million tax returns and other forms, including more than 160 million individual income tax returns.[25] At the same time, IRS officials reported that the agency had difficulty keeping up with the increasing influx of returns, resulting in delays of items such as individual tax refunds.[26]

Without the statute of limitations, IRS agents could become involved in investigations and audits spanning multiple years or even decades, resulting not only in higher administrative costs but also in lower expected returns. Even with increased funding under the Inflation Reduction Act of 2022, the IRS may not have the resources necessary to expand the scope of its review work.[27] The statute of limitations thereby allows the IRS to focus on a smaller subset of recently filed returns, promoting a more cost-efficient system of tax administration and enforcement.

Voluntary Compliance. Finally, the statute of limitations supports our system of voluntary compliance. If individuals were forced to live in fear that the IRS could audit any tax return that they have filed at any point in time, some taxpayers may very well opt not to file at all. In effect, such a system could cause taxpayers to view the IRS like Inspector Javert of *Les Misérables*, who chased Jean Valjean for years for violating parole after being convicted of stealing a loaf of bread.[28] By creating closure for the taxpayer for past actions, the statute of limitations counters the public perception that the IRS investigates taxpayers unceasingly.[29]

HOW THE TAX CLOCK ENABLES TAX AVOIDANCE BY THE RICH

While the tax clock serves important procedural functions, it also weakens the IRS's ability to deter high-end taxpayers from engaging in abusive tax strategies. For several reasons, discussed in the following sections, high-end taxpayers can benefit the most from the current default statute of limitations period. They have more opportunities to engage in complex transactions and structuring that can hide noncompliance from the IRS, and that can make it difficult for the IRS to figure out what they were up to in time to beat the clock.

Tax Clock Limits IRS Review

The most significant tax enforcement obstacle created by the statute of limitations is the time limit that it imposes upon the IRS to review tax returns and assess additional taxes and penalties. An expired statute of limitations prevented the IRS from pursuing tax deficiencies in several high-profile controversies involving overstatement of basis,[30] such as in the case of *United States v. Home Concrete & Supply, LLC*,[31] which the US Supreme Court decided in the taxpayer's favor.

Although Congress later revised the relevant statute in response to the Court's decision in this case,[32] by the time of this legislative change, many large business taxpayers, including the taxpayer in *Home Concrete*, were able to take advantage of the shorter time limit. Accordingly, as the statute of limitations clock had run out, the IRS could not restart it and assess additional tax liability. Further, the *Home Concrete* case also demonstrated how the current statute of limitations is only extended in narrowly defined circumstances, which are often avoidable by sophisticated taxpayers.

Time limits on the IRS disproportionately benefit high-end taxpayers. As IRS officials have reported, high-end tax avoidance is among the most challenging types of noncompliance for the IRS to detect, as high-end taxpayers can use more complex strategies, including creating multiple entities in different jurisdictions, compared to tax strategies used by most taxpayers.[33] High-end taxpayers who claim questionable tax positions are often aware that time may run out before the IRS detects them.[34] As one tax advisor has explained, when he informs his clients that statute of limitations period has expired, "we high-five them."[35]

Taxpayers Control the Clock

Another feature of the current law that provides advantages to taxpayers is that taxpayers have the power to decide when to start the tax clock. The starting point of the statute of limitations hinges on an action of the taxpayer, rather than on an action of the IRS.[36] On the date that a taxpayer files a tax return, or is deemed to have done so, the statute of limitations period begins to run,[37] and continues to do so unless it is suspended, such as when the IRS mails the taxpayer a statutory notice of deficiency.[38] As taxpayers who engage in aggressive tax planning hope to avoid facing audit and additional tax liability or penalties, they seek to start the tax clock as quickly as possible.

High-end taxpayers often attempt to avoid detection and challenge by filing tax returns with the IRS that are sufficient to start the tax clock. One type of tax planning in which well-advised high-end taxpayers often take the statute of limitations into account involves intrafamily transfers of wealth through gifts. By filing a gift tax return with the IRS, high-end taxpayers may limit the ability of the IRS to question whether the value of the gift is accurate, such as in the transfer of land or stock in a closely held corporation.[39]

Sophisticated advisors frequently highlight the relevance of the statute of limitations when advising clients, and advise them to time the filing of tax returns accordingly. For instance, as one law firm informed its clients regarding the need to file gift tax returns:

> A gift's value may be questioned by the IRS if the gift giver fails to file a gift tax return. Tax law limits the time the IRS can question the valuation of a gift to three years after it's been given. If an adequate gift tax return is filed, the clock begins to run on the statute of limitations. After three years, the IRS can no longer question a gift's valuation, and the gift is considered free and clear of any claims the IRS may have on it.[40]

In these and other examples, as long as the taxpayer provides enough information to satisfy the filing requirement, the taxpayer controls the timing of the start of the statute of limitations. In the case of a complex tax return, IRS agents can have even less time to flag potentially abusive items for audit before the tax clock stops.

Limited Retroactive Filing Obligations

To address the imbalance between the resources of the IRS and high-end individual and business taxpayers, policymakers have created rules and policies that require retroactive tax filings and extensions of the statute of limitations.

For example, under current law, if the IRS designates a specific abusive tax shelter as a listed transaction after taxpayers have used it to claim tax benefits, taxpayers are still required to disclose participation in the tax strategy within ninety days of the designation with the IRS Office of Tax Shelter Analysis.[41] If the taxpayer fails to file the required reportable transaction disclosure form, then the statute of limitations with respect to the transaction will not expire before a specific date: one year after the earlier of either (1) the date when the IRS is furnished the required information or (2) the date that a material advisor of the taxpayer provides the information to the IRS.[42] The purpose of this rule is to prevent taxpayers from escaping IRS detection and challenge simply because they participated in abusive tax strategies prior to the IRS's designation of those strategies as listed transactions or transactions of interest.

The interplay of the statute of limitations and the retroactive filing requirements, however, creates additional opportunities for high-end taxpayers to avoid IRS detection and enforcement. While the retroactive filing requirements are designed to provide transparency from the taxpayer to the IRS, they contain an exception that again encourages high-end taxpayers to start the tax clock: The retroactive filing requirement only applies if the relevant statute of limitations is still open at the time of tax-shelter designation by the IRS.[43]

As a result of this exception, high-end taxpayers can file tax returns that reflect tax benefits from aggressive or even abusive tax strategies that are not yet reportable transactions to start the running of the statute of limitations. Years later, if the IRS designates any of these transactions as listed transactions or transactions of interest, and if the relevant statute of limitations has already expired, these taxpayers will not be obligated to disclose the transactions to the IRS retroactively.[44] Further, the IRS has confirmed that in these cases, the statute of limitations will not be reopened or extended.[45]

"Substantial Compliance" Can Start the Tax Clock

Taxpayers may also start the statute of limitations clock by filing tax returns that provide minimal details regarding the underlying transactions and supporting tax analysis. Under the "substantial compliance" doctrine, the filing of a tax return is sufficient to start the statute of limitations as long as the return satisfies four minimal requirements: "First, there must be sufficient data to calculate tax liability; second, the document must purport to be a return; third, there must be an honest and reasonable attempt to satisfy the requirements of the tax law; and fourth, the taxpayer must execute the return under penalties of perjury."[46]

This lenient rule does not require the information on tax returns to be correct. Nor does it require taxpayers to provide the IRS with detailed explanations of the positions claimed on their returns. As an internal IRS presentation regarding this doctrine states, "[a] return that meets these four requirements will be considered valid and trigger the running of the statute of limitations even if it contains other inaccuracies or omissions."[47]

High-end taxpayers can take advantage of the substantial compliance doctrine. While aggressive and abusive tax planning exploits ambiguities or distorted readings of the tax law, tax returns themselves often contain limited explanations for the tax positions claimed. For example, during the 2012 presidential election, commentators speculated on the possible reasons why candidate Mitt Romney's financial disclosure statement revealed that his tax-deferred retirement account had a value of approximately $100 million, even though taxpayers face strict annual limitations regarding contributions to these types of accounts.[48] At the same time, these same commentators cautioned that Romney's returns did not contain statements that would allow for full analysis of these issues.[49] As it was pointed out, this was permissible: As long as Romney's returns showed an "honest and reasonable" attempt to comply with the law, and met the other requirements of the substantial compliance doctrine, the statute of limitations started to run from the time he filed them.

This principle has been upheld by the courts, who have often sided with taxpayers in statute of limitations disputes where the taxpayer filed tax return documents that provided enough information for the IRS to investigate and question the taxpayer's claimed tax positions, even if they rested on questionable grounds.[50]

Taxpayers May Deny Extensions

Sometimes the IRS has little time left on the tax clock when it discovers a taxpayer's questionable tax position. If the IRS detects a potentially improper tax position toward the end of the applicable limitations period, the IRS often requests that the taxpayer grant the IRS an extension.[51] In many cases, taxpayers comply with this request, rather than risk encouraging IRS agents to issue an aggressive notice of deficiency quickly.[52] Taxpayers who agree to provide the IRS with more time sign a "consent to extend the time to assess tax" form, which specifies the new date by which the IRS may assess additional tax.[53] In this way, taxpayers can use the ticking tax clock as a tactic to solicit concessions from the IRS or to limit an investigation.

Where the tax disputes involve high-end taxpayers and complex tax-avoidance strategies, some taxpayers may attempt to delay the audit process, or even refuse to extend the statute of limitations period altogether. Others may be willing to provide the waiver, but only on the condition that the IRS narrow the scope of the audit. In these situations, high-end taxpayers retain negotiation leverage due to the very existence of the initial time limit: They exercise this power by agreeing to a conditional waiver, reaching an agreement with the IRS as to the end date[54] and the specific issues that the IRS may continue to review during the extension period.[55] For this reason, tax advisors who specialize in working with high-income taxpayers have commented that "it is almost always preferred to sign a limited extension with a specified expiration date ... rather than an indefinite extension."[56]

In some extreme cases, high-end taxpayers refuse to grant the waiver at all. In the reported 2012 audit of Georg Schaeffler over a $5 billion deficiency, for instance, Schaeffler allegedly threatened to refuse to grant the IRS an extension.[57] As one practitioner has commented, in tax disputes involving high-end taxpayers, "[p]art of the process of dealing with these audits is delay, delay, delay."[58]

REPROGRAMMING THE TAX CLOCK

As we have demonstrated, high-end taxpayers often manipulate the statute of limitations to avoid detection and challenge by the IRS. These taxpayers, and their advisors, benefit from these time-related restrictions on the IRS's ability to review their tax returns and assess additional tax.

High-end taxpayers can avoid participating in transactions and activities that may trigger an extended statute of limitations, such as listed transactions; and, if they do, they can file the required disclosure to start the clock.[59] They can also avoid failing to disclose entire items of income from their tax returns, and instead disclose just enough to avoid the longer six-year statute of limitations that applies to substantial omissions. Further, most high-end taxpayers, especially those who use sophisticated third-party advisors, can avoid engaging in tax planning that meets the subjective legal definition of tax fraud, which could cause the tax clock to never stop.

As part of a comprehensive effort to address aggressive and abusive tax planning by high-end taxpayers, policymakers should adjust the length of the statute of limitations based on the economic characteristics of the taxpayer. In contrast to recent proposals, which would apply only when specific acts occur, such as tax deficiencies that exceed certain thresholds,[60] policymakers should instead make adjustments based on the means of the taxpayer. In the following section, we show how policymakers could tailor the statute of limitations to high-end taxpayers, argue that our approach offers advantages over both current law and recent legislative proposals, and consider and respond to potential objections.

Incorporating Means Adjustments

Instead of extending the statute of limitations based solely on specific activities, policymakers should also extend the statute of limitations based on the taxpayer's income or wealth. For example, in the case of any individual taxpayer with adjusted gross income of $2 million or more, or aggregate net assets of $10 million or more, policymakers could revise the default review period in which the IRS could assess additional tax liability to six years – instead of the three years under current law[61] – from the filing of the taxpayer's return. This extended statute of limitations would for the most part not depend on any specific traits of the deficiency, such as the type of transaction or its magnitude. As long as the taxpayer's income or wealth reached the applicable threshold, the IRS would have more time to review and assess additional tax liability with respect to the taxpayer's return. All other taxpayers would still face the default three-year statute of limitations.[62]

Low-Value Underpayment Exception. The adjustments to the statute of limitations period that we have proposed could also include exceptions for low-value underpayments. For instance, high-end taxpayers with an aggregate underpayment of less than $50,000 could be exempt from the means-adjusted extended statute of limitations. By providing a low-dollar threshold for this exemption, policymakers could alleviate the potential for high-end taxpayers to claim that they may face excessive IRS scrutiny for tax positions they claimed long ago. Yet this exception would still allow the IRS additional time to review complex, high-value tax-avoidance strategies that are often the subjects of tax controversies involving the rich.

Interaction with Activity-Based Rules. Like other activity-based tax compliance rules, the current rules extending the statute of limitations period in the case of certain taxpayer activities serve an important role in the tax compliance system, notwithstanding their problems. In this area as well, policymakers can adopt a layered approach that would adjust the statute of limitations based on characteristics of both taxpayers and their activities, and build upon the law's current activity-based adjustments for particularly abusive transactions. For example, if policymakers desire to focus on tax returns that reflect substantial omissions,[63] they could extend the IRS's time to review returns filed by high-end taxpayers from the six years under current law[64] to nine years. All other taxpayers would remain subject to the six-year statute of limitations for substantial omissions.

Means-based adjustments, such as these, would enhance the current activity-based tax-shelter rules. Under current law, if a taxpayer fails to disclose participation in a listed transaction to the IRS, the statute of limitations does not expire until one year after the taxpayer (or the taxpayer's material advisor) discloses participation in the transaction to the IRS.[65] If, however, the default statute of limitations for a taxpayer has *already* expired by the time the IRS designates a tax strategy that the taxpayer has used as a listed transaction, the limitations period is not reopened or extended.[66] Means-based adjustments, however, would allow the statute of limitations period to be extended for high-end taxpayers specifically. This would allow notices of a listed transaction or a transaction of interest to remain in effect for longer periods, thereby reducing pressure on the IRS to issue notices quickly.

In any event, a key objective of policymakers should be to increase the statute of limitations period for high-end taxpayers, while retaining the features of current law for all other taxpayers. These examples are illustrative, and policymakers could calibrate the degree of the time adjustments to balance between two competing considerations: providing closure for past offenses and allowing sufficient time for the IRS to make assessments.

Advantages over Current Law

The statute of limitations that is currently in effect, which includes special rules for certain activities and offenses, applies uniformly to all taxpayers regardless of their individual characteristics or circumstances. By taking into account the economic attributes of taxpayers, such as their income or wealth, our proposal offers several advantages over both current law and recent legislative proposals. Not only would it aid the IRS in its detection and deterrence efforts regarding high-end tax noncompliance, but it would also close some loopholes that these taxpayers take advantage of, such as the "substantial compliance" exception. It would also serve to increase taxpayer morale by signaling to the public that it is important to give the agency more time to go after especially abusive cases. These advantages and others are highlighted in the following subsections.

Detection. At a minimum, extending the statute of limitations for high-end taxpayers would provide the IRS with additional time to review tax returns and identify specific tax positions for further review. As we have argued, the ticking tax clock benefits high-end taxpayers in particular because the complexity of the tax strategies that underlie deductions, credits, and exclusions that they may use might not be immediately apparent to IRS officials.

For instance, when high-end individual taxpayers engage in transactions that generate tax losses, if they do not submit the special required disclosure forms, the only information that IRS agents can observe from tax returns is the taxpayer's claimed tax loss on the required schedule.[67] To provide another example, when high-end taxpayers engage in new tax-avoidance strategies that are not yet in widespread use, by the time IRS officials become aware of them, the statute of limitations for these taxpayers' returns may have already expired.[68]

Treasury officials have noted that "[c]omplex audits in the largest cases require extensive factual development by multidisciplinary teams of revenue agents, tax law specialists, economists, engineers, and other IRS personnel."[69] They further report that, as a result of the three-year default statute of limitations, among other factors, "[c]ritical issues may not be identified until late in the process of an examination, and in many cases further development often cannot be pursued due to time and resource constraints."[70] Our proposal would automatically provide the IRS with more time for detecting noncompliance in cases of taxpayers who engage in the most complex forms of tax planning.

Substantial Compliance. Our proposal would also serve as a counterweight to the ability of high-end taxpayers to exploit the "substantial compliance" doctrine, which governs when taxpayers are considered to have satisfied their tax return filing obligations.[71]

Again, the filing of the tax return is the key act that starts the tax clock.[72] As we described, high-end taxpayers are often motivated to provide only enough information on their tax returns to meet the substantial compliance requirement and start the tax clock. For example, when the tax-shelter disclosure rules first took effect, the IRS reported that aggressive taxpayers attempted to file inadequate disclosure forms in order to avoid penalties and start the statute of limitations.[73] Especially in the case of gifts by high-end taxpayers, tax advisors emphasize the importance of filing a gift tax return in order to limit the IRS's time for review.[74] Implicit in some of this advice is that if the clock starts ticking, the IRS may not identify a potential deficiency before time runs out.[75]

Since high-end taxpayers can unilaterally decide when to start the running of the statute of limitations period, our proposal would counter this advantage by providing the IRS with additional time to review tax returns in which the use of abusive tax strategies may not be immediately apparent.

Deterrence. By introducing means-based adjustments to the statute of limitations, our proposal would enhance the ability of IRS officials to deter high-end abusive tax planning ex ante. As long as IRS officials state that they plan to use the additional time to increase review of high-end taxpayers' returns, those taxpayers should become aware that the likelihood of IRS detection of abusive tax positions has increased. Even if policymakers do not apply other means-based adjustments, either to tax penalties or to the use of tax advice, as we have proposed in prior chapters, this change alone would increase not only the probability of detection but also the expected costs of high-end tax noncompliance.

As an additional benefit, the statute of limitations periods can allow policymakers to keep penalty rates at modest levels without compromising their deterrent effect. In the expected return model of tax compliance,[76] extending the statute of limitations periods increases the chances of detection, which in turn increases the expected cost from tax penalties.

Perceptions of the IRS and Tax Morale. Means-based adjustments to the statute of limitations would also address public perceptions that the IRS cannot challenge cases of abusive tax planning because of expired time limits. Whether or not the allegations in the 2018 *New York Times* report on the tax returns of President Trump and members of his family are accurate, dozens of other news sources highlighted the impact of the statute of limitations on further investigation by the IRS.[77] As Steven Rosenthal, Senior Fellow at the Urban-Brookings Tax Policy Center, noted in response to questions regarding the 2018 report and the statute of limitations, "Practically speaking, I would not expect the IRS to be pursuing this one."[78]

In contrast to current law, means-based adjustments would empower the government to signal to all taxpayers that it now possesses an enhanced tax enforcement tool – time itself – which it can deploy in its review of the tax returns of high-end taxpayers.

Harder to Avoid. In its fiscal year 2024 revenue proposals, the Treasury noted that the three-year default statute of limitations creates detection and enforcement obstacles for IRS officials when the tax returns involve complex strategies.[79] The Treasury stated that "extending the statute of limitations for complex cases would provide IRS with enhanced agility and flexibility in evaluating and staffing its case inventory and appropriately allocating its limited enforcement resources."[80]

To implement this goal, in 2023, the Treasury proposed that Congress should provide for a special six-year statute of limitations if a taxpayer omits more than $100 million from their gross income on a return.[81] While the Treasury highlighted the relevance of the statute of limitations to tax enforcement, our proposal would apply more broadly because it would not depend upon the magnitude of tax deficiencies or omissions from income.

First, by focusing only on the size of the omission from gross income, the Treasury would create an opportunity for taxpayers to avoid the extended statute of limitations. For instance, they could respond to this rule by engaging in tax strategies that do not cause them to approach this threshold, or by engaging in separate tax-avoidance strategies that spread over multiple years. Our proposed means-adjusted statute of limitations, however, would be harder to avoid because it would require high-end taxpayers to significantly understate their overall adjusted gross income or net wealth for the year in question.

Second, by targeting "omissions" from income, high-end taxpayers could avoid the extended statute of limitations by reporting either *some* amount of income, even small amounts, or information related to tax strategies. This approach would be consistent with taxpayers' responses to the "substantial omission" exception to the default statute of limitations under current law.[82] Our proposed means-based adjustments, on the other hand, would not require high-end taxpayers to omit any specific amounts of income in order for the IRS to have more detection time.

Finally, by extending the statute of limitations period for omissions only when taxpayers omit more than $100 million of income, the 2023 Treasury proposal would likely apply primarily to corporate taxpayers rather than to individuals. As Treasury implies in its explanation of the proposal, the new rule, if it went into force, would likely primarily apply in audits of large corporations involving transfer pricing issues and complex cross-border transactions.[83] Again, our proposal is significantly broader. By introducing means adjustments based on income or net wealth, along with exceptions for low-value underpayments, our proposal would enable the IRS to have additional time when reviewing the tax returns of high-end individuals, not just large corporations.

Complementing Other Tax Compliance Rules. Finally, introducing means adjustments to the statute of limitations rules can interact with other elements of the tax compliance system to improve their effects and to address other challenges the IRS faces. For example, in some circumstances, extending the statute of limitations period for high-end taxpayers can give the IRS more time to implement other activity-based rules through regulatory action so it can avoid challenges under the Administrative Procedure Act.[84]

Additional Considerations

The most likely concern that a means-adjusted statute of limitations raises is that it could be perceived as depriving high-end taxpayers of procedural fairness and equal treatment under the law.[85] An extended statute of limitations increases the potential that any high-end taxpayer, even one who is compliant with the tax law, could face potentially intrusive audits that stretch several years in the past. Not only would these taxpayers be exposed to the potential for greater IRS assertions of tax deficiencies than other taxpayers, but they would also be subject to increased compliance burdens, including recordkeeping and documentation.[86] By applying different review periods to different groups of taxpayers, this proposal could face criticism that it subjects certain taxpayers to increased scrutiny based on economic status rather than potential culpability.

We agree that policymakers should not introduce rules and procedures that unfairly burden certain taxpayers. Yet, in the case of a means-adjusted statute of limitations, this concern would be mitigated by a number of considerations. First, the small-underpayment exemption would prevent the extended tax clock, and accompanying recordkeeping requirements, from occurring in situations involving low-dollar tax deficiencies. At the same time, it would not be restricted to applying only when individual taxpayers underreport extremely large amounts of income, resulting in unusually large tax deficiencies. This would be the result under the Biden Administration's 2023 proposal for a $100 million omission from the income threshold.[87]

In addition, while the statute of limitations provides taxpayers with closure and repose, it does not implicate core aspects of access to justice in the same manner as other procedural rules. For the same reason, repose is not commonly understood to be a core rule of law principle, but rather a practical concession to the challenges of enforcing the law across time.[88] Even if the IRS were to receive additional time to review certain tax returns, as we have proposed, high-end taxpayers would still enjoy the right to receive a statutory notice of deficiency, pursue an appeal with the IRS Appeals Division, petition the US Tax Court, and, if necessary, appeal judicial decisions.[89] Further, in instances of fraud or failure to file a tax return, the statute of limitations already stays open indefinitely under current law. Yet these current exceptions do not substantially restrict access to justice, but instead help to deter noncompliance and create a fair playing field between taxpayers and the IRS.

More generally, differential treatment of high-end taxpayers in this area may be justified on account of their access to different tax planning strategies and opportunities to avoid detection. This means-based adjustment would be designed to equalize the effect of the statute of limitations rules rather than to make them less equal. As we have discussed, the business affairs of many high-end taxpayers are more complex and difficult for the IRS to review than those of taxpayers whose income consists largely of wages.[90] Accordingly, high-end taxpayers also present a greater resource mismatch with the IRS, in terms of participation of tax accountants and lawyers in planning, than other taxpayers.[91]

Congress has, in fact, already applied net worth requirements to taxpayers in other tax compliance rules, such as provisions that govern taxpayers' ability to shift the burden of proof in civil tax controversies to the IRS.[92] Different statute of limitations periods based on adjusted gross income or net wealth are in line with these other means-based adjustments. By taking into account differences between groups of taxpayers through varying statutory review periods, the IRS may ultimately apply more equitable enforcement of the tax law against these taxpayers in practice.

NOTES

1. I.R.C. § 6501(a).
2. *See* David Barstow et al., *Trump Engaged in Suspect Tax Schemes as He Reaped Riches from His Father*, N.Y. TIMES (Oct. 2, 2018), https://www.nytimes.com/interactive/2018/10/02/us/politics/donald-trump-tax-schemes-fred-trump.html.
3. *Id.*
4. *Id.*
5. *Id.*
6. Michael Mechanic, *A Tax Guru Explains Why Donald Trump May Finally Be in Trouble*, MOTHER JONES (Jan. 10, 2023), https://www.motherjones.com/politics/2023/01/donald-trump-tax-returns-cheating-audit-irs-fraud-losses/ (quoting Steven Rosenthal).
7. I.R.C. § 6501(a).
8. *Id.*
9. I.R.C. § 6501(b).
10. I.R.C. § 6501(a).
11. *See, e.g.*, I.R.C. § 7502.
12. I.R.C. § 6501(a).
13. *Id.*
14. I.R.C. §§ 6212(a), 6213(a).
15. I.R.C. § 6503(a).
16. *Id.*
17. *Id.*
18. I.R.C. § 6501(e).
19. *Id.*
20. *Id.*
21. *See, e.g.*, IRS, *Filing Past due Tax Returns*, https://www.irs.gov/businesses/small-businesses-self-employed/filing-past-due-tax-returns.
22. I.R.C. § 6501(c)(1), (2).
23. I.R.C. § 6501(c)(10).
24. Rev. Proc. 2005-26, 2005-1 I.R.B. 965; Treas. Reg. § 301.6501(c)-1(g)(2) (providing that the rule extending the period until a year after disclosure "does not apply to any period of limitations on assessment that expired before the date on which the failure to disclose the listed transaction under Section 6011 occurred").
25. IRS, Pub. 55-B (Rev. 3-23), 2022 DATA BOOK, at 4 tbl. 2 (2023).
26. *See* IRS News Release IR-2022-11 (Jan. 12, 2022) (quoting National Taxpayer Advocate Erin M. Collins as stating, "While my report focuses primarily on the problems of 2021, I am deeply concerned about the upcoming filing season .... Paper is the IRS's Kryptonite, and the agency is still buried in it.").
27. Inflation Reduction Act of 2022, H.R. 5376, 117th Cong., Pub. L. No. 117-169, 136 Stat. 1818 (2022).
28. VICTOR HUGO, LES MISÉRABLES (1862).

29 *See* MICHAEL I. SALTZMAN & LESLIE BOOK, IRS PRACTICE AND PROCEDURE 5.01 (2d ed. 2020).
30 *See, e.g.*, Beard v. Comm'r, T.C.M. 2009-184 (2009), *rev'd*, 633 F.3d 616 (7th Cir. 2011), *cert. granted and vacated*, 566 U.S. 971 (2012); Bakersfield Energy Partners, LP v. Comm'r, 568 F.3d 767, 768 (9th Cir. 2009). *Cf.* Salman Ranch, Ltd. v. Comm'r, 647 F.3d 929, 943 (10th Cir. 2011) (rejecting petitioner's argument that statute of limitations had lapsed).
31 566 U.S. 478 (2012).
32 I.R.C. § 6501(e)(1)(B).
33 *See* Letter from Charles P. Rettig, Comm'r, IRS, to Sen. Ron Wyden (D-OR) 2, 4 (Sept. 6, 2019), https://www.documentcloud.org/documents/6430680-Document-2019-9-6-Treasury-Letter-to-Wyden-RE.html.
34 *See, e.g.*, Jesse Eisinger & Paul Kiel, *Gutting the IRS: How the IRS Was Gutted*, PROPUBLICA (Dec. 11, 2018), https://www.propublica.org/article/how-the-irs-was-gutted; *see also Statute of Limitations: When Taxpayers Can Tell the IRS, "You Snooze, You Lose,"* BARNES LAW LLP (May 7, 2016), https://www.barneslawllp.com/blog/statute-limitations-taxpayers-can-tell-irs-snooze-lose.
35 Eisinger & Kiel, *supra* note 34.
36 I.R.C. § 6501(a).
37 *Id.*
38 I.R.C. § 6503(a).
39 *See, e.g.*, Anthony Vittiello et al., *Gift Tax Returns & IRS Examination*, CPA J. (Jan. 2017), https://www.cpajournal.com/2017/01/21/gift-tax-returns-irs-examination/.
40 *Start the clock on your gift tax statute of limitations*, VINCENT & ROMEO, LLC (Nov. 13, 2015), https://www.elderlawcolorado.com/blog/2015/11/start-the-clock-on-your-gift-tax-statute-of-limitations/.
41 Treas. Reg. § 1.6011-4(e)(2)(i).
42 I.R.C. § 6501(c)(10).
43 *Id.*
44 *Id.*
45 Rev. Proc. 2005-26, 2005-17 I.R.B. 965.
46 Beard v. Comm'r, 82 T.C. 766, 777 (1984).
47 IRS, THE MEANING OF "SUBSTANTIALLY COMPLETE" WITH REFERENCE TO INTERNATIONAL INFORMATION RETURN PENALTIES (2017), https://www.irs.gov/pub/int_practice_units/iga_c_17_03_01_02.pdf.
48 *See, e.g.*, William D. Cohan, *What's Really Going on with Mitt Romney's $102 Million IRA*, ATLANTIC (Sept. 10, 2012), https://www.theatlantic.com/politics/archive/2012/09/whats-really-going-on-with-mitt-romneys-102-million-ira/261500/; Lynnley Browning, *How Did Romney's IRA Grow So Big?*, REUTERS (Jan. 23, 2012), https://www.reuters.com/article/us-usa-campaign-romney-ira-idUSTRE80N04E20120124.
49 *See, e.g.*, William D. Cohan, *The Secret behind Romney's Magical IRA*, BLOOMBERG (July 15, 2012), https://www.bloomberg.com/view/articles/2012-07-15/the-secret-behind-romney-s-magical-ira; Tim Dickinson, *Mitt Romney's Tax Dodge*, ROLLING STONE (Oct. 12, 2012), https://www.rollingstone.com/politics/politics-news/mitt-romneys-tax-dodge-126974/ (interviews with Victor Fleischer and Daniel Shaviro).

50 *See, e.g.*, Emanouil v. Comm'r, T.C.M. 2020-10 (2020); Joel N. Crouch, *Using the Substantial Compliance Doctrine to Defeat the IRS*, MEADOWS COLLIER (Aug. 31, 2020), https://www.meadowscollier.com/using-the-substantial-compliance-doctrine-to-defeat-the-irs.
51 IRS, PUB. 1035 (REV. 9-2017), EXTENDING THE TAX ASSESSMENT PERIOD (2017), https://www.irs.gov/pub/irs-pdf/p1035.pdf.
52 *Id.* ("If you choose not to sign the consent, we will take steps that will allow us to assess any tax we determine to be due.").
53 *See* IRS, Form 872 (Consent to Extend the Time to Assess Tax).
54 For example, this date could be six months from the date of the waiver.
55 *See, e.g.*, Joe Marchbein, *Consent to Extend the Statute of Limitation*, Tax Adviser (July 1, 2009), https://www.thetaxadviser.com/issues/2009/jul/consenttoextendthestatuteoflimitation.html; Charles P. Rettig, *Tax Practitioners Guidebook: Picking Up Table Scraps*, 114 TAX NOTES 1007, 1010 (2007).
56 Rettig, *supra* note 55.
57 Eisinger & Kiel, *supra* note 34.
58 Graham Kates, *In Trump's Approach to Tax Audits, A Familiar Legal Strategy: Delay*, CBS NEWS (Dec. 22, 2022), https://www.cbsnews.com/news/trump-tax-audit-legal-strategy/ (*quoting* forensic accountant Bruce Dubinsky).
59 *See, e.g.*, LINDA Z. SWARTZ & JEAN MARIE BERTRAND, CADWALADER LLP, TO DISCLOSE OR NOT TO DISCLOSE: TAX SHELTERS, PENALTIES, AND CIRCULAR 230 IN 2015 5-6 & n. 17 (2015), https://www.cadwalader.com/uploads/books/d09bc22416d46ea1af862b33ebf77de8.pdf (advising corporate clients regarding the disclosure requirements and statute of limitations).
60 *See* DEP'T OF TREASURY, *infra* note 68 and the accompanying text.
61 I.R.C. § 6501(a).
62 *Id.*
63 I.R.C. § 6501(e).
64 *Id.*
65 I.R.C. § 6501(c)(10).
66 Rev. Proc. 2005-26, 2005-1 I.R.B. 965; Treas. Reg. § 301.6501(c)-1(g)(2) (providing that the rule extending the period until a year after disclosure "does not apply to any period of limitations on assessment that expired before the date on which the failure to disclose the listed transaction under Section 6011 occurred").
67 *See, e.g.*, IRS, Form 1040 Schedule D (Capital Gains and Losses).
68 *See* DEP'T OF TREASURY, GENERAL EXPLANATIONS OF THE ADMINISTRATION'S FISCAL YEAR 2024 REVENUE PROPOSALS 178 (2023).
69 *Id.*
70 *Id.*
71 *See supra* note 46 and the accompanying text.
72 I.R.C. § 6501(a).
73 *See, e.g.*, Joshua D. Blank, *Overcoming Overdisclosure: Toward Tax Shelter Detection*, 56 UCLA L. REV. 1629, 1667 (2009); *see also* Michael Kosnitzky, *Protective Filings for Hedge Funds after the Jobs Act*, 109 TAX NOTES 817, 817 (2005) (describing inadequate protective filings made by hedge funds).

74 See, e.g., Vittiello et al., *supra* note 39; Jay A. Soled et al., *Rethinking the Penalty for the Failure to File Gift Tax Returns*, 141 TAX NOTES 757, 759 n. 28 (2013) ("[N]oncompliant taxpayers always risk a future audit.").
75 See Vittiello et al., *supra* note 39.
76 See Chapter 6, section "Tax Penalties and Deterrence."
77 See, e.g., Michael Collins, *IRS Unlikely to Pursue Tax Fraud Allegations against Donald Trump and Family, Experts Say*, USA TODAY (Oct. 3, 2018), https://www.usatoday.com/story/news/politics/2018/10/03/trump-taxes-irs-unlikely-probe-fraud-claims-detailed-newspaper/1515405002; Irina Ivanova, *Trump Likely Couldn't Be Prosecuted for Tax Fraud – Even If the Times Report Is True*, CBS NEWS (Oct. 3, 2018), https://www.cbsnews.com/news/trump-couldnt-be-prosecuted-for-tax-fraud-even-if-what-the-new-york-times-reported-is-true; Claudia Koerner, *New York Officials Are "Vigorously" Reviewing a Report That Trump Committed Tax Fraud*, BUZZFEED NEWS (Oct. 3, 2018), https://www.buzzfeednews.com/article/claudiakoerner/trump-taxes-investigation; Bess Levin, *"Beyond the Law": Should Trump's Tax Chicanery Land Him in the Clink?*, VANITY FAIR (Oct. 3, 2018), https://www.vanityfair.com/news/2018/10/beyond-the-law-should-trumps-tax-chicanery-land-him-in-the-clink; Annie McDonough, *Why Hasn't New York Charged Donald Trump for Tax Fraud?*, CITY & STATE N.Y. (May 9, 2019), https://www.cityandstateny.com/articles/policy/criminal-justice/why-hasnt-new-york-charged-donald-trump-with-tax-fraud.html.
78 Collins, *supra* note 77 (quoting Steven Rosenthal).
79 See DEP'T OF TREASURY, *supra* note 68.
80 *Id.*
81 *Id.*
82 See, e.g., *Home Concrete & Supply, LLC*, 566 U.S. 478.
83 See DEP'T OF TREASURY, *supra* note 68.
84 For a discussion, see Chapter 3, section "A Complementary Approach."
85 That is, this adjustment might be viewed as interfering with principles of due process and access to justice.
86 See IRS, *How Long Should I Keep Records?* (Sept. 29, 2020), https://www.irs.gov/businesses/small-businesses-self-employed/how-long-should-i-keep-records; Bob Carlson, *How Long Should You Keep Tax Returns? Longer Than You Think*, FORBES (July 9, 2018), https://www.forbes.com/sites/bobcarlson/2018/07/09/how-long-should-you-keep-tax-returns-longer-than-you-think.
87 See DEP'T OF TREASURY, *supra* note 68.
88 See Chapter 4, section "Generality and the Rule of Law."
89 See, e.g., I.R.C. § 6213(a).
90 See Letter from Charles P. Rettig, *supra* note 33.
91 *Id.*
92 I.R.C. § 7491(a)(2). For a discussion, see Chapter 3, section "Means Adjustments in Current Tax Compliance Rules."

9

Tax Information Reporting

Tax information reporting is an essential element of the tax compliance system.[1] When individuals earn wages from their employers,[2] accrue interest in their bank accounts,[3] or receive Social Security benefits,[4] the IRS usually knows. In these types of transactions, a third-party intermediary, often an employer or a bank, files an information return with both the individual taxpayer and the IRS, and, in many cases, withholds taxes owed by the taxpayer.[5] Not surprisingly, when income is subject to third-party information reporting, and is visible to the IRS, tax compliance is extremely high. The IRS estimates that when income is subject to substantial information reporting, approximately 95% of it is reported properly to the IRS, and that the level of compliance jumps to approximately 99% when income is subject to both substantial information reporting and withholding.[6] On the other hand, where income is subject to little or no information reporting, the IRS estimates that tax compliance is only about 55%.[7]

Despite the power of tax information reporting to maximize the IRS's ability to collect taxes owed, these rules also contain significant gaps. High-end taxpayers can often earn their income through transactions that do not require a third party to file tax information reports with the IRS. Individuals who earn their income primarily through wages, on the other hand, are subject to tax information reporting through the filing of IRS Form W-2 (Wage and Tax Statement) by their employers.[8] Consequently, the tax information reporting regime in the United States can be characterized as two-tiered, where high-end taxpayers often escape scrutiny from the IRS and have the opportunity to avoid or evade taxes, while most other taxpayers have the bulk of their annual income automatically reported to the IRS by someone else.

Policymakers have attempted to address tax information reporting gaps by expanding the types of transactions that financial institutions must report to the IRS. For example, in May 2021, the Biden Administration released a proposal that would create a comprehensive financial account information reporting regime.[9] Under the proposal, banks and other financial institutions would report to the IRS information about any business or personal account, including banking, loan, and investment accounts, with fair market value and gross cash flow of $600 or more (later revised to $10,000).[10] The rationale, according to the Treasury Department, was to provide greater "visibility of business income" and "enhance the effectiveness of IRS enforcement measures and encourage voluntary compliance."[11] Further, it noted that financial institutions already report information regarding accounts, such as interest payments, to the IRS, as well as suspicious activity to other agencies.[12] Despite these stated goals and policy arguments, the proposal encountered significant resistance from legislators, taxpayers, and financial institutions and, ultimately, did not appear in legislation considered by Congress.[13]

This chapter demonstrates how the activity-based approach to information reporting often allows high-end taxpayers to engage in noncompliance with the tax law, while other taxpayers face significant automatic IRS scrutiny. It also shows that the government's approach to tax information reporting applies almost exclusively to specific activities, ranging from methods of earning income to designated transactions. This approach is consistent with the government's design of other tax compliance rules that apply to certain types of activities, such as the use of tax shelters, offshore bank accounts, and non-economic substance transactions to avoid tax liability.[14]

THE ROLE OF TAX INFORMATION REPORTING

Tax information reporting plays a critical role in encouraging individuals to comply with the tax law and file their tax returns correctly. Both first and third parties can provide two general types of information to the IRS. First, reporting parties can provide the IRS with primary information used to calculate substantive tax liabilities, such as the taxpayer's income and transactions. They can also provide the IRS with additional information that can assist in tax administration and enforcement but does not directly factor into calculating tax liabilities, such as general information regarding the taxpayers or their activities, all of which may indicate or enable noncompliance.

Third-Party Information Reporting Rules

The Internal Revenue Code and Treasury Regulations contain dozens of third-party information reporting rules. Information returns supply the IRS with data that can be matched to items that taxpayers self-report to the IRS on their tax returns that may affect their tax liability.[15] Below is a non-exhaustive description of some of the major information reporting requirements that apply under current law, organized into the following categories: compensation; investment and sales; non-compensation payments; and retirement and health benefits.

Compensation for Goods or Services. Some of the most common third-party information reporting rules apply when an individual or entity pays compensation in exchange for goods or services. Every employer engaged in a trade or business that makes payments to an employee in exchange for services, whether in cash or in-kind compensation, must file IRS Form W-2 (Wage and Tax Statement) for the employee.[16] This requirement applies when the employer withheld any income, Social Security, or Medicare tax, or when the employer paid $600 or more in wages and did not withhold any income, Social Security, or Medicare tax.[17]

Outside of the employment context, persons engaged in a trade or business who pay an independent contractor at least $600 in exchange for services must file an information return, IRS Form 1099-NEC (Nonemployee Compensation) or IRS Form 1099-MISC (Miscellaneous Income). In addition, "payment settlement entities" must file IRS Form 1099-K (Payment Card and Third Party Network Transactions) for persons who earn at least a threshold dollar amount of reportable payments in exchange for goods or services.[18] Once legislation enacted in 2021 goes into effect, these entities, which include credit card companies, banks, and online sharing and auction sites, will be required to file the information return for any individual who receives at least $600 in gross earnings during the year (decreased from a higher threshold under prior law of $20,000 in gross earnings and more than 200 transactions during the year).[19] This statutory change extends third-party information reporting to many individuals who earn even a small amount of income through online platforms, such as Uber, eBay, and Etsy.

Investment Income and Transactions. Individuals are also subject to third-party information reporting when they engage in certain investment activities. Financial institutions provide IRS Form 1099-INT (Interest Income) to each person who receives at least $10 of interest income during the year.[20] Corporations file information returns, such as IRS Form 1099-DIV (Dividends and Distributions), when they pay at least $10 in gross dividends and other stock distributions during the year.[21] In addition, the IRS receives information returns when taxpayers engage in sales or dispositions of assets. For example, when a taxpayer sells stock, securities, and other debt instruments through a broker, the broker must file IRS Form 1099-B (Proceeds from Broker and Barter Exchange Transactions), which reports information such as the date the asset was acquired, the cost basis, the proceeds from the sale, and the date the asset was sold.[22]

For tax returns required to be filed after December 31, 2023, digital asset brokers are also required to file IRS Form 1099-B upon a person's sale or exchange of digital assets, such as Bitcoin and other cryptocurrency.[23] This new reporting rule will require platforms such as Coinbase to report the gross proceeds from any sale of digital assets, together with the customer's name, address, and phone number, to the IRS.[24]

Finally, persons who purchase real estate during the year are required to report the gross proceeds from the sale on IRS Form 1099-S (Proceeds from Real Estate Transactions). This requirement, however, is subject to a number of exceptions, such as sales of personal residences.[25]

Offshore Accounts. In some cases, a third party is also obligated to file an information report with respect to a taxpayer's financial account balances. FATCA generally requires third-party "foreign financial institutions" (FFIs), such as banks, to report the account balances and other information regarding their US account holders[26] on IRS Form 8966.[27] Congress enacted FATCA in 2010 with the purpose of gathering the necessary information to prevent taxpayers from avoiding tax liabilities by holding assets in offshore accounts.[28]

Miscellaneous Payments. Taxpayers are also subject to third-party information reporting when they make or receive a variety of other miscellaneous payments. For example, when a bank or other financial institution is paid mortgage interest of at least $600 during the year, the institution is required to file IRS Form 1098 (Mortgage Interest Statement) with respect to the individual making those payments.[29] Similarly, when a financial institution, governmental unit, or educational institution is paid interest of at least $600 during the year on a student loan, it must file IRS Form 1098-E (Student Loan Interest Statement).[30]

Retirement and Health Benefits. Taxpayers who receive retirement and health benefits are also subject to third-party information reporting by financial institutions and their employers. When individuals receive distributions from profit-sharing or retirement plans, IRAs, annuities, and pensions, whether or not any amount of federal income tax was withheld, the financial institutions making the distributions are required to file IRS Form 1099-R (Distributions from Pensions, Annuities, Retirement or Profit-Sharing Plans, IRAs, Insurance Contracts, etc.).[31]

Regarding health benefits, a business that provides minimum essential health insurance coverage to an individual during the calendar year must file an information return reporting the coverage, IRS Form 1095-B (Health Coverage).[32] Similarly, institutions that administer tax-favored accounts related to healthcare, such as Health Savings Accounts (HSAs), must report all distributions to individuals from these accounts on specific information returns.[33]

First-Party Information Reporting Rules

The tax rules also require the taxpayers themselves to report information to the IRS, which are characterized broadly as forms of "first-party" information reporting. For example, the annual tax return filings – such as the income tax returns for individuals (IRS Form 1040),[34] corporations (IRS Form 1120),[35] partnerships (IRS Form 1065),[36] and estates and trusts (IRS Form 1041)[37] – are first-party information reports. These forms require reporting of the primary information that is used to calculate tax liabilities, as well as additional information that can assist in tax administration and enforcement. For example, IRS Form 1040 requires reporting of items of income and deductible expenses, together with other information that does not directly factor into this calculation.[38] Beginning in 2020, for example, the IRS included a question on IRS Form 1040 asking whether the taxpayer transacted in virtual currencies during the taxable year.[39]

Beyond tax return filings, the IRS also requires additional first-party financial information reports that assist with tax administration and enforcement, even though the information reported does not directly affect the calculation of tax liabilities. For example, both US individuals and certain entities with significant "specified foreign financial assets" must file IRS Form 8938 (Statement of Specified Foreign Financial Assets) listing the value of these assets.[40] For these purposes, specified foreign financial assets include non-US financial accounts, financial contracts and securities issued by foreign counterparties, and stock or other interests in foreign entities.[41] Taxpayers subject to IRS Form 8938 reporting must identify any such assets and their maximum value during the taxable year.[42]

To minimize imposing collateral compliance burdens on taxpayers who are not the proper subjects of heightened first-party information reporting, the Internal Revenue Code and Treasury Regulations apply wealth-based thresholds that exempt less-wealthy taxpayers from IRS Form 8938 reporting obligations. In general, individuals must file the IRS Form 8938 only if they hold specified assets with an aggregate value in excess of $50,000, or an aggregate value of $75,000 at any time during the year.[43] These thresholds double to $100,000 and $150,000, respectively, for married couples filing a joint return.[44] Individuals living abroad must file the form only if their specified assets exceed $200,000 at the end of the taxable year, or $300,000 at any time during the year.[45] These thresholds similarly double to $400,000 and $600,000, respectively, for married couples filing a joint return.[46]

How Information Reporting Enhances Tax Compliance

A closer look at the IRS analysis of the tax gap discussed in Chapter 1 reveals that the overwhelming majority of unpaid tax dollars are due to underreporting of income (approximately $352 billion out of the $441 billion gross tax gap).[47] Much of this figure is attributable to underreported business income, including that earned by individuals in the cash economy.[48] Further, though the distribution of tax noncompliance among taxpayers based on income is difficult to discern, one recent study estimates that tax noncompliance by the top 1% of earners alone accounts for 30% of the tax gap.[49]

While the IRS's estimates of the annual tax gap paint an image of high rates of overall tax compliance (approximately 84%),[50] the rate of compliance varies significantly depending upon whether the income is subject to information reporting rules. According to government reports, when taxpayers are subject to information reporting and withholding at the source, the tax compliance rate is approximately 99%.[51] When taxpayers are subject to information reporting only, the rate is approximately 95%.[52] And when taxpayers are subject to neither information reporting nor withholding, the IRS estimates that the compliance rate is as low as 37%.[53] Based on these figures, IRS officials have concluded that third-party information reporting directly impacts the level of compliance for specific types of income. As IRS Commissioner Charles Rettig noted in 2021, the lack of third-party information reporting rules is a "significant reason" for the existing annual gross tax gap, and that "tax compliance is far higher" when income is subject to third-party information reporting.[54]

Why does tax compliance in the United States vary so dramatically between transactions where income is subject to information reporting and those where it is not? Three major explanations relate directly to information reporting: (1) such reporting allows the IRS to receive information from centralized third parties involved in arms' length transactions with the taxpayer; (2) it empowers the IRS to detect noncompliance by the taxpayer; and (3) it influences individual taxpayers' perceptions of the probability of IRS audit.

Centralized Third Parties. One explanation for the efficacy of information reporting is that centralized third parties, such as employers or financial institutions, rather than individual taxpayers, are responsible for collecting and transmitting information about payments and other transactions to the IRS.[55] These third parties are often already maintaining business records, such as payroll and inventory accounting.[56] For example, unlike many average individual wage earners, employers maintain financial accounting reports that include information about wages as part of their ordinary business operations. The tax information reporting rules piggyback on these records. Where the third party complies with the information reporting requirements and has engaged in an arm's length transaction with the taxpayer, an information return provides the taxpayer and the IRS with an independent confirmation of the amount of a taxpayer's income and expenses. Therefore, these centralized third parties assist tax administration and enforcement by providing independent and standardized confirmation of taxpayer transactions.

IRS Detection and Enforcement. Where income is subject to third-party information reporting, the IRS can compare and analyze reported information to detect potential tax noncompliance. Before the introduction of third-party information reporting and withholding in the 1940s, IRS agents could verify a taxpayer's reported income only by auditing the individual taxpayer's return and requesting substantiating documentation.[57] When the IRS receives an information return from a third party, such as IRS Form W-2 (Wage and Tax Statement), it can quickly compare the wage information reported on this form with the wage information that the taxpayer reported on IRS Form 1040 (US Individual Tax Return).[58] The IRS has confirmed that one of the methods it uses to select tax returns for further scrutiny are those in which "payer reports, such as Forms W-2 from employers or Form 1099 interest statements from banks, do not match the income reported on the tax return."[59]

Perceived Audit Probability. When taxpayers think that their income information is well hidden, they may be less fearful of an IRS audit. Studies find that third-party information reporting influences taxpayers' perceptions of the probability of an IRS audit. For instance, in 2020, the IRS audit rate for individual income tax returns was approximately 0.2%.[60] However, despite this low overall audit rate, third-party information reporting rules cause many taxpayers to believe that the chance of an IRS audit is significantly higher if they fail to report income correctly. For example, individual taxpayers estimated that, if they were to file false returns, the probability that their tax returns would be audited by the IRS was 48%.[61] Likewise, in its annual study of taxpayer attitudes, in 2020 the IRS found that approximately 63% of individual taxpayers reported that "[f]ear of an audit" either had somewhat of an influence or had a great deal of influence on their decision to pay their taxes honestly.[62]

TAX INFORMATION REPORTING AND HIGH-END TAXPAYERS

The reach of the tax information reporting rules is not only sprawling but also ever-expanding. According to IRS data, in 2021, over 3.9 billion information returns were filed with the IRS.[63] By 2029, the agency expects to receive approximately 5.2 billion information returns per year.[64] A closer look, however, shows that these rules also contain significant gaps. The rules apply to specific transactions in which third-party intermediaries are required to collect information and submit it to the IRS. But in situations that do not involve these transactions, the information reporting is either ineffective or does not apply at all.

We argue that the gaps in the tax information reporting rules are the result of the government's application of these rules to specific activities. As we discuss in the following section, this approach allows high-end taxpayers in particular to avoid IRS audit and challenge. In response, we argue that policymakers should expand the scope of the tax information reporting rules to increase visibility with regard to not only specific activities but also the personal economic characteristics of the taxpayers who pursue them, such as their income and wealth. As we argue, closing the tax information reporting gap will, in the end, help close the tax gap itself.

Opportunities for Avoiding Tax Information Reporting

A common explanation for high rates of tax noncompliance by high-end taxpayers is that these individuals are not subject to third-party information reporting on significant amounts of their income.[65] Some economists have argued that increasing tax information reporting requirements that apply to high-end taxpayers could generate as much as $2 trillion over a ten-year period.[66] To date, government officials have not offered specific examples of strategies that high-end taxpayers use to escape information reporting rules.[67] Therefore, we offer several specific examples, based on the tax-avoidance research, of common ways in which high-end taxpayers earn income without being subject to third-party information reporting requirements.

Business Income

High-end taxpayers can often structure their businesses and other income-producing activities to avoid third-party information reporting. The most basic strategy is to earn income through a self-owned and self-operated business. When individuals earn wages from an employer, the employer files an information return and withholds tax from the payment to the employee. However, this type of third-party information reporting does not apply to individuals who own and operate their own businesses, either as sole proprietorships or through business entities, rather than work as employees. Studies find that business income is highly concentrated at the top of the income distribution, and "pass-through" business income earned through non-taxable entities is even more concentrated among the highest earners.[68]

For a simple example, consider a wealthy individual who owns and manages several apartment buildings and has multiple tenants in each building. The tenants of the buildings pay rent to the landlord each month, but they are not required to file information returns with the IRS or the landlord as a result of these payments.[69] Specifically, there is no "IRS Form 1099-RENT" or other analogue to the types of information returns that individuals receive when they earn wages or interest.[70] Consequently, when landlords file their tax returns, they essentially have an unchecked opportunity to underreport income they received through rent payments. Several studies confirm that rental income is subject to high rates of underreporting by taxpayers.[71] Further, there is no third-party reporting for many of the expenses that the landlord may incur, such as payments for routine repairs and maintenance of the properties.[72]

When a taxpayer, such as the owner of the apartment buildings in this example, controls the reporting of both income and expenses to the IRS, there is a high potential for tax noncompliance. This potential is magnified when taxpayers participate in cash economy businesses where there is *no* information reporting of income and expenses.[73] As Natasha Sarin has commented, "If you are a normal person who makes a wage, your tax compliance is 99 percent. If you are a rich person who earns dividend income and real estate income and runs a proprietorship, your compliance rate could be as low as 45 percent."[74]

For high-end taxpayers, the availability of pass-through entities, such as partnerships, subchapter S corporations, and LLCs, only increases opportunities to avoid IRS scrutiny. When high-end taxpayers earn income through such entities, not only do they benefit from the lack of third-party information reporting, but they also benefit from the IRS's lack of auditing of these entities. One study has found that IRS agents substantially under-detect tax evasion involving pass-through entities.[75] As one of the authors of the study, Gabriel Zucman, described the results, "random audits uncover very little pass-through business tax evasion, even though the complexity of these businesses can facilitate substantial evasion."[76] Consequently, in addition to not facing the type of third-party information reporting rules that apply to individuals who earn wages, high-end taxpayers who use pass-through entities often escape IRS review during audits.

Offshore Bank Accounts

Hiding assets in offshore bank accounts is another common strategy that high-end taxpayers have used to evade taxes. As with pass-through entities, this is generally possible because of the lack of information reporting to the IRS by banks and other financial institutions.

For decades, high-end taxpayers have diverted earnings from US sources into offshore trusts and bank accounts, whether through the deposit of cash funds or smuggling of tangible assets, such as diamonds concealed in tubes of toothpaste.[77] These schemes only worked because financial institutions outside of the United States, such as UBS, a large international bank that is based in Switzerland, used local bank secrecy rules as a reason for not reporting information about these accounts to the IRS.[78]

As we discussed in Chapter 2, Congress enacted FATCA in 2010.[79] Under this legislation, financial institutions must report identifying and account balance information for their US account holders to the IRS.[80] Noncomplying financial institutions are subject to a 30% withholding tax on certain US-source payments.[81] In addition, from 2009 through 2018, the IRS entered into settlement agreements with over 50,000 US taxpayers who participated in the agency's Offshore Voluntary Disclosure Program (OVDP).[82] Following these actions, since 2014, over 100 countries have adopted the "common reporting standard," under which they agree to automatically share information regarding the bank and financial account holdings of other countries' residents, such as account numbers and balances.[83]

Despite all these developments, some high-end taxpayers still evade taxes in the United States through the use of offshore bank accounts. Academic researchers and IRS officials have estimated that the IRS fails to collect tens of billions of dollars each year due to this activity.[84] Through leaks of financial and tax information in the *Panama Papers* in 2016[85] and the *Pandora Papers* in 2021,[86] the public learned how thousands of ultra-wealthy taxpayers and politicians continued to maintain offshore bank accounts, even after the enactment of FATCA and the introduction of the common reporting standard. For example, in October 2021, journalists reported on offshore accounts of US billionaires, including Robert Brockman, who had been charged in 2020 with a $2 billion federal tax evasion case.[87]

The US Department of Justice has continued to announce indictments of high-end taxpayers who have hidden assets in offshore accounts.[88] And in 2021, a whistleblower accused Credit Suisse, another Swiss-based bank (which was acquired by UBS in 2023[89]), of continuing to assist US taxpayers in avoiding tax through such strategies, even though the bank had entered into a settlement with the US in 2014 in which it pleaded guilty, paid fines of $2.6 billion, and committed to close any accounts of recalcitrant account holders.[90] As these examples illustrate, the answer to the question of whether FATCA has been fully effective in combating offshore tax evasion is, at the very least, uncertain.

Virtual Currency and Digital Assets Transactions

Like offshore bank accounts, virtual currency and digital assets offer high-end taxpayers another opportunity to evade taxation without being subject to effective third-party information reporting. In 2021, IRS Commissioner Charles Rettig identified tax evasion through virtual currency transactions as a significant reason that the tax gap could be as high as $1 trillion each year.[91] In this case as well, Congress has adopted an activity-based approach to information reporting by seeking to adjust the reporting rules for taxpayers who engage in certain digital asset transactions.

Under current law, the IRS treats virtual currency, such as Bitcoin and Ethereum, as property, resulting in ordinary income treatment when taxpayers receive it in exchange for services and capital gain or loss treatment when they sell or exchange it.[92] As discussed earlier, starting for tax returns filed after December 31, 2023, digital asset brokers, such as Coinbase, will be required to file IRS Form 1099-B (Proceeds from Broker and Barter Exchange Transactions) when their customers sell or exchange Bitcoin and other cryptocurrency.[93] Further, under legislation enacted in 2021, individuals engaged in a trade or business and businesses that receive digital assets worth more than $10,000 will be required to file currency transaction reports, IRS Form 8300 (Report of Cash Payments over $10,000 Received in a Trade or Business), just as they do when they receive such amounts in cash.[94]

While Congress has attempted to increase the visibility of digital transactions to the IRS, significant opportunities remain for avoiding information reporting through virtual currency and digital asset transactions, especially by high-end taxpayers. For example, some high-end taxpayers engage in transactions worth upward of millions of dollars through wallet-to-wallet transfers, rather than through services such as Coinbase.[95] The absence of an intermediary, including a digital platform, reduces the likelihood that all significant virtual currency transactions will yield information returns to the IRS. Another potential loophole is that the legislation does not appear to directly address situations where individuals exchange one virtual currency, such as Bitcoin, for another virtual currency.[96]

Trading partners who are similarly motivated can help each other avoid reporting by transacting through a virtual market. For example, in exchanges involving virtual currency, the filing of the currency transaction report may, in some cases, depend upon the cooperation of the other party. If the transaction involves an exchange of virtual currency for virtual currency, both parties may have an incentive not to file an information report, thereby sharing the benefits from any tax avoidance. In this case, the buyer may not comply with the tax information reporting rules in exchange for a reduced price from the seller. And in some cases, such as wallet-to-wallet transfers, a party may not be able to obtain the information necessary to file the required information return.[97] As one practitioner has commented, "If Treasury and the IRS say that we're going to do that verification exactly like for cash, it's going to be really hard to comply."[98]

As described in Chapter 1, Treasury has consequently faced challenges in implementing these rules in a way that would effectively target the intended activities without imposing undue burdens on taxpayers and third parties.[99] Most importantly, Treasury has faced delays in issuing guidance, including on the critical question of which parties will be deemed to be brokers subject to the new information reporting rules.[100]

Use of Business Entities

High-end taxpayers can also escape information reporting by earning income indirectly, through certain types of business entities. Under the current law, when a person engaged in a trade or business pays another party (who is not an employee) $600 or more in exchange for services, that person must file an information return, such as IRS Form 1099-MISC (Miscellaneous Information) or IRS Form 1099-NEC (Nonemployee Compensation).[101] However, under the applicable regulations, if the service provider is a corporation rather than an individual, this reporting requirement does not apply.[102] As a result, with few exceptions, when a subchapter S corporation receives payments and other compensation in exchange for services, the payor does not file an information return with the IRS.[103]

This exception to the information reporting rule offers an opportunity for individuals to engage in tax avoidance and evasion without raising the possibility of IRS detection. Some scholars have proposed that the government should close this loophole, rather than allowing "individuals inclined to evade taxes ... to form a wholly owned corporation simply to avoid receiving information reports."[104] However, an additional consideration, which is not emphasized in the literature, is that this exception likely benefits high-end taxpayers disproportionately. In order to take advantage of it, individuals must have the knowledge to pursue the strategy, the resources to hire advisors in order to incorporate, and the ability to manage ongoing compliance costs of operating in corporate form.

Disguised Dividends

High-end taxpayers can also evade tax and information reporting when they extract disguised dividends from corporations they control. Under US tax law, when a subchapter C corporation makes a distribution of cash or other property to its shareholders, the distribution may be taxable to the shareholders as a dividend.[105] When this occurs, the corporation is required to file an information return, IRS Form 1099-DIV (Dividends and Distributions), with the shareholders and the IRS.[106]

As students in an introductory corporate tax course learn, however, sometimes the form of a transaction may be inconsistent with its substance, especially in cases of abusive tax avoidance and evasion.[107] For example, one abusive transaction that many high-end taxpayers have attempted is to direct a wholly owned subchapter C corporation to make a "loan" of cash to the shareholder rather than the distribution of a dividend.[108] This technique enables the shareholder to claim that the distribution is not taxable because they are only "borrowing" the money, even though the IRS or a court may later recharacterize it as a taxable "disguised dividend."[109]

In addition to the general tax-avoidance motivation, this "lending" strategy enables the shareholder to avoid information reporting by the corporation. Since the corporation treats the distribution as a loan, it does not issue the shareholder an IRS Form 1099-DIV, as this is only required when the corporation pays a dividend.[110] Further, even if the shareholder pays interest to the corporation, whether at market rates or not, the shareholder is also not required to file the interest information report, IRS Form 1099-INT (Interest Income), because this requirement does not apply when the interest payee is a corporation.[111]

High-end taxpayers may pursue other similar strategies that would also avoid information reporting requirements, such as by claiming that transfers from their wholly owned corporations are reimbursements for expenses the shareholders incurred on behalf of the corporation.[112] While the IRS should continue to challenge situations where taxpayers mischaracterize dividend payments, the absence of information reporting by either the corporations or the shareholders may prevent the IRS from discovering that the transactions have occurred.

Payroll Taxes

High-end taxpayers can also use business entities to manipulate the character of their reported income and, as a result, their information reporting and withholding obligations. By forming a subchapter S corporation, high-end taxpayers can control the extent to which they report their earnings as compensation income. For a simple example, an individual who receives compensation as an investment fund manager might earn $10 million each year. If the individual's wholly owned subchapter S corporation, rather than the individual, receives the payments, the corporation may designate only $200,000 of this amount as the individual's salary. In this case, only the $200,000, not the entire $10 million, would be designated as compensation income and would be subject to payroll (Social Security and Medicare) taxes.

On occasion, the IRS has challenged taxpayers who have engaged in such subchapter S corporation strategies on the basis of their failure to satisfy the "reasonable compensation" requirement;[113] however, in many cases, the IRS has neither audited nor challenged high-end taxpayers who have used this tax-avoidance technique. Numerous high-end taxpayers have allegedly used this strategy, including several politicians, such as former Speaker of the House Newt Gingrich,[114] former US Senator John Edwards,[115] and, prior to winning the 2020 presidential election, former senator and vice president Joe Biden.[116] Congress has considered legislative proposals, including the *Build Back Better Act*, that would have prevented taxpayers from using this strategy and potentially raised $250 billion in revenue over a ten-year period, but as of 2022, Congress has not enacted them.[117]

Not all taxpayers have these opportunities to control how their earnings are reported to the IRS. When wage earners receive their paychecks, for instance, their employers automatically characterize the payments as compensation for services, which requires them to file information returns, as well as to withhold federal income taxes and, up to the statutory caps, payroll taxes.

Sales, Exchanges, and Dispositions

Finally, high-end taxpayers have greater opportunities to avoid effective third-party information reporting when they engage in sales, exchanges, and dispositions of property. When average investors purchase and subsequently sell shares of stock through a broker, such as through their Vanguard brokerage accounts, they receive an information return, IRS Form 1099-B (Proceeds from Broker and Barter Exchange Transactions), which reports their cost basis and the proceeds from the sale.[118] Some high-end taxpayers, on the other hand, often participate in transactions that are not subject to comparable third-party information reporting and, in certain cases, may exploit this feature to underreport taxable gains and overreport taxable losses.

One example of this kind of transaction is when high-end taxpayers sell shares of a subchapter S corporation. When they do this, they do not receive an information return that states their cost basis in their shares.[119] Specifically, as a result of the complexity of the applicable law, the IRS does not require the subchapter S corporation to provide the shareholder with an overall basis figure on the annual IRS Schedule K-1 (Form 1120-S).[120] Similarly, when a taxpayer sells a partnership interest, the IRS Schedule K-1 (Form 1065) does not contain an overall outside basis figure either.[121]

As another example, when high-end taxpayers purchase stock or assets in situations not involving a broker, such as a direct purchase from another shareholder of a closely held corporation, they may not receive an information return at all, which allows them to later claim an inflated cost basis in a subsequent sale.[122] Further, in a situation in which a buyer and seller collude, such as by agreeing to not file an information return like the IRS Form 1099-S or the IRS Form 8300 in exchange for a lower purchase price, the IRS will not receive any third-party information return that a sale has even occurred.

Consequently, unlike what happens when the average taxpayer sells stock that they purchased through a brokerage account, the IRS does not receive information returns that computers can quickly compare to taxpayers' self-reported gains or losses on their individual tax returns.

THE CASE FOR A MEANS-ADJUSTED APPROACH

As we have argued throughout this book, there is a viable alternative to focusing exclusively on specific activities in designing information reporting rules. Instead, policymakers could also require more general tax information reporting when a taxpayer's income or wealth exceeds a threshold amount. Further, as has been the case with each of the other examples we have provided, introducing means-adjusted information reporting rules would provide several tax administration and enforcement benefits.

The first, and most obvious, benefit would be to improve the IRS's ability to catch those who do not comply with the tax laws. By supplementing the tax information reporting rules under current law with means adjustments tied to income or wealth, the IRS would cast a wider net to capture the tax-avoidance and evasion strategies that high-end taxpayers pursue. When these taxpayers manipulate the content of information returns, such as by underreporting business income, they often do so because there is no arm's length third-party intermediary that is required to report information to the IRS. However, if the IRS could access more general information about high-end taxpayers' financial affairs, such as by reviewing inflows and outflows of capital, it could identify situations where there are discrepancies between information reported by the third-party intermediary and the taxpayer.

A second reason to incorporate our means-adjusted model is that it would be harder for high-end taxpayers to avoid more general information reporting requirements that apply to actors rather than to their specific activities. Under current law, high-end taxpayers can simply avoid meaningful third-party information reporting by failing to engage in covered activities, such as earning wages. Instead, high-end taxpayers can use vehicles that are not subject to third-party information reporting requirements, such as subchapter S corporations and partnerships.

Policymakers could close gaps like this by empowering the IRS to observe and analyze more general categories of financial information for high-end taxpayers. The types of tax noncompliance that IRS agents may discover as a result of such red flags could include information regarding tax strategies that the IRS has *not*, up to that point, specifically designated as abusive, such as "listed transactions" or "transactions of interest."[123] Under this broader means-adjusted approach to information reporting, the IRS would assume a more proactive, rather than reactive, approach to tax-avoidance and evasion strategies than it can under the current law. Further, as the empirical literature has demonstrated, the introduction of more general, means-adjusted information reporting rules could deter high-end taxpayers from pursuing the most blatant forms of tax evasion, such as underreporting income from wholly owned businesses.

The third reason for implementing a means-adjusted approach is that it would reduce the inequity of current tax information reporting rules. Today, hundreds of millions of individual taxpayers who earn income in ways that involve third-party intermediaries, such as employers and financial institutions, are subject to omnipresent, automated information reporting.[124] As some scholars have explained, the tax compliance of these taxpayers is so high because they have essentially no opportunity to avoid or evade taxation on much of their income.[125] These taxpayers, which include the vast majority of low- and middle-income individuals, face a heightened probability of IRS audit if they fail to report information to the IRS in a manner consistent with that of these intermediaries.

The inequities inherent in the current system are especially stark when it comes to the racial impact of tax enforcement. As we discussed in Chapter 1, an investigation by *ProPublica* in 2021 found especially high IRS audit rates in predominantly Black low-income counties in the South.[126] Professor Dorothy Brown has argued that even though about half of the EITC recipients nationally are white, the *ProPublica* reports show that "[p]redominantly Black counties have higher audit rates than predominantly white ones because of the large number of EITC claimants living there."[127] In response to this apparent systemic injustice, scholars and policymakers have called for investigation by Congress and the IRS into the racial distribution of IRS audits.[128]

By contrast, high-end taxpayers, who are disproportionately white,[129] more often control their own sources of income and methods of earning it. They operate in a different system, in which they have more options to underreport income, and to do so without detection. By implementing general means-adjusted information reporting rules, high-end taxpayers could be subject to a similar risk of detection and enforcement as most other taxpayers.

In Chapter 10, we propose that policymakers should supplement current law by introducing means-adjusted information reporting rules that apply when taxpayers' income or wealth exceeds threshold amounts. We provide policymakers with several models and examples of how they could introduce means-based adjustments to the information reporting rules.

NOTES

1 I.R.C. §§ 6041–6050Y (Information Concerning Transactions with Other Persons). *See* IRS, PUB. 1415 (REV. 9-2019), FEDERAL TAX COMPLIANCE RESEARCH: TAX GAP

Estimates for Tax Years 2011–2013 3 (2019); Theodore Black et al., *Federal Tax Compliance Research: Tax Year 2006 Tax Gap Estimation* 4, IRS Research, Analysis & Statistics Working Paper (2012), https://www.irs.gov/pub/irs-soi/06rastg12workppr.pdf. For discussion, see Leandra Lederman, *Reducing Information Gaps to Reduce the Tax Gap: When Is Information Reporting Warranted?*, 78 Fordham L. Rev. 1733 (2010); Leandra Lederman, *Statutory Speed Bumps: The Roles Third Parties Play in Tax Compliance*, 60 Stan. L. Rev. 695, 697–99 (2007); Leandra Lederman & Joseph Dugan, *Information Matters in Tax Enforcement*, 2020 BYU L. Rev. 145; Joel Slemrod, *Cheating Ourselves: The Economics of Tax Evasion*, 21 J. Econ. Persp. 25 (2007); Jay A. Soled, *Homage to Information Returns*, 27 Va. Tax. Rev. 371 (2007); Manoj Viswanathan, *Tax Compliance in a Decentralizing Economy*, 34 Ga. St. U. L. Rev. 283, 296–306 (2018).

2 I.R.C. § 6041(a); IRS, Form W-2 (Wage and Tax Statement).
3 I.R.C. § 6049; IRS, Form 1099-INT (Interest Income).
4 I.R.C. § 6050F; IRS, Form SSA-1099 (Social Security Benefit Statement).
5 *See, e.g.*, Treas. Reg. § 1.6041-1(a)(1)(i) (payments required to be reported).
6 IRS, *supra* note 1, at 14 fig. 3.
7 *Id.*
8 *See* I.R.C. § 6041(a); IRS, Form W-2 (Wage and Tax Statement).
9 *See* Dep't of Treasury, General Explanations of the Administration's Fiscal Year 2022 Revenue Proposals 88–90 (2021), https://home.treasury.gov/system/files/131/General-Explanations-FY2022.pdf; Dep't of Treasury, Fact Sheet: Tax Compliance Proposals Will Improve Tax Fairness While Protecting Taxpayer Privacy (Oct. 19, 2021), https://home.treasury.gov/news/press-releases/jy0415 [hereinafter Fact Sheet] (detailing the Biden Administration's revised tax compliance proposals); *see also* Dep't of Treasury, The American Families Plan Tax Compliance Agenda (2021), https://home.treasury.gov/system/files/136/The-American-Families-Plan-Tax-Compliance-Agenda.pdf.
10 Dep't of Treasury, General Explanations of the Administration's Fiscal Year 2022 Revenue Proposals, *supra* note 9, at 88.
11 *Id.*
12 *Id.*; *see also* Letter from Janet L. Yellen, Sec'y, Dep't of Treasury, to Richard E. Neal, Chairman, Comm. on Ways and Means (Sept. 14, 2021) (discussing the Biden Administration's proposals and goals). For a description of the original proposal, see Charles O. Rossotti et al., *Shrinking the Tax Gap: A Comprehensive Approach*, 169 Tax Notes Fed. 1467, 1473–75 (2020) (proposing the new Form 1099 for financial institutions).
13 *See, e.g.*, Sarah Kolinovsky & Trish Turner, *Biden Admin Backs Down on Tracking Bank Accounts with over $600 Annual Transactions*, ABC News (Oct. 19, 2021), https://abcnews.go.com/Politics/biden-admin-backs-tracking-bank-accounts-600-annual/story?id=80665505; Andrew Keshner, *Biden Wants IRS to Monitor People's Bank Accounts More Closely – Will It Catch Tax Cheats, or Invade Privacy?*, MarketWatch (Oct. 12, 2021), https://www.marketwatch.com/story/biden-administration-wants-irs-to-monitor-peoples-bank-accounts-more-closely-will-it-catch-tax-cheats-or-invade-privacy-11633560204 (describing controversy regarding proposal).
14 *See generally* Joshua D. Blank & Ari Glogower, *Progressive Tax Procedure*, 96 N.Y.U. L. Rev. 668 (2021); Joshua D. Blank & Ari Glogower, *The Trouble with Targeting Tax*

Shelters, 74 ADMIN. L. REV. 69 (2022); Joshua D. Blank & Ari Glogower, *The Tax Information Gap at the Top*, 108 IOWA L. REV. 1597 (2023).

15 For discussion, see Lederman, *Reducing Information Gaps to Reduce the Tax Gap*, supra note 1, at 1740 (discussing complete reporting); IRS, FS-2006-10, FACT SHEET: THE EXAMINATION (AUDIT) PROCESS (2006), https://www.irs.gov/pub/irs-news/fs-06-10.pdf.
16 Treas. Reg. § 1.6041-1(a)(1)(i) (payments required to be reported).
17 Treas. Reg. § 1.6041-1(a)(1)(i)(A), (B).
18 I.R.C. § 6050W(a).
19 American Rescue Plan Act of 2021, H.R. 1319, 117th Cong., Pub L. 117-2, § 9674, 135 Stat. 185 (codified at I.R.C. § 6050W(e)). In December 2022, the IRS announced that it would delay the implementation of this new reporting requirement and that the 2022 calendar year would be regarded as a "transition period for purposes of IRS enforcement and administration" of the new rules. IRS Notice 2023-10 (Revised Timeline Regarding Implementation of Amended Section 6050W(e)).
20 I.R.C. § 6049; IRS, Form 1099-INT (Interest Income).
21 IRS, Form 1099-DIV (Dividends and Distributions).
22 IRS, Form 1099-B (Proceeds from Broker and Barter Exchange Transactions).
23 I.R.C. § 6045(c)(1)(D). For discussion, see Daniel Hemel, *Decrypting the Crypto Reporting Proposal in the Bipartisan Infrastructure Bill*, SUBSTANCE OVER FORM (Aug. 3, 2021), https://substanceoverform.substack.com/p/decrypting-the-crypto-reporting-proposal.
24 I.R.C. § 6045(c)(1)(D). For discussion, see *New Cryptocurrency Reporting Requirements*, MORRISON & FOERSTER (Dec. 21, 2021), https://www.mofo.com/resources/insights/211221-new-cryptocurrency-reporting-requirements.
25 I.R.C. § 6045(c)(1)(D). IRS, Form 1099-S (Proceeds from Real Estate Transactions); IRS, Instructions for Form 1099-S.
26 I.R.C. § 1471(b). FFIs who fail to comply with these rules may be subject to additional withholding of 30% on US source payments. I.R.C. § 1471(a).
27 IRS, Form 8966 (FATCA Report). For discussion, see also Chapter 2, section "Activity-Based Rules."
28 *See* Joshua D. Blank & Ruth Mason, *Exporting FATCA*, 142 TAX NOTES 1245, 1245 (2014).
29 I.R.C. § 6050H(a); IRS, Form 1098 (Mortgage Interest Statement).
30 I.R.C. § 6050S(a)(3); IRS, Form 1098-E (Student Loan Interest Statement).
31 I.R.C. § 6047; IRS, Form 1099-R (Distributions from Pensions, Annuities, Retirement or Profit-Sharing Plans, IRAs, Insurance Contracts, etc.).
32 I.R.C. § 6055(a); IRS, Form 1095-B (Health Coverage).
33 *See* IRS, Form 1099-SA (Distributions from an HSA, Archer MSA, or Medicare Advantage MSA).
34 *See* IRS, Form 1040 (US Individual Income Tax Return).
35 *See* IRS, Form 1120 (US Corporation Income Tax Return).
36 *See* IRS, Form 1065 (US Return of Partnership Income).
37 *See* IRS, Form 1065 (US Income Tax Return for Estates and Trusts).
38 *See* IRS, Form 1040 (US Individual Income Tax Return).
39 *See* IRS, *supra* note 34; *see also* William Hoffman, *Latest Form 1040 Asks for More Income Information*, TAX NOTES TODAY FED (Dec. 14, 2020), https://www.taxnotes.com/tax-

notes-today-federal/tax-system-administration/latest-form-1040-asks-more-income-informa
tion/2020/12/14/2d9mm.
40 *See* IRS, Form 8938 (Statement of Specified Foreign Financial Assets). For the statutory rules requiring for the filing of this statement, see I.R.C. § 6038D(a), (f).
41 I.R.C. § 6038D(b); *see also* Treas. Reg. § 1.6038D-3 (defining financial accounts and other specified foreign financial assets).
42 I.R.C. § 6038D(c); *see also* Treas. Reg. § 1.6038D-5 (guidelines for valuing specified foreign financial assets based on their current fair market value).
43 I.R.C. § 6038D(a); Treas. Reg. § 1.6038D-2(a)(1).
44 Treas. Reg. § 1.6038D-2(a)(2).
45 Treas. Reg. § 1.6038D-2(a)(3).
46 Treas. Reg. § 1.6038D-2(a)(4).
47 IRS, *supra* note 1, at 8 fig. 1.
48 *Id.*
49 *See* Rossotti et al., *supra* note 12, at 1468 (based on data in Jason DeBacker et al., *Tax Noncompliance and Measures of Income Inequality*, 166 TAX NOTES 1103 (2020)); *see also* Andrew Johns & Joel Slemrod, *The Distribution of Income Tax Noncompliance*, 63 NAT'L TAX J. 397, 406 tbl.3 (2010); Jesse Eisinger & Paul Kiel, *Gutting the IRS: The IRS Tried to Take on the Ultrawealthy. It Didn't Go Well*, PROPUBLICA (Apr. 5, 2019), https://www.propublica.org/article/ultrawealthy-taxes-irs-internal-revenue-service-global-high-wealth-audits.
50 IRS, *supra* note 1, at 8 fig. 1, 15 tbl.1.
51 *Id.* at 14 fig. 3.
52 *IRS Oversight: Treasury Inspector General for Tax Administration: Testimony before the Comm. on Appropriations, Subcomm. on Fin. Servs., and Gen. Gov't*, 116th Cong. 8 (2019).
53 *Id.*
54 CHARLES RETTIG, IRS, A CLOSER LOOK: IMPACTING THE TAX GAP (Apr. 23, 2021), https://www.irs.gov/pub/foia/ig/cl/tax-gap-for-web.pdf.
55 *See* Lederman, *Reducing Information Gaps to Reduce the Tax Gap*, *supra* note 1, at 1739–41; Lederman & Dugan, *supra* note 1, at 160–82; Susan C. Morse, *Ask for Help, Uncle Sam: The Future of Global Tax Reporting*, 57 VILL. L. REV. 529 (2012); Susan C. Morse et al., *Cash Businesses and Tax Evasion*, 20 STAN. L. & POL'Y REV. 37 (2009); Mark D. Phillips, *Individual Income Tax Compliance and Information Reporting: What Do the U.S. Data Show?*, 67 NAT'L TAX J. 531, 531–68 (2014) ("Taxpayers are largely compliant in self-reporting third-party 'matched' income."); Slemrod, *supra* note 1.
56 *See* GOV'T ACCOUNTABILITY OFF., GAO-21-102, BETTER COORDINATION COULD IMPROVE IRS'S USE OF THIRD-PARTY INFORMATION REPORTING TO HELP REDUCE THE TAX GAP 1739–41 (2020).
57 *See* Current Tax Payment Act of 1943, Pub. L. 78-68, 57 Stat. 126 (1943). For discussion, see *Getting to Know the IRS W-2 Form*, AM. BAR ASS'N (Nov. 27, 2018), https://www.americanbar.org/groups/public_education/publications/teaching-legal-docs/getting-to-know-the-irs-w-2-form/; Jay Soled, *The IRS's Voluntary Disclosure Program: Need for Codification*, 37 GA. ST. U. L. REV. 957, 967 (2021).
58 *See* IRS, *supra* note 15.
59 *Id.*

60 See IRS, Pub. 55-B (Rev. 3-2023), 2022 Data Book (2023), https://www.irs.gov/statistics/soi-tax-stats-all-years-irs-data-books.
61 See John T. Scholz & Neil Pinney, *Duty, Fear, and Tax Compliance: The Heuristic Basis of Citizenship Behavior*, 39 Am. J. Pol. Sci. 490, 497–98 (1995); *see also* Harold G. Grasmick & Wilbur J. Scott, *Tax Evasion and Mechanisms of Social Control: A Comparison with Grand and Petty Theft*, 2 J. Econ. Psych. 213, 222 (1982) (37.9% of individuals believed they would be caught if they attempted to evade tax).
62 IRS, Pub. 5296 (Rev. 4-2021), Comprehensive Taxpayer Attitude Survey (CTAS) 2020 (2020), https://www.irs.gov/pub/irs-prior/p5296–2021.pdf.
63 IRS, Pub. 6961 (Rev. 8-2021), Calendar Year Projections of Information and Withholding Documents for the United States and IRS Campuses 2021 Update 4 tbl. 1 (2021), https://www.irs.gov/pub/irs-prior/p6961–2021.pdf (projecting 3,915,607,000 information returns made in 2021).
64 IRS, Pub. 6961, *supra* note 63, at 5, tbl. 2.
65 *See, e.g.*, Natasha Sarin & Lawrence H. Summers, *Shrinking the Tax Gap: Approaches and Revenue Potential*, 165 Tax Notes Fed. 1099 (2019).
66 *Id.*
67 *See* Dep't of Treasury, General Explanations of the Administration's Fiscal Year 2022 Revenue Proposals, *supra* note 9, at 88; Dep't of Treasury, The American Families Plan Tax Compliance Agenda, *supra* note 9, at 20; Dep't of Treasury, Fact Sheet, *supra* note 9.
68 Michael Cooper et al., *Business in the United States: Who Owns It, and How Much Tax Do They Pay?*, 30 Tax Pol'y & Econ. 91 (2016).
69 For discussion, see Viswanathan, *supra* note 1, at 16–17.
70 *See* I.R.C. §§ 6041–6050Y (Information Concerning Transactions with Other Persons).
71 *See* IRS, *supra* note 1, at 21; IRS, Pub. 1415, Federal Tax Compliance Research: Tax Gap Estimates for Tax Years 2008–2010, 19 (2016) (reporting net misreporting percentage of 62% for rents and royalties).
72 For discussion, *see* Morse et al., *supra* note 55.
73 *See id.*
74 Emily Stewart, *The Trump Tax Scandal Is an Indictment of the President – and the System*, Vox (Sept. 28, 2020), https://www.vox.com/policy-and-politics/21492209/donald-trump-income-taxes-ny-times-evasion-avoidance (quoting Natasha Sarin).
75 *See* John Guyton et al., *Tax Evasion at the Top of the Income Distribution: Theory and Evidence*, Nat'l Bureau Econ. Rsch., Working Paper No. 28542 (2021).
76 Daniel Reck, *Sophisticated Tax Evasion by the Super-Rich*, London Sch. of Econ. & Pol. Sci. (Sept. 7, 2021), https://www.lse.ac.uk/research/research-for-the-world/economics/sophisticated-tax-evasion-by-the-super-rich.
77 *See* Mark Hosenball & Evan Thomas, *Cracking the Vault*, Nat'l Whistleblower Ctr. (Mar. 23, 2009), https://www.whistleblowers.org/news/cracking-the-vault/.
78 For discussion, see *Tax Haven Abuses: The Enablers, the Tools and Secrecy – Vol. 1 of 4: Hearing before the Permanent Subcommittee on Investigations*, 108th Cong. 1 (2006).
79 I.R.C. §§ 1471–1474; Hiring Incentives to Restore Employment Act, H.R. 2847, 111th Cong., Pub. L. 111–147, § 501, 124 Stat. 71, 97–99 (2010).

80 Payments include US source interest and dividends and gross proceeds from the sale of assets that generate US dividends and interest. I.R.C. §§ 1471(a), (c), 1473(1).
81 See id. For discussion, see Blank & Mason, *supra* note 28, at 1247; Shu-Yi Oei, *The Offshore Tax Enforcement Dragnet*, 67 EMORY L.J. 655 (2018); J. Richard Harvey Jr., *Offshore Accounts: Insider's Summary of FATCA and Its Potential Future*, 57 VILL. L. REV. 471 (2012); J. Richard Harvey Jr., *FATCA – A Report from the Front Lines*, 136 TAX NOTES 713 (2012); Leandra Lederman, *The Use of Voluntary Disclosure Initiatives in the Battle against Offshore Tax Evasion*, 57 VILL. L. REV. 499 (2012); Young Ran (Christine) Kim, *Considering "Citizenship Taxation": In Defense of FATCA*, 20 FLA. TAX REV. 335 (2017).
82 See DEP'T OF TREASURY, CONTROL NO. LB&I-09-1118-014, MEMORANDUM FOR DIVISION COMMISSIONERS (2018); IRS News Release IR-2018-176 (Sept. 4, 2018), https://www.irs.gov/newsroom/irs-offshore-voluntary-compliance-program-to-end-sept-28 (IRS: Offshore Voluntary Compliance Program to end Sept. 28).
83 See OECD, *Automatic Exchange of Information (AEOI): Status of Commitments* (June 9, 2023), https://www.oecd.org/tax/automatic-exchange/commitment-and-monitoring-process/AEOI-commitments.pdf.
84 See Guyton et al., *supra* note 75; *Written Testimony of the Internal Revenue Service before the Senate Finance Committee, Subcommittee on Taxation and IRS Oversight on the Tax Gap* (2021) (estimating $46 billion in revenue loss due to offshore bank accounts in 2019).
85 See INT'L CONSORTIUM OF INVESTIGATIVE JOURNALISTS, *The Pandora Papers: Offshore Havens and Hidden Riches of World Leaders and Billionaires Exposed in Unprecedented Leak* (Oct. 3, 2021), https://www.icij.org/investigations/pandora-papers/global-investigation-tax-havens-offshore/.
86 See INT'L CONSORTIUM OF INVESTIGATIVE JOURNALISTS, *The Panama Papers: Exposing the Rogue Offshore Finance Industry* (Apr. 3, 2016), https://www.icij.org/investigations/panama-papers/.
87 See, e.g., *"Pandora Papers" Reveal Billions Hidden by the Rich and Powerful*, CBS NEWS (Oct. 4, 2021), https://www.cbsnews.com/news/pandora-papers-billions-hidden-tax-rich/ (discussing Robert T. Brockman); Chas Danner, *Leak Exposes Massive Trove of Documents Detailing Offshore Wealth*, N.Y. MAG. (Oct. 3, 2021), https://nymag.com/intelligencer/2021/10/pandora-papers-massive-trove-of-offshore-data-exposed.html.
88 See, e.g., DEP'T OF JUSTICE, *Offshore Compliance Initiative*, https://www.justice.gov/tax/offshore-compliance-initiative.
89 Press Release, UBS Group AG, UBS Completes Credit Suisse Acquisition (June 12, 2023), https://www.ubs.com/global/en/media/display-page-ndp/en-20230612-ubs-credit-suisse-acquisition.html.
90 See Katie Benner & Michael Forsythe, *Whistle-Blower Says Credit Suisse Helped Clients Skip Taxes after Promising to Stop*, N.Y. TIMES (Mar. 13, 2021), https://www.nytimes.com/2021/03/13/business/whistle-blower-credit-suisse-taxes.html.
91 See Alan Rappeport, *Tax Cheats Cost the U.S. $1 Trillion per Year, I.R.S. Chief Says*, N.Y. TIMES (Apr. 13, 2021), https://www.nytimes.com/2021/04/13/business/irs-tax-gap.html (quoting IRS Commissioner Charles Rettig).
92 See IRS Notice 2014-21, 2014-16 I.R.B. 938; Rev. Rul. 2019-24; IRS, *Frequently Asked Questions on Virtual Currency Transactions*, https://www.irs.gov/individuals/international-taxpayers/frequently-asked-questions-on-virtual-currency-transactions.
93 See *supra* note 24 and accompanying text.

94 I.R.C. § 6050I(d); Infrastructure Investment and Jobs Act, H.R. 3684, 117th Cong., Pub. L. 117-58, §. 80603(b)(1)(B), 135 Stat. 429.
95 *See, e.g.*, Greg Iacurci, *Cryptocurrency Poses a Significant Risk of Tax Evasion*, CNBC (May 31, 2021), https://www.cnbc.com/2021/05/31/cryptocurrency-poses-a-significant-risk-of-tax-evasion.html.
96 *See Senate-Passed Infrastructure Bill Would Impose Information-Reporting Requirements on Sales of Cryptocurrency and Other Digital Assets*, EY (Aug. 19, 2021), https://taxnews.ey.com/news/2021-1538-senate-passed-infrastructure-bill-would-impose-information-reporting-requirements-on-sales-of-cryptocurrency-and-other-digital-assets.
97 *See* Marie Sapirie, *Implementing the New Crypto Reporting Guidance*, 173 Tax Notes 1058 (2021).
98 *Id.* (quoting Megan L. Brackney).
99 *See* Chapter 3, section "The Limitations of Activity-Based Rules."
100 *See* Lauren Loricchio, *Crypto Reg Delay Ruffles Lawmakers*, 179 Tax Notes Fed. 2066 (2023).
101 IRS, Instructions for Forms 1099-MISC and 1099-NEC.
102 Treas. Reg. § 1.6041-3(p)(1).
103 *Id.*
104 *See* Joseph Bankman, *Eight Truths about Collecting Taxes from the Cash Economy*, 117 Tax Notes 506 (2007) Lederman, *Reducing Information Gaps to Reduce the Tax Gap*, *supra* note 1, at 1744–48.
105 *See* I.R.C §§ 301(a), 301(c).
106 IRS, Form 1099-DIV (Dividends and Distributions).
107 *See, e.g.*, Lewis R. Steinberg, *Form, Substance and Directionality in Subchapter C*, 52 Tax Law. 457 (1999).
108 *See, e.g.*, Weigel v. Comm'r, T.C.M. 1996-485 (1996).
109 *See, e.g., id.*; Alterman Foods, Inc. v. United States, 611 F.2d 866 (1979); Levy v. Comm'r, 30 T.C. 1315 (1958). *See also* Albert B. Ellentuck, *Using Loans to Extract Cash from a Closely Held Corporation*, Tax Advisor (Jan. 1, 2015); John W. Lee, *Shareholder Withdrawal-Loan or Dividend: Repayments, Estoppel, and Other Anomolies*, 12 Wm. & Mary L. Rev. 512 (1971).
110 *See* IRS, Instructions for Form 1099-DIV (Dividends and Distributions).
111 Treas. Reg. § 1.6049-4(c)(1)(A); IRS, Instructions for Form 1099-INT (Interest Income).
112 *See, e.g.*, Santos v. Comm'r, T.C.M. 2019-148 (2019).
113 *See* IRS, FS-2008-25, Fact Sheet: Wage Compensation for S Corporation Officers (2008), https://home.treasury.gov/news/press-releases/jy0415. For discussion, see Robert W. Wood, *Payroll Taxes and S Corporations (Again)*, Wood LLP (Mar. 2012), http://woodllp.com/Publications/Articles/pdf/Payroll_Taxes_And_S_Corps.pdf.
114 *See Newt Gingrich's Tax Payments Questioned*, Acct. Today (Jan. 23, 2012), https://www.accountingtoday.com/news/newt-gingrichs-tax-payments-questioned.
115 *See* Mark Koba, *How the Gingrich-Edwards Tax Loophole Works*, CNBC (Mar. 5, 2014), https://www.cnbc.com/2014/03/05/cnbc-explains-the-gingrich-edwards-tax-loophole.html; Walter D. Schwidetzky, *The John Edwards S Corp Tax Shelter: Is the IRS Winning the Battles but Losing the War?*, TaxProf Blog (Sept. 6, 2013), https://taxprof.typepad.com/taxprof_blog/2013/09/schwidetzky.html.

116 Richard Rubin, *Joe Biden Used Tax-Code Loophole Obama Tried to Plug*, WALL ST. J. (July 10, 2019), https://www.wsj.com/articles/joe-biden-used-tax-code-loophole-obama-tried-to-plug-11562779300.
117 *See* Chuck Marr & Samantha Jacoby, *Build Back Better Requires Highest-Income People and Corporations to Pay Fairer Amount of Tax, Reduces Tax Gap*, CTR. ON BUDGET AND POL'Y PRIORITIES (2021).
118 IRS, Form 1099-B (Proceeds from Broker and Barter Exchange Transactions).
119 For discussion, see TAXPAYER ADVOC. SERV., 2015 ANNUAL REPORT TO CONGRESS 394 (2015).
120 *See id.*
121 *See* IRS, Form 1065 (Schedule K-1). For discussion, *see* James Alm & Jay A. Soled, *Tax Basis Determinations, Pass-through Entities, and Taxpayer Noncompliance*, 40 OHIO N. U.L. REV. 693 (2014); James Alm & Jay A. Soled, *Tax Basis Reporting Should Be Required for Passthrough Entities*, 150 TAX NOTES 1358 (2016). In 2020, the IRS issued guidance that would require partnerships to use one of two alternative methods to report capital accounts on Schedule K-1 for years ending on or after Dec. 31, 2020. IRS Notice 2020-43; IRS Notice 2021-13.
122 *See* IRS, Instructions for Form 1099-B (Proceeds from Broker and Barter Exchange Transactions) (requiring participation of broker).
123 Treas. Reg. § 1.6011-4(b)(2), (6).
124 *See* IRS, PUB. 6961 (REV. 8-2021), CALENDAR YEAR PROJECTIONS OF INFORMATION AND WITHHOLDING DOCUMENTS FOR THE UNITED STATES AND IRS CAMPUSES 2021 UPDATE 4 tab. 1 (2021).
125 *See, e.g.*, Lederman, *Reducing Information Gaps to Reduce the Tax Gap*, *supra* note 1.
126 *See* Paul Kiel & Hannah Fresques, *Where in the U.S. Are You Most Likely to Be Audited by the IRS?*, PROPUBLICA (Apr. 1, 2019), https://projects.propublica.org/graphics/eitc-audit. *See also* Kim M. Bloomquist, *Regional Bias in IRS Audit Selection*, 162 TAX NOTES 987 (2019).
127 Dorothy A. Brown, *The IRS Is Targeting the Poorest Americans*, ATLANTIC (July 27, 2021), https://www.theatlantic.com/ideas/archive/2021/07/how-race-plays-tax-policing/619570/.
128 *See, e.g.*, Jeremy Bearer-Friend, *Colorblind Tax Enforcement*, 97 N.Y.U. L. REV. 1 (2022) (arguing that general institutional vulnerability to racial bias necessitates the need for data regarding tax enforcement and race); Brian Faler, *Taxes May Not Be Colorblind, and Critics Say More Data Could Prove It*, POLITICO (Mar. 16, 2021), https://www.politico.com/news/2021/03/16/race-taxes-irs-476371; *see also* Dorothy A. Brown, *Race and Class Matters in Tax Policy*, 107 COLUM. L. REV. 790, 821 (2007) (arguing for greater "empirical data concerning the racial demographics of who benefits from the EITC"); Steven Dean, *Beware the Unintended Consequences of Biden's New IRS Spending*, N.Y. DAILY NEWS (May 5, 2021), https://www.nydailynews.com/opinion/ny-oped-beware-the-unintended-consequences-of-bidens-irs-spending-20210505-ty6iwne2eneupocy26mnkcd2au-story.html.
129 *See* Chye-Ching Huang & Roderick Taylor, *How the Federal Tax Code Can Better Advance Racial Equity*, CTR. ON BUDGET AND POL'Y PRIORITIES (2019); DOROTHY A. BROWN, THE WHITENESS OF WEALTH (2021); Dorothy A. Brown, *What ProPublica Missed about Taxing Rich White Men*, MEDIUM (June 13, 2021), https://profdabrown.medium.com/what-pro-publica-missed-about-taxing-rich-white-men-992cadod19aa.

10

Closing the Tax Information Gap

What type of information would aid the IRS's ability to enforce the tax law and detect noncompliance? How should policymakers design income and wealth thresholds that would trigger such requirements? Who should provide the information to the IRS – individual high-end taxpayers, third-party intermediaries, or both?

In this chapter, we outline the advantages and limitations of both third-party and first-party reporting requirements, in light of the preceding discussion in Chapter 9. We also evaluate reform possibilities. In general, third-party information reporting can utilize the knowledge that third parties have of the taxpayers' activities in relation to specific transactions. However, the taxpayers themselves, as first parties, have the most complete knowledge of their own general economic circumstances, as well as any criteria that are needed to implement a means-adjusted approach to tax compliance.

We begin by evaluating the Biden Administration's 2021 bank information reporting proposal as an example of a third-party information reporting reform. Then, we provide a model for introducing first-party information reporting from high-end taxpayers regarding their finances through an annual wealth reporting form, which we call the *Annual Net Asset Statement*. We describe the possibilities and challenges of introducing such a form and show how there is precedent for this type of reporting in both tax and nontax contexts.

Next, we introduce a hybrid system that incorporates both first- and third-party information reporting and explain how this system would have offered an alternative approach to the Biden Administration's 2021 proposal for reporting inflows and outflows from financial accounts. As we argue, a hybrid first- and third-party information reporting system can utilize the unique advantages of both types of reporting, while also addressing the limitations of each approach. Under the hybrid system that we propose, a first-party taxpayer would directly inform a third-party bank whether the taxpayer is subject to these heightened information reporting rules.

Finally, we describe how this framework for understanding the importance of both a taxpayer's means and specific activities in information reporting – and the roles of both first and third parties – can help improve the tailoring of penalties for noncompliance in two areas: with information reporting obligations and in the use of audit resources. We explain how a means-adjusted approach can improve the operation of these information reporting rules and complement the activity-based focus in current law.

THIRD-PARTY INFORMATION REPORTING

Third-party information reporting plays an essential role in tax administration and compliance. Centralized third parties such as brokers and financial institutions have valuable first-hand knowledge of the taxpayers' transactions and activities, and often have the administrative capacity to report this information efficiently. Further, these third parties do not have the same economic "stake" in tax noncompliance as their clients, and therefore often have less of an incentive to misreport or hide the taxpayer's taxable activities from the IRS than the taxpayer does.

Notwithstanding these advantages, the IRS also cannot depend on third-party information reporting alone to close the tax information gap. Third parties have different substantive compliance obligations than taxpayers, and lesser culpability in the noncompliance of the taxpayers with whom they transact.[1] As a result, the tax system cannot impose the same types of penalties and sanctions on third parties that it can impose on the taxpayers themselves.

The types of information available to third parties also necessarily determine – and limit – the effect of third-party information reporting as a means to increase tax compliance. Most critically, third-party information reporting alone cannot completely close the tax information reporting gap, because these third parties can only provide information as to a taxpayer's specific activities and account holdings.

Because third parties can only observe certain activities of the actor, third-party reporting rules also encounter the same limitations of other activity-based rules, including the risk of imposing collateral burdens on the wrong actors while enabling sophisticated actors to avoid these rules. That said, third-party information reporting of specific activities – regardless of the characteristics of the taxpayer – nonetheless serves a critical role in tax administration and enforcement. This type of reporting can notify the IRS of transactions that it would not otherwise detect, thereby allowing the agency to identify discrepancies between the third-party's information reports and the taxpayer's own tax reporting.

Third-party information reporting of specific activities, however, also encounters the same general limitations of other activity-based tax compliance rules. In many cases, sophisticated taxpayers can avoid the application of these rules by simply changing the form of their tax-avoidance activities to avoid triggering reporting requirements. On the other hand, if policymakers limit opportunities to avoid these activity-based rules by defining them too broadly, this measure can have the adverse effects of unduly burdening taxpayers who are compliant or who are otherwise not the proper priorities for tax enforcement.

Means adjustments to these rules could resolve this challenge by accounting for characteristics of the taxpayers and not just their activities. Third parties, however, are less likely to have complete knowledge of the taxpayer's complete economic circumstances, which would be necessary for these means adjustments. Of course, third parties may have knowledge of certain activities that partially signal the taxpayer's economic circumstances, and that may serve as proxies for a taxpayer's income or wealth. For example, some of the specific activities subject to third-party information reporting under current law are disproportionately – and in some cases exclusively – engaged in by higher-income taxpayers with access to sophisticated financial and legal advice.[2] Beyond these specific activities, financial intermediaries such as brokers, investment managers, and banks also have additional sources of knowledge as to a client's economic circumstances, such as their account balances or assets held with the intermediary. In all these cases, however, the third parties' knowledge of the taxpayer's economic circumstances will be defined and limited by the scope of the taxpayer's transactions with that third party.

The difficulties in defining the information reporting thresholds under FATCA[3] illustrate this inherent tension in third-party information reporting design, which results from the limited knowledge third parties have of a taxpayer's complete economic circumstances. As discussed earlier, FATCA generally requires third-party FFIs, such as banks, to report information regarding their US account holders to the US Treasury.

Therefore, in designing the thresholds for information reporting required under FATCA, policymakers faced a variation of the "Goldilocks problem" introduced in Chapter 3: They needed to define rules that were broad enough to minimize avoidance opportunities, but also narrow enough to avoid unduly burdening the wrong set of taxpayers. For example, the FATCA rules currently exempt FFIs from reporting depository accounts with an aggregate value of $50,000 or less.[4] Policymakers had to define a threshold that was low enough to prevent easy avoidance, since taxpayers could easily avert a high threshold that only narrowly targeted the highest accounts by splitting their offshore holdings among multiple accounts. This splitting strategy would have allowed taxpayers to undermine the objectives of FATCA, by exploiting the fact that any third-party FFI can only be expected to have knowledge of accounts held by the taxpayer with their firm, but cannot be expected to have knowledge of the taxpayer's other assets or activities.

Setting a relatively low threshold of $50,000 subjected a broader range of accounts to this third-party information reporting system, and thereby limited the availability of splitting strategies. However, by solving this problem it encountered a different challenge. In many cases, this lower threshold covering a broader range of accounts imposed disproportionate burdens on fully compliant and lower-income taxpayers who had legitimate reasons to hold assets in offshore accounts. For example, Professor Shu-Yi Oei has documented how FATCA casts a "wide reporting net" that applies to a "broad swath of taxpayers" and "not just deliberate tax cheats," including not only inbound immigrants but also US taxpayers living abroad.[5] Professor Oei argues further that FATCA, together with related offshore asset disclosure programs, impose "uniformly harsh penalties on heterogeneous taxpayers" while often providing insufficient punishment for major offenders.[6]

THE BIDEN ADMINISTRATION'S BANK TAX REPORTING PROPOSAL

The Biden Administration's bank tax reporting proposal illustrates the critical importance of third-party information reporting to tax administration and enforcement. At the same time, the proposal exemplifies the challenges in designing effectively tailored activity-based tax compliance rules that could properly address the challenge of high-end tax avoidance. In this case as well, defining the scope of covered activities too broadly can impose heavy burdens on taxpayers and third parties, while narrower definitions can enable taxpayer avoidance and undermine the reform's effect.

In 2021, the Biden Administration attempted to expand the scope of information reporting to include more general information regarding inflows to and outflows from taxpayers' bank accounts and other financial accounts.[7] The Treasury's Fiscal Year 2022 revenue proposals included proposed legislation that was based on a prior set of recommendations for shrinking the federal tax gap that had been offered by Charles O. Rossotti, Natasha Sarin, and Lawrence Summers.[8]

Under the Treasury's *General Explanation's of the Administration's Fiscal Year 2022 Revenue Proposals*, banks and other financial institutions would be required to report to the IRS comprehensive financial account information, such as gross inflows (receipts) and outflows (transfers) that occurred during the year, for any business or personal account, including banking, loan, and investment accounts, subject to certain exceptions.[9] The new rules would apply to all taxpayers, irrespective of wealth or income, but would exclude accounts with a gross cash flow of less than $600 or a fair market value of less than $600.[10] The proposal would also apply to payment settlement entities, not just bank accounts, and would include reporting on "gross purchases, physical cash, as well as payments to and from foreign accounts, and transfer inflows and outflows."[11] This low threshold would have applied to a broad scope of accounts, thereby preventing taxpayers from avoiding the application of these rules by splitting up their financial activities among multiple smaller transactions and accounts.

While the proposal as originally structured would apply to "all business and personal accounts" above the de minimis threshold, the Treasury stated that its proposed financial account reporting regime was designed to enhance the IRS's ability to enforce the tax law against wealthy and high-income taxpayers specifically.[12] By providing the IRS with information about inflows and outflows to a taxpayer's bank account, Treasury officials argued that the proposal would allow the IRS to identify potential tax noncompliance.[13] Treasury officials reinforced this argument with the illustration of a taxpayer with $10,000 of annual income, but $10 million of inflows to and outflows from their bank account.[14] They argued that by mandating that banks share this information with the IRS, Congress could allow the IRS to "target its enforcement activities on those who are actually evading their tax obligations."[15] Under the Treasury proposal, individual taxpayers would also be required to report corresponding information regarding their bank accounts and other financial accounts on a new line on the annual personal income tax return, IRS Form 1040 (US Individual Income Tax Return).[16] Treasury officials estimated that the new third-party information reporting regime would generate approximately $460 billion in revenue over a ten-year period.[17]

In response to the Treasury's proposed financial account reporting rules, critics raised several concerns with the measure. First, opponents argued that the financial account reporting measure was overbroad, as it would affect millions of average taxpayers, not just millionaires and billionaires, and would thereby impose collateral burdens on those who are compliant, or who otherwise fall outside the proper priorities, for the heightened tax enforcement measures.

In October 2021, twenty-one Democratic members of Congress wrote a letter to then Speaker of the House Nancy Pelosi, in which they expressed concern with "the significant burden and potential unintended consequences" from the reform, and argued that even a higher $10,000 threshold would still affect many other taxpayers who "are not the wealthy tax evaders who are the stated targets of this proposal."[18] Similarly, Representative Jason Smith, who served at the time as the House Budget Committee Republican Leader, commented that the financial accounting reporting measure would "set up millions of middle class families, farmers, small businesses, and gig economy workers for potential audits and legal battles against a powerful federal agency with a troubling history of abusing that power."[19] In December 2021, the Joint Committee on Taxation estimated that the proposed measure would apply to at least 40 million (27%) and less than 134 million (90%) of taxpayers reporting less than $400,000 of taxable income each year, stating further that the average of this range was 87 million (60%) of such taxpayers.[20]

The measure was criticized for other reasons as well. Representatives of financial institutions, for example, argued that the measure would create logistical difficulties. The Credit Union National Association (CUNA), the largest national trade organization representing credit unions, stated that the proposal would cause smaller credit unions "to be especially burdened."[21] Opponents of the measure also argued that increased financial account reporting would violate the privacy of taxpayers. As then House Minority Leader Kevin McCarthy argued, the proposal would empower "87,000 new IRS agents to spy on your bank account. It's invasive, unconscionable, and will impact nearly every American."[22]

Following weeks of criticism from opponents throughout the summer of 2021,[23] Treasury attempted to narrow its proposal. In October 2021, Treasury attempted to respond to concerns regarding overbreadth by modifying the proposed threshold for reporting account information from $600 to $10,000 in annual outflows and inflows, and by including an exemption for outflows and inflows for wages and federal program benefits.[24]

This higher threshold significantly narrowed the taxpayers and accounts subject to this rule; however, it ended up triggering the opposite challenge. With a higher threshold, as well as a narrower scope of activities subject to the rule, taxpayers could more easily avoid the application of the rule by splitting up their transactions among a greater number of accounts.

In connection with this change, the Treasury also offered a detailed "fact sheet" that directly addressed the most common critiques of the proposed rules.[25] In response to criticism that the measure would create logistical challenges for financial institutions, the Treasury stated that these institutions would only be required to add two figures to the information that they already provide to the IRS under current law, such as the amount of interest paid to account holders.[26] It addressed industry concerns by stating that "it is implausible that a requirement to add two pieces of information on a report that is already sent by financial institutions to the IRS could be onerous."[27] Further, the fact sheet, in an attempt to assuage privacy concerns, offered assurances that the scope of information financial institutions would share with the IRS would be "extremely limited" and would not include information about individual transactions.[28]

Despite the Treasury's sustained efforts to convince policymakers and the public, Congress did not adopt, or even formally consider, the financial account reporting measure in tax legislation. Those objecting to the reform argued that even this higher $10,000 threshold would still impose collateral burdens on taxpayers who are not "the wealthy tax evaders who are the stated targets of this proposal."[29] By the time the House passed the *Build Back Better Act* in November 2021, the measure had been excised from the legislation.[30] It was also absent from the revised tax provisions in the Senate version of the legislation.[31] As of February 2022, the Biden Administration and Democratic members of Congress appeared to have abandoned the proposed financial account reporting proposal in favor of narrower third-party information reporting and withholding proposals.[32]

The experience with the Biden Administration's bank information reporting proposal illustrates not only the critical importance of third-party information reporting but also the challenges in designing these systems. These reforms could provide crucial information to aid in tax enforcement, prevent erosion of the income tax base from noncompliance, encourage voluntary compliance, and raise substantial revenue.[33] At the same time, because the proposed reform would have relied upon the third parties' limited knowledge of the taxpayers' specific transactions and activities, it also encounters the same general challenges in designing activity-based tax compliance rules. Specifically, they must be effectively tailored to properly address the challenge of high-end tax avoidance while also avoiding collateral burdens to compliant or lower-income taxpayers.

FIRST-PARTY INFORMATION REPORTING

The Biden Administration's bank reporting reform illustrates both the advantages and limitations of third-party information reporting. First-party information reporting by the taxpayers themselves presents an alternative set of challenges and opportunities. Unlike third parties, taxpayers generally have the most complete knowledge of their own transactions and economic circumstances.

Why would a noncompliant taxpayer ever assist with information reporting requirements that could help the IRS detect their noncompliance? First-party information reporting by taxpayers faces the same limitations that give rise to the challenge of tax noncompliance in the first place: As the primary obligor of their own tax liabilities, taxpayers have a direct economic incentive to underreport not only their actual tax liability, but also any corresponding information the IRS may need to determine that liability. As a result, first-party information reporting by the taxpayers themselves can only play a limited role in a system intended to improve taxpayer compliance.

Notwithstanding this basic limitation, first-party information reporting still plays a valuable role in tax administration. Reforms to expand this type of reporting can leverage its advantages to help close the tax information gap. Specifically, first-party information reporting enables the IRS to utilize the taxpayer's own knowledge of their transactions and economic circumstances in order to improve tax enforcement and the detection of noncompliance. When designed properly, this type of information reporting can also avoid the noncompliance incentives that taxpayers would otherwise encounter when reporting their substantive tax liabilities.

How can taxpayers who engage in aggressive or abusive tax planning aid tax enforcement by providing information reports regarding their own financial affairs? Importantly, the tax rules require individual taxpayers to report not only the primary information that is used to calculate substantive tax liabilities, but also additional information that assists with tax administration and enforcement. Individuals subject to these different first-party information reporting rules will face different incentives to underreport or misreport financial information, depending on both their consequences and their design.

Regarding the information used to determine substantive tax liabilities, such as items of taxable income or deductions on IRS Form 1040, every additional dollar of income a taxpayer underreports will generally translate into additional marginal dollars of tax savings. In this case, a taxpayer will generally realize an economic advantage from underreporting as much as they possibly can, and their decision regarding how much to underreport will depend upon several factors, including their intrinsic motivation to pay taxes,[34] the direct costs they may incur to enable underreporting, the likelihood of detection, and the potential costs of tax penalties and other sanctions if they are caught. A progressive tax system – where taxpayers with greater income pay tax at proportionally higher rates – can compound these economic incentives for higher earners to underreport, to the extent that additional dollars of income that *are* reported would result in proportionally larger tax liabilities.

In the cases of other first-party information reporting requirements, however, underreporting marginal dollars of income or wealth can have lesser consequences, or no consequences at all. For example, to determine whether to file IRS Form 8938 (Statement of Foreign Financial Assets), taxpayers must first determine whether they meet the asset thresholds in the statute and regulations, which is more than $50,000 on the last day of the tax year for a single taxpayer. Assume a single taxpayer living in the US has $51,000 in actual specified foreign financial assets. If the taxpayer underreports their assets' value by $1,000, this underreporting would, in and of itself, not directly affect the taxpayer's substantive tax liabilities for the year (as would underreporting $1,000 of income on IRS Form 1040). Rather, underreporting their assets by $1,000 could only enable the taxpayer to avoid an obligation to file the IRS Form 8938. That said, this underreporting could still create a distinct advantage for the taxpayer, because it could, in turn, indirectly affect the taxpayer's ultimate tax liabilities, since avoiding the IRS Form 8938 reporting could enable the taxpayer to hide underreporting of substantive tax liabilities from IRS detection more effectively.

In some cases, non-reporting of a certain amount of assets or economic activity could have no effect at all on the taxpayer's compliance obligations. For example, assume in the alternative that the same taxpayer has $60,000 in specified foreign financial assets, and fails to disclose and report $1,000 in assets, instead reporting only the first $59,000 in assets. In this case, the underreporting of the marginal $1,000 of asset value would have no effect at all on the taxpayer's obligation to file the IRS Form 8938, since they will still report applicable assets in excess of the compliance threshold. Unlike in the case of underreporting of substantive tax liabilities – where every marginal dollar of non-reported income results in additional tax avoided – the taxpayer can only avoid the application of the IRS Form 8938 compliance by failing to disclose enough asset value, or $10,000, to fall below the threshold. As a result, underreporting up to $10,000 of the taxpayer's assets will have no direct effect on the taxpayer in changing their compliance obligations.

More generally, this example illustrates how measuring income or wealth for use as a threshold in determining the application of certain compliance rules – such as the obligation to file IRS Form 8938 – creates different and often lower incentives for taxpayers to underreport these items. A taxpayer with a total income far above the threshold may have no incentive or ability at all to hide enough income to claim that they are below the threshold for application of the IRS Form 8938 reporting requirements.

As described previously, information from first-party reporting can be used in various ways, such as for calculating substantive tax liabilities, for determining the application of certain compliance rules, or for other uses in tax compliance and enforcement. These different uses will also affect the taxpayer's incentive to underreport items used for their respective purposes.

This distinction among the uses of information from first-party reporting – and consequent differences in the taxpayer's underreporting incentives – also has implications for the feasibility of a reform that would require first-party wealth reporting. In recent years, policymakers have proposed new wealth tax reforms, which would require taxpayers to not only report their net wealth holdings but also pay substantive taxes based on these amounts.[35]

The debate over these wealth tax reforms has primarily focused on the challenges in accurately valuing assets, and on the opportunities taxpayers can use to avoid taxes by undervaluing or underreporting their asset holdings.[36] Scholars have argued that a wealth tax could use simplified valuation methodologies, which could reduce – but not eliminate – the opportunities for tax avoidance and the administrative burdens required to value a broad scope of assets on an annual basis.[37] For example, a wealth tax reform could use a combination of data from asset dispositions and market valuations, imputed returns to cost basis, third-party information reports such as from financial institutions and asset managers, and asset appraisals to approximate the value of assets in different classes.[38]

REFORM PROPOSAL: AN ANNUAL NET ASSET STATEMENT

As an alternative to implementing a substantive federal wealth tax, policymakers could instead implement a means-adjusted wealth information reporting requirement. We propose an *Annual Net Asset Statement*, which would require taxpayers with net assets above certain thresholds to report these assets and their approximate values. However, taxpayers who submit this statement would not have to pay substantive tax liabilities based on these asset valuations, like they would under a substantive wealth tax reform.

In effect, this proposal resembles an expanded version of the current IRS Form 8938 (Statement of Specified Foreign Financial Assets). Like that form, the *Annual Net Asset Statement* could minimize the compliance burden on lower-wealth taxpayers, by similarly requiring only those taxpayers with assets above a certain value threshold to file the report. For example, the *Annual Net Asset Statement* could only be required for taxpayers who hold assets with an aggregate value of $10 million or more, or who have earned income of $2 million or more in the prior year. Unlike Form 8938, however, it could serve as a broader wealth information return, and require reporting of assets regardless of whether they are held in the US or abroad.

The *Annual Net Asset Statement* would not face the same avoidance challenges as would a substantive wealth tax reform, since taxpayers would not have the same immediate economic incentive to underreport every marginal dollar of wealth. As a result, this reform would not necessarily need taxpayers to provide precise valuations.

Consequently, the *Annual Net Asset Statement* could take greater advantage of simplified valuation methods for hard-to-value asset classes. Alternatively, in some cases, taxpayers could be wholly exempted from reporting these valuations at all. For example, taxpayers could be required to only report their cost basis for hard-to-value assets, or to only provide descriptive accounts of these assets without attributing any value to them. A first-party wealth information return such as this could also take advantage of the valuations that taxpayers have received from third parties. For example, the wealth information return could require taxpayers to report valuations of nontraded or irregularly traded financial interests, such as in private equity and hedge funds, or of digital assets, which are already provided by third-party investment managers.[39]

The *Annual Net Asset Statement* rules could also adopt a more flexible approach in defining the thresholds used to determine when a taxpayer is subject to these rules. For example, like in the case of Form 8938, the threshold can be defined by reference to either an aggregate value at the end of the year or the highest asset value at any time during the year.[40] A substantive wealth tax reform could not adopt a similarly flexible approach to asset valuation, especially if it is considered improper to impose a substantive tax liability on the basis of an asset's peak value in this way.

Additionally, the *Annual Net Asset Statement* could improve tax administration and enforcement by allowing the IRS not only to more accurately detect patterns indicating noncompliance, but also to focus audit resources more effectively. Further, tax scholars have also observed that wealth reporting could allow for a more accurate analysis of trends in tax noncompliance and in economic inequality, thereby improving fiscal policy.[41] As we describe in the following section, first-party information through the *Annual Net Asset Statement* could also be used improve the design of third-party information reporting rules.

A HYBRID APPROACH

Each of the third-party and first-party information reporting mechanisms discussed in the previous sections encounters different limitations. Third parties do not always have complete knowledge of the taxpayers' complete economic circumstances, but only of their specific activities. As a result, third-party information reporting faces the same challenge as that of other activity-based compliance rules: The scope of the activities subject to these rules must be defined broadly enough to prevent easy avoidance, but narrowly enough to avoid improperly burdening the wrong taxpayers. First-party information reporting, in contrast, faces a different limitation, in that taxpayers may be unreliable sources on their own taxable activities. Indeed, this is the problem giving rise to the need for tax enforcement and detection of noncompliance in the first place.

In contrast to current law, we propose a hybrid first- and third-party approach to information reporting, which can utilize the advantages of each while also accounting for their limitations. This reporting system could be implemented in two stages. First, taxpayers with income or assets above certain threshold would be subject to additional third-party information reporting requirements. These taxpayers with income or assets above the threshold amounts would be required to report or certify their status to the applicable third parties, thereby confirming that they are subject to the third-party information rules. In effect, this hybrid system would use means-adjusted criteria reported by first parties (the taxpayers themselves) to determine the applicability of additional activity-based reporting by third parties such as financial institutions.

For an illustration, this model for a hybrid first- and third-party information reporting system could have served as an alternative to the Biden Administration's bank reporting reform. As described previously, this reform would have required banks to report gross inflows and outflows from accounts, at a threshold amount that was $600 initially and was subsequently increased to $10,000. An alternative system could have only required this third-party bank flow reporting for taxpayers with income or assets above specified thresholds. Financial institutions could collect this information directly from the account holders, who would in effect be required to certify whether they are subject to these heightened information reporting rules or not.

In this example, these account holders could be required to self-certify to the financial institution that their reported adjusted gross income for the prior year or in recent years did not exceed a specified threshold, such as $2 million, or that the total net value of their financial assets does not exceed a specified threshold, which could be set, for instance, at $10 million. This hybrid system could be implemented in conjunction with the *Annual Net Asset Statement*, which would require high-end taxpayers to report an estimated value of their assets to the IRS.

This model of first-party certification would not be new to the tax system. The current tax compliance rules already use first-party certifications to notify third parties of the application of heightened third-party tax compliance rules. For one example, taxpayers provide information to employers on IRS Form W-4 (Employee's Withholding Certificate) to notify their employers of their economic circumstances, thereby defining the third-party employers' withholding obligations.[42] Similarly, taxpayers must report information regarding their economic circumstances to third-party payors on IRS Form W-9 (Request for Taxpayer Identification Number (TIN) and Certification), including a certification regarding whether they are subject to FATCA reporting or backup withholding.[43]

In effect, this hybrid system would draw from the advantages of both first- and third-party information reporting, while also accounting for the limitations of each. As described earlier, banks do not have complete knowledge of their account holders' economic circumstances and can only observe their specific transactions or account balances. A hybrid first- and third-party system, in contrast, utilizes taxpayers' first-person knowledge of their own economic circumstances to determine when the additional third-party information reporting rules would apply. Consequently, this approach could utilize a lower transaction threshold for the third-party information reporting – in order to prevent avoidance through transaction-splitting – without encountering the concern of unduly burdening lower-income taxpayers subject to rules with lower threshold amounts.

This hybrid system would help avoid the challenges with information reporting requirements that are designed too broadly or too narrowly. The income or asset thresholds for determining the application of these rules could be set at a level that is high enough to exclude lower- or middle-income taxpayers, but also low enough that the wealthiest taxpayers could only avoid these rules by failing to report a substantial portion of their income or wealth. That is, under this proposal, taxpayers with income or wealth far above the threshold amounts would not experience any marginal effect from underreporting their last dollars of income or wealth for purposes of the threshold determination, as they would under a substantive income tax or a wealth tax. In effect, this hybrid system would utilize the advantages of third-party information reporting systems, while also providing these third parties with the information otherwise unavailable to them and which is necessary to design more effectively targeted third-party information reporting requirements.

Because the income and wealth calculations used for purposes of the thresholds would not affect substantive tax liabilities, this hybrid system could also minimize the compliance burdens on first parties and reduce their tax-avoidance opportunities. Taxpayers could certify to third parties whether an income-based threshold applies based on the taxpayer's own income tax filings from prior years, which would not require any additional calculations of their income for purposes of the certification. Similarly, taxpayers with wealth far above a wealth-based threshold would not have to undertake the exercise of actually valuing their assets, if they are certain that the threshold exemption for taxpayers with low asset holdings would not apply. For many high-end taxpayers, the threshold for exemption from reporting would not be high enough to induce them to attempt to game their reporting of income or assets. Only taxpayers on the margins, with a net asset value or income near the threshold levels, would have an incentive to try and avoid meeting them.

For the same reasons, this approach would allow policymakers even greater flexibility in determining the calculation of income and wealth used for purposes of these thresholds. For example, the income-based threshold could be based on a taxpayer's adjusted gross income,[44] which would limit taxpayers' opportunities to avoid the application of these rules by claiming improper below-the-line deductions or expenses.[45] As in the case of IRS Form 8938 and the *Annual Net Asset Statement*, the wealth threshold used in this approach could use a simplified method based on a taxpayer's maximum asset value at any point during the taxable year, without facing the concern that a maximum value would be an improper basis for determining substantive liabilities as under a wealth tax reform.

NONDISCLOSURE PENALTIES

Every first-party or third-party information reporting system also needs enforcement measures – including penalties and audits – to deter and detect noncompliance by anyone who is subject to the applicable reporting requirements. A hybrid first- and third-party information reporting system could also provide policymakers with greater flexibility in setting penalty amounts at levels that can improve their deterrent effect. Policymakers face distinct challenges in setting penalties for nondisclosure of specific information that does not directly affect substantive tax liabilities, regardless of whether they use a percentage-based model or a fixed-amount model. The amount of percentage-based penalties – such as the accuracy-related penalties on income-tax underpayments[46] – vary with the amount of underreported income or other factors used as the base for determining the penalty. As a result, higher-income taxpayers will typically face a higher penalty amount, to the extent they tend to have more underreported income at stake and to the extent that the income would generally be taxed at higher progressive rates. Fixed-amount penalties, in contrast, impose the same absolute penalty burden on all taxpayers. As a result, these penalties will almost always have a relatively lower deterrent effect for wealthier taxpayers.[47]

Policymakers cannot impose percentage-based penalties in all cases. Fixed-amount penalties are often more appropriate for nondisclosure of information that does not directly affect tax liabilities, or for other acts of noncompliance. Designing fixed-amount penalties for activities encounters a basic tension, however, since the penalties must be set high enough to effectively deter high-income taxpayers, but low enough to avoid imposing disproportionately high burdens on low-income taxpayers. Here, as well, means-adjusted criteria can allow policymakers more flexibility in setting penalty levels and in reconciling this tension. For example, Section 6038D of the Internal Revenue Code can provide substantial penalties for noncompliance with IRS Form 8938 reporting requirements, while at the same time minimizing the risk of overburdening lower-income taxpayers, because these requirements only apply to wealthier taxpayers with substantial foreign assets above the threshold levels.

A hybrid first- and third-party information reporting system can similarly offer policymakers greater flexibility in setting fixed-amount penalties at amounts that are high enough to have a significant deterrent effect while also avoiding the risk of collateral burdens on lower-income taxpayers. For example, a hybrid first- and third-party variation of the Biden Administration's bank reporting proposal, which incorporates income- and asset-based thresholds certified by the account holders, could allow for more accurately tailored penalties on both the first parties (the account holders) and the third parties (the financial institutions). Because these additional information-reporting requirements would only apply to wealthy taxpayers, the system could allow for higher fixed-amount penalties for noncompliance, which are necessary to effectively deter this class of taxpayers, while avoiding the risk of imposing collateral consequences or burdens for less-wealthy account holders, as they would not be subject to these rules.

Audits also play a critical and necessary role in ensuring compliance with both tax compliance rules and the proper reporting and payment of substantive tax liabilities. A hybrid system that accounts for both the actor and their activities can allow the IRS to focus a greater proportion of audit resources on substantial acts of noncompliance by high-end taxpayers, as indicated by characteristics of both the actor and their activities. Conversely, accounting for a broader scope of data on both actors and activities can allow the IRS to avoid unnecessary intrusions and audits when they would not be warranted.

NOTES

1 The potential penalties for third parties who fail to comply with information reporting requirements are typically limited, as compared to the potential penalties for failing to report and remit primary tax obligations. For example, the general penalty for failure to file an information return is $310 (adjusted for inflation), even if that information corresponds to a significantly higher potential tax liability. I.R.C. § 6721(a); Rev. Proc. 2022-38, 2022-45 I.R.B. 1 (inflation adjustments).
2 See, e.g., I.R.C. § 6111 (disclosure obligations for material advisors of reportable transactions); § 6707A(c) (definition of reportable transactions).
3 I.R.C. §§ 1471–1474.
4 I.R.C. § 1471(d)(1).
5 Shu-Yi Oei, *The Offshore Tax Enforcement Dragnet*, 67 EMORY L.J. 655, 706–08 (2018).
6 *Id.* at 708–09.
7 *See* DEP'T OF TREASURY, GENERAL EXPLANATIONS OF THE ADMINISTRATION'S FISCAL YEAR 2022 REVENUE PROPOSALS 88–90 (2021), https://home.treasury.gov/system/files/131/General-Explanations-FY2022.pdf; DEP'T OF TREASURY, FACT SHEET: TAX COMPLIANCE PROPOSALS WILL IMPROVE TAX FAIRNESS WHILE PROTECTING TAXPAYER PRIVACY (Oct. 19, 2021), https://home.treasury.gov/news/press-releases/jy0415 [hereinafter FACT SHEET] (detailing the Biden Administration's revised tax compliance proposals); DEP'T OF TREASURY, THE AMERICAN FAMILIES PLAN TAX COMPLIANCE AGENDA (2021), https://home.treasury.gov/system/files/136/The-American-Families-Plan-Tax-Compliance-Agenda.pdf.
8 Charles O. Rossotti et al., *Shrinking the Tax Gap: A Comprehensive Approach*, 169 TAX NOTES FED. 1467, 1473–75 (2020).
9 DEP'T OF TREASURY, GENERAL EXPLANATIONS OF THE ADMINISTRATION'S FISCAL YEAR 2022 REVENUE PROPOSALS, *supra* note 7.
10 *Id.*
11 *Id.*

12 *Id.*
13 *Id.*
14 Dep't of Treasury, Fact Sheet, *supra* note 7.
15 *Id.*
16 Dep't of Treasury, General Explanations of the Administration's Fiscal Year 2022 Revenue Proposals, *supra* note 7, at 88–90.
17 Dep't of Treasury, The American Families Plan Tax Compliance Agenda (2021), 20, https://home.treasury.gov/system/files/136/The-American-Families-Plan-Tax-Compliance-Agenda.pdf; Natasha Sarin, *The Case for a Robust Attack on the Tax Gap*, Dep't of Treasury (Sept. 7, 2021), https://home.treasury.gov/news/featured-stories/the-case-for-a-robust-attack-on-the-tax-gap.
18 *See* Letter from 21 Democratic Members of Congress, to Nancy Pelosi, Speaker of the House, US House of Representatives, and Richard Neal, Chairman of the Ways & Means Comm., US House of Representatives 1 (Oct. 27, 2021), https://www.nafcu.org/system/files/files/House%20Dem%20IRS%20Letter%20FINAL.pdf.
19 Press Release, Budget Comm., Tax Scorekeeper Confirms Millions of Americans Making Less Than $400,000 Would Have Accounts Targeted under Biden IRS Spying Scheme (Dec. 7, 2021), https://budget.house.gov/press-release/tax-scorekeeper-confirms-millions-of-americans-making-less-than-400000-would-have-accounts-targeted-under-biden-irs-spying-scheme.
20 Letter from Thomas A. Barthold, Chief of Staff, the Joint Comm. on Tax'n, Congress of US, to Hon. Jason Smith, Rep., US House of Representatives (Dec. 3, 2021), https://budget.house.gov/wp-content/uploads/2021/12/117-0809-fjs.pdf.
21 *Increased IRS Reporting "Risky and Unnecessary" for Consumers*, Credit Union Nat'l Ass'n (Oct. 6, 2021), https://news.cuna.org/articles/119980-increased-irs-reporting-risky-and-unnecessary-for-consumers.
22 Kevin McCarthy (@GOPLeader), Twitter (Nov. 9, 2021, 7:46 PM), https://twitter.com/gopleader/status/1458234464862101508?lang=en.
23 *See, e.g.*, Scott Horsley, *Biden's Proposal to Give IRS More Info on Bank Accounts Faces Criticism*, NPR (Oct. 2, 2021), https://www.npr.org/2021/10/02/1042667366/bidens-proposal-to-give-irs-more-info-on-bank-accounts-faces-criticism; Naomi Jagoda, *Democrats Face Growing Storm over IRS Reporting Provision*, Hill (Oct. 16, 2021), https://thehill.com/policy/finance/577017-democrats-face-growing-storm-over-irs-reporting-provision/; Callie Patteson, *"This Is Screwed Up": Manchin Says IRS "Snooping" Won't Be in Final Biden Bill*, N.Y. Post (Oct. 26, 2021), https://nypost.com/2021/10/26/sen-manchin-says-irs-snooping-wont-be-in-final-biden-bill/.
24 Dep't of Treasury, Fact Sheet, *supra* note 7; *see also* Sarah Kolinovsky & Trish Turner, *Biden Admin Backs Down on Tracking Bank Accounts with over $600 Annual Transactions*, ABC News (Oct. 19, 2021), https://abcnews.go.com/Politics/biden-admin-backs-tracking-bank-accounts-600-annual/story?id=80665505.
25 Dep't of Treasury, Fact Sheet, *supra* note 7.
26 *Id.*
27 *Id.*
28 *Id.*
29 *See* Letter from 21 Democratic Members of Congress, *supra* note 18.

30 *See* Build Back Better Act, H.R. 5376, 117th Cong.
31 *See* CONG. RSCH. SERV., R46998, SENATE FINANCE COMMITTEE TAX PROVISIONS IN THE BUILD BACK BETTER ACT (2021).
32 *See, e.g.*, Build Back Better Act, H.R. Rep. No. 117-130, pt. 3, § 138402 (Application of Backup Withholding with Respect to Third-Party Network Transactions).
33 *See* DEP'T OF TREASURY, GENERAL EXPLANATIONS OF THE ADMINISTRATION'S FISCAL YEAR 2022 REVENUE PROPOSALS, *supra* note 7, at 88; DEP'T OF TREASURY, THE AMERICAN FAMILIES PLAN TAX COMPLIANCE AGENDA, *supra* note 7, at 88.
34 *See* Marjorie E. Kornhauser, *A Tax Morale Approach to Compliance: Recommendations for the IRS*, 8 FLA. TAX REV. 599 (2007).
35 For recent proposals, see Elizabeth Warren, Senator, *Ultra-Millionaire Tax*, WARREN FOR SENATE (Mar. 3, 2022), https://elizabethwarren.com/plans/ultra-millionaire-tax (proposing a wealth tax with rates reaching 6% on net wealth above $1 billion); Bernie Sanders, Senator, *Tax on Extreme Wealth*, BERNIE SANDERS (Mar. 3, 2022), https://berniesanders.com/issues/tax-extreme-wealth/ (proposing a wealth tax with rates reaching 8% on net wealth above $10 billion). For wealth tax reforms proposed by scholars, see BRUCE ACKERMAN & ANNE ALSTOTT, THE STAKEHOLDER SOCIETY 94–112 (1999); THOMAS PIKETTY, CAPITAL IN THE TWENTY-FIRST CENTURY 515–18, 524–30 (Arthur Goldhammer trans., 2014); Emmanuel Saez & Gabriel Zucman, *Progressive Wealth Taxation*, 2019 BROOKINGS PAPERS ON ECON. ACTIVITY 437, 437 (2019); David Shakow & Reed Shuldiner, *A Comprehensive Wealth Tax*, 53 TAX L. REV. 499, 500–31 (2000).
36 For discussion, see Ari Glogower, *Comparing Capital Income and Wealth Taxes*, 48 PEPP. L. REV. 875, 894–98 (2021); James R. Repetti, *Commentary: It's All about Valuation*, 53 TAX L. REV. 607 (2000); Leandra Lederman, *Valuation as a Challenge for Tax Administration*, 96 NOTRE DAME L. REV. 1495 (2021).
37 *See generally* David Gamage et al., *How to Measure and Value Wealth for a Federal Wealth Reform*, ROOSEVELT INST. (Apr. 2021).
38 *See* Glogower, *supra* note 36, at 894.
39 *See, e.g.*, INSTITUTIONAL LTD. PARTNERS ASS'N, QUARTERLY REPORTING STANDARDS BEST PRACTICES (2016).
40 *See* IRS, Form 8938 (Statement of Specified Foreign Financial Assets).
41 *See, e.g.*, PIKETTY, *supra* note 35, at 518–19; Emmanuel Saez & Gabriel Zucman, *The Rise of Income and Wealth Inequality in America: Evidence from Distributional Macroeconomic Accounts*, 34 J. ECON. PERSP. 3, 11 (2020).
42 *See* IRS, Form W-4 (Employee's Withholding Certificate).
43 *See* IRS, Form W-9 (Request for Taxpayer Identification Number and Certification).
44 I.R.C. § 61.
45 I.R.C. § 63(a).
46 I.R.C. § 6662.
47 For discussion, see Chapter 6, section "Tax Penalties in Current Law."

Conclusion

The federal tax system in the United States supports the welfare of its citizens, sustains the economy, and advances basic principles of fairness. Its future, however, depends in large part on the functioning of its tax compliance rules. Policymakers must take a new look at these rules and address several important questions regarding how they can be redesigned to address the challenges of high-end tax noncompliance that this book describes.

First, in light of new pressures and uncertainties, how can the IRS most effectively execute its mission to "enforce the law with integrity and fairness to all?"[1] The IRS plays an essential role in administering and enforcing the substantive tax rules. The agency's operations convert the substantive tax rules from mere words on pages to the tax revenues that fund public expenditures.

Robust IRS enforcement is necessary to sustain the tax system, but enforcement alone is not sufficient. High-end taxpayers operate within a system of porous tax compliance rules, which can give them an upper hand against the IRS at every step in the tax compliance process, from information reporting and return filing through dispute litigation. The IRS also faces evolving obstacles to performing its mission, including new administrative law hurdles, uneven funding from Congress, and ongoing political scrutiny.

Second, how can the tax compliance system adapt to taxpayers' transactional innovation? Fueled by new technology and high-powered advisors, well-resourced taxpayers can use complex structures to avoid scrutiny by the IRS, and to take advantage of intricacies and ambiguities in the law. High-end taxpayers can also often sidestep the tax compliance system's current activity-based rules, which target activities that indicate or enable noncompliance. Well-advised taxpayers can often benefit the most from tax compliance rules that apply in the same way to all taxpayers, regardless of their means or their avoidance opportunities. Because of these issues, policymakers have struggled to design tax compliance rules that can effectively narrow the tax gap without imposing new burdens on other taxpayers.

Last, how should we design tax compliance rules during a time of uncertain prospects for substantive tax reform? For instance, efforts to reform the rules to tax large fortunes progressively would require new approaches to taxing capital income or wealth.[2] Yet these reforms would only be sustainable and effective if they were implemented in connection with new measures to prevent high-end avoidance of the new rules. On the other hand, Congress also may not be able to implement these major substantive tax reforms, in part due to uncertainty as to whether the Supreme Court would uphold the changes. In this scenario, measures to improve high-end tax compliance may be policymakers' best option to shore up revenue collection and prevent further erosion of the progressive tax base.

The unique challenges of high-end tax noncompliance make all these questions harder to answer. This noncompliance costs the public hundreds of billions of dollars in lost tax revenue each year, which the nation needs for critical public investments and for reining in an escalating national debt. Tax noncompliance at the top also subverts the progressivity of the tax system, erodes taxpayer morale, and raises the stakes for substantive tax reform. Effectively preventing modern forms of high-end tax noncompliance will require new thinking about the tax compliance system, as well as novel solutions.

The three stories as presented in the Introduction exemplify these pressing challenges for tax compliance. The 2022 congressional report investigating President Donald Trump's tax returns found that the IRS faced not only a web of complex transactions but also a wall of high-powered legal counsel.[3] The Biden Administration's 2021 proposal to expand bank information reporting ran aground on objections that it would burden the wrong activities and taxpayers.[4] Even Congress's historic $80 billion investment in the IRS prompted threats of repeal and concerns that the agency would use the new funding to target and harass taxpayers.[5]

In recent years, policymakers have prioritized cracking down on high-end tax avoidance and countering these challenges to the US tax system. In a letter accompanying the IRS's 2023 strategic operating plan, IRS Commissioner Daniel Werfel emphasized that the agency would need new capacities to "unpack the complex filings of high income taxpayers" so that "Americans have confidence that all taxpayers, regardless of means, are doing their part to meet their responsibilities under our tax laws."[6]

This book offers a new direction for the tax compliance system that can help to realize this goal, and a new approach to addressing the long-standing challenge of high-end noncompliance. Our proposed system of means adjustments would adjust the operation of the tax compliance rules based on taxpayers' economic circumstances, and not just based on their specific activities. These adjustments would proactively account for the advantages that high-end taxpayers enjoy under the current tax compliance rules, and they would also create a more robust and effective tax compliance system. Further, they would enhance the impact of the current activity-based rules and IRS enforcement procedures, while redressing the limitations of these conventional responses to high-end tax noncompliance.

As we have described, policymakers can design means adjustments in a way that would make the tax compliance rules more fair and more equal in their application to taxpayers of all wealth and income levels. These rules would not single out certain taxpayers for harsher treatment or more compliance burdens but, rather, would account for the ways in which a taxpayer's financial resources can often enable their tax noncompliance. For the same reason, these adjustments can be designed to advance basic principles of fairness in legal design and constitutional guarantees of equal treatment and due process.

Means-adjusted tax compliance rules can also help the IRS perform its mission more effectively. As the agency tasked with administering and enforcing the tax laws, the IRS often faces political threats and public mistrust. Embedding means adjustments into the structure of the tax compliance laws can alleviate the burden on the IRS to be the primary arbiter of fairness in tax administration. Through these adjustments, Congress can publicly express principles of fairness by enacting them through the legislative process, and give the IRS new tools for combatting high-end noncompliance and enforcing the tax laws fairly.

We have also offered a practical guide for how policymakers can implement these adjustments, as well as how they would interact with features of current law, to build a more robust and effective tax compliance system. This book has focused in detail on how means adjustments could improve four areas of the tax compliance rules: (1) civil tax penalties; (2) tax advice and its relevance to the "reasonable cause" defenses to certain civil tax penalties; (3) the statute of limitations on assessment; and (4) tax information reporting rules. We do not detail every possible application for means adjustments in the tax compliance system in this book. The same general principles outlined here could also be applied by policymakers to other areas of tax compliance, particularly when such adjustments could similarly counteract the advantages of high-end taxpayers.

While our book provides a framework of key design considerations, policymakers would still have flexibility when introducing means-adjusted tax compliance rules. They would also have many decisions left to make. For example, they would need to determine the specific thresholds used for making the adjustments, as well as which rules to adjust and to what degree. We have offered guideposts that policymakers can use when making these decisions, rather than hard and fast rules. Future research on taxpayer behaviors and avoidance opportunities can also help to fine-tune and optimize the adjustments we propose here.

The concept of means-adjusted tax compliance rules is not a "silver bullet" that can fully solve the complex challenges of high-end noncompliance on its own. Rather, we argue that by relying primarily on conventional approaches, policymakers have not fully considered how the tax compliance rules can be designed to maximize their effect. A layered approach, which combines IRS enforcement, activity-based rules, and means adjustments, offers the greatest promise to effectively ensure that all taxpayers are paying their fair share.

We urge our readers to take a fresh look at our tax compliance system, and to imagine how it could be reformed to meet today's challenges. We hope that this book has offered a start down this path, and new ideas to help narrow the tax gap at the top.

NOTES

[1] IRS, *The Agency, Its Mission and Statutory Authority* (Nov. 15, 2023), https://www.irs.gov/about-irs/the-agency-its-mission-and-statutory-authority.

[2] *See* Chapter 1, section "Why the Distribution of Noncompliance Matters."

[3] HOUSE COMM. ON WAYS & MEANS, REPORT ON THE INTERNAL REVENUE SERVICE'S MANDATORY AUDIT PROGRAM UNDER THE PRIOR ADMINISTRATION (2017–2020) (Dec. 20, 2022).

[4] *See, e.g.*, Letter from 21 Democratic Members of Congress, to Rep. Nancy Pelosi (D-CA) and Rep. Richard Neal (D-MA) (Oct. 27, 2021); *see also* Chapter 10, section "The Biden Administration's Bank Tax Reporting Proposal."

[5] *See, e.g.*, H.R. 23, Family and Small Business Taxpayer Protection Act, 118th Cong. (2023); *see also* Jeff Carlson, *House Passes Measure Clawing Back Nearly $80 Billion from IRS*, THOMSON REUTERS (Jan. 11, 2023), https://tax.thomsonreuters.com/news/house-passes-measure-clawing-back-nearly-80-billion-from-irs/; *see also* Chapter 3, section "Limitations of Increasing IRS Funding."

[6] Letter from Daniel I. Werfel, Commissioner of Internal Revenue to Treasury Secretary Janet Yellen, IRS Inflation Reduction Act Strategic Operating Plan, Apr. 5, 2023.

Index

2022 Midterm Election, 2, 66
activity-based rules, *See* tax compliance rules
Administrative Procedure Act (APA), 27, 77–79, 83, 88, 154, 195
administrative rulemaking, 75–81
   interpretation and implementation, 76
   means adjustments (proposed), impact on, 83–84
   statutory and judicial constraints, 76, 83–84
Annual Net Asset Statement (proposed), 223–36
   administration and enforcement, improving, 232
   as a first-party wealth information return, 232
   fiscal policy, improving, 232
   Form 8938, similarity to, 231
   thresholds, 232
   valuation methods, 232
Anti-Injunction Act (AIA), 77–78
anti-tax advocates, 109
Aristotle, 102–4
asset classes, alternative, 72
Astor, William B., 4
attorney's fees, 167–68
   fee-shifting rule, 89
   tax counsel, billing methods for, 29
audits
   benefits of written tax opinions during, 169
   of complicated vs. simple tax returns, 26, 68, 153, 169, 193, 208
   correspondence, 20, 25, 68
   increasing, as a means of boosting tax enforcement, 133
   as an IRS function, 48
   IRS Wealth Squad, conducted by, 143
   low-income taxpayers, 8, 215
   of pass-through entities, 26, 208
   perceived probability of, 207
   racial distribution of, 22, 49, 215
   rate drops due to funding constraints, 54
   reduced frequency, in response to lobbying, 143
   statute of limitations, 186, 193, 195
   taxpayer fear of, 66, 133, 152, 207, 227
   taxpayer privacy, 195
   of wealthy taxpayers, increasing frequency of, 20

Bakija, Jon, 21
banks, *See* financial institutions
Batchelder, Lily, 54
Becker-Bentham fine deterrence model (of sanctions), 46, 69, 82, 106, 139, 147
behavior (of taxpayers), *See* taxpayer behavior
behavioral incentives (of taxation), 107
benefits (of tax compliance), *See* tax compliance benefits
Biden Administration
   bank tax reporting proposal (2021), 75, 201, 226–29, 233, 235, 240
   tax reform proposal (2023), 196
Biden, Joseph R., 2, 153, 213
Bitcoin, 28, 203, 210, *See also* cryptocurrency
Bloomberg, Michael, 2
Blumkin, Tomer, 109
bonds, 4
BOSS (bond and option sales strategy), 71, *See also* Son of BOSS
Brockman, Robert, 209
brokers
   defining, for information reporting purposes, 74
   of digital assets, 210
   reporting obligations, 55, 72, 203, 211, 213
   taxpayer transactions, first-hand knowledge of, 224–25

243

Brown, Dorothy, 22, 215
Buffet, Warren, 2
Build Back Better Act, 213, 228
business entities
  corporations, 26, 49, 55, 123–24, 138, 195, 203–4, 211–12
  corporations (closely held), 213
  LLCs, 77, 167, 208
  partnerships, 26, 49, 172, 204, 208, 213–14
  sole proprietorships, 208
  subchapter C corporations, 163, 175, 211–12
  subchapter S corporations, 128, 138, 172, 208, 211–14

CARDS (custom adjustable rate debt structure), 71
carried interest, *See* income
cash economy, 205, 208
charitable contributions
  conservation easements, 172
charitable remainder annuity trusts (CRATs), 26
Chevron doctrine, 76
Chirelstein, Marvin, 167
CIC Services, LLC v. IRS, 77–79, 81
Circular 230 Regulations Governing Practice before the Internal Revenue Service, 50–51, 167–68, 177
civic duty, as taxpayer motivation, 45
civil tax penalties, 3, 5, 39, 41, 46–47, 51–52, 81, 88, 113, 123–24, 131, 141–55, 161–67, 173, *See also* sanctions (for noncompliance)
  categories, 142–43
  chance of detection and enforcement, 146
  defenses against, 3, 5, 123, 144, 161, 163–66, 177–78
  defenses, proposed changes to, 172–77
  delinquency, 142
  inaccuracy, 142
  limited IRS enforcement of, 143
  negligence, 164
  percentage vs. fixed amount, 142
  reasonable basis defense, 51, 166, 170–71, 174–75, 177
  reasonable cause and good faith defense, 5, 51, 151, 161, 164–67, 170–78
  reasonable reliance on tax advice, 165–66, 170
  risk aversion, deterrent effect, 145
  self-adjusting penalties (Alex Raskolnikov proposal), 147
  subjective vs. objective factors, 144, 163
  substantial authority defense, 177
  substantial understatements, 165
clean vehicle credit, 41
Coinbase, 210
Compaq Computer v. Commissioner (Fifth Circuit case), 73, 83

Congress, 228
  Byrd rule, 76
  constitutional taxing and spending power, 76, 83
  cryptocurrency, regulating, 72
  economic legislation, Supreme Court deference regarding, 105
  inquiries into EITC correspondence audits, 8
  IRS appeals for legislative action, target of, 70
  IRS funding legislation enacted, 54, 66
  IRS funding rescinded, 55, 66–67
  IRS funding, political aspects of, 66–67, 82
  IRS oversight legislation enacted, 67
  IRS policy, influence over, 67
  IRS, criticism of, 26
  Joint Committee on Taxation, 128, 152, 227
  means adjustments (proposed), requirement of legislative implementation, 154
  nondelegation doctrine, limitations imposed by, 76
  policy riders, use of, 68
  tax legislation, process for enactment, 76
  tax reform legislation enacted, 2–3, 26, 74, 87, 153
  tax reform legislation, political realities of, 86–87
  traditional approaches to addressing tax noncompliance, limitations of, 154
  Treasury Department, division of labor with, 75, 133
  visibility of digital transactions to IRS, attempts to increase, 210
Congressional Budget Act of 1974, 76
Congressional Budget Office (CBO), 28, 65
Constitution, United States, 42, 75, 101, 125, 153, *See* Congress – constitutional taxing and spending power
  designation of legislative power (tax), 76
  due process, 8, 52, 89, 101, 105–6, 110, 112, 125, 153, 196, 241
  equal protection, 8, 101, 105–6, 110, 112, 125, 153, 241
  Necessary and Proper Clause, 76
corporate tax rate
  adjustments, distributional effects of, 40
corporations, *See* business entities – corporations
cost basis, 203, 213–14, 231–32
credit card companies, 203
Credit Suisse, 209
Credit Union National Association (CUNA), 227
credits, *See also* Earned Income Tax Credit (EITC)
  child and dependent care, 126
  education, 126
Crenshaw, Ander, 66

Index

criminal tax penalties, 52, 78, 106, 124, 142, *See also* sanctions (for noncompliance)
cryptocurrency, 13, 26–29, 55, 72, 74, 128, 138, 152, 203, 210–11

day fines, 108
declining marginal utility, 21, 110, 129, 140, 145
deductions
    qualified business income, 162
Department of the Treasury, *See* Treasury Department
detection (by the IRS), *See also* tax noncompliance, *See* multiple headings under Internal Revenue Service (IRS)
digital assets, 16, 72, 74, 203, 210–11, 232, *See also* cryptocurrency
digital currency, *See* cryptocurrency
discretion, in tax-rule enforcement, 74
disguised dividends, 212
dividends, *See* income – dividends
Doran, Michael, 148
double distortion principle, 106–9
due process, *See also* Taxpayer Bill of Rights (TBOR), *See* Constitution, United States

Earned Income Tax Credit, 20
Earned Income Tax Credit (EITC), 8, 22, 24–25, 68, 90, 126, 172, 215
    correspondence audits, 8
eBay, 203
Edwards, John, 213
efficiency optimization (law and economics), 106
employee trusts (as listed transactions), 78
Equal Access to Justice Act, 89
equal protection, *See* Constitution, United States
estate tax, 109
Ethereum, 210
Etsy, 203
ex ante (before the fact) legal rules, 7, 41, 48, 69, 82, 85, 111, 141, 146–47, 194
ex post (after the fact) legal rules, 7, 41, 48, 69–70, 114, 141, 146
excises, 4
executive compensation, 26
expected monetary outcome model (of tax penalties), 145
expected utility model (of tax penalties), 145

Federal Register, 77
Field, Heather, 29
financial institutions, 1, 47, 201, 203–4, 206, 209, 225–26, 233, *See also* foreign financial institutions (FFIs)
Finland, 108

first-best vs. second-best legal design, 109
first-mover advantage (in interpreting new tax laws), 31
Foreign Account Tax Compliance Act (FATCA), 72, 209–10, 225–26, 233
    account splitting, undermining objectives of, 225
foreign accounts, *See* offshore accounts
foreign entities
    interest in, reporting rules, 205
foreign financial assets, underreporting of (example), 230
foreign financial institutions (FFIs), 204, 225
formal equality, 102
Forms, *See* (Form name) under Internal Revenue Service (IRS)
Fuller, Lon L., 102
fund managers
    classification of earnings as "carried interest," 31
    fees, reporting of (hypothetical), 149

Galler, Linda, 162
Gangl, Katharina, 23
Gates, Bill, 2
Gemmell, Norman, 69
generality principle (rule of law), 102
gifts, 188, 193
Gingrich, Newt, 213
Global High Wealth Industry Group, *See* Internal Revenue Service (IRS) – Wealth Squad
Government Accountability Report, 26
government benefits
    means-tested, 105
    reporting requirements, 228
    Social Security, 201
    Social Security disability, 106
    Supplemental Nutrition Assistance Program (SNAP), 105
Gowder, Paul, 104
Graetz, Michael, 109
Gregory v. Helvering, 14–29
Guyton, John, 26, 28

Hasseldine, John, 69
health benefits (reporting requirements), 204
Health Savings Accounts (HSAs), 204
hedge funds, 128, 232
Holmes, Oliver Wendell, Jr., 45
House of Representatives, 2, 76, 228
    Appropriations Committee, 66
    Budget Committee, 227
    Committee on Ways & Means, 1, 26, 29, 66, 183

Index

income
  business, strategies to avoid reporting, 208–9, 214
  capital, 13, 24, 28, 126, 128, 151, 172, 210, 214, 240
  from capital, 203–4
  carried interest, 31, 162
  cash economy, 205
  dividends, 208, 211–12
  goods or services, compensation for, 202–3
  Health Savings Accounts (HSAs), 204
  interest, 50, 138, 201–4, 206, 208, 228
  from labor, 28, 39, 128
  miscellaneous, 203–4
  qualified small business stock (QSBS), 162
  real estate, 208
  rental, 208
  retirement benefits, 204
  wages and salaries, 25, 28, 45, 50, 126, 138, 172, 196, 201, 206, 208, 212–14
income distribution
  law and economics, principles of, 106
  level assessments, impact on tax noncompliance research, 16–20
  scale, lower end of, 8, 20, 43, 73, 85, 89–91, 151–52
  scale, top of, 5, 17, 128–30, 145, 208
  through taxation, high administrative costs of, 109
income shielding (by wealthy taxpayers), 24
Inflation Reduction Act (IRA), 3, 54, 65–66, 132, 153, 169, 186
information reporting, *See also* Biden Administration – bank tax reporting proposal (2021)
  centralized third parties, benefit of, 206
  digital assets, 210–11
  financial statements, 205
  first-party, benefits of, 229
  first-party, incentive to underreport, 229
  gaps in, 201
  hybrid first- and third-party model (proposed), 223–36
  information, uses of, by the IRS, 231
  requirements, by category, 202–5
  specific activities, focus on, 202
  tax compliance rates, effect on, 201, 206
  tax returns, 204–5
  third-party reporting, limits of, 224
  two-tiered nature of (by level of wealth), 201
in-kind wealth transfers, 138
insurance
  advice from sophisticated tax counsel (against IRS tax challenges), 29, 162–63, 174
  health, 204
  life insurance policy (as income-shielding vehicle), 24, 56
  micro-captive (as income-shielding vehicle), 77, 79
  policy distributions as taxable income, 204
  tax (against potential liabilities), 29
Internal Revenue Code (IRC), 13, 31, 41–42, 48–49, 51–52, 56, 75, 77, 87, 90, 127, 132, 142, 144, 150, 162–65, 171, 202, 205, 235
Internal Revenue Service (IRS), 50
  "dirty dozen list," **2023** 26
  Strategic Operating Plan **2023**, 8
  abuses of power, fear of, 67, 196
  administrative rulemaking, challenges of, 75–81
  agents, highly skilled, benefit of, 54, 69, 152
  Appeals Division, 196
  Appeals Office, 5
  Commissioner, 8, 16, 20, 22, 25, 27, 30, 54, 67–68, 70, 153, 206, 210, 240
  cybersecurity, 54
  Data Book, 143, 148
  detection of tax avoidance, 25, 72, 202, 212–14
  discretion, exercise of, 65–69
  Discriminant Index Function (DIF), 49
  dispute resolution, 25
  enforcement efforts, recognition of limits of, 70
  enforcement resources, historical lack of, 153
  establishment of (1862), 76
  examination resources, 8
  Form 1040, 49, 204, 206, 227, 229–30
  Form 1041, 204
  Form 1065, 204
  Form 1065, (Schedule K-1), 213
  Form 1095-B, 204
  Form 1098, 204
  Form 1099, 50
  Form 1099-B, 203, 210, 213
  Form 1099-DIV, 203, 212
  Form 1099-INT, 203, 206, 212
  Form 1099-K, 203
  Form 1099-MISC, 203, 211
  Form 1099-NEC, 203, 211
  Form 1099-R, 204
  Form 1099-S, 203, 214
  Form 1120, 204
  Form 1120-S (Schedule K-1), 213
  Form 8275, 165, 175
  Form 8275-R, 165
  Form 8300, 210, 214
  Form 8886, 50
  Form 8918, 50
  Form 8938, 49, 205, 230–32, 234–35
  Form 8966, 204
  Form W-2, 28, 50, 201, 203, 206
  Form W-4, 45, 233
  Form W-9, 233

functions, 48
funding of, 2–3, 38, 40, 53–55, 65–69
guidance, assessment of penalties, 154
guidance, sub-regulatory, 80
Internal Revenue Service Restructuring and Reform Act of 1998, 67
investment in, impact on tax gap, 69
Large Business and International (LB&I) Division, 20
mission of, 43, 48–49, 239
National Taxpayer Advocate, 23, 45, 66, 68, 73, 85
Notice 2007-83, 78
Notice 2016-66, 77–78
Office of Professional Responsibility (OPR), 50
Office of Tax-Shelter Analysis, 188
Offshore Voluntary Disclosure Program (OVDP), 73
rules, equitable enforcement of, 8, 152, 202
special interest groups, influence over, 80–81
Tax Exempt and Government Entities Division, 132
tax gap, estimation of, 15–16
taxpayer trust in, 23, 43, 55, 85, 132, 152
technology modernization, 70
Treasury Department, role in, 76
Wealth Squad, 30, 54, 143
wealthy taxpayers, differential treatment of, justifications, 196
investment managers, 212, 225, 232

Jim Crow, 104
Joint Committee on Taxation, *See* Congress
Justice Department, 209

Kamin, David, 54
Kaplow, Louis, 21, 106
Keen, Michael, 69
Kornhauser, Marjorie, 45

law and economics, 106
Lederman, Leandra, 21, 53–54, 67
legislation, 2–3, 26, 54, 66, 70, 72–77, 83, 86, 105, 133, 153–54, 202–3, 209–10, 213, 226, 228, *See also* Congress
life insurance, *See* insurance
Liscow, Zachary, 109
listed transactions, 39, 50, 55–56, 71, 73, 75, 78–80, 88, 151, 164, 175, 186, 189, 191–92, 214
LLCs, *See* business entities – LLCs
loans
 to shareholders, rather than taxable dividend distributions, 212
lobbying, 80–81, 109

Logue, Kyle, 147
Lord, Samuel, 4
Luttmer, Erzo F. P., 23

Mann Construction v. *United States* (Sixth Circuit case), 78
Margalioth, Yoram, 109
Marian, Omri, 72
material advisors, 50, 55, 77, 142, 185, 189, 192, *See also* Internal Revenue Service (IRS) – Form 8918
Mathews v. *Eldridge*, 106
Mazur, Mark, 65
McCarthy, Kevin, 227
means adjustments (proposed), *See also* tax compliance rules – means adjustments (proposed)
 actor characteristics, focusing on, 225
 adjustment thresholds, 128–31
 advantages of, 81–87
 Annual Net Asset Statement (proposed), 223–36
 arguments for, 6–7
 civil tax penalties, justification for, 146
 civil tax penalties, selecting for application, 149–51
 costs, minimizing, 82
 criminal tax procedure rules, special considerations, 113
 design considerations for tax compliance rules, 123
 deterrent effect, equalizing, 108
 distributional equity, promoting, 109
 double-distortion principle, influence of, 114
 due process and equal protection, considerations for, 8, 112, 125, 153–54
 effect of IRS enforcement, improving, 88
 equalizing effects, 82, 112, 152
 fairness, 101–15
 information reporting, 214–15
 legal advice, impact on, 178
 legislative implementation, requirement of, 154
 means adjustments in current tax system, examples of, 88
 noncompliance defenses, applicability to, 173–77
 political durability, 86
 political feasibility, 86
 preemptive implementation, advantages of, 83
 procedural due process considerations, 113
 reasonable cause and good faith defense, applicability to, 173, 176
 reducing cooperation with IRS, threat of, 131
 statute of limitations, 191–97

means adjustments (proposed), (cont.)
  statutory implementation of, 83
  system design questions for policymakers, 122
  tax compliance rules, impact on
    implementation of, 123
  tax compliance rules, proposal for, 81–91
  tax morale, impact on, 85
  Taxpayer Bill of Rights (TBOR), consideration
    of, 113
Medicaid, 19
Medicare taxes, 203, 212
micro-captive insurance, *See* insurance
Minow, Martha, 104
monetary fines, *See* sanctions (for noncompliance)
  deterrent effect of, 108
monetized installment sale structures, 26
Murdoch, Rupert, 2
Musk, Elon, 2

national debt, 240
National Taxpayer Advocate, *See* Internal Revenue
  Service (IRS) – National Taxpayer Advocate
New York Times, 4, 123, 183, 194
noncompliance, *See* tax noncompliance
nondelegation doctrine, 76
notice and comment rulemaking, 77–79, 154

Obama, Barack H., 132
occupational licensing, 105
Oei, Shu-Yi, 73, 226
offshore accounts, 11, 25–26, 28, 72–73, 128, 131, 152,
  172, 202, 204, 209–10, 220, 225–26
Offshore Voluntary Disclosure Program (OVDP),
  209

Panama Papers, 209
partnerships, *See* business entities – partnerships
pass-through entities, *See* business entities –
  partnerships
payroll taxes, 213
Pelosi, Nancy, 227
planning drift (in interpreting new tax laws), 31
Posner, Eric, 47
preliminary injunctions
  IRS notices, preventing going into effect, 79
PricewaterhouseCoopers, 124
private equity funds, 31, 232
pro se litigants, 90
progressive taxation, 4–5, 7, 10, 20–21, 23, 41, 54,
  85–86, 88, 101, 109–11, 129, 133, 146, 154, 230,
  235, 240
ProPublica, 2, 22, 31, 66, 143, 152, 215
public finance, 7
public investments, 240

qualified small business stock (QSBS), *See* income

Raskolnikov, Alex, 147
Rawls, John, 102
reasonable compensation requirement (subchapter
  S corporations), 213
red flags, 165, 173, 214
reportable transactions, 39, 50–51, 55–56, 75,
  77–80, 88, 142–43, 148–49, 151, 186, 189
reporting, tax information, *See* information
  reporting
retirement accounts
  as a means of shielding wealth, 24
retirement benefits (reporting requirements), 204
Rettig, Charles P., 8, 16, 20, 25, 27, 68, 70, 206, 210
Romney, Mitt, 189
Rosenthal, Steven, 194
Rossotti, Charles O., 18, 54, 67–68, 226
rule of law, 101–5

S corporations, *See* business entities – subchapter
  S corporations
sanctions (for noncompliance), 42, 46–47, 70, 82,
  84, 113, 124, 130, 132, 139, 148, 150, 154, 174,
  230, *See also* civil tax penalties; criminal tax
  penalties; Becker-Bentham fine deterrence
  model (of sanctions)
  Finland, 108
  nonmonetary, 47
  third parties, not available for, 224
  variable fines, 108
Sarin, Natasha, 16, 18, 65, 208, 226
Schaeffler, Georg, 169, 190
Schickel, Richard, 143
Schierenbeck, Alec, 113
Schizer, David, 30
scrutiny tests (due process and equal protection
  violations), 105
Secretary of the Treasury, 153
securities, *See also* stocks; bonds; business entities
  collusion between buyer and seller, transactions
    in, 214
Shapiro, Ian, 109
Shavell, Steven, 106
Shaviro, Daniel, 41
Shulman, Douglas, 30
Singhal, Monica, 23
Slemrod, Joel, 10, 14, 17, 21, 40, 69–70, 114, 140, 146,
  148
Smith, Jason, 66, 227
social, 21
social norms, as taxpayer motivation, 45
Social Security, *See* government benefits
Social Security taxes, 203, 212

Index 249

social welfare, 239
sole proprietorships, *See* business entities – sole proprietorships
Solum, Lawrence, 102
special interest groups
   IRS, influence over, 80–81
Speck, Sloan, 31
speeding, fines for, 103, 106–8
statute of limitations
   complex cases, extension of (2023, Treasury Department proposal), 194
   complex tax returns, limited IRS review of, 69, 88, 187–88
   conditional waiver, 190
   effect on audit of Donald J. Trump's tax returns, 183
   extension of period, granted by taxpayer, 190
   function, 183, 187
   generally, 6, 183–97
   listed transactions, rule regarding, 188, 192
   longer period (proposal), 82, 85, 88, 191
   longer period (proposal) – detection advantage, 192
   longer period (proposal) – due process and equal protection considerations, 195
   longer period (proposal) – low-value underpayment exception, 192
   longer period in substantial omission and fraud cases, 6, 127, 185, 191
   reportable transactions, 186
   retroactive filing requirements, interplay of, 189
   start of statutory period, impact of return filing date, 184, 187–88
   substantial compliance doctrine, 189–90
statutes, *See* legislation
Stobie Creek Investments, LLC v. United States (Federal Circuit case), 167
stocks, 4, 213
   subchapter S corporation, selling shares of, 213
Strauss, David, 103
subchapter C corporations, *See* business entities – subchapter C corporations
subchapter S corporations, *See* business entities – subchapter S corporations
Summers, Lawrence, 16, 18, 226
Supplemental Nutrition Assistance Program (SNAP), 105
Supreme Court of the United States, 14, 77, 105, 154
Sutherland, George (US Supreme Court Justice), 14
Switzerland, 209
syndicated conservation easements (as listed transactions), 26, 79

tariffs, 4
tax advice, 161–83, *See also* material advisors; tax planning
   Circular **230** rules, 50, 167
   complicated statutes and regulations, 162
   confidence level, 166
   conflicts of interest, prohibition against, 167
   as a contractual term requirement, 163
   disregard of rules and regulations, as defense against, 165
   due diligence requirements, 169
   formal written tax opinion, 162
   as insurance against IRS tax challenges, 162–63
   law firms, reasons for high prices, 168
   legal conclusion, 166
   legal uncertainties, 163
   negligence, as defense against, 164
   as a "penalty shield," 81, 144
   possible tax treatment, 162
   potential tax risks, 162
   reasonable basis defense, required for, 164
   reasonable basis for factual and legal assumptions (standard), 166
   reasonable cause and good faith defense, required for, 164
   reporting obligations, 78
   as representative of "resource imbalances," **169**
   requirements, 166–67
   sophisticated, 25, 29–30, 123, 129, 150, 168
   substantial understatement, as defense against, 165
   Technical Advice Memoranda (IRS publication), 49
   use in tax liability defenses, 163–66
   wealthy taxpayers, disproportionately helpful to, 70–71, 144, 167–72, 196, 211
tax advisors, *See* tax advice; material advisors
tax collection, 40
tax compliance benefits, 47–48, 84
tax compliance norms, 45
tax compliance rates, 205
tax compliance rules, 39
   activity-based rules, as a quick-response mechanism, 73
   activity-based rules, broadly vs. narrowly defined, 74
   activity-based rules, generally, 3, 55–57
   activity-based rules, legislation vs. regulation, 73, 75, 83–84
   activity-based rules, problems of, 71–75
   changes to, as impacting return-examination time, 70
   changes to, saving enforcement costs, 70, 82

tax compliance rules (cont.)
  current benefits to high-end taxpayers, 19
  current law, 3
  definition, 5
  deterrent effect, 70, 215
  dispute procedures, 52
  distributive function of, 108, 111–12, 115, 154
  enforcement of, by IRS, 40, 65, 152
  fee-shifting, net asset test for, 89
  general applicability, 64–65
  means adjustments (proposed), 81–87
  noncompliance, social costs of, 84–85
  proposed adjustments, overview of, 6–7
  role and function in current system, 31–38
  for tax advisors, 50–51
  Treasury Regulations, 48
  unequal effects, 64–65, 73–74, 82
  wealthy taxpayers, burden on, 7, 125, 130, 133, 152
tax compliance, estimation of, 201, 205–7
tax compliance, voluntary vs. involuntary, 45–46
tax counsel, *See* tax advice
Tax Court, *See* US Tax Court
Tax Cuts and Jobs Act of 2017, 162
tax evasion
  deterrence of, through means-adjusted penalties, 153
  effect on tax morale, 23
  Foreign Account Tax Compliance Act (FATCA), effect on, 210
  pass-through structures or income, 26, 138, 152, 172, 208
  tax progressivity, undermining, 21, 23
  vs. tax avoidance, 14
  wealthy taxpayers, engaging in, 2, 9, 17, 26, 28, 30, 54, 85, 211–12, 214–15
tax gap
  closing at the top, difficulties of, 143
  definition and estimation of, 15–16
  narrowing, through IRS funding, 71
  reasons for, 206
  recovery of, as a means of funding federal programs, 19
tax information, reporting of, *See* information reporting
tax insurance, *See* insurance
tax liability
  minimization of, 13
  underpayments, 3, 5–7, 41, 51, 56, 74, 89, 123, 126, 130–31, 142, 144, 149–51, 164, 173, 176, 191, 195, 235
  underreporting, 3, 17–18, 27, 128, 141, 143, 146, 205, 208, 214–15, 229–31, 234
  understatements, 7, 42, 51, 131, 143, 148, 150, 165–66, 171, 177

tax morale, 7, 10, 22–23, 45, 85, 139, 151, 174, 194
tax noncompliance
  definition of, 13
  Detection Controlled Estimate (DCE) adjustment, 17
  detection, low probability of, 143, 215
  discouraging through tax penalties, 141
  distribution of, 16–19
  effect on tax morale, 23
  financial costs, 141
  history, 4
  social costs, 84–85
  stigma, leveraging to encourage compliance, 47
  third parties, lower stake in (related to information reporting), 224
  by wealthy taxpayers, 2, 9, 214
tax opinions, *See* tax advice
tax penalties, *See* civil tax penalties; criminal tax penalties
tax planning, *See also* tax advice
  aggressive or abusive, 128–29, 153, 161, 168–69, 173, 177, 188–89, 191, 194, 229
  versus clear tax noncompliance, 14
  complex, 29–30, 124, 129, 193
  costs of, 69
  gifts, 188
  as an industry, developments in, 73
  tax opinions or advice, role in, 167
  wealthy taxpayers, disproportionate access to, 196
Tax Policy Center, 53, 194
tax preparers, 142, 162
  fees, 51, 168
tax reform
  barriers to, 23–24
  uncertainty of (Supreme Court), 240
tax returns
  audit rates, 207
  and data privacy, 47
  disclosure of, 47
  of Donald J. Trump, 1, 4, 26, 29, 67, 128, 240
  filing requirement, 3, 51, 124, 204
  gifts, 188
  landlords, 208
  limited examination of, 169
  prioritizing for audit, 49, 131, 206
  public inspection of (in the 1800s), 4
  publicizing, 2
  return rate, IRS data on, 207
  of wealthy taxpayers, 8, 26, 133, 152, 195
tax shelters, 75, 80, 86, 128, 149, 151, 154, 164, 188, 192–93, 202, *See also* listed transactions
  battle against, 71

Compaq Computer v. *Commissioner* (Fifth Circuit case), 73
contingent liability structures, 71
Son of BOSS, 167
written tax opinions, role of (historically), 167
tax strategies, abusive, 72
tax structuring
sophisticated, 25
tax systems approach (Slemrod), 40
taxation, social costs of, 40
tax-exempt organizations, 132
Taxpayer Advocate Service, 52–53
taxpayer behavior, 39–41, 69, 72–73, 114, 123, 147, 241
Taxpayer Bill of Rights (TBOR), 52–53, 113, 125, *See also* Constitution, United States – due process
taxpayers
  experience, knowledge, and education (related to negligence defense), 152, 164
  low-income, 8, 20, 43, 68, 73, 85, 89–91, 126, 151–52, 172, 174, 215, 235
  motivation to pay taxes, 45
  procedural protections for, 7, 196
third parties, *See* information reporting
third-party advice, *See* tax advice
tiered entities, 28
tiered partnerships, 25
Torgler, Benno, 23
transactional complexity, 71–72
transactions lacking economic substance, 74
transactions of interest, 50, 71, 75, 77–80, 88, 189, 192, 214
transfer pricing, 26
Treasury Department, 1, 26, 42, 50, 75, 83, 175, 178, 193–95, 202, 211, 225–28
  establishment of (1789), 76
  Inspector General for Tax Administration (TIGTA), 20, 132, 143
  Regulations, 48, 55, 77, 151, 154, 164–65, 171, 202
  Secretary, 153

Trump, Donald J., 1, 4, 26, 29–30, 67, 128, 152, 169, 183, 194, 240
trusts, 24, 26, 78, 204, 209, *See also* charitable remainder annuity trusts (CRATs)
TurboTax, 169, 172

US Tax Court, 5, 196
  Golsen rule, 90
  S cases, 90
Uber, 203
UBS, 209
underpayments, *See* tax liability – underpayments
underreporting, *See* tax liability – underreporting
understatements, *See* tax liability – understatements

Vanderbilt, Cornelius, 4
Vanguard, 213
variable fines, 108
Viard, Alan, 24
virtual currency, *See* cryptocurrency

Wall Street Journal, 133
Wallace, Clinton, 80
Warren, Elizabeth, 24
wash-sale rules (IRC Section 1091), 31
wealth reporting, *See* Annual Net Asset Statement (proposed)
Wealth Squad, *See* Internal Revenue Service (IRS) – Wealth Squad
wealth tax, 24, 127–28, 231–32, 235
welfare economics, 21
Werfel, Daniel (Danny), 8, 22, 240
West, Robin, 102, 104

Yellen, Janet, 153
Yitzhaki, Shlomo, 14, 40, 69, 114, 146

Zelenak, Lawrence, 167
Zolt, Eric, 147
Zuckerberg, Mark, 2
Zucman, Gabriel, 2, 208

Milton Keynes UK
Ingram Content Group UK Ltd.
UKHW020153281124
451683UK00010BA/101